D0883265

Optical Computing

A Survey for Computer Scientists

To my parents,
who were much less surprised than I was when it
turned out that their little boy was writing a book.

Optical Computing

A Survey for Computer Scientists

Dror G. Feitelson

The MIT Press
Cambridge, Massachusetts
London, England

Publisher's Note

This format is intended to reduce the cost of publishing certain works in book form and to shorten the gap between editorial preparation and final publication. Detailed editing and composition have been avoided by photographing the text of this book directly from the author's prepared copy.

© 1988 Massachusetts Institute of Technology

All rights reserved. No part of this book may be reproduced in any form by any electronic or mechanical means (including photocopying, recording, or information storage and retrieval) without permission in writing from the publisher.

Printed and bound in the United States of America.

Library of Congress Cataloging-in-Publication Data

Feitelson, Dror G.

    Optical computing: A survey for computer scientists.

    Bibliography: p.
     Includes index.
     1. Optical data processing. I. Title.
    TA1630.F45 1988   621.36'7'0285 87-35704
    ISBN 0-262-06112-0

Rok   Sosič

Contents

III THE IMPACT OF OPTICAL COMPUTERS

Figures

Tables

Preface

Most surveys are written by prominent researchers, leaders in their field. They usually try to mention all the relevant literature, with detailed examples from the specific work of the author. The structure and technical language are meant for other researchers in the field or in related fields.

This survey is somewhat different. It was written by an outsider, for outsiders. More specifically, it attempts to present the subject of optical computers from a computer science point of view; the emphasis is not on optical techniques and devices but rather on applications and implementations of computer concepts. The object in writing this survey was to create an awareness of the subject in the computer science community. This review should therefore be seen as an introduction to a new field, and can be used as a source of material for a seminar. On the other hand, it can also be used as a textbook in optical computing courses.

The study of optical computers is quite wide. Many different and unrelated things have been dubbed "optical computing" or "optical data processing" over the years. This volume is the first attempt to survey all of the main topics. The field is still immature; in many cases numerous ideas have been brought up as solutions to a given problem, but none has been shown to be superior to the others. Therefore all the choices have to be surveyed. The wide scope of this book is an additional factor that makes it suitable for use as a textbook.

When surveying such a large field, one is faced with the dilemma of what to include. In this survey, the *what* has been augmented by the *how* and the *why*. Many compromises were made in the process. While readers who are looking for a brief introduction may find the description of optical implementations tedious, others who decide to start work in this field are sure to conclude that this survey is superficial.

There is no optical computing journal; the references for this survey come from a multitude of publications. An effort was made to use widely accessible and even popular publications, not only the more professional ones. The citations in the text should provide an adequate starting point for anyone who is interested in further details.

Structure of the book

An effort has been made to make the survey readable, despite the large amount of material. Each section starts with a general idea and then goes into the technical details. Readers who are not interested in the finer points of the optical implementations are urged to skip to the beginning of subsequent sections, where a new topic will be presented.

The chapters are organized according to the following graph:

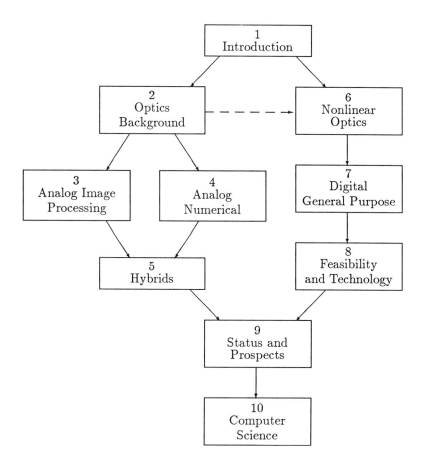

The first chapter introduces the field of optical computing. The rest are divided into three parts. Part I deals with special purpose optical processors: chapter 2 gives a general background in optics, chapter 3 deals with image processing and signal processing, chapter 4 with numerical processing, and chapter 5 surveys hybrid systems. Part II considers the possibility of a general purpose digital optical computer: chapter 6 is about nonlinear optics, chapter 7 reviews different optical approaches to the realization of computer components, and chapter 8 deals with feasibility and technological issues, including the possible use of integrated optics. Part III discusses the impact of optical computers: chapter 9 looks at where they are now and where they are headed, while chapter 10 relates optical computers to computer science.

Future editions

No additional editions of this book are planed at present. However, it should be remembered that optical computing is a very dynamic field; new developments may soon render the current edition inadequate. If and when this happens a new edition will be offered. In view of this prospect, readers are urged to send in any comments whatsoever, relating to content, style, errors or inaccuracies in the text, missing topics or references, etc. Such comments should be addressed directly to the author (at the Computer Science Department, Hebrew University of Jerusalem, 91904 Jerusalem, Israel) or to the publisher (The MIT Press, Acquisition Department, 55 Hayward St., Cambridge, MA 02142).

Units

The metric system is used throughout this work. The important units are:

length	m	Meter	
	μ	Micron	(10^{-6} of a meter)
	Å	Angstrom	(10^{-10} of a meter)
time	s	Second	
frequency	Hz	Hertz	(the reciprocal of time)
energy	J	Joule	
power	W	Watt	

The basic units may be prefixed by a symbol that denotes a power of ten. The most useful ones are:

f	femto-	10^{-15}
p	pico-	10^{-12}
n	nano-	10^{-9}
μ	micro-	10^{-6}
m	milli-	10^{-3}
c	centi-	10^{-2}
K	Kilo-	10^{3}
M	Mega-	10^{6}

For example, "μs" denotes a microsecond, which is 10^{-6} of a second.

Acknowledgements

This work was started when the author was a summer student at The Weizmann Institute of Science (supported by the Karyn Kupcinet fund) and then blossomed into an M.Sc. thesis; most of the work was carried out in this capacity (supported by a scholarship from the computer science department at The Hebrew University). Many thanks are due to the two open-minded advisors who supervised this unconventional work and significantly contributed to its final shape: Profs. Danny Dolev and Larry Rudolph. Danny Dolev encouraged me to investigate the connections between optical computers and computer science; this later evolved into Chapter 10 and part of Chapter 9. Larry Rudolph contributed many ideas that appear throughout the text, and suffered through numerous preliminary versions of the manuscript. He also provided material help in getting this book published.

The environment at The Hebrew University greatly contributed to this work; fruitful discussions with Avi Wigderson and Michael Ben-Or were important for the section about theoretical computer science. Talks with Michael Rabin and Yehoshua Sagiv, as well as with Yizhak Yacobi of the physics department and Mickey Cohen and Shelly Glaser of the Weizmann Institute, are also gratefully acknowledged. Joseph Goodman reviewed the preliminary version of the manuscript for The MIT Press, and John Caulfield reviewed the final version; their support and corrections were helpful in creating this book. Finally, the MIT press staff and especially Terry Ehling and Robert Bolick are thanked for their dedicated work.

This book was typeset with LaTeX, and printed on an Apple LaserWriter Plus. The computer science department is thanked for providing these facilities. About a third of the original artwork was done with the LaTeX "picture" environment; the rest was drawn by Zehava Cohen and Elana Elah.

Chapter 1

Introduction

1.1   Why optics?

It is unquestionable that computers play a major role in modern life. They are used for everything — from chores such as producing business letters, to controlling weapon systems and traffic lights. All these computers, from the humblest PC to the largest supercomputer, are basically similar: their hardware is based upon VLSI circuits, etched in silicon. Their architectures are based on processing units that operate on data kept in the memory. They run sequential programs that specify exactly what to do at each step. Broadly speaking, they are Von Neumann electronic computers.

These computers have come a long way in the past three or four decades. They are flexible and convenient. We have a lot of experience with them. We know how to make them work. In most applications (e.g., word processing and controlling traffic lights) they are very good and efficient. It is unlikely that they will be replaced by any new technology in the near future. There are, however, some cases where conventional electronic computers do not live up to requirements. These cases usually involve great masses of computation, e.g., image processing and the simulations of fluid dynamics.

The realization of the limitations of conventional computers has given rise to various research efforts that attempt to create machines of new types. One idea revolves around "fifth-generation" computers that will incorporate ideas from artificial intelligence and logic programming. Another is concerned with parallel computers. This survey deals with a totally different concept, one that departs from electronics altogether: the concept of *optical computing*.

The field of optical computing is quite broad, and includes many different ideas and possibilities. Regrettably, it is not well defined; nearly any operation in which an optical device or phenomenon has been used for information processing or some computation has been dubbed "optical computing". A taxonomy of optical computing research is given in appendix A. I will try to cover all the important examples in this work.

The following is a partial listing of those points that make optical computing appealing:

- *Direct image processing.*
  Images are naturally thought of in terms of optical systems and light beams.

Certain image processing functions may be carried out by specific optical systems directly on the image, with no need for sampling, quantization, and such. These optical systems operate faster and with better resolution than their electronic counterparts.

- *Massive parallelism and connectivity.*
  The problems preventing the ultimate speeding up of conventional computers do not arise from the inadequate speed of the basic elements. Rather, interconnection issues are the limiting factor. Optical communication allows for unheard of new ideas: millions of data channels may operate in parallel, each with a bandwidth much greater than that of any electronic link.

- *Speed.*
  The possibilities of special purpose systems and massive parallelism give rise to high speed in data processing. This is important in modern applications, where the amount of data that has to be sorted out increases all the time. For example, more than 10 years ago NASA had already estimated that a space station would produce some 55,000 images daily for weather forecasting, pollution control, land use mapping, and earth resources mapping [111]. This would overwhelm any conventional computation facility.

- *Immunity to EMI.*
  The electrons circulating in a conventional computer are susceptible to electromagnetic interference (EMI) [730]. In electronically noisy locations, and possibly also in nuclear battlefields, they fail. Optical computers, on the other hand, will continue to function undisturbed.

- *Size and cost.*
  Optical systems tend to be smaller, lighter, and simpler than equivalent electronic computers. Hence they may also be expected to cost less.

The above list is quite impressive — but the fact is that optical computers are not in wide use today. The main reason for this state of affairs is that, for lack of investment, most optical processing systems never got beyond the feasibility-demonstration stage. Another is that most people simply don't know what can be done with optical systems, and therefore don't try to use them. This book is an attempt to fill in this lack of knowledge and awareness.

1.2   A brief history

The "ancient" history of optical computing is linked, to a large extent, to that of radar systems [418]. The need to process the vast amount of data supplied by radars used in mapping was the motivating force behind early optical signal processing research efforts. Conversely, many ideas developed by the radar community were later found useful in optical computation (e.g., holography [417]). The first optical processing systems are described in [555, sect. 1.00].

Optical computing received a great push from the invention of the laser in 1960. The characteristics of this light source allowed numerous new operations to be realized by optical means. These operations were analog in nature, and are best described by the term "signal processing". Unlike electronic signal processing systems, which have one (temporal) degree of freedom, typical optical processors have two (spatial) degrees of freedom; the data is a 2-D image. One of the basic operations that can be performed on images in laser light is the Fourier transform. Numerous applications grew out of this ability.

During the time that conventional electronic computers were being developed, sporadic efforts were also being made to realize digital logic by optical means. These efforts did not amount to much for two reasons. One was the success of conventional electronic Von Neumann computers. They answered the world's computational needs. They were flexible and easy to program. They gave results that were accurate to any desired degree. When this is compared to the basically analog optical systems, with their new and immature technologies and potentially problematic operation, it is clear why investments in optical computing have been comparatively small.

The second reason was the indecisiveness of the optical computing community. Electronic computers received a great push from the invention of the transistor and development of the integrated circuit, ideas that won wide acceptance. In optical computing, on the other hand, the quest for materials and technologies was far from over. And as long as there is no chosen technology, there is no single channel in which to invest massive development effort. As a consequence, none of the ideas have to date been brought to the final stages of development and production.

1.3   Current trends

Today there are two distinct trends in optical computing: That of special purpose analog systems, and that of general purpose digital optical computers.

Special purpose analog optical computers are again divided into two classes: those that deal with image and signal processing, and those that deal with numerical processing. Image processing systems have been around longer, and have had some successes. As noted above, the word "computer" might be misleading in this context; actually we are talking of optical systems that accept one beam of light as input, manipulate it, and finally produce an output beam of light. These systems exploit various physical phenomena from the field of optics, such as the ability to perform 2-D Fourier transforms. They are usually very specific and unflexible, but well adapted to their tasks. Numerical processors do not manipulate beams of light — rather they deal with arrays of numbers, represented by multiple points of light. The repertoire of operations relates to linear algebra and matrix operations. As many problems may be formulated in such terms, these systems are relatively general purpose (though of course not as general purpose as a conventional programmable electronic computer). Both classes are typically coupled to a front-end electronic computer.

New developments in analog optical systems are still being pursued today, with the support of major institutions like NASA, DARPA and SDIO [509,646,481]. It is hoped that as electronic computers approach their limits, optical systems will provide a viable alternative.

The first part of this book is dedicated to these systems. The background required for understanding analog optical systems is surveyed in chapter 2. The two classes of analog optical computers, or rather of analog optical data processing systems, are the subject of chapters 3 and 4. Chapter 5 discusses systems that combine analog optical computers with electronic computers.

General purpose digital optical computers have become a major research topic only in recent years. They are usually based on nonlinear optical effects. Generally speaking, these systems try to mimic existing electronic computers: logic gates, memory elements, and such are implemented using optical devices. The goal is to create a general purpose digital computer that will be comparable to electronic ones, but better in some significant way, e.g., it might be much faster. The architecture of these computers is expected to be a parallel one. At the moment only prototypes of the basic elements exist.

The second part of this book covers general purpose digital optical computers. It begins with chapter 6, which is about nonlinear optics. The implementations of computer components are surveyed in chapter 7. Chapter 8 then deals with the realization of these machines by means of integrated optics circuits.

The final part of the book surveys the impact optical computers have on the computing industry and computer science. Chapter 9 deals with the current status of optical processing systems, and with the prospects for the future. Chapter 10 appraises the influence of optical computers on computer science. This influence consists of new concepts and new devices that have to be accommodated, and will remain even if complete optical computers should not be realized.

Bibliographical notes

The literature on optical computers includes a number of books and numerous scientific papers. The books cover only the older analog processing systems. The most prominent are:
□ Goodman / Introduction to Fourier Optics [260] — Actually an optics book, it provides an excellent introduction to the optical theory of analog optical processing.
□ Preston / Coherent Optical Computers [555] — A survey oriented toward engi-

neering issues of analog optical systems utilizing coherent light.

□ Yu / Optical information processing [746] — Based on optics theory, both coherent and incoherent.

□ Caulfield (ed.) / The Handbook of Optical Holography [291] — A collection of papers that cover the many uses of holography in optical processing (among other things).

The most important scientific journals are:

▷ Applied Optics ⎫ Most of the original research papers, surveys, and
▷ Optical Engineering ⎭ special issues.

▷ Proceedings of the IEEE — special issues, some reviews.

Other useful journals are:

▷ Optics Letters ⎫
▷ Optics Communications ⎬ Some research papers.
▷ J. Optical Society of America ⎭

▷ IEEE Spectrum ⎫ Surveys and semitechnical articles.
▷ Scientific American ⎭

Additional journals that occasionally carry relevant material are Applied Physics Letters, IEEE Journal of Quantum Electronics, IEEE transactions on Information Theory, IEEE transactions on Electron Devices, Laser Focus (a quarterly optical computing newsletter was started in October 1987), Optics News, and Nature. Progress in Optics, which is an annual series of books, occasionally includes in-depth review articles on specific topics in optical computing.

Another important source of information about optical computing is conference proceedings. A number of conferences and topical meetings on different aspects of optical computing are held annually; the proceedings are usually published by SPIE or OSA. These proceedings are rather costly and hard to come by, and their use in preparing this book was kept to a minimum. Abstracts are usually listed in the Journal of the Optical Society of America.

I

SPECIAL PURPOSE
OPTICAL PROCESSORS

The first part of this book deals with special purpose optical processors. While many of the systems that are described are analog in nature, this is not always the case; a number of systems that utilize digital encoding in order to improve accuracy have been proposed lately. Therefore it was felt that a division between special purpose and general purpose systems would be more meaningful than a division between analog and digital systems.

The first chapter in this part, chapter 2, supplies the necessary background in classical optics. It may be skipped by readers who have this knowledge, or readers that are not so interested in the technical details. Chapter 3 surveys the large number of image processing and signal processing systems that have been devised over the years. These include operational devices, such as synthetic aperture radar imagers, as well as new ideas still awaiting implementation. Chapter 4 reviews the newer field of optical numerical processing, with an emphasis on matrix processors. All of these systems are still in the prototype stage. Finally, chapter 5 is about hybrid systems, i.e., combinations of optical and electronic devices; most of the optical special purpose processors are not self-supporting.

Chapter 2

Background in Optics

Optical computers are based, of course, upon phenomena related to optics and light. Therefore some background is necessary before delving into the details and intricacies of optical computers. This chapter will attempt to present the necessary rudiments, with emphasis placed on the points that are important to optical computing, and especially analog optical processing systems. It is not, however, a full course in optics. Readers with a deeper interest are referred to the many textbooks available (see the bibliographical notes at the end of the chapter).

We start with a couple of sections that discuss the basic properties of light, and some basic optical phenomena. The next five sections survey optical systems: first the sources that create a beam of light, then the devices that manipulate the light (including acoustooptical devices), next the fundamental limitations of optical systems, and finally the detectors that translate the light into an electrical signal. The last section is about holography, which is an important technique for the recording and manipulation of the information carried by light beams.

2.1 Light as a wave of electromagnetic radiation

The physics of light is a very interesting subject. Even people with no background in physics have probably heard about the dual nature of light: on the one hand it is composed of elementary particle-like quanta, called *photons*, and on the other it may be regarded as a wave. Readers who are interested in knowing more about this are referred to Feynman's more-or-less popular book about quantum electrodynamics [216]. For our purposes it will suffice to resolve the ambiguity by considering each photon to be a small *wave packet* (top of fig. 2.1). The light wave is then the sum of many photons (bottom of figure).

In the context of optical computers the individual photons are of interest only if there are so few of them that their random fluctuations affect our measurements. The processing power of optics, however, derives from the wavelike properties of light; it only becomes apparent when large numbers of photons[1] are involved, so that random fluctuations cancel out. We therefore turn to a discussion of the properties of waves in general, and electromagnetic waves in particular [214].

---

[1] In many cases it is sufficient to detect about 1000 photons in order to insure reasonable accuracy.

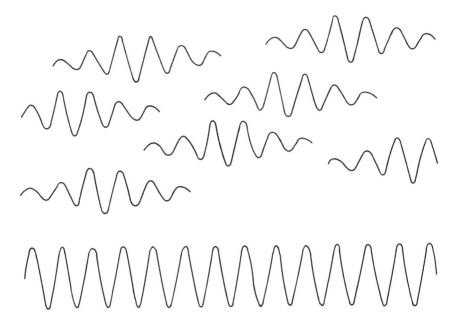

Figure 2.1: *Photons, the elementary quanta of light, may be considered as wave packets (top). When many are present, their combined effect is that of a continuous wave (bottom).*

The most basic property that characterizes a wave is its *frequency*. This is the number of cycles it completes in one second. Electro-magnetic waves come in a wide range of frequencies: FM radio transmission is at about 100 MHz[2], a radar may use 2 GHz, and the frequency of a gamma ray may be 10^{22} cps. *Visible light* occupies a rather narrow band between 10^{14} cps (red) and 10^{15} cps (violet). The special thing about visible light is that our eyes are equipped with sensors that are sensitive to radiation in these frequencies, just as a radio transistor is sensitive to the frequencies of FM radio. The reason both nature and optical computers use this range is that many materials transmit and absorb radiation in these frequencies better than in other frequencies, by means of interactions between photons of radiation and the electrons in the material.

Our eyes do not respond in the same manner to different frequencies of visible light. Rather, different cells in our retina respond to distinct frequencies. This is what gives us the sense of *color* [603]. This term is used also in the field of optics:

---

[2]The useful unit for frequencies in the radio and microwave domains is the *Hertz*, which means one cycle per second (*cps*). KHz is 10^3 cycles, MHz is 10^6, and GHz is 10^9 cycles per second.

when we talk about *polychromatic* light we mean light that incorporates many frequencies. On the other hand *monochromatic* light is spectrally[3] pure light, with only one frequency. For example, the light issuing from a HeNe laser is pure red light — and we say that it is monochromatic.

Another parameter of interest when talking about light is its *wavelength*. This is the distance the light propagates during one cycle. Therefore the wavelength for a given frequency depends upon the *speed of propagation*. This speed in turn depends upon the medium through which the radiation is propagating. The characteristic of the medium that describes the speed of light passing through it is called the *index of refraction*. This is defined as the ratio of the speed of light in vacuum to the speed of light in the material. The refractive index of vacuum is therefore 1; the speed of light in it is approximately 300,000 Km per second. Materials have a higher refractive index, and the speed of light in them is proportionately lower. When light passes obliquely from one medium to another, its change of speed causes a change of direction; this is called *refraction*. Lenses and other optical devices use this phenomenon to change the direction of rays of light. Lenses are actually just specially shaped transparent objects with a different refractive index then their surroundings.

Two additional parameters are needed in order to describe a wave. The first is its *amplitude*, which is the "height" of the wave. The square of the amplitude is called the *intensity* of the wave, and conveys the number of photons in the wave. As each photon is a quantum of energy, the light intensity also indicates how much energy is propagating with the wave. The second parameter is the *phase* of the wave, which stands for the part of the cycle that the wave is in. Absolute phases are of no interest; only the phase of one wave relative to another is of consequence. When we describe a wave by harmonic functions, e.g., sine, one cycle corresponds to 2π radians. A phase difference of $\frac{\pi}{2}$ between two waves then means that one of them lags behind the other by one quarter of a cycle. For computational purposes, the amplitude A and the phase φ are sometimes linked together to form one complex value $Ae^{i\varphi}$: the modulus is the amplitude, and the argument is the phase. This is called the *complex amplitude* of the wave.

When two waves combine, they are said to *interfere*. If the waves have the same frequency, the result depends on their relative amplitudes and phases. If the crests in one wave coincide with the crests in the other, the waves reinforce each other. This is called *constructive* interference. If the crests in one match the throughs in the other, the waves tend to cancel out. This is *destructive* interference (fig. 2.2). In general, one adds up at every point the complex amplitudes of the two waves. In many cases the interference between two waves creates a pattern of alternating bright and dark bands, which correspond to constructive

---

[3]The *spectrum* of a signal, e.g., a beam of radiation, is its structure in the frequency domain. Another way of putting this is to say that the spectrum is the decomposition of the signal into basic frequencies. The spectrum may be calculated by taking the Fourier transform of the signal.

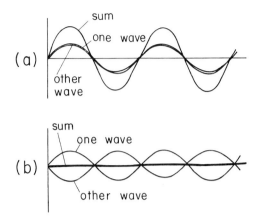

Figure 2.2: *Interference between two waves:*
(a) Constructive interference occurs if they are in phase.
(b) Destructive interference occurs if they are out of phase.

and destructive interference. These bands are called *fringes*.

Electromagnetic waves are a combination of an electric field and a magnetic field, perpendicular to each other and to the direction of propagation. The orientation of the electric field is defined to be the wave's *polarization*. For example, in a horizontally polarized wave the electric field oscillates in a horizontal plane, while the magnetic field oscillates in a vertical plane. This is important when the wave passes through a material which responds differently to the different orientations.

The concept of *wavefronts* is useful when studying how a wave propagates through space. A wavefront is a collection of points with the same phase (or the same optical distance from the source). If the light in adjacent points is propagating in parallel, the wavefront will be a plane, and we speak of a *plane wave*. If the light diverges from a point source, the wavefronts will be spherical surfaces, and we call the result a *spherical wave*.

2.2   Coherence

2.2.1   Definitions

The photons drawn in fig. 2.1 are all in phase with each other. therefore their sum is a wave that can be described by a harmonic function such as $\sin(x)$. We call such light *coherent*. Unfortunately, this is not always the case. In many situations the phase of the photons, and thus of the light wave, changes in a random manner. When this happens, we say the light is *incoherent*. The most important difference between coherent and incoherent light is that mutually incoherent beams *do not interfere*. When two combine, their *intensities* (rather than their complex amplitudes) add up.

We distinguish between two types of coherence in light:

- *Spatial coherence* — the phase relations between different parts of the cross section of the beam are constant; therefore different parts of the cross section can be made to interfere with each other.

- *Temporal coherence* — The phase relations between consecutive wavefronts are constant; therefore a beam can interfere with a delayed version of itself. Temporal coherence is actually equivalent to monochromaticity of the light: it means that the frequency of the light wave is stable and confined to a narrow band.

The boundary between coherent and incoherent light is not clear-cut, and depends on the specific system being discussed. A measure of coherence is the *coherence length* of the light. This is the width of beam over which spatial coherence is maintained, or the distance the light travels before temporal coherence is lost. The path differences in a system must be shorter than the coherence length for the system to be coherent.

2.2.2   Tradeoffs

In optical computing systems, temporal coherence is usually assured, as only monochromatic light sources are used. Spatial coherence or incoherence is, however, an important issue, because the image data is imposed on the cross section of the light beams. Systems using coherent[4] light are easy to describe and understand mathematically, because trigonometric relations and harmonic functions may be used. In addition the light carries more information: both its amplitude and phase can be manipulated. Complex values can thus be represented by the light's complex amplitude. As an example, Fourier transforms of images in coherent light are easy to produce. However, these systems require special and controlled lighting conditions, as natural light sources are nearly always incoherent. An alternative is to use input transducers that accept an incoherent input image and turn it into a coherent one. Such devices will be discussed when we consider spatial light modulators (section 2.4.6).

Incoherent systems, on the other hand, are harder to analyze. Only the light intensity, which is always a positive, real quantity, can be used to convey information. But these systems are more immune to noise, such as dust particles, and are easier to interface with the natural, incoherent world. The light intensity is also much easier to detect and measure than the complex amplitude of a coherent

---

[4]From now on, "coherent" will mean "spatially coherent".

beam. Some indirect methods have therefore been developed in order to represent bipolar or complex data symbolically, using incoherent light. [247]. The two dominant methods are to use multichannel systems or spatial carrier modulation.

Multichannel systems

Multichannel optical systems are conceptually very simple. A bipolar data stream can be represented by two unipolar data streams, one of positive values and the other of negative values. Using this decomposition, bipolar data may be represented by two beams of incoherent light: one's intensity will represend positive data values, and will be zero if the data is negative. The other's intensity will represent negative values, and will be zero where the data is positive. A natural extension to complex signals would use four channels, for the positive and negative values of the real and imaginary parts. However, a more efficient representation is possible by decomposing the complex signal into only three unipolar components [90,261], thus:

$$f = f_1 + f_2 \exp\left(\frac{2\pi i}{3}\right) + f_3 \exp\left(\frac{4\pi i}{3}\right).$$

With this decomposition, f_1, f_2, and f_3 are real and positive.

The different channels are usually separated spatially, i.e., they are situated next to each other in space. another possibility is to use light with a distinct color for each channel [563].

Spatial carrier modulation

A totally different approach to the representation of complex data by incoherent light is to use spatial carrier modulation [431]. the spatial carrier is simply a pattern of high spatial frequency, e.g., a grating of thin parallel lines, imposed on the cross section of the light beam. This is modulated by the complex information signal much as an electromagnetic radio frequency carrier is modulated in radio transmission: the amplitude and phase of different points on the lines are multiplied by the amplitude and phase of corresponding points in the information signal.

The process of representing a complex-valued image by the modulation of a real-valued spatial carrier may be described mathematically as follows: When the grating (i.e., the carrier) is imposed on the cross section of the beam, it is multiplied by the image (i.e., by the information). Then the complex conjugate of the modulated carrier is added, in order to do away with the imaginary part. Finally a constant bias (i.e., an even illumination) is added, in order to compensate for negative values. Though this may seem too complicated to carry out, the techniques used are simple, and combine the three steps into one. The decomposition into three is needed only to explain how the complex values are hidden in the resulting real-valued intensity distribution of the incoherent light.

The (spatial) spectrum of the result contains three components: the bias, centered around zero frequency, and two side bands for the modulated carrier and its conjugate [698]. These components must be distinct in order to enable subsequent decoding. The condition for this is that the spatial carrier frequency must be at least three times higher than the spatial bandwidth of the information signal. Spatial carrier modulation is the basis of holography, as we shall see in section 2.8 and appendix F.

2.3   Sources

The properties of an optical system depend to a large degree upon the source of the light that is being used. This can be a controlled source that is part of the system, or light that comes as input from the outside. Historically, a common source that gave reasonable monochromatic and spatially coherent light was an arc lamp followed by an opaque screen with a pinhole in it. Today, two other sources dominate: *LED*s and *lasers*. There is a basic difference between these sources and the common household incandescent light bulb. In incandescent bulbs a filament is heated, and then it radiates part of its energy. A small part of the radiation happens to be in the visible range. Both LEDs and lasers, on the other hand, depend on certain changes in the energy states of the electrons in the light-source material. Specifically, electrons in high-energy (so-called "excited") states go down to their ground states. In doing so they release an energy quantum in the form of a photon.

A LED (Light Emitting Diode) provides monochromatic — and hence temporally coherent — light. This light, however, is not very coherent spatially [59,500]. A LED's power consumption is minimal and its efficiency is very high when compared with regular lamps. As a consequence it does not heat up very much, which might be important in optical computer implementations. An explanation of how LEDs work is given in appendix E.

A LASER (acronym for Light Amplification by Stimulated Emission of Radiation) outputs an intense, monochromatic, spatially coherent, and very directional beam of light [601,204]. It has therefore become the most popular source in modern coherent systems, and is often used also in incoherent systems (where the light is first diffused in order to remove the coherence). The principle of operation of the laser is explained in appendix D.

The sources discussed above are usually internal to the optical system. To get information "into" the light beam the beam passes through a transparency and becomes modulated (just as a beam of light is modulated by a slide in a slide projector). It is also possible for the system to accept already modulated light as input. An example is the use of self-luminous objects like the screen of a CRT (or a black and white television set), on which the input image is displayed. Such screens are more or less monochromatic, but spatially incoherent. Another

source	wavelength	power consumption	efficiency
home lamp	(white light)	25–100 W	2–4%
mercury arc	5461Å,5770Å,5790Å	10–100 W	5–10%
LED	~ 850 or 1300 nm	~ 10 mW	$\sim 45\%$
HeNe laser	6328Å	0.01–0.1 W	$\sim 1\%$
injection laser	~ 850 or 1300 nm	40–100 mW	30–70%

Table 2.1: *Characteristics of typical light sources.*

option is for light coming directly from the input scene to enter the optical system. Such light is usually neither monochromatic nor coherent, which generally makes it harder to get good performance from the optical system. In some special cases, however, this problem can be solved if it is possible to illuminate the input scene with lasers. One such example is a factory assembly line with an optical system serving as eyes for a robot.

2.4   Basic elements of optical systems

Most optical systems are built out of a small number of basic components, grouped together in various ways. This section describes these basic components, with emphasis on aspects relevant to optical computing.

2.4.1   Mirrors and prisms

Mirrors and prisms are used to change the direction of beams of light in an optical system. The difference is in the technique: mirrors *reflect* the light, while prisms *refract* it. We shall only consider plane mirrors. This involves no loss of generality, as specially shaped mirrors can be regarded as combinations of flat mirrors and lenses.

Mirrors also affect the polarization of the reflected light: it tends to be parallel to the plane of the mirror. This phenomenon is at the base of Polaroid sunglasses, which avoid bright reflections by blocking out horizontally polarized light.

In prisms, the angle of refraction also depends on the wavelength. Thus they can be used to obtain a spectral analysis of polychromatic light. In optical computers using monochromatic light, this property is not important.

2.4.2 Beam splitters

The information in an optical system is carried by beams of light. It is often necessary to split a beam of light into two, or to join two beams into one. Both these functions are carried out by beam splitters. A beam splitter is actually just a semitransparent mirror. Part of the light that hits it is reflected, as in an ordinary mirror; the rest goes through it without changing direction. To join beams, the two input beams are directed in such a way that the reflected part of one of the beams and the passing part of the other beam come out together.

The problem with this configuration is that half of the energy is always lost, because both beams are split and we only use one part of each. This can be avoided by using polarization beam splitters, which reflect all the light in one polarization and transmit all the light in the orthogonal polarization. With proper control of the polarization, lossless operation may be achieved.

2.4.3 Gratings

A (thin) grating is a set of fine, straight parallel lines on a transparency. Like mirrors, gratings may be used to change the direction of a beam of light. However, with a grating the beam is also split into a number of beams that go in different directions. In each of the beams, the exact change in direction depends on the wavelength of the light, as it was in prisms. Thus a grating too may be used to obtain the spectral analysis of polychromatic light.

As we said, a grating is simply a set of thin, parallel lines, Alternatingly transparent and opaque [339, chap. 17]. When a coherent beam of light impinges upon a grating, it can be considered as equivalent to a set of coherent, long, linear light sources. The light from these sources interferes. In certain directions the *path differences* for light coming from adjacent sources (i.e., adjacent lines) is an integral multiple of the wavelength, and *constructive* interference occurs. These are the directions in which we get beams of light. In other directions *destructive* interference occurs, and the waves tend to cancel out. More generally, the directions in which constructive interference takes place must satisfy (fig. 2.3 (a)):

$$d \sin \theta = n \, \lambda \qquad \text{(Bragg's law)},$$

where d is the grating spacing
        λ is the wavelength
        n is an integer, called the *diffraction order*.

Note that this assumes the incident light beam is perpendicular to the grating (so all the lines oscillate in phase).

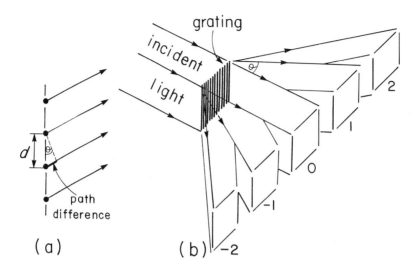

Figure 2.3: *Bragg diffraction:*
(a) Constructive interference depends on a path difference which is an integral number of wavelengths.
(b) Many diffraction orders may be produced.

Diffraction analysis

It is worthwhile to note the method used to analyze what happens to light that passes through a grating. We know the light distribution at plane A (the grating), and want to find out what the light distribution is at plane B, some distance away. To do so we consider plane A to be composed of many individual light sources (in the case of the grating, these are arranged in lines). The light from these sources interferes, and creates a so-called *diffraction pattern*[5] at plane B. To calculate it, we simply calculate the result of the interference at each point in plane B, i.e., the sum of the contributions from all the sources in plane A:

$$B(x,y) = \int\limits_{-\infty}^{+\infty}\!\!\!\int A(\xi,\eta)\, h(x,y,\xi,\eta)\, d\xi\, d\eta,$$

where $h(x,y,\xi,\eta)$ is a complex function that gives the illumination at point x,y in plane B resulting from an illumination of one unit at point ξ,η of plane A.

---

[5]The term *diffraction* is somewhat hard to define; it means both the interference of light coming from multiple sources (or an extended source), and the change of direction of a beam of light as a result of being partitioned into many points that interfere with each other.

The case of an evenly illuminated grating is easy, and allows some shortcuts: the symmetry of the problem dictates that the contributions will cancel each other in all but a few specific directions. In the general case it can be quiet difficult to derive an expression for $h(x, y, \xi, \eta)$, and hence various approximations are used. The most useful ones are the *Fresnel* diffraction formula, used when the distance from A to B is large enough, and the simpler *Fraunhofer* diffraction formula, used when the distance is much larger. Diffraction analysis is a basic procedure in classical optics and is treated extensively in all textbooks, e.g., [260, chap. 4].

Thick gratings

If the grating is *thick*, i.e., it is a set of parallel plane surfaces, the situation is slightly different. A light beam impinging on such a grating is reflected by each surface individually. If the angle between the beam and the surfaces is just right, constructive interference will occur between the reflections. The result will be a very strong diffraction. At other angles the diffraction will be very weak. The angle at which strong diffraction occurs is called the *Bragg angle*, and it satisfies $\sin \theta = \frac{n\lambda}{2d}$ (see fig. 2.10). This phenomenon is of major importance in volume holography and some acoustooptical devices, as well as in the diffraction of x-rays from crystals.

Acoustooptic devices [571,267,380]

Gratings need not be stable and tangible like most other devices; in fact it is quite common to use an acoustic wave as a grating. An acoustic wave propagating in a crystal causes a periodic deformation of the crystal. This deformation usually results in a periodic change of the refractive index of the crystal. The velocity of the acoustic wave is always much lower than that of light waves. Therefore we may say that to a good approximation a light wave passing through the crystal "feels" a standing periodic change of the medium — that is, a grating. This grating causes diffraction of the light, just like any other grating would. Such phenomena in which light is scattered by interaction with acoustic waves are called *Brillouin scattering*. This topic is elaborated in section 2.5.

2.4.4   Lenses

Lenses are well known to everyone from daily experience (If not, go out now and try to burn a piece of paper by concentrating the sun's rays on it with a magnifying glass). However, their full power does not come into play in everyday conditions. In optical systems, and in the context of optical computers in particular, lenses have three main uses (table 2.2): to create wide collimated beams of light, to cast images, and to perform Fourier transforms.

Collimators and beam expanders

A collimated beam is a plane wave of limited extent; this is a straight, parallel beam of light that does not change its diameter. Convex lenses may convert a diverging beam from a point source into a collimated one, or convert a collimated beam into a converging one[6]. Concave lenses do the opposite: they convert a converging beam into a collimated one, and a collimated beam into a diverging one. Combinations of convex and concave lenses are used to change the diameter of a collimated beam within an optical system.

Fourier transforms

The Fourier transform is extremely important in signal analysis, and as we shall see it also has many uses in optical computing. In short, it generates the spectrum of the input signal, which is the representation of the signal in the frequency domain. A definition of the Fourier transform and an explanation of its properties is given in appendix C.

Let us consider a thin convex lens of focal length f, illuminated by a beam of coherent light. We place a transparency with transmittance $g(x, y)$ at the front focal plane (i.e., at a distance f in front of the lens). We take $g(x, y)$ to be a complex function, so it can be expressed as

$$g(x, y) = |g(x, y)| \, e^{i\varphi(x,y)}.$$

Using a transparency with transmittance $g(x, y)$ means that right after the transparency the light's amplitude will be $|g(x, y)|$ and its phase will be $\varphi(x, y)$. In other words, the transparency modulates the complex amplitude of the light (see page 11). We now investigate the light distribution in the *back* focal plane of the lens, i.e., at a distance f behind it. We designate the complex amplitude of this light distribution by $G(u, v)$ (we use coordinates x, y for the front focal plane and u, v for the back focal plane, to avoid confusion. See left side of fig. 2.4). If we use the relations

$$\nu_x = \frac{u}{\lambda f} \qquad \nu_y = \frac{v}{\lambda f},$$

it turns out that $G(\nu_x, \nu_y)$ is the Fourier transform of $g(x, y)$. G is of course also a complex function, just as g is.

In short, your magnifying glass[7] can perform an analog 2-D Fourier transform with the speed of light. Note that it is the *spatial modulation* of the beam that is being analyzed. ν_x and ν_y are spatial frequencies. This has nothing to do with the temporal frequency of the light in the beam, which is monochromatic anyway.

---

[6] Actually, this may be taken as the definition of an ideal convex lens.

[7] The truth is that lenses only perform the Fourier transform to *first approximation*; They have to be perfectly engineered in order to give good results. A household magnifying glass is only capable of a very crude approximation.

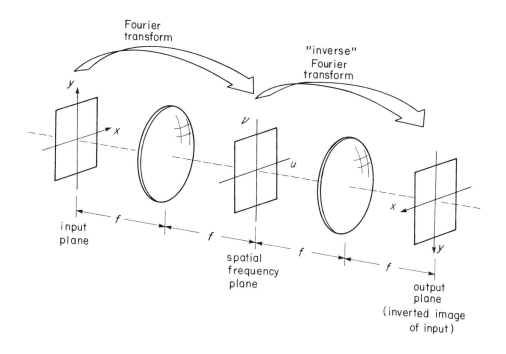

Figure 2.4: *Configuration of a Fourier-transform system of lenses.*

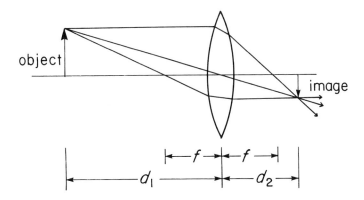

Figure 2.5: *Imaging by a lens.*

As an example, think of what would happen if a point source is placed at the focus of the lens. It is rather intuitive that a parallel beam of light will emerge at the other side. In particular, the back focal plane will receive even illumination. This is an optical analogue of the well-known fact that the Fourier transform of a delta function is a constant. Appendix C gives some more examples, and an explanation of why the Fourier-transform relation always holds.

The inverse Fourier transform is very similar to the original Fourier transform; actually the only change is in the sign of the coordinates. Therefore a lens may also be used in order to obtain the inverse Fourier transform: it actually performs a regular Fourier transform, but if we regard the resulting image as inverted this is equivalent to an inverse transform (fig. 2.4).

Imaging

A better known property of lenses, that holds also for incoherent light, is their ability to form *images* (i.e., distributions of light that resemble that of the source). This is easy to understand with tools from *geometrical optics*. The main idea in geometrical optics is to trace rays of light as they propagate through the optical system, taking into account changes in direction at the various optical elements[8] [339, chap. 8]. To find where an image of an object is formed, different rays emerging from a point in the object are traced. The image of that point is formed at the spot where the rays intersect again. It turns out that if the object is placed at a distance d_1 in front of the lens, the image will be formed at a distance d_2

---

[8]Note the difference between the concepts of a ray of light and a beam of light: a ray has an infinitesimal cross section, while a beam may be quiet wide. A lens only changes the direction of a ray, but it changes the characteristics of a beam (e.g., from a parallel beam to a converging one).

use	operation	configuration
collimating lens	turn a diverging beam of light (from a point source) into a collimated beam	
imaging lens	cast an image of a light distribution in one plane onto another plane	
Fourier-transform lens	create a light distribution that is the Fourier transform of a given light distribution (only with coherent light)	

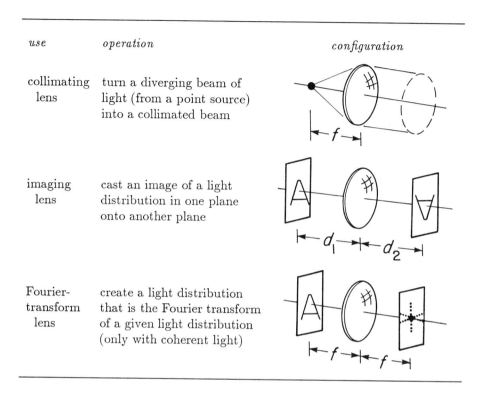

Table 2.2: *Lenses are often called after the function they perform. The three main types are summarized in this table. Note that the lens itself is the same — only the configuration of the system changes.*

behind it, where d_1 and d_2 obey

$$\frac{1}{d_1} + \frac{1}{d_2} = \frac{1}{f} \qquad \text{(the lens law)},$$

where f is the focal length of the lens (see fig. 2.5).

Other properties of lenses

So far we have considered the properties of perfect lenses, working under ideal conditions. But lenses (like many other things in life) are not perfect. An ideal (convex) lens can be defined as one that transforms a plane wave (i.e., a parallel beam of light) into a spherical wave that converges to the focus. With a real lens, the focus will always be slightly smeared. A collective name for all the reasons for this imperfection is *aberrations*. When designing an optical system it is of course very important to understand the different aberrations and to compensate for them. This is done by employing systems of lenses with aberrations that cancel each other. Some ideas may be found in [188]. We will tend to ignore this problem.

Another unspoken understanding has been that the lens exhibits identical behavior in all the axes, i.e., that there is no distinction between the x and the y axes. While this is true for the common spherical lenses, it need not be true for any lens. A lens that behaves differently in two axes is said to be *astigmatic*. For example, a cylindrical lens is astigmatic: it images (or Fourier transforms) along one axis, but does nothing along the other. Astigmatic lenses are also used to correct those vision problems that arise in humans, when the lens of the eye is not spherical.

2.4.5   Polarizers and analyzers

Polarizers and analyzers are actually the same thing — they are filters that allow light in one polarization only to pass. Light in the orthogonal polarization is blocked. The name "polarizer" is used when the objective is to create a beam of polarized light from a beam with random polarization. The name "analyzer" is used when the object is to check whether the beam of light is in a certain polarization, or to deliberately block light of a certain polarization.

2.4.6   Spatial light modulators

All the optical elements described so far have been used in optical research for centuries. Spatial light modulators (SLMs) are a relatively new addition, and are especially important in optical computing. It is generally agreed that the lack of fast, high-resolution SLMs is the major obstacle that has prevented many optical computing systems from reaching reality.

A spatial light modulator is a device that creates some sort of modulation on the cross section of a beam of light. Usually a uniform beam of light impinges upon the SLM, and a modulated beam of light results. A simple example is a transparency: after passing through a transparency, different areas in the beam's cross section have different intensities. Thus the beam has become modulated.

The dominant use of spatial light modulators is for display systems, such as giant video screens. They also have a few important uses in optical computing:

- *Input transducers.* SLMs are used to convert an incoherent image into a coherent one. The procedure is as follows: the intensity distribution of the incoherent input image is analyzed, and the results are used to create an SLM of the appropriate transmittance. This the SLM is then used to modulate a coherent beam of light [678].

- *Spatial filters or masks.* For example, consider an optical system in which a lens is used to obtain the Fourier transform of an image. If we place an SLM in the back focal plane of the lens, we can filter out a chosen set of spatial frequencies and thus affect the image [336].

- *Page composers.* These are elements that prepare input pages for optical storage systems.

As we shall see, these uses are extremely important in optical computing, and SLMs will pop up continuously throughout the rest of this work. This also explains the large amount of references, which include a few surveys [97,197,222,678,555, chap. 5] and special issues [621,622,527].

The simplest and best-known way to implement an SLM is of course by photography. photographic film has a couple of nice characteristics in this context: it can achieve very good resolution, and it can give a continuous scale of gray tones. However, it is inconvenient to use: it must be exposed under controlled illumination conditions, developed in a darkroom, dried, and finally mounted in the optical system. This procedure suffers from two major drawbacks. First, it is anything but real-time. Second, in some applications the transparency must be positioned with great accuracy, which might be tricky.

What we are looking for is, therefore, a sort of reusable photographic film. We want to be able to expose, develop, and erase it without moving it, and at high speed. The main criteria for comparing different devices and evaluating their performance are [97,197]:

- *Method of writing on (exposing) the SLM.* There are two basic options:

  * To address each point separately, by a scanning electron beam or by individual addressing electrodes.

  * To (optically) cast an image the whole data onto the surface of the SLM.

- *Light.* Any requirements of the light, e.g., if it must have a specific wavelength.

- *Modulation.* What type of modulation is produced (amplitude, phase, polarization, or any combination), and how is it achieved. What is the modulation efficiency?

- *Quality.* This includes resolution, the ability to distinguish between gray levels, output contrast, linearity, uniformity, noise added by the SLM, etc.

- *Time.* This has two aspects:

modulation	realized by	SLM types
amplitude	change of transmittance	photographic film photodichroic materials
phase*	change of shape	thermoplastic micromechanical deformable mirror
	change of density	acoustooptic cell
polarization*	physical effects in crystals	liquid crystal electrooptic crystals magnetooptic materials

* Phase and polarization modulations are sometimes transformed into amplitude modulation. Likewise, polarization modulation can be converted into phase modulation.

Table 2.3: *Underlying techniques for spatial light modulation.*

* How long is a write-use-erase cycle? Many SLMs work at a video rate of 30 Hz (as they were originally developed for display purposes). While this is rather slow, it does allow for the processing of over $2\frac{1}{2}$ million images per day, assuming the actual processing is done in the short time between successive frames.

* How long can the SLM retain the data written on it, i.e., can it serve as a memory device?

• *Operating conditions.* The power consumption, sensitivity, size, temperature range, etc.

Numerous implementations of spatial light modulators have been proposed over the years. None fulfills all the requirements, and there is no agreement as to which is the best. The basic underlying techniques are summerized in table 2.3. We will only mention a few representatives. A comparison between some actual devices is given in table 2.4.

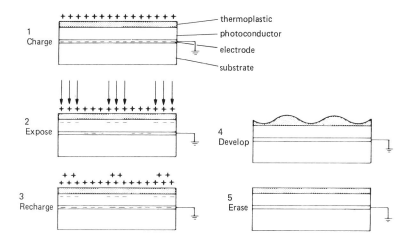

Figure 2.6: *An exposure cycle of a photoplastic device.*
(Reprinted with permission from *Optical Engineering* [160], ©1978)

Photodichroic SLMs

Photodichroic SLMs [92] are similar to photographic film. These are Alkali-Halide
materials (like KCl or NaF) with structural defects called "color centers". These
defects display the photochromic effect: they change color when illuminated with
light of a certain wavelength. A change of color implies that the transmittance
changes. Hence illumination with the right wavelength causes a transmittance
change, and sort of combines the exposure and development stages of photography.
This kind of effect has found an everyday use lately, in the form of sunglasses that
become dark only when there is intense illumination.

A bad thing about photodichroic SLMs is that the wavelength used for reading
the information must be different from the wavelength used to write it — otherwise
the reading will also affect the material. Furthermore, the written pattern tends
to fade out with time and use. Good points are the high resolution obtainable and
the ease of fabrication and use.

Deformable SLMs

A totally different family of SLMs is that of deformable SLMs, such as *photoplastic*
devices [695,160,157]. In these devices an electric field is applied to a thermoplastic
(fig. 2.6). The field strength is modulated by a beam of light that images the input
data on a photoconductor. Then the thermoplastic is heated to its softening point,
and the force applied by the electric field causes a deformation of the plastic.
Upon cooling, the deformation is frozen and will cause phase modulation of a

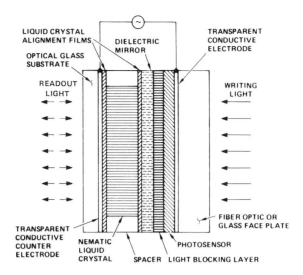

Figure 2.7: *Schematic liquid crystal light valve.*
(Reprinted with permission from *Optical Engineering* [63], ©1978)

readout beam. The deformation can be erased by subsequent heating to a higher temperature.

These SLMs are simple and have good resolution. They also remain operative indefinitely. However, they have a bandpass characteristic and hence cannot record very high or very low spatial frequencies. The cycle time for writing and erasing is rather long. The necessity to dissipate the heat generated in the process is also a disadvantage.

Another type of SLM that actually changes its shape is the *micromechanical* SLM [545,77]. This is an array of miniature leaves, etched with integrated circuit technology. The leaves are charged in correspondence with the input data. The charge exerts a coulomb force on the leaf, and bends it. Consequently, light incident on the array will be reflected at different angles from different leaves.

A similar concept is used in the *deformable mirror* SLM [538,555, chap. 5], which uses a thin membrane suspended above wells rather than small leaves.

Liquid crystal SLMs

A common every-day type SLM is the liquid crystal light valve [308]. One version of this device is what makes the digits of electronic watches stand out (black on a grey background). The principles and physics of liquid crystals (LCs) are quiet complex, and we shall not go into them in detail. Suffice it to say that an LC is a material made of long cigar-shaped molecules that are free to align themselves in various orientations. This alignment can be influenced by applying an electric field. In a watch, the LC is covered by an electrode shaped like a digit. Another electrode is placed below. When a voltage is applied, the molecules align in such a way as to change the polarization of light passing through the LC by 45°. Light coming from the outside passes the LC, hits a mirror and returns through the LC, thus accumulating a polarization change of 90°. The surface of the watch is a polarizer that only allows light of one polarization to enter. After the polarization change, it cannot get out again and the digit appears black. In other places where voltage is not applied the orientation of the molecules is random, the polarization doesn't change, and we see a grey color (not white, because only half the light got in through the polarizer in the first place).

An LC SLM [63,196] (usually called a "liquid crystal light valve" or LCLV) uses the same principle, except that the voltage is not applied by specially shaped electrodes. Instead, it depends on the data written with a beam of light. The device is divided into two parts: the writing beam acts on one side, and the readout beam interacts with the other (fig. 2.7). The mirror that reflects the readout beam is the partition between the two. On the writing side, the mirror is attached to a photoconductor and a transparent electrode that covers the whole surface. The writing light acts on the photoconductor, and allows the electrode to affect the LC. Thus voltage will be applied only in places illuminated by the writing beam. Writing and reading can be done simultaneously, with different light beams. When compared with other SLMs, the LCLV is relatively efficient. The typical response time is about 30 ms, i.e., video rate. Faster devices are, however, being developed [286].

Electrooptic crystals SLMs

A similar family of SLMs are Pockels SLMs [336,318,98,99]. These are based on crystals that change their index of refraction when an electric field is applied to them. The most popular are $Bi_{12}SiO_{20}$ (BSO) and Deuterated KD_2PO_4 (DKDP). The change is different along two axes of the crystal. When light falling on the crystal is polarized so that it has components along both these axes, the components will propagate with different speeds and emerge with a phase difference. Thus linearly polarized light can turn into elliptically polarized light. If this output beam is analyzed by a polarizer that only passes light in a polarization perpendicular to that of the original beam, the output intensity will be proportional to $\sin^2 V$, where V is the applied voltage.

As in liquid crystals, the applied voltage is supplied by two transparent electrodes that sandwich the crystal, and a photoconductor that governs the effect of the electrodes on the crystal[9]. The input data can be written in one of several

---

[9]BSO is itself photoconducting, so a separate photoconductor is not needed.

type	magnetooptic	liquid crystal	electrooptic
name	LIGHT-MOD	Hughes LCLV	E-DKDP
size [cm]	1–5	4.6	5–7.5
resolution [linepairs/mm]	≤ 50	40	40
addressing	electronic x-y	optical imaging	electron beam
switch speed	$\sim 1\mu s$ **per pixel** parallel access to lines	~ 40 ms	33 ms cycle
contrast	1000:1	$> 100:1$	100–1000:1
gray scale	binary	binary	continuous
power/voltage	1 watt	5–10 V. RMS	**6000 V.** electron gun
comments	serial access also possible	video rate	video rate
reference	[589]	[63]	[98]

Table 2.4: *Comparison of some operational spatial light modulators.*

ways: a scanning laser beam can act on the photoconductor, or a scanning electron beam can deposit a surface charge directly on the crystal[10] (fig. 2.8). Alternatively, the whole data can be imaged on the photoconductor.

The advantage of these SLMs is that various operations can be performed on the data, by changing the voltages that act on the crystals. For example, image subtraction can be achieved by using a reversed voltage.

There are a few other types of SLMs based on electrooptical effects in crystals, such as in PLZT [393,404,206], or with added features as in microchannel SLMs

---

[10] In this case a photoconductor is not necessary.

electrooptic	photodichroic	deformable	electrooptic
PROM	—	thermoplastic	photo DKDP
2.5	1–2	1	3
< 100	**10,000** (molecular)	4000	80
optical imaging	optical imaging	optical imaging	optical imaging
30 Hz	—	**250 ms cycle** (slow)	**1000** frames/sec
$10^3 - 10^4$:1	—	200:1	1000:1
continuous	continuous	continuous	continuous
4000 V. across crystal	—	20 erg/exposure	100 V.
video rate	fades out with use	bandpass characteristic	
[318]	[92]	[160]	[99]

[718,605]. The details of these variations are beyond the scope of this review.

Magnetooptic matrix

Our last example is an SLM comprised of a matrix of elements, each of which is addressed individually by electronic means. In this SLM [589], each element is a small ferromagnet. When light transverses this magnet, its polarization is rotated by 45° (this is called the Faraday effect). The direction of rotation depends on the direction of magnetization. Therefore light passing through elements with opposite magnetization will come out with a 90° polarization difference. A polarizer can

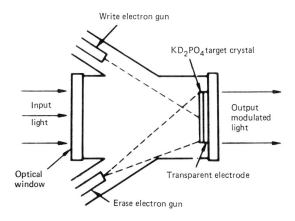

Figure 2.8: *An electron-beam addressed DKDP electrooptic SLM.*
(Reprinted with permission from *Optical Engineering* [98], ©1978)

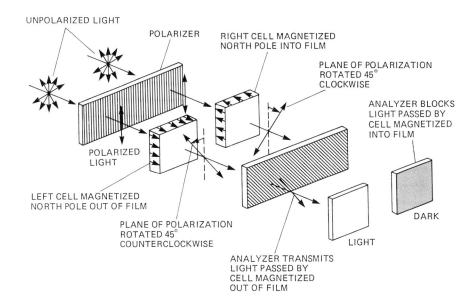

Figure 2.9: *Operation of a magnetooptic SLM.*
(Reprinted with permission from *Optical Engineering* [589], ©1983)

turn this into a binary intensity difference (fig. 2.9).

Magnetooptic matrix SLMs are limited by addressing speed and wiring complexity. These limitations cause matrices of more than 128×128 elements to be impractical, so that the resolution is quite poor. Another problem is that they do not allow for grey levels. Several ideas have been proposed in order to circumvent this last drawback. One is to combine elements of different sizes. Another is to cascade a few SLMs in order that their combined transmittance will have more discrete values.

2.5 Acoustooptic systems

A special kind of optical systems is those which involve interactions with acoustic waves. This combination is distinguished by the following points:

- The acoustic waves themselves may also undergo any physical process that is characteristic of waves, e.g., interference. in particular, the acoustic waves may carry information and may perform some data-processing operation [76].

- In acoustooptic systems, time tends to be the free variable, rather than space. Therefore acoustooptic systems are useful for *systolic* architectures and for the analysis of time signals. They are usually one-dimensional rather than two-dimensional.

This section starts with a short treatise of the interactions between light waves and acoustic waves, known collectively as *Brillouin scattering*. The exploitation of these interactions for optical processing is also mentioned. This includes a brief paragraph on acoustooptic SLMs. Then transducers, which are used to generate acoustic waves, are discussed. The question of materials with good acoustooptic properties [691] is not addressed.

2.5.1 Acoustic waves and Brillouin scattering

Generally speaking, acoustic waves are waves of deformation in a material medium (acoustic waves cannot propagate in vacuum). The deformation usually takes one of two basic forms (or a combination of them) [372]: either periodic *compression* and *rarefaction* of the medium, or a periodic *shearing* movement to the left and right[11]. We will only discuss the first kind.

When an acoustic wave exists in a medium, a snapshot of the medium will reveal a regular spatial alternation between regions where the density is higher than the average and regions where it is lower than the average. Because of the

---

[11] The first kind is called a *longitudinal* wave, because the particles of the medium move in the line of the wave's propagation. The second kind is called a *transverse* wave. Transverse waves cannot exist in liquids or gasses.

high speed of light, when compared with the speed of acoustic waves[12], a light wave passing through the medium will "see" just such a snapshot. In other words, from the light's point of view, the medium has the characteristics of a phase grating. The interaction between the light and this grating, known as Brillouin scattering [6,571,380,373], causes various effects of deflection, modulation, and frequency shifting of the light.

The exact interaction depends on the relative angle between the light wave and the acoustic wave. Three distinct possibilities are of importance: when the waves are perpendicular to each other, when they are collinear, and when the direction of the light wave satisfies the Bragg diffraction condition.

Bragg diffraction

We begin with the Bragg diffraction, because of its relative importance and usefulness in acoustooptic processing. This type of diffraction occurs when the acoustic beam is wide relative to the wavelength of light. In this situation the abovementioned grating behaves like an array of reflective *surfaces*[13]. The surfaces are those where the density of the medium is maximal, and they are reflective because (light) waves tend to be partially reflected when they pass from a medium with one density to a medium with another density (this is the reason why light is reflected from the surface of a pond, or from a sheet of glass). The light that is reflected from successive surfaces interferes. Constructive interference (and thus strong diffraction) occurs only if the light impinges on the surfaces at the *Bragg angle*, defined by

$$\theta = \arcsin \frac{\lambda}{2\Lambda},$$

where λ is the wavelength of the light

Λ is the wavelength of the acoustic wave, and thus the separation between the surfaces.

This is so because when the light comes at this angle, the path differences between reflections from successive surfaces is exactly one (light) wavelength (fig. 2.10).

When the angle in which the light comes differs from the Bragg angle, the diffraction efficiency falls. Note, however, that the Bragg angle depends on the wavelength of the *acoustic* wave. This can be used to modulate the intensity of the deflected light beam: the light beam will come at a predetermined angle, but the acoustic wavelength will change [151,267]. It should be clear that this scheme only works within a limited range of acoustic frequencies, centered around the frequency corresponding to the angle of incidence.

---

[12]Typical speeds for acoustic waves in crystals are of the order of 6 $^{mm}/_{\mu s}$, which is 6 $^{Km}/_{sec}$ [690]. The speed of light in vacuum is $300,000$ $^{Km}/_{sec}$, and in a crystal about half of this.

[13]In other words, it is a *thick* grating.

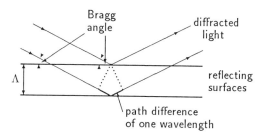

Figure 2.10: *When light impinges on a set of surfaces at the Bragg angle, the path differences for successive reflections is exactly one wavelength.*

The diffraction efficiency also depends on the contrast, or difference, between the high- and low-density regions. Thus the deflected light intensity may also be modulated by changing the amplitude of the acoustic wave.

Raman-Nath or Debye-Sears diffraction

This type of diffraction happens when the light wave is exactly perpendicular to the acoustic wave, and the acoustic frequency is relatively low (so that the width of the acoustical beam is not much more than the acoustical wavelength). It is somewhat similar to diffraction from a *thin* grating, as described in section 2.4.3, although the mechanism is different: here we have a grating that changes the phase in a cyclic manner, rather than changing the amplitude. Typically, more diffraction orders exist than in the case of Bragg diffraction. This phenomenon too may be used to modulate the intensity of light beams.

Collinear waves

When the acoustic and light waves propagate in the same direction, the surfaces created by the acoustic wave cause the light to bounce back and forth between them. Thus a *resonator* is formed. If the acoustic wavelength Λ is exactly an integral multiple of half the optical wavelength $\frac{\lambda}{2}$, constructive interference will occur in the forward direction. Otherwise most of the light will be reflected backwards. Such a configuration can therefore be used as a *band-pass filter* [150]. Note that here we speak of filtering the light's *temporal* frequency. This has nothing to do with the spatial filtering mentioned previously.

Doppler shift

In the above description we treated the acoustic wave as if it was a stationary grating. This is actually not true — as the acoustic wave propagates, its "grating surfaces" move. This causes a small change in the frequency of the diffracted light (again, this is the temporal frequency). This change may be regarded as a Doppler shift[14]. The amount of change depends on the acoustic wave frequency and on the diffraction order. For example, in the Bragg diffraction case, the diffraction order is ±1. Therefore the light frequency is either incremented or decremented by the acoustic frequency, depending on their relative directions [380,6,150,267].

2.5.2   Acoustic transducers

As we shall see in section 3.5, the acoustic waves in acoustooptic processing systems often reproduce received RF (radio frequency) signals. Acoustic transducers are the means by which the electronic waveforms are converted into acoustic waves. These transducers exploit the *piezoelectric effect* which occurs in some crystals (e.g., $LiNbO_3$) [150].

Bulk transducer

In order to generate an acoustic wave that will propagate through some medium, a piezoelectric crystal is attached to the end surface of the medium. Such crystals display the piezoelectric effect: when an electric voltage is applied to them, their shape is deformed. Conversely, when they are deformed, an electric potential may be measured between their sides. Hence the application of an alternating voltage to the crystal will cause it to vibrate. These vibrations cause periodic compressions in the attached medium, which propagate in the form of acoustic waves.

Interdigital transducer

In various applications it is more convenient to use surface acoustic waves (SAW), i.e., acoustic waves that propagate along the surface of the medium [372,660], rather than bulk acoustic waves. These waves are also generated by a piezoelectric crystal, but the electrodes that apply the voltage are different. Instead of having two electrodes on opposite sides of the crystal, two electrodes with interleaved prongs are laid on its surface. When a periodic electrical signal is applied, a SAW is generated. The prongs are spaced according to the desired acoustic wavelength, and the waves generated by successive pairs reinforce each other.

Input/output characteristic

It should be noted that the above transducers can operate both as generators and as detectors of acoustic waves. This is a direct result of the two-way nature of the

---

[14]A Doppler shift is a change of the apparent frequency of a wave as a result of relative motion between the transmitter and the receiver.

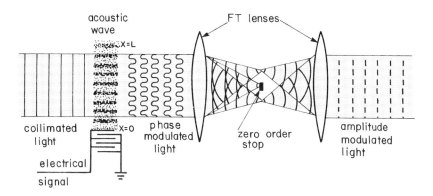

Figure 2.11: *Schlieren filtering turns a phase modulated light beam into an amplitude modulated one.*

piezoelectric effect: a voltage causes a deformation, and a deformation causes a voltage.

2.5.3   Acoustooptical spatial light modulators

A very common use of acoustooptic devices is to spatially modulate the cross section of a beam of light in accordance with a temporal electrical signal. This is done as follows [642,454,579]. The electrical signal $f(t)$ activates an acoustooptic transducer, which generates an acoustic wave. This acoustic wave is an exact replica of the original electrical signal. Therefore the density of the medium may be described by $f(x - vt)$, where v is the propagation speed of the acoustic wave, and $x = 0$ at the transducer.

The density of the medium affects its index of refraction. Therefore light passing through the medium perpendicularly to the acoustic wave will become phase modulated: parts of the beam that pass through an area of higher density will suffer a larger delay. The light will then be described by[15]

$$g_t(x) = e^{i\alpha f(x - vt)},$$

where α is the modulation factor. Assuming α is small, we can approximate this by

$$g_t(x) \approx 1 + i\,\alpha\,f(x - vt),$$

---

[15]Recall that a phase change is represented by an imaginary exponential factor (page 11). The subscript t is included to stress the fact that this spatial modulation is also time dependent.

i.e., a constant bias level plus a spatial amplitude modulation factor proportional to f. An amplitude modulated beam will therefore be obtained by filtering out the zero-frequency bias term. This is easy to do by Fourier-transforming with a lens and blocking the center of the resulting light distribution. Another Fourier transform will produce the desired light distribution, which is amplitude modulated by f, albeit it is also attenuated and phase shifted:

$$g_t'(x) \approx i\,\alpha\,f(x-vt) = \alpha\,f(x-vt)\,e^{i\frac{\pi}{2}}.$$

This filtering action is sometimes called "schlieren filtering".

The one-dimensional character of acoustooptic devices does not preclude them from use in optical systems that operate on light beams with a two-dimensional cross section. For example, a multichannel system might use a different one-dimensional acoustooptic modulator in each channel. The advantage of using such devices are that they are readily available, have a higher bandwidth, and are much cheaper [570].

2.6   Fundamental limitations

Optical systems that manipulate modulated beams of light aren't all- powerful — there are some fundamental limitations as to what they can do. These limitations relate to the amount of information that can be handled and to the accuracy with which it is handled.

2.6.1   Diffraction-limited systems and the space-bandwidth product

The most basic and unavoidable limit arises from the fact that the propagation of beams of light is governed by the phenomenon of diffraction. The aperture from which the light issues may be regarded as an extended source. Denote its diameter by D. Let us assume, for simplicity, that all the points in this source oscillate in phase. The extent of the beam of light is then dictated by the occurrence of constructive interference between light rays coming from distinct points [168, sect. 9.5]. The beam's intensity is maximal at the center, and falls off away from it. We can approximate the beam boundary by finding where destructive interference occurs. Let us regard the source as made up of two parts, each of extent $\frac{D}{2}$. We pair off the points in one half with the corresponding points in the other. The light from each pair interferes destructively in the direction θ so that the path difference is $\frac{\lambda}{2}$, half a wavelength (see fig. 2.12): this direction is given by $\theta = \arcsin\frac{\lambda/2}{D/2}$. Using a small-angle approximation, we may state that the angular width of the beam is of the order of $\theta \approx \frac{\lambda}{D}$. In short, a beam of light is never perfectly collimated; it always diverges slightly.

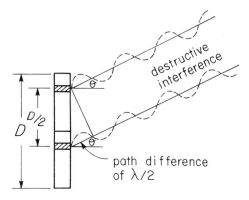

Figure 2.12: *Diffraction between rays coming from distinct points in a source limits the angular extent of a beam of light.*

The inherently divergent character of light beams has far-reaching implications in optical systems. It sets a limit to the number of resolvable points in the cross section of a beam of light: points that are too small spread out and mix with each other as the beam propagates, thus becoming indistinguishable. The total number of distinguishable points is given by the *space-bandwidth product* (SBW) of the optical system: the space is the cross section area, and the bandwidth is the highest spatial frequency that can be handled by the system (actually the square of the highest frequency, because the cross section is two-dimensional). For example, the SBW of the lens of a 35 mm camera is approximately 10^6. High precision optical systems used in optical processors may pass 10^{10}.

This limit, set by the diffraction of light, cannot be avoided. However, the space-bandwidth product of an optical system might be even lower than the limit imposed by the diffraction. This is usually the result of aberrations in the optical elements. When very high-quality optical elements are used, so that the aberration limits are smaller than the diffraction limit, we get a *diffraction-limited* system. This is the best that can be done; further improvement of the quality of the optical elements will not help.

2.6.2 Dynamic range

The data is introduced into optical processing systems by *analog* modulation of the light. The range of possible values, as well as how fine its division is, are limited by various properties of the optical system.

A basic limiting factor is noise, i.e., random and unintentional changes in the light. Noise may result from quantum effects, from statistical properties of the light[16], and from dirt and dust. Aberrations and nonuniformities of the optical elements also contribute to the noise. As it is desired that the noise have as little effect as possible on the data processing, the signal-to-noise ratio must be high. Hence the noise level sets a limit on the smallest intensities and phase changes that can be used — smaller ones would be too susceptible to influence by the noise.

At the other end of the scale, there is also a limit on the highest intensity that can be used. The reason is that optical systems are typically used for linear processing. In reality, however, these systems are only linear to the first approximation[17]. When high intensities are involved, nonlinear effects start to come into play. In such a situation, the system no longer performs the processing it is supposed to.

The ratio of the highest usable intensity to the lowest usable intensity is called the *dynamic range* of the system. This also gives the approximate number of intensity levels that can be distinguished. Typical optical systems have a dynamic range of a few hundreds, which implies that when data values are represented by analog intensities the obtainable accuracy is roughly equivalent to that of 8-bit binary numbers.

2.7   Detectors

The information in an optical computing system is conveyed by modulated beams of light. Naturally, so is the output. What you do with it depends on the specific implementation. In some cases the total light intensity is important. In other cases the light distribution in the output is of importance. There are a number of methods to detect and/or record the output.

2.7.1   Detecting light intensity

There are four main types of devices that are used to detect light intensity [476, 228].

PIN photodiodes

These diodes have an opening that gives access to incident photons. The photons excite electrons in the P area of the diode and create electron-hole pairs (a full explanation is given in appendix E). These charge carriers are separated by an electric field, and so a photocurrent is formed. The photocurrent is usually very weak, and it must be amplified before it can be used for anything.

---

[16]Recall that a light wave is composed of individual photons. The arrival rate of photons follows Poisson statistics.

[17]Coherent systems are linear in the complex amplitude; incoherent systems are linear in the intensity.

Avalanche photodiodes (APD)

The principal here is the same as in PIN diodes. The difference is that the applied voltage is much higher, so that the diode operates near its breakdown point. As a result, electron-hole pairs are accelerated to such a degree that they receive enough energy to create additional electron-hole pairs. In this way the photocurrent is amplified while still in the diode.

Photoconductors

A photoconductor is an insulating material that becomes conducting when light falls on it. It may be used to detect light by being placed between two transparent electrodes. If light is present, the photoconductor will conduct, and current will flow from one electrode to the other. In the absence of light, there will be no current. Devices using this principle are rare; they are less developed and less efficient than the photodiodes described above.

Photomultipliers (PMTs)

The incident light in a photomultiplier falls on a photocathode and causes the release of some electrons. These electrons are accelerated through a chain of electrodes (called "dynodes"), causing the emission of more and more electrons along the way. The photocurrent that finally reaches the anode is highly amplified. The problem with photomultipliers is that they are bulky and require very high voltages. They are therefore seldom used in optical computing or optical communications systems.

2.7.2   Detecting light distributions

Photography

The oldest and best known method of recording a distribution of light intensities is to photograph it on film. This creates a transparency with transmittance that is more or less inversely proportional to the light intensity. This method is good when high resolution is needed and when the data must be stored for extended periods. Its drawbacks are that it is inconvenient and time-consuming, and has linearity and dynamic range problems.

Detector arrays

A completely opposite approach is to detect the optical output signal in real time, and convert it to an electrical signal that may be stored or otherwise manipulated. One method of doing so is by using an array of small detectors, like the photodiodes described in the preceding section. These devices translate the intensity of the light falling on them to a voltage. Such an array gives a real-time output for all pixels in parallel, but usually has rather low resolution. For example, an array of 128×128 detectors already needs individual connections for 16,384 detectors.

Vacuum tube video cameras [158,225]

The dominant use of video cameras is of course in television, but transforming an image into a video signal can be very handy also in optical computing. In vacuum tube cameras, an image is formed on the face of the tube. This image is then read out by a scanning electron beam. The output signal is therefore a serial raster scan of the image. The resolution is usually better than that of detector arrays, but nowhere near that of film. A typical resolution is about 500 points across the whole image.

CCDs (Charge-coupled devices) [10,225]

This is another technology used in video cameras. The basic feature of CCDs is that small packets of charge can be moved across the device, by manipulation of voltages on electrodes. In a CCD video camera, the input image creates a charge distribution by the electro-optic effect, and this charge distribution is passed to the CCD. The CCD is organized as a matrix of elements, representing pixels, and each acquires its own local charge. These charges are then shifted out of the CCD in an orderly manner, line by line, to obtain a raster scan of the image.

2.7.3   Phase loss

All detectors react only to the energy conveyed by light; in other words, they measure the *intensity* of the light, and not the complex amplitude, so that phase information is lost. This can be a big problem in those coherent optical systems where part of the information is represented by the phase. As an example, consider the case of obtaining the Fourier transform of an image by use of a lens. If we try to detect the Fourier transform in the back focal plane of the lens, we will only get the *power spectrum* of the image, instead of the spectrum itself.

If we are interested in the complex amplitude, therefore, we need resort to indirect methods. One possibility is to use interferometric methods. This means that we cause the light we are interested in to interfere with some other, known beam of light, and deduce the complex amplitude from the interference pattern. Another is to use homodyne detection, in which the detection device compares the phase of the incoming light with the phase of an internal reference light wave [430]. Such detectors are now in advanced stages of development.

2.8   Holography

The dominant method for recording both the amplitude and the phase of an image is holography. Holography was introduced in 1948 by Gabor [235,236,237,417], as a method of lensless imaging to be used in electron microscopy. However, it was only in the early '60s that Leith and Upatnieks modified the technique and made it a generally accepted and useful tool [413,414,415,416], using the newly invented lasers. Today holography is a basic and important part of optics, and it is indispensable for optical computers. See the bibliographical notes for additional references.

2.8.1   Wavefront recording and reconstruction

A hologram is usually recorded on photographic film, which, of course, only responds to intensity. Therefore holography is a method that represents a complex-valued image by a real, positive-valued one. Indeed, holography is actually equivalent to the spatial carrier modulation discussed in section 2.2.2. This equivalence is shown in appendix F. Here we will show how a hologram records the wavefront of a modulated beam, and how this wavefront is subsequently reconstructed.

The basic idea in holography is to have the object beam, which is the beam whose wavefront we wish to record, interfere with a reference beam of known amplitude and phase. If the beams are mutually coherent, the interference pattern depends both on the amplitudes and on the phase relations of the beams. Specifically, if we denote the complex amplitude of the object beam by O, and the complex amplitude of the reference beam by R, the intensity pattern recorded on the film will be

$$\mid O + R \mid^2 = \mid O \mid^2 + \mid R \mid^2 + O^*R + OR^*,$$

where X^* denotes the complex conjugate of X. As we see, the fourth term is directly proportional to O, which is what we want to record. As a fringe benefit, we also record O^*.

The transmittance of the developed hologram is (inversely) proportional to the recorded intensity pattern. We denote the proportionality factor by β. In order to reconstruct the wavefront, we illuminate the hologram with a beam identical to the reference beam. This is called the *readout* beam. The beam will become modulated by the transmittance of the hologram, and we get

$$(\beta|O + R|^2)R = \beta|O|^2R + \beta|R|^2R + \beta O^*RR + \beta OR^*R$$

$$= \beta(|O|^2 + |R|^2)R + \beta R^2O^* + \alpha O.$$

If R is a uniform plane wave, $\alpha = \beta RR^*$ is just a scalar, and O is reproduced.

Unfortunately we also get two more terms that we did not want. Obviously we must be able to separate the terms for the process to be practical. This separation

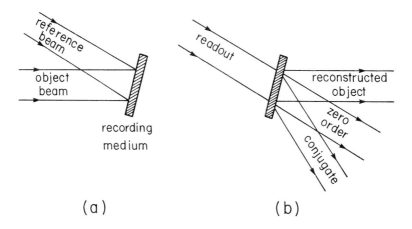

(a)   (b)

Figure 2.13: (a) Recording a hologram.
(b) Reconstruction from a hologram.

is achieved by having the object and reference beams come from different directions. Let us use a simple example to see why this helps. Assume that both the object and reference beams are uniform plane waves. When two plane waves meet at an angle, and a film is introduced to record their interference pattern, the result is a set of parallel lines (i.e., a grating)[18]. Later, when the reconstruction beam impinges upon this grating, it is diffracted (as we saw in section 2.4.3) and split into a number of beams. The direction of the zero-order diffraction term is the same as that of the reconstruction beam. The first-order diffraction terms flank it at approximately the same angle to both sides, and there might be higher-order diffraction terms at larger angles.

When the object beam is not a plane wave the picture is more complicated, but the principle is the same. The hologram can be seen as a special, very complicated, diffraction grating. When it is illuminated by the readout beam, there are three main resulting beams. One is the zero-order term, represented by $\beta(|O|^2 + |R|^2)R$ in the formula. This is an attenuated continuation of the incident readout beam R. The other two are first-order terms. At one side of the zero-order term we get the reconstructed object beam, represented by αO. On the other side is the conjugate beam, represented by $\beta R^2 O^*$ (fig. 2.13 (b)). In order for the different beams to be distinct and not overlapping, the angle between the reference and object beams (at the recording stage) must be big enough. This depends on the spatial bandwidth of the signal and on the wavelength.

---

[18] This is the spatial carrier mentioned above.

2.8.2 Holographic optical elements

The whole discussion so far has concerned using holograms to record wavefronts originating from existing objects. However, this is not the only use of holograms. In the context of optical computing, holograms have numerous other, more important applications. These applications revolve around the fact that a hologram can be viewed as an optical element, in that it can change the direction of rays of light in an arbitrary fashion [83,84,149,448,300]. This point deserves further elaboration. A regular, spherical lens has a global behavior pattern. All parts of an incident plane wave are deflected in accordance with a global scheme, so that they all pass through the focus. A hologram is not like that (or rather, doesn't have to be like that). In a hologram, each part of the beam is amplitude and phase modulated individually. This can be done in accordance with a global pattern, so a hologram can also operate as a regular lens, but it can also be arbitrary.

Holographic optical elements (HOEs) have some advantages over the classical optical elements. The important ones are [134]:

- Flexibility. Weird and wonderous optical elements are relatively easy to implement holographically, while they might be practically impossible to implement in any other way. Examples are:
    * Optimal low-aberration lenses [359].
    * A multifocus lens [427].
    * A cylindrical lens with a varying focal length [125].
    * Aspheric optical elements [208].
    * Low-loss arbitrary optical elements [47].

- The simplicity of fabricating HOEs applies also to conventional optical elements, which implies that they too might be cheaper and easier to reproduce with this technology.

- HOEs tend to be smaller and lighter than regular optical elements.

2.8.3 Computer generated holograms

Holograms with arbitrary diffraction patterns cannot be created by the usual photographic procedure, as the patterns do not arise from an existing wavefront. Therefore they have to be computer generated [298,327]. This is typically done in four steps:

1. The desired diffraction pattern is computed. This is the complex function $g(x,y)$ that represents the amplitude and phase we want the light to have immediately after it passes through the hologram. This is the most computationally intensive step.

2. A real, positive function that represents $g(x, y)$ is computed. This reflects the fact that a hologram encodes a complex function by an intensity pattern. However, CGHs do not necessarily employ spatial carrier modulation. A few possible methods are discussed later in this section.

3. The result is plotted on some output device, usually a binary (black/white) plotter (recently laser printers have also been put to use). Alternatively, it may be displayed on a CRT and photographed.

4. The plot is reduced to its final size and used to make a transparency.

There are several fine points about this procedure:

- The resolution of a photographic hologram is about 1500 lines per mm. Thus a 20×20 cm hologram has about 9×10^{10} resolution elements! [239]. Such resolution is not achievable in a computer generated hologram. The reasons are both the amount of computation involved in creating the diffraction pattern, and the limited resolution of the plotting and reduction apparatus. The achievable resolution with conventional devices is about $10^3 - 10^4$ lines in each dimension [448], i.e., a total of no more than 10^8 pixels and usually much less. Only devices that employ an electron-beam to write the hologram can achieve a resolution comparable to that of photographic holograms [24]. The quality achieved by the obtainable resolution depends on the coding scheme [575].

- The plotting device is usually binary, i.e., black/white. Therefore the complex function must be represented directly by a binary pattern, or else some halftoning technique must be used [727]. A good candidate is pulse-density-modulation coupled with error diffusion [298]. It turns out that the lack of grey tones is actually an advantage: it greatly simplifies the photo-reduction process, because linearity is not important, and it allows for easy mass reproduction [80]. Binary holograms are also more efficient, and produce less noise in the reconstructed object beam [651].

- CGHs usually just represent quantized, discrete samples of the desired function. This introduces some quantization noise [327,93]. The quantization noise may be reduced by iterative adjustments [220].

Encoding methods

Several methods for the representation of the complex diffraction pattern (step 2 above) have been proposed. They are now described, and then summarized in table 2.5.

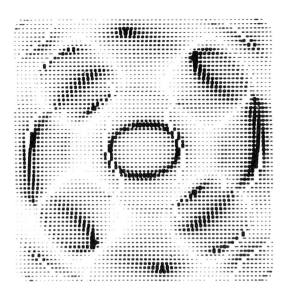

Figure 2.14: *A computer generated hologram made with the detour phase method.* (Reprinted with permission from *Applied Optics* [437], ©1967)

- The interference of a spherical wave originating from a point and a plane reference wave creates a pattern of concentric circles called a *Fresnel zone plate* (fig. F.1. See appendix F for the derivation). A hologram of a nonexisting object can therefore be created by superimposing FZPs for the various points of the object [619,721].

- A simple and elegant way to create the required light distribution is to use the fact that the reconstruction beam is a plane wave that hits the hologram at an angle. Such a configuration causes a cyclic change of the phase across the plane of the hologram. The desired light distribution is obtained by partitioning the hologram into minute squares, and drawing a small transparent slit in each one. The position of the slit is determined so as to pass light with the desired phase. Its size is determined by the desired amplitude (fig. 2.14). This is called the "detour phase" method [78,80,437,440,409].

- A somewhat similar method first decomposes the complex function into four real, positive components[19] [410,327]:

$$g = g_1 - g_3 + ig_2 - ig_4.$$

---

[19]It is also possible to use only three components [90].

Figure 2.15: *Synthetic interferogram CGH.*
(Reprinted with permission from *Optical Engineering* [83], ©1975)

This sum can also be regarded as a result of *phase shifting* the different components:

$$g = g_1 + g_2 e^{i\frac{\pi}{2}} + g_3 e^{i\pi} + g_4 e^{i\frac{3\pi}{2}}.$$

If a Fourier hologram is being created (i.e., the image will be viewed only through a Fourier-transform lens), these phase shifts may be realized by sampling the four components in different points. This works because in a Fourier transform, spatial shifts are translated into phase changes. In other words, each sampling cell is divided into four subcells, with transmittance proportional to $g_1 \ldots g_4$. This is called the "delayed sampling" method.

- A hologram is actually a special case of an *interferogram*, i.e., a recording of the interference pattern of two waves. This is usually a set of alternate bright and dark lines, called fringes, that indicate the places where constructive and destructive interference has occurred. A CGH can therefore be made by creating a synthetic interferogram. When a constant-amplitude wave $e^{i\varphi(x,y)}$ interferes with a plane reference wave $e^{i2\pi\frac{\sin\theta}{\lambda}x}$, constructive interference occurs along lines that satisfy

$$2\pi\frac{\sin\theta}{\lambda}x - \varphi(x,y) = 2\pi n$$

type	preparation	gray levels	comments	ref
superimposed FZP	multi-exposure photo	continuous	limited number of points	[619]
detour phase	plotter output	binary	both phase and amplitude are quantized	[80]
delay sampling	CRT display	continuous	Fourier hologram	[410]
synthetic interferogram	CRT display	binary	phase only	[411]
kinoform	bleached photo of plotter output	plot—continuous final result— transparent	phase only, special film treatment	[423]
ROACH	bleached photo on triple-emulsion film	continuous	special film, special treatment	[156]

Table 2.5: *Comparison of computer generated hologram methods.*

(where n is any integer). The locations of these lines are computed, and they are plotted on an output device [409]. When simple wavefronts are concerned, this type of CGH gives a striking demonstration of the fact that a hologram is actually a slightly deformed grating (fig. 2.15).

- The above methods all reconstruct the required wavefront by diffraction from a light beam that impinges upon the CGH at an angle. As in regular holography, additional diffraction orders are also created. Therefore the diffraction efficiency in these methods is limited: The input light must always be divided among the different output beams. A *kinoform* achieves higher efficiency (which may reach 100%) by direct phase modulation of normally incident light [423,424] — a configuration that results in just *one* on-axis diffraction order.

This is done as follows. The *phase* of the desired wavefront is computed (modulo 2π), plotted, and photographed. The film is then bleached [157] — a process in which the dark grains are removed. Thus an emulsion with varying density is transformed into an emulsion with varying thickness, which serves as a phase filter. The process must be carefully controlled so that the maximal difference in thickness will cause a phase delay of exactly 2π.

A more sophisticated setup, which uses film with three emulsions which are exposed individually by light of different colors, allows the amplitude to be controlled as well [156]. This is called "ROACH" — referenceless on-axis complex hologram.

Multifacet holograms

A simpler way is which to achieve low-resolution synthetic holograms is to create multifacet holograms. These are holograms that are divided into numerous small cells, called *facets* (typically there are about 1000). Each facet manipulates the light falling on it in a manner that is independent of neighboring facets. The facets are created optically, like conventional holograms, one at a time. A computer controls the process until all facets are exposed [125,126].

Summary

Optical computers use light to convey information. Light is an electro-magnetic wave that is characterized by its frequency, wavelength, amplitude, phase, polarization, and degree of coherence. Light sources used in optical computers are semiconductor LEDs and lasers. Information is imposed on a light beam by modulation of its cross section; this is done by spatial light modulators (SLMs). The information content of a beam of light is limited by the system's space-bandwidth product and by its dynamic range. Light beams are manipulated by various optical elements, e.g., beam-splitters, gratings, lenses, and polarizers. In particular, lenses can form a light distribution that is the Fourier transform of another light distribution. The intensity of a light beam may be detected by a photodiode. The intensity distribution in an image is detected by a detector array or a TV camera. The amplitude and phase in an image can be recorded by an interferometric method such as holography. Computer generated holograms can create the wavefronts of nonexisting objects, or realize arbitrary optical elements.

Bibliographical notes

Numerous textbooks on optics have been written; the following are the most commonly used:
□ Jenkins & White [339] — Basically a geometrical optics point of view, but wave optics and quantum optics are also treated.

□ Born & Wolf [67] — A rigorous mathematical approach based on Maxwell's equations of electromagnetic fields. An exhaustive text, for those who want an in-depth treatment.

□ Feynman, Leighton & Sands [217, chap. 26–36] — Optics in the context of electromagnetic waves, quantum phenomena, and vision.

□ Goodman [260] — Fourier optics. Includes issues in optical data processing.

□ Hecht (& Zajac) [306] — beautifully illustrated treatment of basic properties of light and optical effects.

The attitude of modern physics towards light is aptly described in Feynman's book on QED [216]. More intuitive descriptions are gathered in a collection of readings from Scientific American [398]. Lasers are also treated in this collection, as well as in numerous other publications (e.g., [421]). Each January issue of Laser Focus contains a survey of the last year's developments in lasers, for those who wish to be very up-to-date.

The classical optical elements are treated in optics textbooks (especially Jenkins & White [339]). The fullest review of SLMs is by Casasent [97]. Neff [509] mentions a few recent attempts to realize SLMs with a frame rate exceeding 1 KHz. A table of commercially available SLMs may be found in the survey by Bell [54].

Brillouin scattering is treated in Born & Wolf [67, chap. XII]. Uses of acoustooptic systems, as well as their theory, may be found in a special issue of the proceedings of the IEEE [5].

An encyclopedic coverage of holography (theory, techniques and applications) is provided by the Handbook of Optical Holography [291]. A shorter, very clear treatment is given in the book by Caulfield and Lu [127]. The article by Leith and Upatnieks in Scientific American [416] is an excellent introduction to the field. Most optics books also include a chapter about holography.

Chapter 3

Optical Image and Signal Processing

One of the basic endeavors of physics is to give a precise mathematical description of natural phenomena. In the field of optics, the phenomena in question are related to light and its interactions with various materials and optical elements. These interactions are usually far from trivial, and thus the mathematical description may also be quite complicated. As an example, consider the Fourier-transform property of a lens (see section 2.4.4 and appendix C). When we say that a lens takes the Fourier transform of the light distribution in its front focal plane, and displays the result in the back focal plane, what we actually mean is that given a certain light distribution $f(x, y)$ in the front focal plane of a lens, the resulting light distribution in the back focal plane may be *described mathematically* as the two-dimensional Fourier transform of $f(x, y)$.

Most optical systems are linear, i.e., there is a linear functional relationship between the input light distribution and the output light distribution. The most general form of this functional relationship is [562]:

$$g(x', y', t') = \iiint f(x, y, t) \, h(x, y, t; x', y', t') \, dx \, dy \, dt, \qquad (3.1)$$

where f is the input light distribution, which depends on the input spatial coordinates x, y and on the time t

        g is the output light distribution, in terms of the spatial coordinates x', y' and the time t'

        h describes the optical system, by specifying the effect of $f(x, y, t)$ on $g(x', y', t')$ for every possible combination of x, y, t, x', y', t'.

In most cases, however, only space *or* time integration is used, rather than integration over all three variables. Returning to the Fourier-transform example, this is a case where we do not utilize the option of time integration, and therefore t and t' are redundant. The kernel h for the Fourier transform is

$$h(x, y, x', y') = e^{-i2\pi(xx' + yy')}.$$

This chapter and the one following it are about the use of optical systems to perform some sort of nontrivial computation or processing. Actually this is just a small conceptual shift: instead of regarding the mathematics as a description of

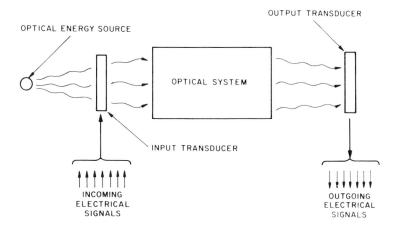

Figure 3.1: *Schematic optical signal processor.*
(Reprinted with permission from Preston/**Coherent Optical Computers** [555], ©1972 McGraw-Hill)

the optics, look at the optics as a means to compute the mathematics. In other words, if the desired computation can be described by a formula like eq. 3.1, all we have to do is to create an optical system that realizes h, feed it with light modulated according to f, and read out the result g (fig. 3.1). For example, the optical system needed for the Fourier transform turns out to be very simple — it is just a lens[1]. In other cases we might need an optical system of greater complexity.

The main advantage of such optical systems is their speed [557]. An optical two-dimensional Fourier transform of a 1000×1000 point image takes a few nanoseconds (the time needed by light to traverse the system). The same computation on a digital computer requires some 10^8 operations (using the FFT algorithm), so the optical system is working at a rate equivalent to more than 10^{16} operations per second! [250]. This extraordinary feat is not so much a consequence of the high speed of light as of the *inherent parallelism* of the system: The whole image goes through the lens at the same time, and all the output points are created simultaneously.

Optical signal processing systems also have some drawbacks and limitations:

- If the input signal is not an optical signal, it must be translated into an optical form by some sort of *input transducer*[2]. The speed of the input

---

[1] "Just a lens" might be misleading; if a high quality transform is required, the lens should be designed carefully and polished to fine tolerances.

[2] Typical input transducers are SLMs (spatial light modulators), discussed in section 2.4.6.

transducer may severely limit the throughput of the optical system.

- If the desired output is not an optical image but rather an electronic signal, an output transducer is also needed.

- Macroscopic physical systems are *analog* in nature, i.e., there is no quantization of values [557]. The accuracy of optical processors is therefore limited by the accuracy with which it is possible to modulate the input light, and the accuracy with which it is possible to measure the output light. The obtainable accuracy is usually equivalent to no more than 8 bits. In other words, the dynamic range of these systems is small.

- The information content of modulated light beams is limited by the space-bandwidth product of the system (see page 39).

- Optical signal processors are *special purpose*: each optical system is characterized by the functional relationship h between its input and output; it can only perform the operation described by eq. 3.1. When another operation is desired, a new optical system is needed. Thus an optical signal processor can either form a complete special purpose computer, if its function is useful enough, or else it can be a special-purpose accelerator that is part of a larger computer system. But it cannot serve as a general purpose computer.

The balance of this chapter describes operations related to image and signal processing that are achievable with special purpose analog optical systems. First and foremost are operations based on the Fourier transform: spectral analysis, convolution, and correlation. These operations typically involve *spatial filtering* in the Fourier domain — which is the hallmark of analog optical processing [517,172]. Applications that use this include picture deblurring and synthetic aperture radar imaging. Then some other linear and even nonlinear transforms are discussed. Next we turn to RF signal analysis, which also utilizes the time variable. The next chapter then describes numerical operations that are achievable with analog optical processors. This includes, for example, methods for performing operations from the algebra of matrices. Chapter 5 deals with hybrid systems, which combine special purpose analog optical systems with general purpose digital electronic computers.

3.1   Spectral analysis and filtering

The frequency spectrum of a signal is obtained, by definition, as a result of Fourier-transforming the signal. Knowledge of the spectrum is an important tool in signal analysis. As we shall see in section 3.2.7, it can also serve for pattern recognition. This is true both for radio signals and for two-dimensional spatial signals (i.e.,

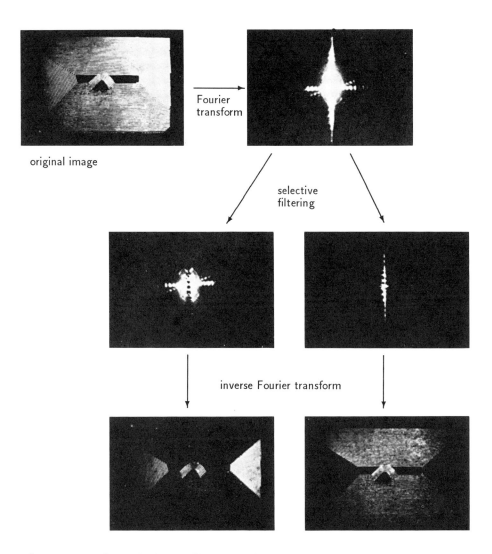

original image

Fourier
transform

selective
filtering

inverse Fourier transform

Figure 3.2: *Effects of selective filtering in the spatial frequency domain. The image is an aerial picture of a wheat field at harvest.*
(Adapted with permission from *Optical Engineering* [336], ©1974)

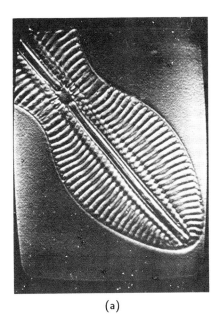
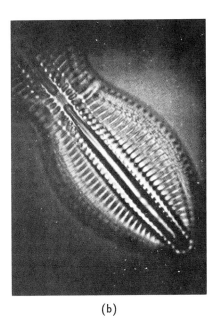

(a)   (b)

Figure 3.3: *Real-time increase of depth of field.*
(a) Regular microscopic image of a diatom.
(b) With increased depth of field.
(Reprinted with permission from *Optica Acta* [302], ©1977)

images). As we have seen, a two-dimensional spatial Fourier transform is easy to
obtain in coherent-light optical systems by passing the light through a lens (see
section 2.4.4 and appendix C).

The fact that the spatial frequency spectrum of an image appears as a physically tangible light distribution allows for the easy manipulation of the different
spectral components [517]. In particular it is easy to implement high-pass filters (a
disk that blocks the central, low-frequency part of the spectrum), low-pass filters
(an opaque screen with a hole that only allows the low frequencies through), or
directional filters (an opaque screen with wedges cut out [336,678]; see fig. 3.2). It
is also easy to filter out a periodic noise, which manifests itself as a point in the
spectrum. More sophisticated filters are discussed in the following sections.

Increase of depth of field

An interesting application for spectral filtering is the increase of depth of field
[302,303]. In many situations, and notably in microscopic photography, the object
depth is greater than the depth of field. As a result parts of the image are always

THE DEVELOPMENT OF RADAR DURING WORLD
WAR II BROUGHT RADAR FROM A LABORATORY
CONCEPT TO A MATURE DISCIPLINE IN JUST
A FEW SHORT YEARS. SINCE 1945 RADAR
TECHNOLOGY HAS BECOME SO SOPHISTICATED
THAT THE BASIC RECTANGULAR PULSE RADAR
SIGNAL IS NO LONGER SUFFICIENT IN THE
DESIGN OF MANY NEW RADAR SYSTEMS.
MORE COMPLEX RADAR SIGNALS MUST BE
TAILORED TO SPECIFIC REQUIREMENTS.

(a)

(b)

Figure 3.4: *Pattern recognition by cross-correlation.*
(a) The scene is a paragraph of text; the model is the word RADAR.
(b) In the correlation output (after thresholding), the six locations of the word are indicated. The dots at right show the vertical resolution.
(Reprinted with permission from the *Proceedings of the IEEE* [102], ©1979 IEEE)

out of focus (fig. 3.3 (a)). The out-of-focus parts are smeared to different degrees. They do not contain any sharp lines; hence they do not contain any high spatial frequencies. We may conclude that all the high-spatial-frequency content of the picture comes from the focused part only. Therefore a high-pass filter will enable us to see only the focused part, and block out the unfocused part.

To obtain a whole focused image, the camera's focus is changed during the exposure: it scans the entire object, so that at the beginning the point nearest to the camera is in focus and at the end the point farthest away is in focus. The image is high-pass filtered, so that at any instant only the in-focus part is imaged on the film. Thus when the focus is changed, additional focused parts are accumulated, and finally a complete in-focus picture is constructed. An example of the outcome is given in fig. 3.3 (b).

3.2 Pattern recognition

Perhaps the most widely researched application of analog optical processing systems is that of pattern recognition by cross-correlation [422]. The basics of this subject were laid down by VanderLugt in 1964 [699], and it has seen many interesting developments since then. The central position that this subject holds in the field of analog optical processing warrants the somewhat lengthy and detailed treatment of this section.

The problem may be stated as follows: given an input scene, determine whether or not a known object appears in it, and, if it does, where it is. The object is of course obscured by other objects and by the background (collectively called the "noise"). Representing the input scene by $g(x, y)$ and the object (usually termed the "model") by $s(x, y)$, the cross-correlation of these functions will give us the desired answer: if $s(x, y)$ is indeed a subscene of $g(x, y)$, a *correlation peak* will appear. The position of the peak will indicate the position of the model in the scene. If s is not a part of g, all the correlation values will be low. Fig. 3.4 is an example of text correlation: the word "radar" was the model that was searched for in the paragraph (a). Its six locations are indicated by points of light in the output (b).

We begin our in-depth review of the subject with a discussion of what cross-correlation is, and how it answers our needs. Next comes a description of an optical correlator. This is followed by a discussion of some problems, e.g., rotation and scale invariances, and a section about pattern recognition using incoherent light. Then pattern recognition by a different method, namely feature extraction, is described. We end with a few examples of optical pattern recognition systems using cross-correlation and other methods. Prominent among these examples is the realization of character recognition.

3.2.1   Cross-correlation

The cross-correlation of two functions $g(x, y)$ and $s(x, y)$, denoted $f = g \star s$, is defined by[3]

$$f(x', y') = \int\limits_{-\infty}^{+\infty}\!\!\!\int g(\xi, \eta)\, s^*(\xi - x', \eta - y')\, d\xi\, d\eta, \qquad (3.2)$$

where s^* is the complex conjugate of s.

We can understand the meaning of $f(x', y')$ as follows. Take the two functions g and s, and displace one relative to the other by x' in the x direction and by y' in the y direction. Now check the correlation, or conformity, between them, i.e., how similar they are. $f(x', y')$ is a measure of the degree of similarity after a relative displacement of x' and y'.

The integral over all space in eq. 3.2 is the means by which the similarity is measured. This is best viewed as a weighted sum, where one function is used to weigh the values of the other. If the functions are identical, or at least very similar, large values will receive large weights, while small values only get small weights. Negative values will have negative weights, so they too will contribute to the sum. The sum will be dominated by the large absolute values, and will be

---

[3]The customary definition uses $s^*(\xi + x', \eta + y')$ rather than $s^*(\xi - x', \eta - y')$. We use minus signs, because this is what we can compute optically. For all practical purposes, the two definitions are equivalent.

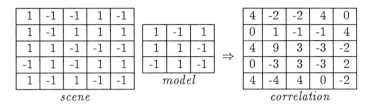

Figure 3.5: *A numerical example of the cross-correlation of two discrete functions. The scene and model are taken as ±1 for simplicity. The highest absolute value of the correlation (9 at center left) indicates the location of the center of the model in the scene.*

very large. If the functions have no resemblance, on the other hand, large values may receive small weights while small values get large weights. Negative values or weights might cancel the contributions of positive ones. Thus the overall sum in this case will be much smaller. an example is given in fig. 3.5.

When the functions are complex-valued, as in our case, we must multiply one function by the *complex conjugate* of the other. This way when the functions are identical, we accumulate the squared modulus at the different points. As the squared modulus is a positive, real number, we are guaranteed to get a large sum. If we were to just multiply the functions, the different points would contribute complex values to the sum, and these might cancel out.

3.2.2   Coherent optical frequency-plane correlator

In an optical system, the correlation peak will be represented by a bright point of light in the output light distribution. We start with a simple argument that shows how the object's light distribution in the input might produce a point of light in the output. Consider a hologram that records the interference pattern of the object beam with a reference beam that is a spherical wave diverging from a point source, rather than a plane wave (fig. 3.6 (a)). In the normal reconstruction procedure, the reference beam is reproduced and used to illuminate the hologram (fig. 3.6 (b)). If we look into the reconstructed object beam, we see a virtual image of the original object. The recording process of holography is, however, perfectly symmetric. Therefore if we reproduce the object beam and illuminate the hologram with it, the reference beam will be reconstructed (fig. 3.6 (c)). If we now look into the reconstructed reference beam, we will see a point of light — the virtual image of the point source. If the object does not appear in the input scene, the reference beam will not be reconstructed, and we will not see a point of light.

The above description depends on the exact reproduction of the object beam. Therefore the claim that we will see a point of light is valid only if the input scene is exactly identical to the model. A small displacement will be enough in order

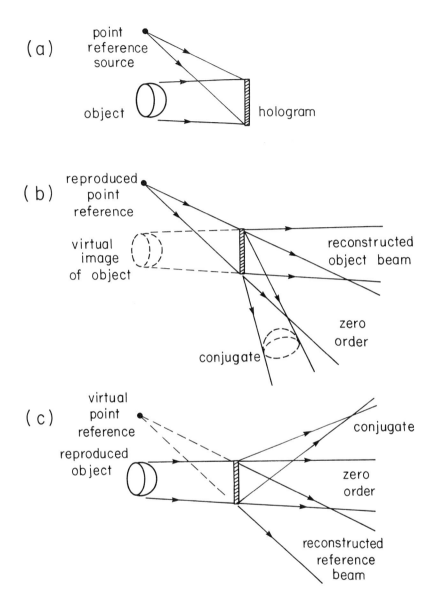

Figure 3.6:

(a) Recording a hologram with a reference from a point source.

(b) Reconstruction by reproducing the reference beam.

(c) Reproducing the object beam reconstructs the reference beam, and a point of light appears.

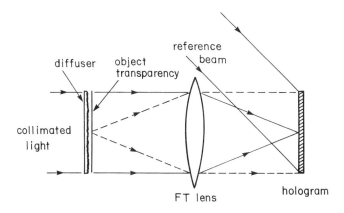

Figure 3.7: *Recording a Fourier hologram.*

to destroy the reconstruction[4]. This problem is solved, however, if we use the
Fourier transform of the object rather than the object itself. This helps because
the Fourier transform of the object is always centered around zero frequency, no
matter where the object is located. The name "frequency-plane correlator" derives
from the fact that the interaction between the input and the stored model occurs
in the frequency plane, i.e., after they are Fourier transformed.

Matched filtering

The hologram will therefore be a *Fourier hologram*, i.e., a hologram recording
the light distribution that represents the Fourier transform of its object's light
distribution. If the object (in our case a transparency with transmittance $s(x, y)$)
is physically available, the hologram may be created optically: simply insert a
Fourier transform lens between the object and the hologram in the recording stage
(fig. 3.7). If not, the hologram may be generated by computer, as described in
section 2.8.3 [78].

An interesting property of the Fourier transform is that when three functions
f, g and s are related by eq. 3.2, their respective Fourier transforms F, G and S
are related by

$$F(\nu_x, \nu_y) = G(\nu_x, \nu_y)\, S^*(\nu_x, \nu_y)$$

i.e., the Fourier transform of the correlation is just the point multiplication of
the Fourier transform of one function by the complex conjugate of the Fourier

---

[4]A small displacement of the point reference in a regular reconstruction will not destroy it — but
it will produce a slightly distorted and displaced object beam. The problem here is that we cannot
provide the necessary small distortion when we move the object.

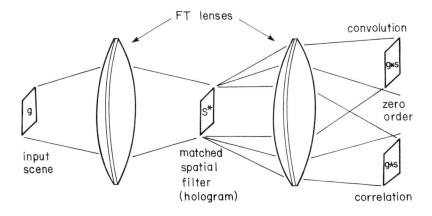

Figure 3.8: *Optical processor for correlations and convolutions.*

transform of the other.

This explains how the frequency-plane correlator works. Recall that when a hologram records a light distribution S, it also records S^* (see page 43). The hologram therefore acts as a *spatial filter*, whose transmittance is $S^*(\nu_x, \nu_y)$ [699,172, 698,385]. This means that when the light representing $G(\nu_x, \nu_y)$ passes through the hologram, it is modulated by $S^*(\nu_x, \nu_y)$. The light distribution after the filter is therefore $G(\nu_x, \nu_y) S^*(\nu_x, \nu_y)$. A second lens then takes the inverse Fourier transform. Thus the result $f(x, y)$ appears in the output plane[5]. As the hologram also records S and a bias term, there are two additional outputs: the convolution of g and s, and a zero-order term (fig. 3.8).

If the model $s(x, y)$ is indeed present in the input scene $g(x, y)$, a bright spot of light appears in the corresponding place in $f(x, y)$. This follows from the derivation in the last couple of pages: the bright spot simply indicates a high correlation value. It can also be explained directly (fig. 3.9) [385,102,260, p. 179]. Assume that the input to the correlator is $s(x, y)$. After modulation by the filter we then get $S(\nu_x, \nu_y) S^*(\nu_x, \nu_y)$. But this is the squared modulus of S, i.e., a *real* positive value. Hence the phase across the beam is constant (see page 11), so this represents a plane wave. The second lens focuses this plane wave to a point on the correlation plane. In other words, the effect of the system is to *concentrate* the energy of the signal to one point, while leaving the noise smeared. This increases the signal-to-noise ratio (SNR), and facilitates the detection of the presence of the signal in the distracting noise.

The optical system depicted in fig. 3.8 may also be described in terms of linear

---

[5]The coordinates are not reversed as they were in fig. 2.4 because of the way we defined the correlation.

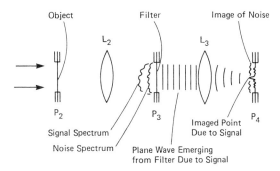

Figure 3.9: *How the correlation peak is formed.*
(Reprinted with permission from *Applied Optics* [385], ©1965)

systems (see appendix B). Comparing eq. 3.2 with eq. B.1, we see that the impulse response of this system is

$$h(x, y, x', y') = s^*(x - x', y - y').$$ (3.3)

A filter with such a relation between its impulse response and some signal $s(x, y)$ is said to be *matched* to that particular signal. This term was coined some 40 years ago, when electrical engineers were looking for linear systems that would identify an echo of a radar pulse in a received RF signal. It turned out that matched filters maximize the SNR of the output peak, assuming a uniform noise distribution [688,689]. Note that matched filtering is simply a *technique* to implement the cross-correlation operation. Therefore the claim that matched filters are the best possible supports our case in favor of the use of cross-correlation. We will see later, however, that if the noise is correlated with the signal in some way, rather than being white noise, then cross-correlation (and matched filters) do not perform too well.

3.2.3 Shift, rotation, and scale invariance

As mentioned above, the optical correlator we are discussing is *shift invariant*: if the object we are looking for, $s(x, y)$, moves across the input scene $g(x, y)$, the correlation peak tracks it across the output $f(x, y)$. This shift invariance is the result of using a correlation function defined in Cartesian coordinates, and from its realization by a Cartesian Fourier transform. When the object moves, its power spectrum does not change; only the phase of its Fourier transform changes. As a result, the shape of the correlation peak does not change — only its position does.

Regrettably, our system is not rotation or scale invariant. If the object appears in $g(x, y)$, but in a different orientation of scale than in the model $s(x, y)$, we will

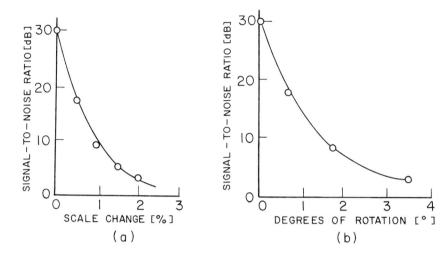

Figure 3.10: *Deterioration of the correlation peak as a function of (a) change of scale and (b) rotation. Note that the ratio of the peak to its surroundings is measured in dB, which is a logarithmic unit.*
(Reprinted with permission from the *Proceedings of the IEEE* [108], ©1977 IEEE)

not get any correlation peak. fig. 3.10 shows the deterioration of the peak as a function of the rotation or scale change [109]. A few ideas have been proposed to overcome these difficulties. Rotation invariance and scale invariance are usually treated individually, as they are orthogonal properties [56].

Moving components

The simplest solution to the lack of rotation invariance is to rotate the filter. When the orientation of the filter matches that of the input, a correlation peak will appear. Similarly, putting the input plane *behind* the lens, instead of at the front focal plane, and changing the distance from the filter to the back focal plane, changes the effective scale. A correlation peak will appear only when the distance (and hence the scale) is just right [700,109].

These methods are not very attractive, as they require mechanical motion of some component and thus are slow and complicated. It should be noted that the movement must be done to within very strict tolerance, as the exact placing of the filter is crucial (see page 72).

A set of filters

Another solution is to have a set of filters that depict the model in various orientations and sizes, to be used in parallel (alternatively, a filter that depicts a set of models may be used) [91,412,283,276]. The correlation peak will appear only in the channel using the filter that happens to match the input. If the object is limited to rotations in the plane (e.g., items on a conveyor belt or airplanes on a runway), and the possible scale changes are small, the number of filters may be kept manageably low. However, the need for multiple channels is still a drawback as it requires a much larger system (large total space-bandwidth product), and reduces the output light intensity in each channel. In addition, multiple outputs must be scanned for the correlation peak.

Circular harmonics

Rotation invariance may be achieved by decomposing the image into circular harmonics. This is best described using polar coordinates. The decomposition is then

$$f(r, \theta) = \sum_{m=-\infty}^{\infty} f_m(r) \, e^{im\theta}. \tag{3.4}$$

The radial functions that serve as coefficients to the different circular harmonic orders are defined by

$$f_m(r) = \frac{1}{2\pi} \int_0^{2\pi} f(r, \theta) \, e^{-im\theta} \, d\theta.$$

It is clear that if the object is rotated by θ_0 degrees around the origin, the moduli of the functions $f_m(r)$ are not affected; only the relative phases in the sum of eq. 3.4 change by $e^{im\theta_0}$.

The key to rotation-invariant correlation is the use of *only one* circular harmonic component for the matched filter [319,320,27]. As correlation is a linear operation, the correlation of one component with the whole body is equivalent to the sum of the individual correlations of that component with all the components. The correlation of the chosen component with any other component gives a low output. The correlation with itself, however, gives a high absolute value that is also rotation invariant; the rotation only changes the *phase* in the correlation peak, but it does not change the peak intensity. The reason that regular correlation is not rotation invariant is that the matched filter uses the whole object, i.e., all its circular harmonic components. When the input object is rotated, the phases of the correlations of the different circular harmonic orders change by different amounts, and tend to cancel out rather than to sum up to a large correlation value [320].

To summarize, the steps in rotation-invariant correlation with this method are:

1. Calculate the circular harmonics of the object you are looking for. The origin for the calculation is chosen so that the maximal correlation value after rotation will appear at the origin [319].

2. Choose one component of the circular harmonic decomposition as the model. The chosen component should have low correlation with the expected noise, so as to give good discrimination [321,26].

3. Make the matched filter. This is the complex conjugate of the Fourier transform of the chosen component, as in regular correlations. Note that the matched filter must be a *computer generated* hologram, as we cannot physically isolate the chosen component.

4. Use the filter to perform the correlation, as described on page 62. An example of the results is given is fig. refcircfig.

The use of only one component is, of course, a limitation that degrades the performance: only part of the information about the object is being used. Various schemes have been proposed in order to use several components in parallel and to combine the results [737,322].

Coordinate transforms

A more sophisticated approach is to use a geometrical transformation of the coordinates so that rotation or scale differences become shifts [725]. Then the normal shift-invariant correlator may be used. This method allows one to decide whether or not the object appears in the input plane, and at what orientation and scale. It does *not* provide the position of the object within the input [566,104].

The geometrical transformation that provides rotation invariance is a simple transformation to *polar coordinates*:

$$r = \sqrt{x^2 + y^2}, \qquad \theta = \arctan\left(\frac{y}{x}\right).$$

With these coordinates, rotations of the scene are represented by shifts in the θ direction.

The geometrical transformation that provides scale invariance is the *Mellin transform* [105,106]. In one dimension, it is defined as

$$M(u) = \int_0^\infty f(x)\, x^{u-1}\, dx.$$

This may also be written as

$$M(u) = \int_0^\infty f(e^{\ln x})\, e^{u\,\ln x}\, d(\ln x),$$

which, after a change of variable to $t = \ln x$, is the Fourier transform[6] of $f(e^t)$ (see eq. C.1) [744]. The optical realization of the Mellin transform will therefore

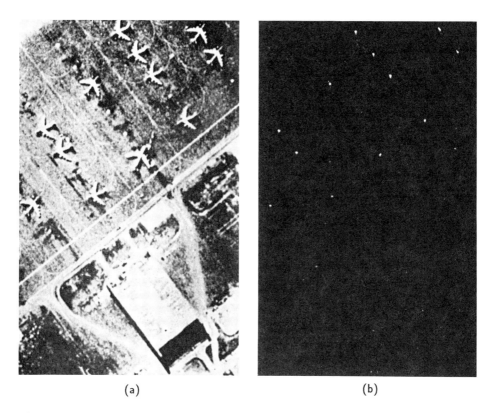

(a)   (b)

Figure 3.11: *Rotation-invariant correlation by use of circular harmonics. The sixth harmonic component was used to identify airplanes parked on a runway.*
(a) The input image: the airplanes appear in different orientations.
(b) The output: all the airplanes are identified.
(Reprinted with permission from *Applied Optics* [321], ©1983)

consist of two stages: first a logarithmic change of the coordinates, and then a Fourier transform.

The Mellin transform is helpful because when the original function f is scaled, the modulus of its Mellin transform does not change; only a phase factor is added. Positional, rotational, and scale-invariant correlation is achieved by the following procedure [107,108], that uses the above transformations (fig. 3.12):

1. The input scene is Fourier transformed and detected. This gives the squared modulus of the Fourier transform, which is oblivious to the position of the object in the scene. It is centered about the origin.

---

[6]Here u is taken to be a *radial* frequency, which is 2π times the regular frequency.

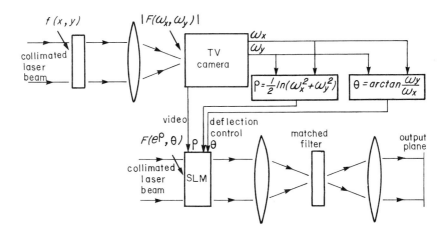

Figure 3.12: *Geometrical transforms are realized by control of the deflectors that scan the image. The transformed image is then used as the input for the correlator.*
(Adapted with permission from *Applied Optics* [107])

2. A geometrically transformed image of the detected Fourier transform is fed to an SLM, which serves as an input transducer to a regular correlator. The geometrical transform may be realized by controlling the deflectors that determine the scanning of the image. It includes both the transformation from Cartesian to polar coordinates, and the logarithmic transform along the r coordinate (A Mellin transform along the θ coordinate is not needed, as it does not change when the input is scaled). This method is depicted in fig. 3.12. Alternatively, a computer generated hologram can realize the transformation to $(\ln r, \theta)$ coordinates without scanning [593,122].

3. The first thing the regular correlator does with its input is to Fourier transform it. The Fourier transform along θ gives us the rotation invariance. The Fourier transform along r completes the Mellin transform.

4. The Fourier transform of the input falls on a matched spatial filter (MSF). In our case, this is the complex conjugate of a model that has received the same handling: Fourier transform — squared modulus — polar coordinates — Mellin transform.

5. After the filter, the light distribution represents the point multiplication of the transformed input and the filter. A nice thing about the Mellin transform is that this multiplication represents the Mellin transform of the correlation of the original functions [52]. Therefore an inverse Mellin transform will

provide us with the desired correlation peak. As the Mellin transform is a combination of a logarithmic scaling and a Fourier transform, we can make do with an inverse Fourier transform which is simple to do optically. The lack of exponential scaling just means that a scale difference of α at the input will move the correlation peak by $\ln \alpha$ instead of by α.

Following this procedure, a correlation peak appears if a rotated and/or scaled version of the model had been incorporated in the input scene. The peak's displacement from the origin indicates the relative rotation and scale[7].

3.2.4 Interclass discrimination and intraclass recognition

Rotation and scale invariances are a special case of a more general problem. In real life situations we usually cannot expect the viewed object to be perfectly identical to the model: it might be distorted in some way (e.g., scaled or rotated), or it could even be genuinely different, but "belonging to the same class". For example, E, E, **E**, and E all belong to the class of capital Es, and we would like a character recognition system to recognize them as such in spite of intraclass variance. F and B, however, although similar, belong to other classes. We would therefore like our recognizer to discriminate against them.

Matched filters do not perform well when faced with such problems [712]. They sometimes hardly notice small but crucial differences, e.g., between E and F. On the other hand, they are sometimes oversensitive to "meaningless" differences, e.g., between E and E. The reason is that matched filters just implement the cross-correlation operation — they assume each and every point in the model has equal importance. While this is good policy when faced with distracting *white* noise, it is not good in the cases cited here. In order to distinguish between E and F, for example, we should emphasize the importance of the bottom horizontal bar. In order to recognize both E and E, we should de-emphasize the slant and the serifs.

The training set

A basic difficulty with the desire for interclass discrimination and intraclass recognition is the need to define exactly what we want. The way to get around this is to use a *training set*, i.e., a set of examples. The training set includes objects from all the classes; the objects within each class display typical intraclass variances.

For notational convenience, assume K classes and M examples from each class. The recognizer's output will be symbolically displayed in a K-dimensional space: class i will be indicated by the unit vector in the ith dimension, $\mathbf{e}_i$. The inputs

---

[7]Actually a double peak appears, because when an object is rotated by θ_0 degrees it is as if part of it is shifted by θ_0 along the θ axis, and another part is shifted by $2\pi - \theta_0$ in the opposite direction [107].

will be encoded as vectors too; we denote the jth example of class i by $\mathbf{t}_{ij}$. We want to create a set of linear operators, L_k, so that[8] $L_k \mathbf{t}_{ij} \approx \delta_{ik}$ for all i, j, and k. The output will be $\sum_k (L_k \mathbf{t}) \mathbf{e}_k$, i.e., a vector whose coordinates are given by the operators operating on the input $\mathbf{t}$. Note that all training-set elements of class i produce vectors which are very close to $\mathbf{e}_i$, while the outputs for elements of other classes lie far away; this is the basis of the classification. Assuming that the training set faithfully represents the classes, other inputs will also be classified correctly.

Filters for discrimination

The different operators L_k are usually implemented by cross-correlations with different models. These models are synthesized in some special way from the training set. A simple method that works well is a linear combination of "average" objects. We illustrate this by an example with two classes. A training set of 10 songbirds and 10 fish is given (fig. 3.13 (a,b)). From this the average bird and the average fish are calculated. Now two models are generated (fig. 3.13 (c)): one is the average bird minus the average fish; it recognizes all birds and discriminates against all fish. The other is the average fish minus the average bird; it does the opposite [279,280,309]. Random noise can also be played down if it can be characterized statistically; in such a situation the noise is simply formulated as another class, which is always discriminated against [281].

Other, more sophisticated methods have also been proposed; these include generalized matched filters [132,133,136,309] and synthetic discriminant functions [118,119,124,581,347,317]. The differences between these methods are mostly technical, and will not be surveyed here.

A basic problem with all these filters is their efficiency, i.e., how much of the input light intensity is concentrated into the correlation peak. Good discrimination requires the use of high spatial frequencies, in which the objects differ. Most of the light energy, however, is to be found in the low spatial frequencies. Therefore discriminating filters tend to have low signal-to-noise ratios, and vice versa [140, 581]. The only solution to this problem is the use of phase-only filters, which are more efficient [348].

3.2.5   Additional problems

Invariance and discrimination might be the most noticeable problems of optical pattern recognition by cross-correlation, but they are not the only ones. Here are a few other problems:

---

[8] $\delta_{i,k} = \begin{cases} 1 & \text{if } i = k, \\ 0 & \text{otherwise.} \end{cases}$

(a)

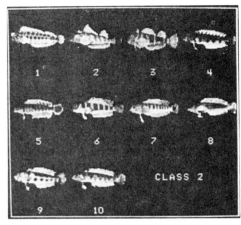

(b)

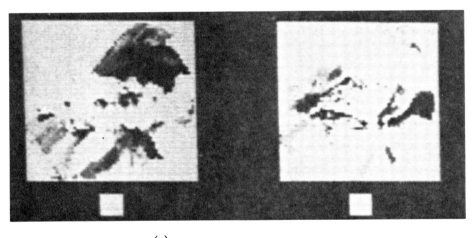

(c)

Figure 3.13: *Interclass discrimination and intraclass recognition.*
(a) Training set of ten songbird images.
(b) Training set of ten fish images.
(c) Discriminating models. These are bipolar; the zero gray level is indicated in the little square at the bottom. lighter gray levels are positive, darker are negative.
(Reprinted with permission from *Applied Optics* [280], ©1984)

- The tolerances in positioning the filter are quite strict — even displacements of a few microns can degrade the performance [701,702,109,283]. One possible solution is to use incoherent light, as shown in section 3.2.6. Another is to use the so called "joint transform correlator". Instead of preparing a hologram of the Fourier transform of the model in advance, a transparency of the model itself is prepared (alternatively, the model may be displayed on a CRT). This is placed next to the input scene in the input plane. Thus both the input and the model are Fourier transformed together, and their transforms fall in exactly the same place [723,102]. An additional advantage of the joint transform correlator is that the model may be displayed on a low-resolution device, which should be much cheaper than the high-resolution device needed for a matched filter. It is also easier to change the model [748].

- Arbitrary distortions might occur in the scene, apart from rotations and scale differences. Such distortions may be handled by appropriate geometrical transforms of the coordinates [104,566].

- Illumination changes also degrade the correlation peak, as they change the input's appearance [283].

- The efficiency of the correlator is defined as the percentage of the signal energy that is actually concentrated into the correlation peak. It turns out that in many cases higher efficiency (and better discrimination) may be gained by using a *phase-only* filter, which does not affect the light intensity [315,316,183,167]. The reason for this is that the phase information is more significant than the amplitude information in a Fourier transform of a scene [519,18]. However, such filters are more sensitive to positioning errors [244].

- The spatial filter introduces some aberrations [700,702].

3.2.6   Pattern recognition with incoherent light

Up to now we have discussed optical correlators that utilize coherent light. These correlators make use of the fact that with coherent illumination, a Fourier-transform relationship exists between the front and back focal planes of a lens. As we saw, this allows for the easy realization of cross-correlations, by spatial filtering in the frequency domain. With incoherent light, the Fourier-transform relationship does not hold. We can only modulate the spatial light *intensity*, which is a real nonnegative quantity. Therefore incoherent optical correlators must operate directly on the images, in the spatial domain.

The reasons for using incoherent rather than coherent light are [435,436]:

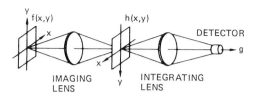

Figure 3.14: *Direct optical correlation of two functions.*
(Reprinted with permission from the *Proceedings of the IEEE* [499], ©1977 IEEE)

- An input transducer is not necessary. Any quasi-monochromatic light source may be used directly. For example, the input may simply be displayed on a CRT or television screen.

- The required mechanical tolerances in placing the components are much relaxed.

Incoherent optical correlation may be carried out in three distinct ways: by scanning systems, by shadow-casting systems, or by spatial-filtering systems. We now survey these three methods in turn, and then address possible improvements to the basic scheme.

Scanning correlators

An incoherent optical system that is a direct realization of the integral in eq. 3.2 is easy to build (fig. 3.14). The input light distribution of intensity $f(x, y)$ is simply imaged on a transparency with intensity transmittance $h(x, y)$. The intensity of the light distribution after the transparency is thus described by $f(x, y) h(x, y)$. This is subsequently collected by a lens and focused on a detector. The detector's output is therefore $\iint f(x, y) h(x, y) \, dx \, dy$, which is the correlation of f and h with no displacement[9].

If we now move either the input f or the filter h, we can scan the whole cross-correlation of f and h. Various one-dimensional, two-dimensional, and multichannel systems of this type have been devised [333,499,250].

Shadow-casting correlators

The whole cross-correlation of f and h may be obtained in parallel by a ridiculously simple configuration (fig. 3.15). In this configuration there are no lenses, so light from every point in the input f reaches every point in the output g. Let's look at all the light that reaches point (x_0, y_0), i.e., the light that is summed up to

---

[9]Recall that f and h are real nonnegative functions, rather than complex-valued functions. This allows us to work with intensities, which are detected easily.

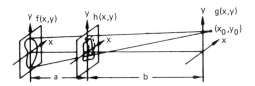

Figure 3.15: *Cross correlation by shadow casting.*
(Reprinted with permission from the *Proceedings of the IEEE* [499], ©1977 IEEE)

create $g(x_0, y_0)$. This light passes through the transparency h on the way. Simple
geometry indicates that the light passing through point (x, y) in h came from point
$\left(\frac{a+b}{b}x - \frac{a}{b}x_0, \frac{a+b}{b}y - \frac{a}{b}y_0\right)$ in f. Therefore the light intensity at g is given by

$$g(x_0, y_0) = \iint f\left(\tfrac{a+b}{b}x - \tfrac{a}{b}x_0, \tfrac{a+b}{b}y - \tfrac{a}{b}y_0\right) h(x, y) \, dx \, dy,$$

which is the cross-correlation of f and h (disregarding a few scale factors).

This configuration has the advantage of not using any optical elements. As a
result it can be used with extremely short wavelengths, such as x-rays or γ-rays.
Other configurations that do include collimating lenses have also been proposed
[499,577,250].

Spatial-filter correlators

The coherent frequency-plane correlator described previously correlates two *complex-valued* functions. The input is represented by the *complex amplitude* of a
coherent light beam, while the model is represented by the complex transmittance
of the hologram. It turns out that a very similar system may be used to correlate
two *positive-valued* functions, where the input is represented by the *intensity* of an
incoherent light beam [577,435,436,431,449].

The convolution and correlation of any two images are obtained incoherently
in the following way[10]. The hologram of the object is recorded as described in fig.
3.6 (note that this is a direct hologram of the object, not a Fourier hologram).
Both the object beam and the reference beam are, of course, coherent. As usual,
after the hologram is developed, the object beam is reconstructed by illuminating
the hologram with a reproduction of the spherical reference beam.

Now suppose we move the point source used for the reconstruction. This
results in a proportional movement of the the reconstructed object beam. If we
are looking into the hologram, this means that we will see the virtual image of
the object move. This is true as long as the movement is not too large, e.g., we
do not move the point source by more than the object size. If the intensity of the

---

[10]This explanation is due to Shelly Glaser.

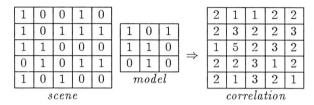

Figure 3.16: *Example of the correlation of nonnegative functions. The correlation peak is much less pronounced than when the functions are bipolar (compare with fig. 3.5).*

object's light distribution is $s(x, y)$, we may summarize by saying that the image produced by a reference of intensity g displaced by ξ in the x direction and by η in the y direction is $g\, s(x - \xi, y - \eta)$.

If we use *two* displaced sources simultaneously, we will therefore get two reconstructed object beams, in slightly different directions. As the light sources are coherent, these beams will interfere with each other, and we will *not* see two images of the object superposed on each other. If we use *relatively incoherent sources*, however, the beams will not interact, and we *will* see two displaced images.

From here it is easy to generalize to an *extended* incoherent source, described by $g(\xi, \eta)$, situated about the original position of the point reference source. Each point in g creates its own reconstruction of s, and all these reconstructions are superimposed with their respective displacements. Contributions to point (x', y') of this superposition come from various combinations of $g(\xi, \eta)\, s(x' - \xi, y' - \eta)$. If we sum them up, it is obvious that instead of a reconstructed object beam we get the convolution of g and s.

When the reproduced reference beam is used to reconstruct from a hologram, both the object beam and a conjugate beam are created. Up to now we treated only the reconstructed object beam, and saw how the combination of reconstructed object beams created by distinct points in an extended source forms the convolution of the hologramed object with that source. A similar analysis of what happens with the conjugate beams produced by distinct points of the extended source shows that they combine to give the cross-correlation of the object with the source. Thus pattern recognition by cross-correlation can be accomplished with a hologram and incoherent light.

Problems and optimization

A few technical problems arise in the incoherent holographic correlation process [251]. As these problems are rather involved, we will not discuss them here. Rather we will only address the following basic problem: as we noted in section 3.2.1, cross-correlation may be regarded as a weighted sum. When both the function and the weights are bipolar or complex, a high correlation value appears only if there is a perfect match. Otherwise the contributions cancel out. If the function and weights are all positive, however, the contributions cannot cancel each other. Therefore we will get high correlation values even when the match is only partial (fig. 3.16). In general, therefore, the correlation peak in an incoherent system will be much less pronounced than in a coherent system.

The situation is aggravated if the model incorporates relatively large areas of nearly constant gray level. If this is the case, a small shift does not change the correlation value by very much. As a result, the correlation peak is smeared out, and it is hard to pin-point the location of the object. The above observation indicates one possible solution, namely edge enhancement. If both the input and the model are edge enhanced, the high values in both images will occur only in thin lines along the edges. A high correlation value will again result if there is a good match, but a small shift will destroy the correlation. Thus the correlation peak will be sharp. The edge enhancement might be carried out by a digital convolution with a small kernel (e.g., the Roberts or Sobel operators [587, chap. 10]. Some additional preprocessing might also be required [734]. All this can be done at video rate.

It should be noted that using an edge-enhanced input and model has the additional advantage of allowing one to correlate images obtained by different sensors and under different conditions. This is because the edge content is a basic feature of the imaged object, more than texture or a certain shadow pattern [734,19].

A better solution is to use a bipolar model, implemented by means of a two-channel system [438] or by spatial carrier modulation [649,234]. In this case the input need not be processed at all, so real-time operation is easier. the model, on the other hand, is operated upon by a Laplacian operator (i.e., a second derivative) [686,20,357]. This produces positive and negative lines on both sides of the image edges. Thus the correlation of the model with a uniform background is zero, and a high correlation value will occur only if the searched-for object is present.

3.2.7   Pattern recognition by feature extraction

All the methods discussed so far may be grouped under the name "pattern recognition by spatial filtering". The basic procedure involved is equivalent to a matching of the input image to a reference, pixel by pixel, and summing the results. A much more "economical" method is to use *feature extraction*: a small number of important and characteristic features are determined, and their values (referred to collectively as the *feature vector*) are used to characterize the input [116].

Feature-extraction methods are appealing because they are simple and reduce the amount of information that is dealt with. They may also incorporate shift, rotation, and scale invariances, by use of features that do not change under these transformations. Even interclass discrimination and intraclass recognition may be

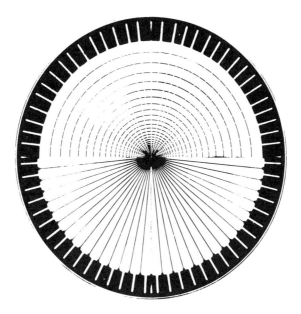

Figure 3.17: *A wedge-ring detector array may be placed in the Fourier plane of an optical system. It is composed of 32 wedge shaped detectors which give information about characteristic orientations, and 32 ring shaped detectors which identify characteristic spatial frequencies.*
(Reprinted with permission from the *Proceedings of the IEEE* [678], ©1977 IEEE. The device is manufactured by Recognition Systems Inc.)

accommodated, by intelligent tailoring of the features that are used. However, they also have their drawbacks. First, some postprocessing is needed in order to decide what the features mean. Second, feature extractors can only work on one object at a time, so an initial step providing segmentation of the input is necessary. The correlators described previously could operate on any number of objects in parallel.

In this section, we review three types of optical feature extractors: those that use the Fourier transform, the chord transform, and moments. We then mention ways to use the feature vector to distinguish between objects.

Spectral features

The spatial frequencies contained in an image are important features that characterize it, and may serve to distinguish between different pictures. It turns out that rather a crude measurement of the characteristic frequencies is usually enough.

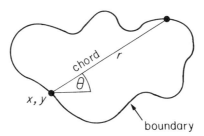

Figure 3.18: *A chord is drawn between two points on the boundary of an object. The histogram of all such chords characterizes the object.*

For example, land uses in an aerial picture may be easily identified. The spatial frequencies that characterize, say, urban areas are totally different from those that are typical in agricultural areas or in a natural landscape [420,557,532].

This is exploited by the "wedge-ring" detector array (fig. 3.17) [115,102,678, 288], which is composed of 64 specially shaped detectors. 32 of the detectors (covering half of the circle) are shaped as radial wedges. The other 32 (in the other half) are concentric rings. When placed in the frequency plane of an optical system (i.e., in the back focal plane of a lens that performs a Fourier transform), the wedge detectors give information about the characteristic orientations in the image, while the ring detectors characterize the spatial frequencies. Hence a set of some 10^6 pixel values, which are individually meaningless, is reduced to a set of 64 meaningful values.

Chord-histogram features

Given an object described by its outline, it may be characterized by the histogram of all chords drawn between all airs of points on the boundary (fig. 3.18). The histogram value $h(r,\theta)$ will be the number of chords with length r and angle θ. Note that $h(r,\theta) = h(r,\theta + \pi)$.

It is tedious to compute the lengths and angles of all the chords; however, the histogram may be generated in a direct and efficient manner. Let us describe the object's boundary by the binary function

$$b(x,y) = \begin{cases} 1 & \text{if } x, y \text{ is on the boundary,} \\ 0 & \text{otherwise.} \end{cases}$$

A chord of length r and angle θ originates from point x, y if and only if $b(x,y)\,b(x + r\cos\theta, y + r\sin\theta) = 1$. The total number of chords with length r and angle θ is therefore

$$h(r,\theta) = \iint b(x,y)\,b(x + r\cos\theta, y + r\sin\theta)\,dx\,dy.$$

A change of variables shows that this can be regarded as

$$h'(\xi, \eta) = \iint b(x, y) \, b(x + \xi, y + \eta) \, dx \, dy,$$

i.e., the autocorrelation of b.

The autocorrelation is easy to produce optically with any of the correlators described in the preceding sections. It is simplest to just correlate the object with itself, without finding the boundary first. The outcome of the autocorrelation is then a *generalized* chord transform, which includes chords between internal points as well as chords between boundary points[11].

The chord transform, like the Fourier transform, does not reduce the amount of data on hand. The chords have to be grouped together in some way in order to create a feature vector. It turns out that the same wedge-ring detector that is used to obtain the main features of the Fourier space may be used to obtain the features of the chord space. The wedge-shaped detectors provide information about typical chord orientations, while the rings tell us about typical chord lengths [117,116].

The advantage of chord features over spectral features is that they are partially invariant under rotation and scaling: the length histogram, $h(r) = \int h(r, \theta) \, d\theta$, is invariant under rotation, provided scale is maintained. The angle histogram, $h(\theta)$, is invariant to scale changes, provided there is no rotation. A combination of both scale and rotation distortions just causes shifts of $h(r)$ and $h(\theta)$.

Moment features

The concept of moments stems from physics, where it characterizes the distribution of mass or charge in an object. It may be transferred to image processing, where it will characterize the distribution of ink in a picture. Formally, the moments m_{pq} of the image are defined by

$$m_{pq} = \int\limits_{-\infty}^{+\infty}\!\!\!\int f(x, y) \, x^p \, y^q \, dx \, dy.$$

The full infinite set of moments completely defines the image [323]. However a rather small finite set is usually sufficient for recognition purposes. Moments are very effective in distortion-invariant pattern recognition. They can be used in either of two ways: one is to generate invariant moments, i.e., moments that will assume the same value regardless of image distortions, and the other is to normalize the image (e.g., by scaling and rotating it) so that the moments reach

---

[11]This has a statistical interpretation: given a point (x, y) in the object, the probability that $(x + r \cos\theta, y + r \sin\theta)$ is also in the object is proportional to $h(r, \theta)$.

predefined values. The first method is good for recognition based on a feature vector; the second as a preprocessing step for a correlator [3].

The invariances of moments are fairly well known, so we shall only mention a few simple examples [323,587, sect. 12.1.3]. The zero-order moment m_{00} is simply the "weight" of the object; it is invariant under translation and rotation. The first-order moments m_{10} and m_{01} define the coordinates of the centroid ("center of mass"): $x_c = \frac{m_{10}}{m_{00}}$ and $y_c = \frac{m_{01}}{m_{00}}$. If the centroid is taken as the origin, all moments become shift invariant (these are called *central* moments). The second-order moments m_{20} and m_{02} may be used to define the principle axis of the body. If this is chosen as the y axis, moments become rotation invariant.

The optical generation of the first $P \times Q$ moments is easy: the object is simply imaged on a transparency with transmittance

$$g(x,y) = \sum_{p=0}^{P} \sum_{q=0}^{Q} x^p y^q \, \cos[(\omega_1 + p\,\omega_0)x] \, \cos[(\omega_1 + q\omega_0)y].$$

This is just a superposition of spatial carriers with different frequencies and orientations, each modulated by a monomial $x^p y^q$, which multiply the image. A Fourier transform then causes each moment to be integrated at a different point, dictated by the spatial frequencies. An array of detectors situated at these points outputs all the moments in parallel [123]. An equivalent but somewhat simpler design is to create multiple images of the input that fall on a set of masks with transmittances $x^p y^q$. The output from each mask is then focused on to a detector by a lens [191].

Postprocessing

The optical processor in a feature-extraction pattern recognizer accepts an image as input and produces a low-dimensionality feature vector as output. A postprocessing stage is then needed in order to evaluate this feature vector, and decide how to classify the image. This is usually done by an electronic computer. A number of algorithms for the classification of feature vectors have been devised [115,116]. Typically the inner products of the feature vector and some other vectors are calculated, and the results are thresholded to see which vector most resembles the feature vector.

3.2.8   Uses of optical pattern recognition

Optical pattern recognition (OPR) may be used in principle in any situation where the need for pattern recognition arises. It becomes especially attractive if the following conditions are met:

- The input and pattern are two-dimensional images.

- Large volumes of data are concerned, e.g., the images are large and numerous.

- Speed is essential, as when real-time recognition is required.

OPR has been suggested in a number of applications, among them character recognition, identification, target registration, tracking, and machine vision.

Optical character recognition (OCR)

Optical recognition of letters of printed text is probably the most popular application of OPR [22,91]. The motivation behind it is the desire to be able to use printed text as input to computers, implementation of automatic mail sorting [447], and so on. It is characterized by the following points:

- Rotation and scale invariance is usually not very important.

- The input is binary-valued, with low noise.

- A large set of models must be recognized — upper and lower case letters, digits, and punctuation marks. If a number of fonts may appear, the set becomes much larger.

- Some of the models are remarkably similar, e.g., 1, l, and I, or 0, O, and Q. This makes discrimination harder.

Implementations usually use multiple filters, so as to correlate all the letters in parallel. The number of filters needed to recognize N characters is $\log N$ [71,135]. Assume that the characters are numbered from 1 to N. A specific matched filter is made for each character; this filter gives an output of "1" for its character and "0" for all the others. Now these filters are combined into a set of $\log N$ compound filters, each of which represents *one bit* in the numbering scheme: compound filter number i incorporates all the filters with numbers whose i^{th} bit is 1. Thus the binary representation of the input character may be read from the outputs of the compound filters. Some sort of feature extraction might be used to improve discrimination.

Noncorrelation methods have also been proposed for automatic recognition of characters. The most prominent is the use of holograms as code translators [238, 437,439,453,506]. In the preparation of these holograms, the reference beam comes from *a number* of point sources. The locations of these sources encode the character being recorded; their combination is different for each character. As shown in fig. 3.6 (c), When the object (in this case, the character) is reproduced, the points are reconstructed in the conjugate beam. Therefore when the light distribution of the character impinges upon such a hologram, a predetermined pattern of light points is produced. These light points fall on a set of detectors. Thus the letter is translated from a continuous spatial light distribution into a binary code, at the outputs of the detectors. A large character set may be recognized by using a multiplexed hologram, that translates all the characters to their respective codes.

A related application is that of optical word recognition. Here the motivation is the search for a keyword in a large data base [110,103]. OPR techniques are especially appropriate in this context when the data base is kept on microfilm. If this is the case, the microfilm is used directly as an input transparency. Thus whole pages may be scanned in parallel without need to read the text.

Identification

Each person carries with himself an unforgeable spatial pattern that uniquely identifies him — namely his fingerprints. It has been suggested that optical pattern recognition systems be used to match the fingerprints of people who enter sensitive places with a bank of the fingerprints of authorized personnel. The input will be a window against which the employee puts his hand; optical systems are needed in order to make the check in real time. Another application is the use of optical correlation to search through the extensive files of the FBI (which already had 175 million records more than 10 years ago) or other police forces [474,456].

Target registration

Numerous papers on the subject of OPR use examples where the model happens to be an airplane or a tank, and it is clear that possible military applications motivate and finance a large part of OPR research [103,54]. Dominant among these applications is the recognition of a target in a scene. This problem is characterized by the following points:

- The model may appear in different sizes, orientations and perspectives.

- Light conditions may vary.

- Real-time operation is essential.

- The optical system should be small, lightweight, and rugged.

A variant of this application is the use of optical pattern recognition for control and alignment, e.g., in an industrial environment or in outer space [646]. In such situations we have the added benefit of being able to influence the target's appearance; for instance we can paint circular (hence rotation-invariant) marks on it, which will be easy to identify [253].

Tracking and motion analysis

As mentioned above, if the object in the input scene moves, the correlation peak in the output also moves. This can be used to track the motion of the object [240].

When a sequence of pictures of a scene is available, parts of early frames may be used as models which are searched for in subsequent frames. This allows one to follow the motion of objects that appear in the scene. A nice example is the analysis of air currents from the motion of cloud formations, as seen in satellite pictures [698]. Certain cloud formations in one frame are chosen as models, and are then located by OPR means in another frame, taken some time later. The displacement of the cloud formations between the frames indicates the direction and velocity of air movement in that area.

Another example is missile guidance. This application combines motion analysis with target registration, both of which can be done by cross-correlation. The motion in this case results from the movement of the missile above the terrain, rather than from the motion of some other object in the scene. The optical correlator must satisfy strict size and weight restrictions in order to be useful in this application [694,190]. An optical correlator that fits into a box with a 6-cm side has been proposed. This tight configuration is achieved by folding the optical axis by means of dove prisms [54].

Machine vision

Target recognition and motion analysis are two important aspects of a machine vision system, e.g., a system that allows a robot to see. Ultimately we would like to create a autonomous system, so that a robot would be able to move about at a reasonable speed with no accidents. OPR based ideas might make this feasible, by alleviating the computational complexity of scene analysis [422,176]. Again, small and lightweight systems are needed.

3.3 Picture deblurring

An optical imaging system is never perfect — the image is always a degraded version of the original. Every amateur photographer knows a few possible reasons for such an outcome: lack of focus, blurring due to relative motion, or too little depth of field. Additional reasons might include aberrations in the optical elements and imaging through a nonuniform medium (e.g., turbulent air). All these effects, however, do not change one basic property of imaging systems — they remain shift-invariant linear systems (see appendix B for definitions). Therefore the combined effect of all the degradations suffered by an image may be described as a convolution: the original is convolved with the point spread function (PSF) of the optical system, to produce the output image. Mathematically

$$g(x', y') = \iint f(x, y) \, h(x' - x, y' - y) \, dx \, dy,$$

where f is the original input

h is the PSF that describes how the optical imaging system spreads
out a point input

g is the produced output.

It should be noted that the information is not completely lost — it is merely
"reshuffled", and displayed in a form that is less obvious to a human observer.
Appropriate processing steps may, however, recover the original input picture, at
least to a large degree.

We begin our discussion with a look at the effects caused by blurring of a
picture. We then describe a method to "undo" these effects, and show an optical
holographic technique for its implementation.

3.3.1   Contrast loss and reversal

Everyone knows what an out-of-focus picture looks like — it is sort of smeared out
and hazy. But most people do not notice the details of what actually happens.
This section provides some insight into this matter.

It turns out that blurring has a different effect on different spatial frequencies
that appear in the picture. We will show this for a simple case, in which the PSF is
such that a point in the input is spread out evenly over an extent a in the output
(fig. 3.19 (a)). In the case of low spatial frequency, where the period is much
larger than a, such spreading does not cause a significant change (b). With higher
spatial frequencies, however, where the period is exactly a, this spreading results
in a *complete loss* of the spatial structure (c). If we look at even higher spatial
frequencies, we see that the spreading causes adjacent crests to overlap. This
creates a *reversal* of the spatial pattern: areas that were relatively dark become
relatively bright, and vice versa (d). As the spatial frequency continues to increase,
these phenomena of loss and reversal reoccur in a cyclic manner. At the same time,
the contrast between the bright and dark areas becomes less pronounced (fig. 3.20
(a)).

In a general picture, the different spatial frequencies are not isolated as in fig.
3.20. Different combinations of them appear throughout the picture. However
areas in which a small range of spatial frequencies dominate do occur. If this
range happens to suffer from contrast reversal, severe errors in the interpretation
of the picture might ensue.

3.3.2   Deconvolution

As mentioned above, the degradation caused by an optical system may be regarded
as a convolution. In the spatial frequency domain (often called "Fourier space"),
convolution turns into pointwise multiplication (see appendix C). Therefore if

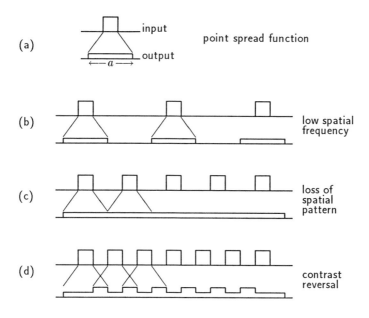

Figure 3.19: *Contrast loss and reversal as a result of blur.*
(a) *A point is spread out over an extent a.*
(b) *Low spatial frequencies are not affected.*
(c) *Some spatial frequencies are totally lost.*
(d) *Other frequencies suffer from contrast reversal.*

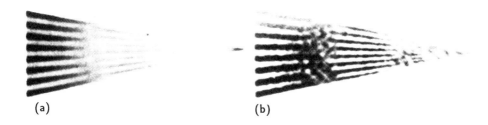

Figure 3.20: *Deconvolution.*
(a) *Blurred radial test pattern. Note the contrast reversal.*
(b) *Deblurred image. Note the improved contrast and the corrected reversal.*
(Reprinted with permission from *New Scientist* [655], ©1971)

F, G, and H denote the Fourier transforms of f, g, and h respectively, we have

$$G(\nu_x, \nu_y) = F(\nu_x, \nu_y) \, H(\nu_x, \nu_y).$$

G is the Fourier transform of the image. H is known (assuming we can test the optical system). Therefore we may obtain the desired F by

$$F(\nu_x, \nu_y) = \frac{G(\nu_x, \nu_y)}{H(\nu_x, \nu_y)}. \tag{3.5}$$

In other words, we need to filter G through a spatial filter with a complex transmittance $\frac{1}{H}$. This is called *deconvolution*.

This filter is a degenerate form of the more general *Wiener filter* [62] defined by

$$\frac{H^*(\nu_x, \nu_y)}{|H(\nu_x, \nu_y)|^2 + \frac{P_n(\nu_x, \nu_y)}{P_g(\nu_x, \nu_y)}},$$

where P_g and P_n are the power spectra of the original signal and any added noise, respectively. If we assume no noise, or at least low noise on the average, the term $\frac{P_n}{P_g}$ may be ignored, and we are left with $\frac{1}{H}$.

Note that this filtering action cannot restore the picture completely; specifically, spatial frequencies where contrast loss has occurred will not be reproduced. This is intuitively clear: when many different spatial frequencies are lost, we cannot expect the system to be able to guess which one should appear in each place. Mathematically, in these frequencies both H and G are zero, so eq. 3.5 is ill-defined.

3.3.3   Optical implementation

The optical implementation of deconvolution is similar to other spatial filtering operations, e.g., correlation. The filter is realized as follows [652,653,654,655,656, 657,658,388]. Note that

$$\frac{1}{H} = \frac{H^*}{HH^*} = \frac{H^*}{|H|^2},$$

where H^* is the complex conjugate of H. Recall that a light distribution falling on a filter is multiplied by the transfer function of the filter. Here we want to multiply it by $\frac{1}{|H|^2}$ and then by H^*. This is accomplished by using two filters in series. $\frac{1}{|H|^2}$ is an amplitude-only filter, i.e., its density causes a decrease of the amplitude of the light passing through it, without inducing any phase change. H^* is a complex filter that also changes the phase (this will correct the contrast reversals). It is realized by means of a hologram, just like the S^* filter used in pattern recognition.

To summarize, the configuration of the system is as follows: the blurred image is Fourier-transformed by a lens. The Fourier transform falls on a sandwich of two spatial filters, that together multiply it by $\frac{1}{H}$ (where H is the OTF of the system, i.e., the Fourier transform of its PSF). The result is Fourier-transformed by another lens. This forms three output beams, as usual. One of the first-order beams will be the deconvolved picture.

An example of the improvement achieved by such filtering is given in fig. 3.20. The method has been used primarily in conjunction with electron microscopes, where it has sometimes improved the resolution by 100% [655,657].

3.4 Synthetic aperture radar imaging

Synthetic aperture radar (SAR) is a technique used in creating aerial terrain images, which are used, for example, in mapping and in searching for mineral resources [202,203]. The apparatus is carried by plane or satellite. It acquires information about the terrain below by sending out radar pulses and recording their echos. It is thus not sensitive to climate or light conditions, which is a distinct advantage over conventional aerial photography. The set of echos produced by a single point encodes the position and reflectivity of that point. In the recording process, the echos modulate the beam of a CRT which exposes a photographic film. The resulting pattern turns out to be a hologram of the terrain — it holds all the information, but does not in itself resemble the original to any degree. Therefore a processing stage is required before the final image is obtained. This processing consists of simply reconstructing an image of the terrain from the hologram [419]. This can be done, of course, with coherent light.

The processing of SAR data is the oldest and most successful application of analog optical processing systems. Research in this field laid down the groundwork that was later used in the development of optical holography. The acceptance of optical techniques for performing this processing has been almost complete: the great majority of images produced over the years have been processed optically. SAR imaging is widely used in military and civilian mapping throughout the world (fig. 3.21) [343].

We begin this section with a short treatise of phased arrays and side looking radar, by which the data is gathered. We then discuss Fresnel zone plates and synthetic apertures, to see how the microwave radar echos create a holographic image. Finally, the optical processing method is described. This description is quite detailed, for two reasons: one is the success and importance of optical processing in this application, and the other is the fact that most popular surveys do not give a full description, while professional papers use mathematical formulations, which can be difficult to follow.

3.4.1 Side looking radar

The geometry for a plane-carried side looking radar is shown in fig. 3.22 [81, 82]. The radar beam illuminates a strip of terrain to one side of the flight path.

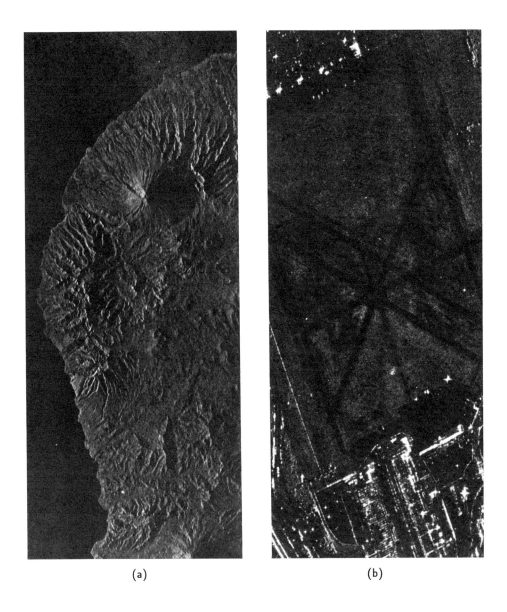

(a)   (b)

Figure 3.21: *SAR images of (a) natural terrain and (b) man-made terrain. Walls and pavements create corners which reflect the radar beam strongly back towards the plane; hence the bright points in the built-up area. Flat surfaces like runways or the sea reflect all the radiation away from the plane; therefore they appear black.*
(Picture courtesy of Goodyear Aerospace Corp. Previously published in *Scientific American* [343])

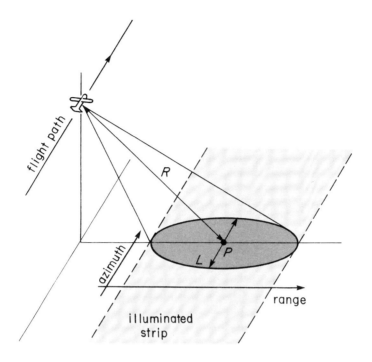

Figure 3.22: *An airborne side looking radar system.*

This is necessary so that the position of reflectors that cause radar echos will be identifiable, without left/right ambiguity [202].

A point p in the illuminated area is identified by its two coordinates: its *range*, or distance perpendicular to the flight path, and its *azimuth*, or "along-track" location. The range R from the plane to the reflecting point is easy to find. Given that the radar pulse propagates with speed c, the time it will take to complete the round trip to the reflector and back is $\Delta t = 2\frac{R}{c}$. Therefore a measurement of the time delay between the transmission of a pulse and the reception of an echo immediately identifies the range of the reflector that caused the echo. The resolution in the range measurement depends only on the length of the pulses that are used.

It is more difficult to pinpoint the along-track location of a reflector. All the reflectors in the illuminated area that have the same range R will create echos that arrive back at the plane simultaneously. Therefore the resolution in the along-track direction is limited by the width of the radar beam (L in fig. 3.22). If we want high resolution, we must be able to *focus* the radar beam, so that it illuminates a very narrow area at each instant. This is done by a synthesized aperture, which simulates a phased array.

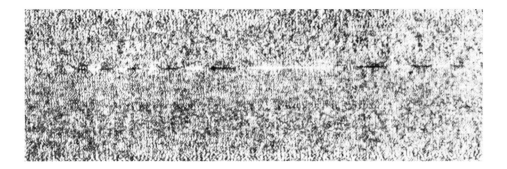

Figure 3.23: *Enlarged portion of a SAR data film. A 1-D FZP created by reflections from an especially strong reflector is clearly seen.*
(Picture Courtesy of Goodyear Aerospace Corp. Previously published in *Scientific American* [343])

3.4.2   The synthetic aperture

The beam may be focused if we use a *phased array* of antennas [75], rather than just one antenna. This is an extensive array of antennas that transmit the radar pulses in a coordinated manner. The phases of the pulses transmitted from the various antennas are carefully controlled. The transmitted pulses interfere with each other. Their relative phases are set so that constructive interference will occur only in one chosen spot, and destructive interference will occur everywhere else. Thus the radar signal is effectively focused to that spot.

The problem with the phased array idea is that a very large array is needed in order to focus the radar beam onto a small area. For example, the desired resolution for terrain images would require an array that is 2000 meters long [419]. Such a large array cannot be accommodated on an airplane. The solution is to use a *synthesized aperture*[12] — instead of having the whole array working at once, we accumulate data from different parts of the array bit by bit. The data is then summed up, to produce the result that would have been obtained by one big array.

This is done by using just one rather small antenna. As the plane advances along its course, the antenna assumes the positions of successive elements in a virtual phased array. It is obvious that the pulses transmitted from the different positions cannot interfere with each other, as they do not exist at the same time. Therefore a record is made of the exact amplitude and phase of the echos received at each position individually. This recording will subsequently be processed to simulate the behavior of a phased array. The recording is accomplished by comparing the echo with a reference wave that is generated in the transmitter,

---

[12]The term aperture, in this context, refers to the whole extent of the array of antennas.

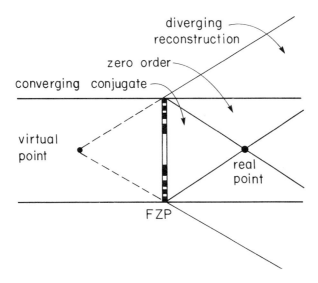

Figure 3.24: *A FZP is a holographic lens. When illuminated by a plane wave, a converging beam and a diverging beam are created.*

together with the original pulse. As the reference maintains its coherence as the plane advances, what we are actually recording is the interference pattern of the echos from the reflecting point with a reference. This is a microwave analog to the recording of a hologram of a three-dimensional object, where each point reflects a light wave that then interferes with a reference wave [375,419].

Let us look for a minute at the interference pattern created in a hologram of one point. The point scatters light in all directions, so the wavefronts of the object beam are spherical. If the reference is a plane wave, the interference pattern will be a *Fresnel zone plate* [239] (abbreviated FZP; see fig. F.1 and appendix F).

Returning to SAR, we see that the echos gathered along the flight course may be regarded as samples along a cross section through the FZP created by interference between the point and the reference. Thus each point contributes a one-dimensional FZP to the data (fig. 3.23). The FZPs belonging to different points in the same range overlap, and therefore the sum looks scrambled. However, the underlying data is still there, just as in optical holography.

3.4.3 Optical processing

The data from the received echos is recorded on film by scan lines on a CRT. Each scan corresponds to all the echos from one pulse. As echos from remote points

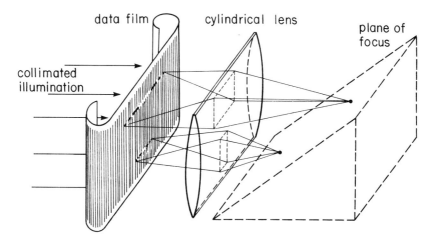

Figure 3.25: *Direct reconstruction from the film that records SAR data creates an image that is tilted relative to the film.*

take longer to arrive, there is a linear connection between the point along the scan and the range. The scans are made across the film. The film is moved between scans, so that subsequent scan lines appear one next to the other. The speed of the film movement is regulated so as to match the speed of the airplane. As a result, the coordinates on the film represent azimuthal position of the plane (along the film), and range to the reflector (across). Note that the data is accumulated by scans *across* the film, but the 1-D FZP relating to a point appears *along* the film, because it is created by multiple echos from the point.

As noted above, the film records one-dimensional holograms of points in the underlying terrain. Therefore it is possible to reconstruct an image of the terrain by simply illuminating the film with a plane wave of coherent light. Consider the reconstruction of one point from a FZP. As always, three output beams are created (fig.3.24). One is the reconstructed beam of light that diverges from the point. Another is the conjugate converging beam. The third is the zero-order continuation of the incident plane wave.

At first glance it seems best to use the conjugate beams, as they already focus the light relating to each point. Actually they only focus it in the horizontal direction (because the FZP is one-dimensional), so a cylindrical lens is needed in order to focus in the vertical direction as well (fig. 3.25). An image of the terrain is indeed created; however, it should be remembered that the original points were at different distances from the airplane. Hence they will be imaged at different distances from the film. The image plane will therefore be tilted, which

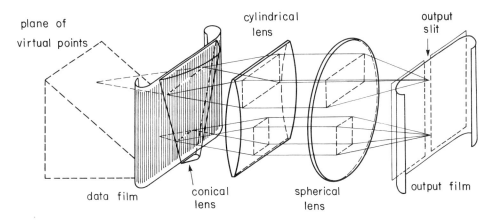

Figure 3.26: *Optical processor for SAR data (see explanation in text). The illumination comes in a collimated beam from the left.*

is inconvenient [386].

The customary[13] configuration for SAR processing therefore creates an image from the diverging beam [419,81,82]; it is depicted in fig. 3.26. The imaging is done in two steps: first a collimated beam is created for each point, and then it is focused. The degree of divergence in the horizontal direction depends on the range (i.e., on the size of the FZP), so a lens with a varying radius is needed — this is the conical lens that is adjacent to the film. The vertical divergence is identical for all points, so a simple cylindrical lens (one focal length away from the film) will do. After both these lenses, the light is collimated; A regular spherical lens then focuses it to a point on the output plane.

When the data film moves, the image also moves. However, points that are at the bottom (near range) move faster than points at the top (far range), just as the scenery from a car window behaves. This makes it hard to record the output. The solution is to use a slit in the output plane, through which the output image is recorded on a film that moves synchronously with the data film.

It is interesting to note that this same configuration can also be interpreted as a multichannel matched-filtering correlator [173]. The pattern we are looking for is the one-dimensional zone plate created by a point in the terrain. It turns out that the matched filter is a quadratic phase filter, with the radius depending on the range. Therefore we need a separate channel for every range, with a separate filter. This is realized by the conical lens. the cylindrical-spherical combination then performs the necessary one-dimensional Fourier transform in all the channels [82].

To summarize, the data gathered by a synthetic aperture radar imaging system is easily processed by a coherent optical processor. The simplicity of the processor (a sequence of three lenses) is striking in contrast with the complexity of the data (a recording of the amplitudes and phases of echos of thousands of pulses). The reason this is possible is that light and microwaves are actually the same thing: namely electromagnetic waves. The light simply reverses the action of the microwaves, at a smaller scale (because of its shorter wavelength).

3.5   Radio-signal analysis

Optical processing systems are inherently suited to the processing of two-dimensional spatial signals, i.e., images. Many important signals, however, are one-dimensional temporal signals — notably radio signals, such as radar. There are two ways to process such signals optically. One is to translate the temporal signal into a spatial signal, and the other is to use the option of time integration, mentioned at the beginning of this chapter (eq. 3.1).

The most common type of device for the introduction of the temporal variable

---

[13]Other configurations have also been proposed, however, as well as digital processing [35,567].

into an optical system is an acoustooptic device (section 2.5) [150,380,267]. As the input signal has only one degree of freedom, time, a one-dimensional acoustooptic device is sufficient. This also means that the two-dimensional capacity of the usual optical systems is unnecessary in this application. Another possibility is to stay with the regular two-dimensional configuration, and use the extra dimension to create a multichannel system [172].

In this section two examples of acoustooptic processing systems are given: one for RF (radio frequency) spectral analysis, and the other for radar pulse compression.

3.5.1   RF spectral analysis

Knowledge of the frequency spectrum is an important tool in the analysis of radio signals. A method for the fast and efficient calculation of the Fourier transform, which produces the spectrum, is therefore desirable. This has been the driving force behind the development of the fast Fourier transform (FFT) [60] algorithm and of various special purpose hardware accelerators designed to calculate the Fourier transform [690].

In coherent optical systems, the Fourier transform is a basic operation: it is the transformation that light passing through a lens is subject to (see section 2.4.4 and appendix C). The advantages of using this phenomenon for spectral analysis are the high speed of the operation, and the extremely large bandwidth of the signals that can be dealt with (up to 10 GHz, as opposed to a ~ 2 MHz upper limit in special purpose digital equipment) [690]. It may be utilized if we just modulate a light beam in accordance with the radio signal we want to analyze — which is what acoustooptic spatial light modulators do. Note that the two-dimensional capacity of the usual optical lens is unnecessary in this application, and indeed most optical spectrum analyzers use planar optical systems, where the beam only has a 1-D cross section (e.g., [14,15,290,478]). The exact configuration is described in section 8.5.3.

If the usual 2-D system is used, a multichannel spectrum analyzer is created. The one-dimensional inputs are stacked one above the other, and an astigmatic lens system creates a stack of their respective Fourier transforms in the output plane. Such a configuration may also be used for the analysis of one extra-high-bandwidth signal, by using the different channels to create a raster scan of the signal and performing a 2-D Fourier transform [677]. This method may be analyzed in terms of the FFT algorithm, which also works by breaking up the input signal into smaller pieces [690].

3.5.2   Radar pulse compression

High resolution in the range measured by a radar depends on short pulses. A large overall range depends on high transmission intensity. The combined requirement of short but intense pulses is hard to achieve. A practical solution is the use of long *coded* pulses. The coding allows for the correlation of the echos with a reference pulse, an operation that pinpoints the exact instant of the echo's arrival. This extraction of an instantaneous time point from the long pulses is termed "pulse compression". As mentioned in section 3.2.2, the correlation may be regarded as an operation that concentrates the signal into a point. As the background noise is not concentrated, this also improves the signal-to-noise ratio. Thus rather faint echos may also be detected.

Acoustooptical systems for pulse compression directly carry out the integral in the definition of the cross-correlation operation (eq. 3.2). There are two basic approaches: one uses space integration, while the other utilizes time integration [642,579].

Space integrating correlator

In this configuration, two acoustooptic cells are used (fig. 3.27 (a)) [642]. The first modulates the light beam according to the received RF signal, that includes the radar echos. This is Fourier-transformed and the zero frequency is blocked, so as to turn the phase modulation into amplitude modulation (see page 38). Another Fourier transform images the spatially modulated light onto the second acoustooptic cell. This cell accepts a time-reversed reference signal as input, but this signal propagates in the opposite direction to the received input signal in the first acoustooptic cell. Thus the two signals slide past each other, to give the correlation function. The light after the second acoustooptical cell is gathered by a lens and focused onto a detector. This is the spatial integration step.

Note that this method requires both the received signal and the reference signal to be present in the apertures of their respective acoustooptic cells simultaneously. Therefore some prior knowledge of the probable time of the echo is needed, and the duration of the pulses cannot be too long.

Time integrating correlator

With this configuration [643,360,112], the input signal is used to modulate the light source (fig. 3.27 (b)). This light illuminates an acoustooptic cell that carries the reference signal. The resulting light distribution is filtered as before, to remove the bias term, and imaged on a detector array. Denoting the input by s_1 and the reference by s_2, the light falling on a detector located at x at instant t is $s_1(t)\,s_2(x+vt)$. If the detector integrates this for the duration that the reference travels across the acoustooptic cell, it will accumulate one term in the correlation of s_1 and s_2. An array of detectors thus accumulates the whole correlation function in parallel.

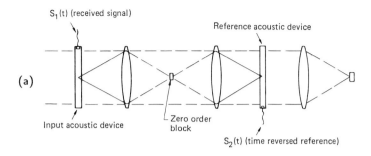

(a)

S₁(t) (received signal) — $S_1(t)$ (received signal)

Reference acoustic device

Input acoustic device

Zero order block

$S_2(t)$ (time reversed reference)

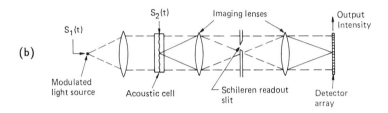

(b)

$S_2(t)$

$S_1(t)$

Imaging lenses

Output Intensity

Modulated light source

Acoustic cell

Schileren readout slit

Detector array

Figure 3.27: *Acoustooptic correlators.*
(a) Space integrating.
(b) Time integrating.
(Reprinted with permission from *Optical Engineering* [642], ©1977)

3.6 Transforms

In the preceding sections we saw that the Fourier transform can be easily realized by optical means. As a result, any shift-invariant linear transform can be implemented. In this section we explore methods for the implementation of other transforms by optical means. It seems that practically any transform *can* be implemented by some optical system, albeit not always in real time [302,265]. We first address pointwise transformations, in which each point in the output depends on only one point in the input. These include arbitrary changes in the gray scale, on one hand, and geometrical transformations of the coordinates, on the other. We then move on to general linear transforms. An important example is the Radon transform, which is useful in tomography. Finally we touch upon nonlinear transforms.

3.6.1 Nonlinear pointwise transforms

The simplest kind of transform is that which just changes the function value at each point. Linear pointwise transforms reduce to multiplication by a constant,

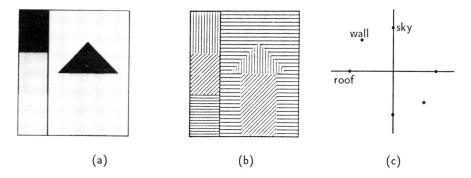

Figure 3.28: *Theta modulation.*
   (a) Original image.
   (b) Theta modulated version.
   (c) Spatial spectrum of theta modulated image.
   (Reprinted with permission from *Applied Optics* [23], ©1965)

which is not very interesting. We therefore turn to nonlinear transforms. These may be accomplished by four different ways: use of nonlinear photographic film, translation to spatial patterns followed by filtering, halftone techniques, and manipulation of TV scans.

Photographic and photochromic methods

Monotonic nonlinear pointwise transformations of a light distribution can usually be realized by recording it on a photographic film, and exploiting the nonlinearities of the film. For example, a high-contrast film may be used to get a thresholding effect. As an alternative, a photochromic material may be used (see page 27 for a short explanation of the photochromic effect) [210]. This saves the need for chemical development.

Intensity to spatial frequency

General nonlinear transforms require some sort of encoding to enable an optical system to distinguish between the different intensities. Better still, the input intensities should be translated into distinct spatial locations, so that they can subsequently be filtered. A conceptually simple idea in this direction is *theta-modulation* [441,23]. The image is encoded by a set of gratings, where the different gray levels are represented by gratings with different orientations (fig. 3.28 (a,b)). A subsequent Fourier transform by a lens will separate the gray levels spatially: each will become a pair of points of light in a certain direction on the unit circle (fig. 3.28 (c)). Any desired nonlinear transformation may now be carried out by filtering these points of light. The decoding step (getting rid of the gratings) is trivial: the grating pattern results from interference between light from the two points that represent each gray level in the Fourier plane. If only one point from each pair is used, while the other is blocked, no grating structure will appear.

Theta modulation has two severe drawbacks: one is that the grating spacing must be much less than the image resolution, so a high space-bandwidth product is required. The other is that it is hard to realize in real time [46]. A feasible alternative is the use of a variable grating mode (VGM) liquid crystal [665]. This is a liquid crystal that creates a grating structure when a voltage is applied to it. The grating period depends on the voltage. When such a liquid crystal is sandwiched with a photoconductor between two electrodes, the voltage on the liquid crystal depends on the light falling on the photoconductor. Hence such a device transforms light intensity into spatial frequency. Again a Fourier transform by a lens separates the gray levels, and enables us to perform arbitrary transformations by manipulation in the frequency plane.

Halftoning techniques

A totally different approach is the use of halftoning techniques. Halftoning is well known from its use in the printing industry: it is the representation of gray levels in a picture by an array of small dots of different sizes [727]. This is actually a form of "pulse width modulation": the width (size) of regularly spaced pulses (dots) is the parameter that conveys the data values sampled at those points. Because of the sampling, the spatial spectrum of a halftone image will include many harmonics, displaced by the sampling frequency. The original data may be reconstructed by low-pass filtering (this is done naturally by the eye) [93, fig. 2].

Normally we would want the dot size to be linearly dependent on the intensity level. A monotonic nonlinearity may be introduced by having a monotonic nonlinear dependence [356,21]. Nonmonotonic nonlinearities may also be accommodated. The idea is simply to use one of the higher-order harmonics of the spectrum in the reconstruction stage, instead of the basic component. The intensity of the higher-order harmonics changes periodically (and therefore nonmonotonically) as the size of the dots increases [650,177,178].

Masking of TV scans [270]

A video camera makes a raster scan of its input image and creates an electrical signal which is analogous to the input intensities encountered along the scan line. This signal is subsequently displayed on the screen of an oscilloscope, with the x axis describing location along the scan line and the y axis showing voltage, and hence intensity of the input. Thus the input intensity is translated into the vertical position of the oscilloscope beam. The oscilloscope screen is then masked with a mask incorporating some horizontal pattern, e.g., a number of horizontal slits in an otherwise opaque mask. The light passing the mask is focused by a lens onto a

detector, whose output is displayed on a video monitor that is synchronized with
the input camera. In the case of a mask made of a number of horizontal slits, light
will pass only when the input intensity matches one of a few specific values; hence
a grey level contour map will be generated on the monitor. Grey-tone masks can
implement any arbitrary nonlinear transformation.

Applications

There are various uses for nonlinear transformations. Three examples are:

- Generation of equidensity lines (isophotes) of an image, i.e., a contour map
  of the gray levels.

- A logarithmic transformation may facilitate the removal of periodic noise. If
  the noise *multiplies* the image (rather than being additive), intermodulation
  elements will appear in their joint spectrum. These will not be removed
  by filtering out the noise frequency and its harmonics. After a logarithmic
  transform, however, the noise becomes additive, and no intermodulation
  terms appear in the Fourier transform [356,353].

- Contrast enhancement of an image may be achieved [405], as well as thresholding.

3.6.2   Geometrical transforms

A different type of pointwise transform does not change the function values, but
rather deforms the coordinates in some way. When an image is scanned point by
point, any geometrical transform can be realized by controlling the deflectors that
regulate the scanning (an example was given on page 68).

Geometrical transforms may also be realized in parallel if we have an imaging
system, and are able to arbitrarily influence the imaging of each point in the
object. It turns out that this is possible (with coherent light) by introducing a
phase filter into the system, which independently modifies the phase at each point
[85,86]. This filter may be viewed as an array of miniature prisms and lenses,
which cause the light from each point in the object to be imaged at an arbitrarily
chosen spot (fig. 3.29). A mathematical analysis shows that in a continuous filter,
the directional derivatives of the phase are translated into shifts.

The most straightforward way to implement the required filter is to shape the
face of an optical element according to the required phase [157]. For example, a
plate of glass of varying thickness will cause light passing through different points
to suffer different delays, and thus to emerge with different phases. Such a filter,
however, is difficult to produce in the general case. Another approach is to use
computer generated holograms [83,84,144]. As stated in section 2.8.3, computer

Rok Sosič

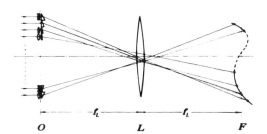

Figure 3.29: *Geometrical transforms may be realized by a phase filter. This is modeled by an array of miniature prisms and lenses, which affect the imaging of each point individually.*
(Reprinted with permission from *Optics Communications* [85], ©1974)

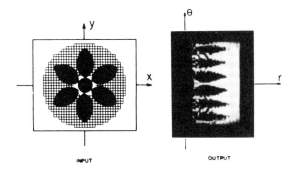

Figure 3.30: *A geometrical transformation from Cartesian to polar coordinates, implemented by a multifacet hologram.*
(Reprinted with permission from *Optical Engineering* [48], ©1983)

generated holograms can implement arbitrary optical elements. This includes, of course, arbitrary phase filters.

The continuous phase filter is necessary in order to realize a continuous transform of the whole field. If a low-resolution transform is sufficient, a simpler method may be used. The field is divided into the required number of cells (typically about a thousand), and each cell is individually directed to its destination. This is done by a multifacet hologram that has a separate facet for each cell [48,126]. An example of a transform from Cartesian to polar coordinates, realized in this way, is given in fig. 3.30.

Applications

Geometrical transforms have many uses. Some examples are:

- Corrections for geometrical distortion, e.g., when an image is displayed on the slightly curved screen of a TV.

- Preprocessing before other filtering, e.g., the transform to $\ln r, \theta$ coordinates needed for rotation and scale invariant pattern recognition (see page 68).

- A method for simplifying optical systems. Geometrical transforms that map many points to one point may alleviate the need for space-integrating optical elements. For example, a wedge-ring detector array (fig. 3.17) may be replaced by a simpler linear detector array if a geometrical transform first maps circles of different radii to a line, and wedges in different orientations to another line [144,121,620].

3.6.3 Shift-invariant linear transforms

As mentioned in appendix B, any shift-invariant linear transform may be written as a convolution. Using the convolution property of the Fourier transform (appendix C), we find that any shift-invariant linear transform may be realized optically by applying the correct spatial filter to the function's Fourier transform. The details of the optical systems and the production of the filters by holographic means were delineated in section 3.2.

3.6.4 Space-variant linear transforms

Volume holography

A space-variant transform is one in which the transformation is different for different points in the field. This means that the transformation cannot be described by one global transfer function. Rather we should sample the input (with a sufficient sampling resolution) and describe a distinct transfer function for each point. We saw that for a shift-invariant system, the transfer function was realized by means of a hologram. What we need for a space-variant system with N^2 sampling points is, therefore, a set of N^2 distinct holograms. This is feasible using volume holograms — holograms that are recorded in a three-dimensional medium [181,717].

The principle behind volume holograms is the same as the principle behind regular, thin holograms. The hologram is a recording of the interference pattern between the object beam and a reference beam. The difference is that in volume holography we record the three-dimensional pattern, rather than just a two-dimensional slice of the interference pattern. as a result, the reconstruction is very sensitive to the angle of the reproduced reference beam: it must be *exactly* the same as the angle of the reference beam used in the recording stage. This allows

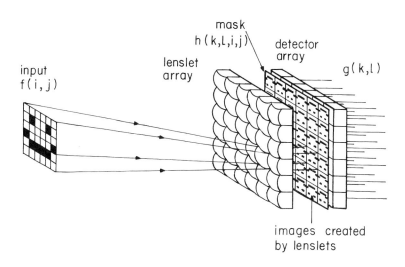

Figure 3.31: *Implementation of a general discrete linear transform with a lenslet array.*

us to multiplex many holograms in the same recording medium: each hologram uses a reference beam from a different angle.

The problem is that the only practical way to create the volume hologram that represents a space-variant optical system is by using the system itself. Thus if the system is physically available, we simply sample the input by using an opaque screen with pinholes in it, and record the hologram by a photographic process. It is impossible, however, to generate a hologram that will behave like an arbitrary, unavailable system.

An alternative that is viable — at least in some cases — is to use multiple amplitude and phase filters, sandwiched together [282]. While the formulation that leads to the calculation of the different filters is not directly related to volume holograms, the outcome is similar: it is a thick optical element that manipulates light coming from different points in different ways.

Lenslet array

A simpler way in which to implement a discrete space-variant linear transform is with a lenslet array. This device is a direct implementation of the definition of a general discrete linear transform, which is

$$g(k, l) = \sum_{}^{N} \sum_{}^{N} f(i, j) \, h(k, l; i, j). \tag{3.6}$$

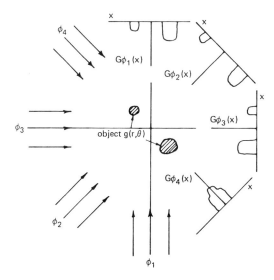

Figure 3.32: *The Radon transform of an object consists of its projections in all possible directions.*
(Reprinted with permission from *Optical Engineering* [256], ©1980)

The configuration is shown in fig. 3.31 [252]. The input f is situated at left. A set of N^2 detectors, one for each element of the output g, is at right. An array of N^2 lenslets (little lenses packed together) creates N^2 distinct images of the input — one on each detector. A mask is placed between the lenslet array and the detector array, and modifies the light distribution falling on the detectors. The mask is divided into N^2 submasks, one for each detector. the submask in front of detector k, l has N^2 small squares, representing the values of $h(k, l; i, j)$ for $i, j = 1, \ldots, N$. When the k, l^{th} lenslet images the k, l^{th} copy of the input on the k, l^{th} submask, the light passing through is proportional to the double sum of eq. 3.6. This is detected by the detector, so the k, l^{th} detector outputs the k, l^{th} element of g.

3.6.5   The Radon transform

The Radon transform [43], because of its importance, deserves special attention. This transform is defined as follows. Our input function $g(x, y)$ may also be represented in a rotated coordinate system, by a different mathematical expression $g_\phi(x_\phi, y_\phi)$, where

$$x_\phi = x \cos \phi + y \sin \phi, \qquad\qquad y_\phi = y \cos \phi - x \sin \phi.$$

For each rotation angle ϕ, let us calculate the projection of $g_\phi(x_\phi, y_\phi)$ on the x_ϕ axis. Designating points on the x_ϕ axis by χ, we get

$$G_\phi(\chi) = \int_{-\infty}^{\infty} g_\phi(\chi, y_\phi) \, dy_\phi.$$

The resulting set of projections is the Radon transform of g (fig. 3.32). Note that Radon space is also two-dimensional: its coordinates are ϕ and χ, in the ranges $0 \le \phi < \pi$ and $-\infty \le \chi \le \infty$.

The Radon transform may be used to reduce the dimensionality of a problem, and thus to simplify it [44]. Its chief importance, however, stems from the fact that imaging techniques that try to extract information about the interior of a three-dimensional object actually only get projections of the object. The best known example is tomography: a planar sheet of radiation is used to investigate a two-dimensional slice from a 3-D object (typically a human being). The intensity of the radiation after it passes through the body in parallel to the y axis is

$$O(x) = I \, e^{-\int g(x,y)\, dy},$$

where I is the (uniform) input intensity

$\quad\quad\quad O(x)$ is the output intensity at point x of the projection

$\quad\quad\quad g(x,y)$ designates the local transmittance of the body at point (x, y) in the slice.

As we see, the detected output depends on on the projection of g on the x axis. More generally, for every direction ϕ we may write

$$\ln(I) - \ln(O_\phi(\chi)) = \int g_\phi(\chi, y_\phi) \, dy_\phi = G_\phi(\chi). \tag{3.7}$$

I is known; $O_\phi(\chi)$ is measured — so $G_\phi(\chi)$ may be calculated. The problem now is to reconstruct $g(x, y)$ from this information. For that we need to perform the inverse Radon transform.

The inverse transform

Here we shall not rigorously derive the inverse Radon transform, but will make do with a short sketch of how it is done (more details may be found in [43,45,256]). Even this requires some mathematical gymnastics. We first note that a point x_ϕ, y_ϕ in a rotated Cartesian coordinate system may also be described in *polar* coordinates. It has radius $r = \sqrt{x_\phi^2 + y_\phi^2}$ and angle $\theta = \phi + \arctan\left(\frac{y_\phi}{x_\phi}\right)$ (fig. 3.33).

We now write g in polar coordinates (this is a third mathematical expression describing the same function; we'll use subscripts $r\theta$ to distinguish it). Using this, we rewrite the projection for angle ϕ. The line of integration is defined by

$$r \cos(\theta - \phi) = \chi. \tag{3.8}$$

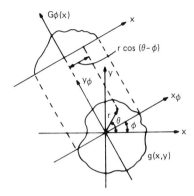

Figure 3.33: *Relations between the rotated Cartesian coordinates and the polar coordinates for describing the Radon transform.*
(Reprinted with permission from *Applied Optics* [277], ©1981)

Therefore

$$G_\phi(\chi) = \int_{-\frac{\pi}{2}}^{\frac{\pi}{2}} \int_{-\infty}^{\infty} g_{r\theta}(r,\theta)\, \delta\left(r\cos(\theta-\phi)-\chi\right)\, r\, dr\, d\theta$$

(it is as if we integrate over all space, but the δ function[14] chooses only the points along the appropriate line). What we are looking for is the inverse of this expression.

An oversimplified way to reconstruct the original object is by backprojection (fig. 3.34): Take the projection $G_\phi(\chi)$ and smear it out again, perpendicularly to the ϕ direction. Do this for all ϕ, and sum up the result. Point r, θ of the object is therefore reconstructed as the sum of $G_\phi(\chi)$ for all ϕ, where χ is defined by eq. 3.8. Formally, this is written as

$$g'_{r\theta}(r,\theta) = \frac{1}{\pi} \int_0^\pi G_\phi\left(r\cos(\theta-\phi)\right)\, d\phi.$$

The result is an approximation of the original object. A better approximation may be obtained by combining this with a filtering action, i.e., a convolution that will remove the trailing "smear marks" created by the naive backprojection. It turns out that the proper choice is

$$g_{r\theta}(r,\theta) = -\frac{1}{2\pi^2} \int_0^\pi \int_{-\infty}^{\infty} \frac{G_\phi(\chi)}{\left(r\cos(\theta-\phi)-\chi\right)^2}\, d\chi\, d\phi. \qquad (3.9)$$

---

[14]The δ function is zero at all points except the origin, and has the property $\iint \delta(r,\theta)\, r\, dr\, d\theta = 1$.

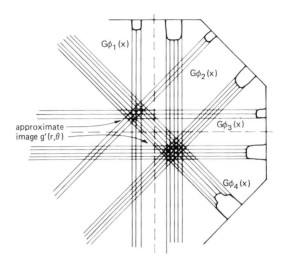

Figure 3.34: *Reconstruction of an object from its Radon transform by backprojection. Compare to the original in fig. 3.32.*
(Reprinted with permission from *Optical Engineering* [256], ©1980)

This should be interpreted as a principle-value integral, i.e., the singular points should be "skipped".

Optical realization

Optical realization of tomographic reconstruction has been motivated by the desire to supply the medical imaging capabilities of CAT[15] scanners at a lower cost. Many different approaches have been proposed [256]. We shall concentrate on one that seems most advanced. We now follow the various steps in the recording and reconstruction process.

Each projection $G_\phi(\chi)$ is recorded as a horizontal line across a film. The response of the recording film is nonlinear, and incorporates the logarithmic transform implied by eq. 3.7. Successive projections are recorded one underneath the other. Thus the coordinates on the film are χ (horizontal) and ϕ (vertical). Note that any single point in the object follows a sinusoidal trajectory on the film (fig. 3.35). The amplitude of the sine wave depends on the point's distance r from the axis, while its phase depends on the point's angular coordinate θ. Such a recording is therefore called a *sinogram* of the object.

---

[15]Acronym for "computer aided tomography".

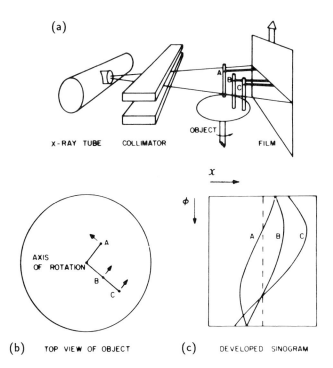

Figure 3.35: *The Radon transform is recorded by a sinogram.*
(a) Successive projections are recorded one under the other to form a sinogram. As the object rotates, the film advances.
(b) Example of a three-point object.
(c) Sinogram produced by the three-point object.
(Reprinted with permission from the *Proceedings of the IEEE* [45], ©1977 IEEE)

The object $g_{r\theta}(r, \theta)$ is reconstructed point after point, in a spiral fashion. We start with a very small r, and slowly increase it. Meanwhile θ completes many cycles. As noted above, each point r, θ is represented by one sine wave on the sinogram. Therefore we must first isolate the correct sine, in order to evaluate $g_{r\theta}(r, \theta)$. There are two methods to do so:

1. Wrap the sinogram on a drum, whose circumference corresponds to the period of the sine waves. The different sines then turn into ellipses in various orientations. When viewed in a specific tilt (ψ in fig. 3.36) and rotation angle (ω_c), exactly one ellipse will appear as a straight line. It can then be isolated by a simple straight slit. The scanning of the image is done by a slow change of ψ (corresponding to scanning along r), and a fast rotation in

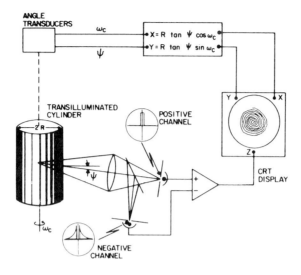

Figure 3.36: *Optical system for the inverse Radon transform, using a drum.*
(Reprinted with permission from the *Proceedings of the IEEE* [45], ©1977 IEEE)

ω_c (which represents θ).

2. Image the sinogram on a mask with a sinusoidal slit in it. Only one sine wave will fit and pass through completely. The sine slit is designed so that its amplitude decreases slowly over a few cycles. Scanning is achieved by simply moving the slit. The quick change of phase corresponds to a fast cyclic change of θ, while the slow change of amplitude translates into a slow scanning of r [277] (fig. 3.37).

These isolation methods are not perfect: when other sine waves intersect the wave we are trying to isolate, they too influence the outcome. This is analogous to the smear marks left in the naive backprojection reconstruction. As indicated in eq. 3.9, the solution lies in a convolution with the function $-\frac{1}{x^2}$. As this has a singularity at $x = 0$, it is approximated by

$$
h(x) = \left\{ \begin{array}{ll} -\frac{1}{x^2} & x > \varepsilon, \\[2ex] \frac{1}{\varepsilon^2} & x < \varepsilon. \end{array} \right.
$$

Using incoherent light, a two-channel configuration must be used in order to implement this bipolar function. The outcome of the negative channel is then subtracted from the outcome of the positive channel, and thus the value of $g_{r\theta}(r, \theta)$ is obtained (figs. 3.36 and 3.37).

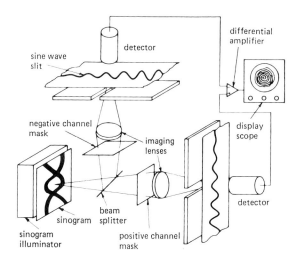

Figure 3.37: *Optical system for the inverse Radon transform, using a sinusoidal slit. This is called a "loop" processor.*
(Reprinted with permission from *Optical Engineering* [256], ©1980)

Fourier transform method

Recall that $G_\phi(\chi)$ is the projection of $g_\phi(x_\phi, y_\phi)$ on the x_ϕ axis. This integrates all the information about how g changes in the ϕ direction, and no information as to how it changes in other directions. Therefore if we take the one-dimensional Fourier transform of $G_\phi(\chi)$, we will find that it is just a slice (in the ϕ direction) through the two-dimensional Fourier transform of $g(x, y)$. This is called the *central slice theorem*.

This theorem forms the base of one of the other optical reconstruction methods [256]. The projections $G_\phi(\chi)$ are Fourier-transformed by an astigmatic lens. They are then combined in a star shape to form the complete 2-D Fourier transform of the object. An inverse Fourier transform by a lens produces an image of the original object. This method, unlike the former one, requires the use of coherent light.

3.6.6   General nonlinear transforms

There is no recipe for the optical implementation of general nonlinear transforms. However, such transforms may often be decomposed into a number of stages, each of which is either a linear transform or a pointwise nonlinear transform. As each of these stages is realizable in optics, as shown in the preceding sections, so is their sum.

Summary

This chapter introduced optical processing systems that operate on images. The data is a 2-D analog light distribution, created by an SLM (coherent) or a CRT (incoherent). As the modulated light beam traverses the optical system, the light distribution is manipulated; hence the output light distribution is a processed version of the input. These optical processors are special-purpose: each can only manipulate the light in one specific way. They have limited dynamic range and limited space-bandwidth product.

The most important operation that coherent analog optical image processing systems can perform is the Fourier transform. This is usually combined with spatial filtering, in which the amplitudes and phases of specific spatial frequencies are changed. Simple applications of spatial filtering include low-pass filtering, high-pass filtering, and periodic noise removal. A more sophisticated application is the realization of the cross-correlation operation, used in pattern recognition. In this case the filter must be matched to the pattern that is being searched for. Deconvolution may also be realized; here the filter is dictated by the transfer function that is to be "undone".

Pattern recognition is the application that has received the most attention. Apart from improvements on the basic matched-spatial-filter approach, other methods that use optical feature extraction have also been devised. Another very important application is synthetic aperture radar imaging, which is used to create aerial pictures of the surface of the earth. Here the data collected by the radar is recorded on film, and the image of the terrain is later constructed optically with a set of specially shaped lenses.

Optical systems may be designed to perform many other transforms, in addition to the classical Fourier transform. These include pointwise nonlinear transformations of the grey levels, geometrical transformations of the coordinates, and general space-variant linear (and even nonlinear) transforms. For example, optical systems that perform the inverse Radon transform have been devised — this is useful for the construction of tomographic images.

Another class of systems is that of signal processors. Conceptually, these are very similar to image processors; the difference is that the data is a one-dimensional temporal signal, rather than a two-dimensional spatial image. Optical processors for such signals are useful especially in conjunction with radar systems.

Bibliographical notes

The basic concepts of spatial filtering were set down by O'Neill [517] and Cutrona et al. [172]. VanderLugt's introduction of arbitrary holographic filters initiated an avalanche of papers on this issue; organized reviews such as those of Goodman [265,260, chap. 7] or VanderLugt [698] make better reading.

Different aspects of pattern recognition are the subject of hundreds of papers — most of them technical and of limited scope. The best reviews of the classic matched-filter methods are probably those by Casasent [102,103]. The newer feature-extraction methods are reviewed in [116]. It seems that there are no comprehensive reviews on rotation and scale invariances or on interclass-discriminating and intraclass-recognizing filters.

Synthetic aperture radar image processing has been reviewed repeatedly; A nice introduction is the article by Jensen et al. in Scientific American [343]. An in-depth review is by Leith and Ingalls [419]. Optically realizable transforms have been reviewed by Häusler [302]. Optical processors for the Radon transform are reviewed by Gmitro et al. [256].

Chapter 4

Optical Numerical Processing

The preceding chapter discussed the processing of continuous, analog images, by analog, usually linear, optical systems. Similar systems are also used for the processing of numerical data, where the numerical values are represented by analog light intensities. The distinction between image processing and numerical processing is somewhat artificial. For example, pattern recognition is easily classified as image processing, while matrix multiplication has the flavor of numerical processing. But how does one classify transforms? While the Radon transform clearly relates to image processing, a general discrete 2-D linear transform by a lenslet array fits better into the context of numerical processing. In this book it was decided to group all the various transforms together, in section 3.6, so as to present a complete and coherent picture. This chapter will deal with other subjects: first come the simple arithmetic operations, then linear algebra and matrix operations, and finally differentiation, integration, and the analog solution of differential equations.

4.1 Simple arithmetic

In the optical systems treated in this section, the data is conveyed by the modulation of the cross section of light beams (just as it was in the applications discussed in the preceding chapter). For simplicity, we shall assume that the modulation is done by a transparency. When coherent light passes through a transparency, its *amplitude* is multiplied at each point by the transmittance of that transparency. In this case the transmittance might be complex, i.e., it might also produce a phase change. When *in*coherent light passes through a transparency, its *intensity* is multiplied by the transmittance, which is real and positive. The question in each case is how to add, subtract, multiply, and divide the transmittances of two transparencies [302].

4.1.1 Addition

Addition is accomplished by modulating two separate light beams, and then combining them with a beam splitter (fig. 4.1 (a)). A beam splitter is actually just a semitransparent mirror. In this case what it does is to let one beam (modulated by f_1) through, and break the other (f_2). Thus the output contains both.

If the light is coherent, the complex amplitudes are added up. This is another way of saying that the light beams interfere. If it is incoherent, on the other hand, the intensities are summed.

4.1.2 Subtraction

With coherent light, the simplest way in which to achieve subtraction is by a phase shift of π, based on the identity $e^{i\pi} \equiv -1$. To do so, a phase plate is inserted into the path of one of the beams (fig. 4.1 (b)) [194]. This is just a flat piece of glass (or a crystal), whose thickness is such that light passing through it suffers a delay of half a wavelength relative to light that does not.

With incoherent light, the two data images must first be imposed on a spatial carrier, i.e., a high-frequency grating. If the carriers are out of phase, the difference between the images will be encoded on a spatial carrier at the output [194,461].

A totally different method for subtraction is to exploit the properties of certain electrooptic spatial light modulators (described on page 29). In such SLMs, a voltage is applied onto a sandwich containing an electrooptic crystal and a photoconductor. When light modulated by a data image falls on this structure, a corresponding spatial charge distribution is created on the crystal. If now the voltage is reversed and a second data image is entered, the final charge distribution will correspond to the difference between the two. This charge distribution governs the transmittance of the SLM, and thus a light beam modulated by the abovementioned difference may be generated. Note that the images must be entered sequentially for this to work; the previous methods were parallel.

4.1.3 Multiplication

Multiplication is the easiest operation — in fact, it does not require any special device or configuration. As mentioned above, when light passes through a transparency it is multiplied by the transparency's transmittance. Therefore if we wish to multiply two data images, we simply use a sandwich of their two transparencies (fig. 4.1 (c)).

4.1.4 Division

As shown already on page 86, division may be regarded as a set of two multiplications [652]:

$$\frac{1}{f} = \frac{f^*}{ff^*} = f^* \frac{1}{|f|^2}$$

(this notation implies coherent light, as f^* is the complex conjugate of f. It is, however, also applicable to incoherent light, where we simply have $f = f^*$). The real-valued $\frac{1}{|f|^2}$ transparency may be created photographically, by use of a film

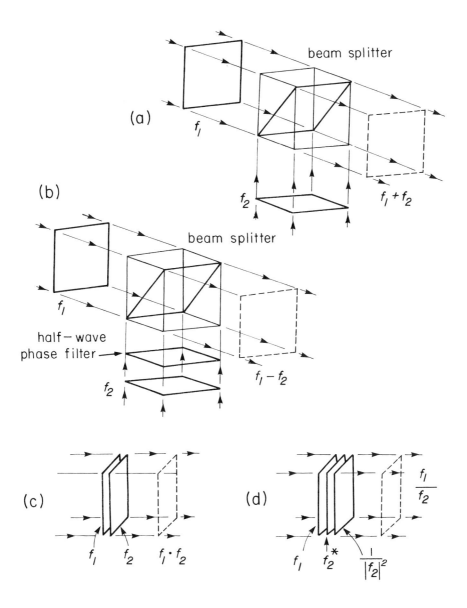

Figure 4.1: *Analog optical arithmetic.*
  (a) Addition: beams are combined with a beam splitter.
  (b) Subtraction: the phase of one beam is shifted.
  (c) Multiplication: A sandwich of two transparencies.
  (d) Division: Three transparencies are used.

with the correct nonlinearity. Luckily some photochromic materials materials also display such nonlinearities, so this can also be done in real time [210].

The quotient $\frac{f_1}{f_2}$ is therefore obtainable by use of a sandwich of three transparencies (fig. 4.1 (d)).

4.1.5   Operations on single values

The use of beam splitters and transparencies allows us to perform arithmetic operations on continuous fields of data (i.e., images) in parallel. In some cases, however, a lesser capability suffices: we could have a light beam whose intensity represents a number, and want to add to or multiply it by another number. This can also be done, as we now show.

The output voltage from a detector is proportional to the total amount of light falling on it; it does not care if the light comes in one beam or in a few distinct beams. Thus it can be used to derive the sum of more than two numbers. This capability for almost unlimited-fan-in addition is one of the strongest points of optical computers.

Multiplication may be done by modulating the intensity of a beam. A modulator can only decrease the intensity; hence the multiplier must be less than 1.

4.2   Evaluation of polynomials

A polynomial in the variable x is an expression of the form

$$p[x] = a_n x^n + a_{n-1} x^{n-1} + \cdots + a_2 x^2 + a_1 x + a_0.$$

This may be rewritten according to Horner's rule thus [374, page 467]:

$$((((a_n x + a_{n-1})x + a_{n-2})x + \cdots)x + a_1)x + a_0$$

The advantage of this representation is that it implies less arithmetic operations.

Given a polynomial p with positive coefficients, and a positive value for x, it is easy to evaluate $p[x]$ by an optical systolic array based on Horner's rule [707]. The extension to complex numbers is straightforward, using a multichannel system. The kth stage of the systolic array will accept an input v_k, multiply it by x and add a_{n-k}, thus forming its output v_{k+1}, which is piped to the next stage. The multiplication is implemented by a modulator. The addition is implemented by a beam splitter, which combines the modulated input beam with a beam issuing from a local source whose intensity is proportional to a_{n-k}.

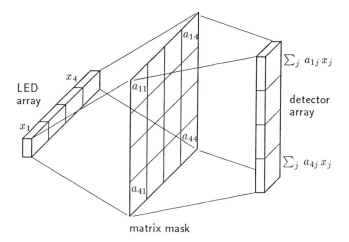

Figure 4.2: *Schematic optical matrix-vector multiplier. The optical components that focus the light are not shown.*

4.3 Matrix operations

Matrices and matrix operations are a fundamental tool in linear algebra, and are therefore extremely important in many fields. A lot of research has gone into algorithms for the efficient execution of matrix operations on digital electronic computers. For example, the multiplication of two $N \times N$ matrices[1], which naively requires $O(N^3)$ steps, can (at the time of writing) be done in $O(N^{2.376...})$ steps [166]. A different research avenue is the quest for special purpose architectures that will compute matrix operations efficiently, e.g., systolic arrays [390]. Special purpose optical systems are also being considered.

4.3.1 Matrix-vector multiplication

The multiplication of a vector $\mathbf{x}$ by a matrix $\mathcal{A}$ is perhaps the simplest of matrix operations. The optical implementation of a parallel, real-time matrix-vector multiplier is straightforward, as shown in fig. 4.2 [263,129]. The input vector is obtained from an array of N LEDs: the light intensity issuing from LED number i is proportional to x_i. The matrix is represented by a transparency, which is divided into N^2 small squares. The transmittance of square i, j is proportional to a_{ij}. An astigmatic lens (not shown) spreads the light from each LED onto the corresponding column in the transparency[2]. Thus the intensity of the light passing

---

[1]See appendix B for the definition of matrix-matrix and matrix-vector multiplication.

[2]A network of fiberoptics may be used instead of a lens. This makes it easier to achieve even

square i, j is proportional to $x_j \, a_{ij}$. Another astigmatic lens collects the light from a whole row, and focuses it onto the corresponding detector. The intensity of the light falling on detector number i is then proportional to $\sum_{j=1}^{N} a_{ij}x_j$. Therefore the output of the detector array represents the product vector.

A striking feature of the above configuration is that all the N^2 scalar multiplications are done in parallel. This results in very high speed — it has been demonstrated that the multiplication of a 100 element vector by a 100×100 matrix may be done in 20 ns [129]. The throughput, however, may be limited if the matrix is to be changed. The transparency representing the matrix would, naturally, be an SLM such as described in section 2.4.6, so that it would be possible to change the values of the matrix elements at will. Today's SLMs, however, fall a few orders of magnitude short of the objective of being able to change more than 10^7 times per second.

Another problem with the above system is that it uses the light *intensity* to represent data, and is therefore limited to data with positive, real values. A multichannel design (section 2.2.2) may, however, be used to work with bipolar [129] or complex-valued [263] data.

Systolic array architecture

An alternative configuration for an optical matrix-vector multiplier is that of a systolic array. A systolic array [390] is a locally connected array of simple, identical computing elements. It is used as a pipeline, with the data units passing in step from one computing element to the next. Each computing element performs a small modification of the data stream as the stream passes through it. An important aspect of this architecture is its use of the *temporal* variable. In optics, the time is introduced by means of acoustooptical devices [578,114].

In the optical systolic matrix-vector multiplier [130,129,100], there are N pulsing LEDs and N detectors. The light pulses from the LEDs are modulated by an acoustooptic device before they are imaged on the detectors. The detectors are integrating detectors, i.e., their output is proportional to the sum of the intensities of the light pulses falling on them.

The pulses generated by LED number i are not of equal intensity — rather they represent the values in row i of the matrix. The acoustooptic modulator is also dynamic — it creates an acoustic wave that modulates successive LEDs according to successive elements of the vector $\mathbf{x}$. The pulse with intensity a_{ij} is created by LED i exactly when the acoustooptic modulator modulates the light from LED i by a factor x_j. Thus detector i receives a pulse proportional to $a_{ij} x_j$. Fig. 4.3 gives an example of how the data is moved in a 4-element multiplier. Several variations of this configuration have also been described in the literature [130,101].

---

illumination of the whole matrix, and reduces crosstalk [95]. However, such a configuration involves unacceptable wiring complexity for large N.

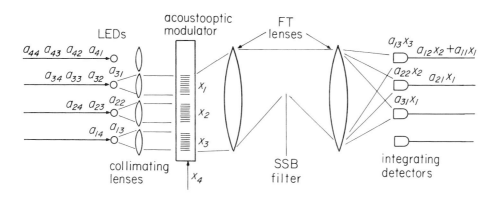

Figure 4.3: *An optical systolic matrix-vector multiplier, for N = 4.*

Comparing the systolic array architecture with the completely parallel device described earlier, the systolic device has the advantage of using 1-D acoustooptic modulators rather than 2-D SLMs. These modulators are simpler, faster, and feature better operation characteristics. Systolic array architecture has the disadvantage of not being completely parallel: the multiplication takes N steps, rather than just 1.

4.3.2   Uses of matrix-vector multipliers

Many important problems may be solved (or at least approximated) by iterative multiplications of a vector by a matrix. This is an attractive use for the fast, parallel optical matrix-vector multiplier, because the matrix need not be changed. The outputs of the detectors are simply used to set the intensities of the LEDs. A few examples to which optical systems have been applied follow.

Finding eigenvalues and eigenvectors [131,711,278]

A vector **v** that only changes in scale when multiplied by a matrix $\mathcal{A}$ (i.e., the relations between its components stay the same), is called an *eigenvector* of the matrix. The scale factor, λ, is called the *eigenvalue*. In short, these two entities are defined by the equation

$$\mathcal{A}\,\mathbf{v} = \lambda\,\mathbf{v}$$

where we have a matrix multiplying a vector on the left-hand side, and a scalar multiplying it on the right-hand side.

If the matrix has N distinct eigenvalues, we can find the largest one by taking an arbitrary vector and iteratively multiplying it by the matrix (this is called "the power method"). The reason is that the eigenvectors form a basis[3], and so the initial arbitrary vector may be decomposed into eigenvector components. When we iteratively multiply by the matrix, the component corresponding to the largest eigenvalue grows faster than the others, until it dominates the scene. when this happens the procedure converges: additional multiplications just change the scale. Therefore in a situation of convergence, we know the largest eigenvalue (the scale factor) and its eigenvector.

Additional eigenvalues may be found by modifying the matrix so that it will no longer enhance the largest eigenvector. Once all the eigenvalues and eigenvectors have been found, this information may be used to invert the matrix.

---

[3]A *basis* is a set of n independent vectors (in an n-dimensional space). Any vector in the space may be seen as a linear combination of the basis vectors. For example, three vectors in the three Cartesian directions x, y, and z form a basis for our regular three-dimensional space.

Solving systems of simultaneous linear equations

A linear equation with n unknowns, $x_1, \ldots, x_n$, is an expression of the form

$$a_1 x_1 + a_2 x_2 + \cdots + a_n x_n = y.$$

If the unknowns must satisfy not one but a system of n independent equations, this can be represented by the matrix equation

$$\mathcal{A}\mathbf{x} = \mathbf{y},$$

where $\mathcal{A}$ is the matrix formed by the coefficients of the equations

$\mathbf{x}$ is the vector of unknowns

$\mathbf{y}$ is the vector of right-hand sides of the equations.

The difference between this and the regular matrix-vector multiplication is that here $\mathbf{y}$ is known and $\mathbf{x}$ is not. $\mathbf{x}$ may, however, be found by an iterative procedure of matrix-vector multiplications, using [563]

$$\mathbf{x}_{t+1} = (\mathcal{I} - \mathcal{A})\mathbf{x}_t + \mathbf{y},$$

where $\mathcal{I}$ is the identity matrix[4]. The answer is obtained when the iterations converge, i.e., when $\mathbf{x}_{t+1} = \mathbf{x}_t$, because then the formula reduces to

$$\mathbf{x} = \mathbf{x} - \mathcal{A}\mathbf{x} + \mathbf{y} \quad \Rightarrow \quad \mathcal{A}\mathbf{x} = \mathbf{y}.$$

The question is, of course, whether or not the iterations converge. It turns out that convergence depends on the eigenvalues λ_i of $\mathcal{A}$, which have to fulfill the condition

$$|1 - \lambda_i| < 1, \qquad i = 1, \ldots, n.$$

The method can be extended, however, to accommodate matrices with arbitrary eigenvalues [264,95].

The size of the optical matrix-vector multiplier needed for solving a general system of linear equations is n. In many applications, however, the matrix of coefficients is *banded*, i.e., only elements in the main d diagonals are important, and all the rest are zero. If this is the case, a systolic matrix-vector multiplier of size d will suffice, regardless of how large n is [100].

Computing the discrete Fourier transform

The Fourier transform, as defined in appendix C, is continuous and extends from $-\infty$ to $+\infty$. The discrete Fourier transform (DFT) [60] is its discrete, bounded version: the continuous image is sampled at N^2 points, and a spectrum of only N^2 discrete components is produced.

---

[4]The identity matrix has 1 along its main diagonal and 0 elsewhere. When multiplied by a vector, the result is the same vector.

Mathematically, a *one-dimensional* DFT may be described as a multiplication of the vector of samples s_m by a matrix $\mathcal{A}$ whose elements are

$$a_{nm} = e^{-\frac{i2\pi nm}{N}}, \qquad n, m = 1, \ldots, N.$$

Such a multiplication can be carried out on an optical matrix-vector multiplier as described above [263].

Simulation of the Hopfield model of neural networks

The Hopfield model of neural networks deals with a fully interconnected network of simple threshold elements [313,314]. These elements are considered as a formalization of neurons — the nerve cells of the brain. Each neuron may be in one of two states: active, denoted by 1, or inactive, denoted by -1. The state of the whole system, comprising N neurons, is described by a vector $\mathbf{s}$, where s_i is the state of neuron number i.

The neurons may influence each other through their synapses, i.e., the connections between them. Not all the connections are identical; rather the mutual influences are given by a matrix $\mathcal{T}$, where $\mathcal{T}_{ij}$ denotes the strength of the influence of neuron j on neuron i. The influences are, however, symmetric.

The dynamics of the system are as follows: each neuron sums the influences of all other neurons on it. The sum of the influences on neuron i is $\sum_j \mathcal{T}_{ij} s_j$. If this sum is above a predefined threshold (typically zero), neuron i will become active. Otherwise it will become inactive. If all the neurons update their state synchronously, these dynamics may be described by the matrix notation

$$\mathbf{s}_{t+1} = \mathrm{sgn}(\mathcal{T}\,\mathbf{s}_t),$$

where

$$\mathrm{sgn}(x) = \left\{ \begin{array}{ll} 1 & \text{if } x \geq 0, \\ -1 & \text{otherwise,} \end{array} \right.$$

is applied to each element of the vector individually. Using this, the evolution of the system may be simulated by an iterative optical matrix-vector multiplier, with thresholding on the feedback loop [209,564,565].

The importance of the Hopfield model lies in the fact that the system of neurons may have some stable states, which repeat themselves under the above dynamics. These stable states are interpreted as states that the system *remembers*. Moreover, it is possible to design a matrix $\mathcal{T}$ so that specific, chosen states will be stable. This is interpreted as *learning*. If the system starts at an arbitrary state, the dynamics will cause it to move to the nearest stable state. This can be viewed as a readout from an associative memory [292]: given a partially correct state, the system finds the nearest memory, and converges to it.

A lot of research is currently being done about the properties and uses of such networks; much of this work involves simulations of the evolution of the systems, given a matrix $\mathcal{T}$ and an initial configuration **s**. Typically the simulated networks are limited to a few dozen neurons, because computations of the evolution of larger systems take too much time. Fast optical matrix-vector multipliers may help alleviate this problem.

Crossbar switch

A crossbar interconnection element is a switch with n inputs and n outputs, which allows any pattern of connections to be made. This too can be described as a multiplication of a vector by a matrix: the vector is the inputs, and the matrix is a binary one with $a_{ij} = 1$ (transparent) if input i connects to output j, and $a_{ij} = 0$ (opaque) if it does not [469,597,598,159].

4.3.3 Matrix-matrix multiplication

Matrix-matrix multiplication may be reduced to matrix-vector multiplication, albeit at a higher dimensionality [39]. Most researchers, however, feel that its importance justifies efforts towards a direct implementation. As in matrix-vector multiplication, there are two approaches: one using systolic arrays, and the other using completely parallel devices.

Systolic arrays

Matrix-matrix multiplication is typically done in systolic array style, and a few optical systolic arrays have been devised. One possible configuration is an extension of the matrix-vector systolic multiplier described on page 118. The vector is expanded into a second matrix by use of frequency multiplexing in the acoustooptic modulator: elements belonging to different rows of the matrix will create superposed gratings of different frequencies. The diffracted light is then decomposed into its constituents by a Fourier transform lens, and the light belonging to each row is focused on a distinct detector [101,129].

Fig. 4.4 shows the details of this configuration for 3×3 matrices. We need 5 LEDs for the 5 diagonals of the first matrix. The different elements on each diagonal are fed to the LEDs one after the other. The second matrix is represented by 3 cells in the acoustooptic modulator — each holds a composite grating for a whole column of the matrix. These composite gratings are each a sum of 3 simple gratings, with 3 distinct acoustic frequencies, representing the elements from the different rows. 3 detectors are positioned so as to detect the light with these 3 spatial frequencies, after it is Fourier-transformed.

A totally different configuration uses outer-product[5] multipliers. It is possible to regard a multiplication of two matrices as a sum of the matrices obtained from

---

[5]The outer-product of two vectors is a matrix whose elements are the products of multiplying all pairs of elements from the vectors.

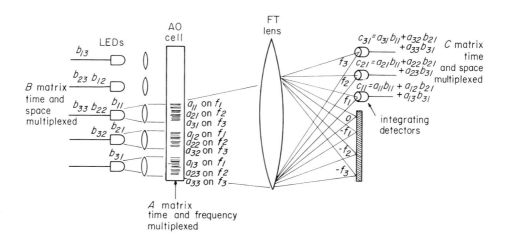

Figure 4.4: *Systolic optical matrix-matrix multiplier.*
(Adapted with permission from *Applied Optics* [101], ©1983)

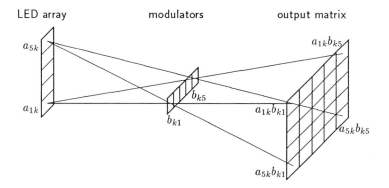

Figure 4.5: *Optical outer-product multiplier for two vectors.*
(Adapted with permission from *Applied Optics* [31], ©1982)

the outer products of the *columns* of the first with the *rows* of the second:

$$\mathcal{A}\,\mathcal{B} = \sum_{k=1}^{N} \mathcal{C}_k,$$

where

$$\mathcal{C}_k = \begin{pmatrix} a_{1k}b_{k1} & \cdots & a_{1k}b_{kN} \\ \vdots & & \vdots \\ a_{Nk}b_{k1} & \cdots & a_{Nk}b_{kN} \end{pmatrix}.$$

An optical outer-product multiplier is schematically depicted in fig. 4.5. Its result may be imaged onto an integrating detector array. By successively feeding the LEDs with the columns of $\mathcal{A}$, and the modulators with the rows of $\mathcal{B}$, the detector array will accumulate the sum $\sum_k \mathcal{C}_k$ [31,33,129].

An alternative configuration is to use two orthogonal sets of one-dimensional acoustooptic modulators, placed one next to the other just before the detector array. The first set incorporates N horizontal modulators; it modulates the uniform incident light in N horizontal stripes, according to one column of $\mathcal{A}$ at a time. The second set is made up of N vertical modulators, and modulates the light vertically in accordance with the rows of $\mathcal{B}$. Thus the output from the detectors is the same [636,129].

Single-step parallel matrix-matrix multipliers

The importance of matrix-matrix multiplication has spurred a research effort with the object of improving on the systolic performance, which is typically $O(N)$ steps. The problem is that each and every one of the elements of the input matrices

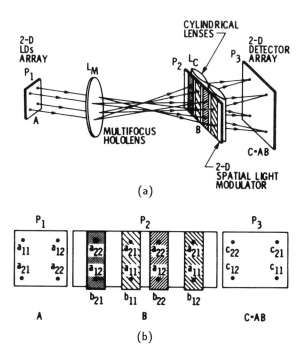

(a)

(b)

Figure 4.6: *Single-step parallel matrix-matrix multiplier.*
(a) General configuration.
(b) Details of planes P_1, P_2 and P_3.
(Reprinted with permission from *Optics Letters* [426], ©1984)

is used in the calculation of N different elements of the output matrix. If we wish to perform all these calculations in parallel, we must therefore *duplicate* the data many times. This is difficult to accomplish electronically, because of fan-out limitations; it is, however, easily accomplished by optical means.

A *single-step* optical matrix-matrix multiplier is shown in fig. 4.6 [426]. Actually this is a direct implementation of the set of equations that define the elements of the product matrix, namely (for 2×2 matrices)

$$c_{11} = a_{11}b_{11} + a_{12}b_{21}, \qquad c_{12} = a_{11}b_{12} + a_{12}b_{22},$$
$$c_{21} = a_{21}b_{11} + a_{22}b_{21}, \qquad c_{22} = a_{21}b_{12} + a_{22}b_{22}.$$

As we can see, the matrix $\mathcal{A}$ is duplicated and multiplied by the elements of $\mathcal{B}$, which appear in adjacent columns. In the optical processor, $\mathcal{A}$ is represented by a LED array. Multiple images of this array are created by a special hololens: this is a holographic lens with many foci, instead of only one. Its action is similar to that of a lenslet array. The images fall on an SLM divided into columns that represent

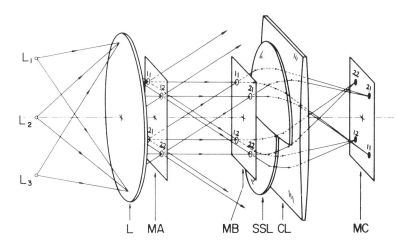

Figure 4.7: *Single-step parallel matrix-matrix multiplier, based on multichannel correlation with a segmented lens.*
(Reprinted with permission from *Optica Acta* [604], ©1975)

the elements of $\mathcal{B}$. Thus all the multiplications are done in parallel. These are finally summed up by a set of cylindrical lenses, to form the output $\mathcal{C}$.

A different approach to this problem, depicted in fig. 4.7, is based on optical correlation. In section 3.2.1 it was stated that the cross-correlation operation is similar to a weighted sum. Each element in the product matrix $\mathcal{C}$ may therefore be regarded as representing the correlation between a row of matrix $\mathcal{A}$ and a column of matrix $\mathcal{B}$. The optical system is a compound multichannel correlator, based on the concept of direct incoherent correlation (see page 73). $2N-1$ light sources are used to create correlations of all the rows simultaneously. A special segmented lens (fig. 4.8) is used to distinguish between correlations relating to different columns.

Triple products

In some applications it is necessary to calculate the product of *three* matrices. With optical systems a special configuration may often be found which does this directly, rather than multiplying only two matrices and then multiplying the product by the third one. The direct system is, of course, faster [101,114,507].

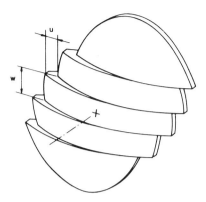

Figure 4.8: *A segmented lens used in the multiplication of* 5 × 5 *matrices.*
(Reprinted with permission from ***Optica Acta*** [604], ©1975)

4.3.4   Uses of matrix multiplication

The ability to perform matrix multiplication in one step is quite exciting, as this
is an extremely basic and important operation. The following are some examples
of its use.

Graph algorithms

One popular representation of **graphs** is that of an *adjacency matrix*. Given a
graph with N vertices, this is an $N \times N$ matrix whose elements are defined by

$$a_{ij} = \begin{cases} 1 & \text{if there is an edge from } i \text{ to } j \text{ or } i = j, \\ 0 & \text{otherwise.} \end{cases}$$

Certain problems in graphs may be solved by operations on this matrix. For
example, connected components may be found by raising this matrix to the Nth
power, which requires $\log N$ matrix multiplications. If $a_{ij} > 0$ in the result, it
means that the vertices i and j are in the same connected component.

Algebraic problems

The great majority of numerical problems solved by computers may be stated in
terms of linear algebra. The solution of these problems typically involves matrix
operations, e.g., finding the determinant or inversion. The parallel algorithms for
the execution of such operations make use of matrix multiplication as an often-
repeated step.

4.3.5   Accuracy and digitization

The algebraic operations discussed in this section are not well suited for analog evaluation. They are numerical in nature. Unlike other operations described in this chapter, they operate on a discrete set of elements rather than on a continuum. And we would typically require a high accuracy from the results. This accuracy is usually not achievable if numbers are simply represented by analog light intensities, because of the low dynamic range of analog optical systems (see section 2.6).

The solution to the accuracy problem is to go digital, as electronic computers have done. This means that data values will be represented by combinations of elementary entities (like bits in a binary electronic computer), each of which may assume one of a prespecified set of distinct values. In this approach the accuracy is limited only by the number of elementary entities that we decide to assign for the representation of each data value.

Systolic matrix-matrix multipliers that use binary, two's complement representation have indeed been proposed [65,271,32]. Designing a parallel digital matrix-matrix multiplier is somewhat more difficult, because a carry may be generated between the bits. The idea is to represent each matrix as a sum of binary matrices, relating to different bit planes. For example,

$$
\begin{pmatrix} 2 & 3 & 6 \\ 5 & 4 & 0 \\ 3 & 7 & 1 \end{pmatrix} = 2^0 \begin{pmatrix} 0 & 1 & 0 \\ 1 & 0 & 0 \\ 1 & 1 & 1 \end{pmatrix} + 2^1 \begin{pmatrix} 1 & 1 & 1 \\ 0 & 0 & 0 \\ 1 & 1 & 0 \end{pmatrix} + 2^2 \begin{pmatrix} 0 & 0 & 1 \\ 1 & 1 & 0 \\ 0 & 1 & 0 \end{pmatrix}.
$$

Then all the possible pairs of binary matrices are multiplied in parallel, and summed up to give the binary representation of the product matrix. The general expression for the multiplication of two r-bit matrices, giving a $2r$-bit product, is

$$
c_{ij} = \sum_k a_{ik}\, b_{kj} \qquad \text{(definition)}
$$

$$
= \sum_k \left(\textstyle\sum_n^r 2^n a_{ik}^{(n)} \right) \left(\textstyle\sum_m^r 2^m b_{kj}^{(m)} \right) \qquad \text{(binary)}
$$

$$
= \sum_k \textstyle\sum_n^r \textstyle\sum_m^r 2^{n+m}\, a_{ik}^{(n)}\, b_{kj}^{(m)} \qquad \text{(open brackets)}
$$

$$
= \sum_\ell^{2r} 2^\ell \, \textstyle\sum_t \underbrace{\textstyle\sum_k a_{ik}^{(t)}\, b_{kj}^{(\ell-t)}}_{\text{element in binary matrix multiplication}} \qquad \text{(rearrange)}.
$$

We see that the grand sum can be partitioned into $2r$ groups of elements, where each group seems to contribute to one bit plane of the product. However, each of these groups is itself a sum (over t), and therefore it might overflow. As a result, the product's bit-plane matrices $\mathcal{C}^{(\ell)}$ must be evaluated in a sequential manner:

each one is generated from a sum of at most r multiplications of input bit matrices, *plus* a carry from the preceding bit-plane matrix $C^{(\ell-1)}$. This observation implies that complete parallelism is lost. Note, however, that the number of steps we need is $2r$: it depends on the desired accuracy, and not on the size of the matrices.

4.3.6   Size limitations

The multiplication of 10×10 matrices can be done on a microcomputer without any difficulty, and at reasonable speed. The possibility of especially fast matrix operations only becomes interesting when very large matrices are involved, for instance matrices with 1000×1000 elements. The optical systems described in this section cannot handle such large matrices; they are limited to matrices in the order of 64×64 or 100×100. The reason is that with larger arrays the nonuniformity of the systems becomes unacceptable, and crosstalk[6] between the different channels degrades the result.

This difficulty may be resolved by *partitioning* the problem into smaller problems, which can be handled [139,40]. This is easily accomplished because of the linear character of matrix operations. Let us take matrix-vector multiplication as an example. If we have a multiplier that can handle input of size N, and the actual input size is $2N$, we must partition the matrix into four submatrices of size $N \times N$ and the vectors into two subvectors of size N. These can now be treated as numbers in a 2×2 problem:

$$A\mathbf{x} = \mathbf{y} \quad \Longrightarrow \quad \begin{pmatrix} A_{11} & A_{12} \\ A_{21} & A_{22} \end{pmatrix} \begin{pmatrix} \mathbf{x}_1 \\ \mathbf{x}_2 \end{pmatrix} = \begin{pmatrix} \mathbf{y}_1 \\ \mathbf{y}_2 \end{pmatrix}.$$

This implies that $\mathbf{y}_1 = A_{11}\mathbf{x}_1 + A_{12}\mathbf{x}_2$, i.e., the first half of the output vector, is obtained by multiplying the top left quarter of the matrix by the top half of the input vector, and adding this the the product of the top right quarter and the lower half. A similar expression gives the bottom half of the output.

It should be noticed that the different parts of the output are independent of each other. Therefore if enough of the smaller multipliers are available, all the output may be generated in parallel. In the case of systolic multipliers, it turns out that a number of small devices are even faster than one full-sized device. However the large number of devices that are required might make the whole scheme unpractical. For instance, if the multiplication of 1000×1000 matrices is required, and only 100×100 multipliers are available, 1000 such multipliers will be needed in order to produce the result in parallel. The accuracy of this result will be limited to a maximum of 8 bits. If digitization is used so as to improve the accuracy to 16 bits, as described in the preceding section, the number rises to an impressive 16,000 multipliers.

---

[6] *Crosstalk* is the leakage of a signal from the channel in which is belongs to a neighboring channel. In this case it means that one element in the output matrix might influence neighboring elements.

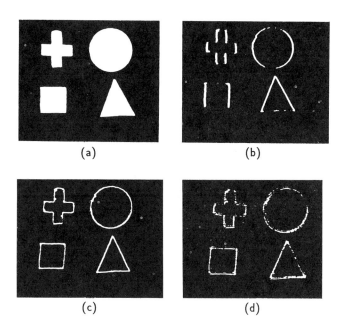

Figure 4.9: *Optical differentiation.*
(a) Initial function $f(x,y)$.   *(c) Result of $\frac{\partial f(x,y)}{\partial x} + \frac{\partial f(x,y)}{\partial y}$.*
(b) Result of $\frac{\partial f(x,y)}{\partial x}$.   *(d) Result of $\frac{\partial^2 f(x,y)}{\partial x^2} + \frac{\partial^2 f(x,y)}{\partial y^2}$.*
(Reprinted with permission from *Optical Engineering* [405], ©1974)

4.4   Differentiation

Given a continuous function of two variables, $f(x,y)$, its partial derivative in, say, the x direction is defined to be

$$\frac{\partial f(x,y)}{\partial x} = \lim_{\Delta x \to 0} \frac{f(x + \Delta x, y) - f(x,y)}{\Delta x}.$$

This may be approximated by choosing a small interval for Δx, creating two copies of f shifted by Δx relative to each other, and then subtracting one from the other.

These actions can be realized by a composite grating, placed in the frequency plane of a coherent optical processor such as the one used for correlations and convolutions (i.e., the grating replaces the matched spatial filter, fig. 3.8). If nothing is present in the frequency plane, such a processor simply images the input light distribution onto the output plane. With a simple grating, three displaced images are created (with sinusoidal gratings, only the zero-order and first-order beams exist). The distance of the first-order images from the optical axis depends on the grating frequency. If we use a composite grating, composed of *two* gratings with slightly different frequencies, the first order will contain two slightly shifted images. If, in addition, the two gratings are out of phase (one with a transparent line at the origin, the other with an opaque line), the difference of the two shifted images will be obtained. This is actually subtraction by modulation of out-of-phase spatial carriers (see page 114). Results obtained by this scheme are presented in fig. 4.9 (a,b). Higher-order derivatives may be obtained by the use of more complex gratings (c,d) [405,738].

Note that the superposition of two out-of-phase gratings creates an opaque block that does not let light through; however, because of the slightly different frequencies, more and more light gets through as the distance from the origin increases. Actually, a filter which is opaque at the origin and becomes transparent as a linear function of the distance, together with a half-wave plate that causes a phase-reversal in the negative frequencies, also implements differentiation. This is an immediate result of the fact that if $F(\nu)$ is the Fourier transform of $f(x)$, then the Fourier transform of $\frac{df(x)}{dx}$ is $\nu F(\nu)$ [172].

4.5   Integration

Integration is a basic property of some optical devices. Therefore optical systems that evaluate the integral of a single-variable or a two-variable function are easy to create. The integrating devices fall into two categories: space-integrating and time-integrating.

4.5.1   Space integration

In this type of device, the function is represented by the amplitude (or intensity) modulation of the cross section of a beam of light; therefore functions of two variables are accommodated. The space-integrating device is simply a lens, which focuses the light to a point. The amplitude (intensity) of the light at the focus is then the integral of the function.

4.5.2   Time integration

In this type of device, the function is represented by the temporal changes in the intensity of a light beam. Therefore it must be a positive function of one variable (time). The time-integrating device is an integrating detector. This is a history-sensitive detector; its output voltage is proportional to the sum of the light falling on it during a certain time, called the *integration period*.

4.6 Analog solutions of partial differential equations

Partial differential equations (PDEs) are used extensively in physics to describe the dynamics of physical systems; in fact, Newton developed the concept of the derivative function for just this purpose. A PDE is an expression that relates different derivatives of a function to each other; the unknown is the function itself. Except for a few special cases, these equations are very hard to solve. Often no analytical solution method is known. Therefore numerical methods are used: given the boundary conditions (how the function looks at the edge of the area of interest) and expressions for the derivatives (which tell how the function changes), the function is built up incrementally. This procedure can be very computationally intensive, especially if high resolution is required.

A much faster solution may be derived by analog means. The idea is to create a physical system that is described by the given equation, force it into the boundary conditions, and then let it go. As the system evolves, it then "solves" the differential equation. The values that the desired function assumes simply have to be measured. The price is paid, of course, in accuracy. There are three error sources:

- The physical system may not behave exactly as described by the differential equation.

- Limited accuracy in the setting of the boundary conditions.

- Limited accuracy in the measurement of the results.

4.6.1 The optical system

Optical systems, which are inherently two-dimensional, lend themselves to the simulation of partial differential equations in two variables[7]. The optical system that is used is a confocal Fabry-Perot resonator [145]. This is an area in space limited by two spherical semitransparent mirrors, which combine the actions of reflecting the light and taking the Fourier transform (recall that a curved mirror may be regarded as a combination of a flat mirror and a lens). The input comes through the top of one mirror, while the output leaves through the bottom of the other (fig. 4.10). Light not exiting at the output returns to the input and is combined with it, thus forming a feedback loop. The light travels somewhat off-axis; in this way the location of the Fourier transform on the forward path, from the input to the output (point A in the figure), is distinct from the location of the Fourier transform on the feedback path (point B). The output light distribution is

---

[7]The variables in the equation may be two spatial variables, or a combination of space and time, or anything else, even though in the optical system both are represented by spatial coordinates.

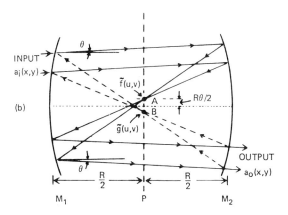

Figure 4.10: *Confocal Fabry-Perot resonator used for the optical analog solution of partial differential equations.*
(Reprinted with permission from the *Journal of the Optical Society of America* [145], ©1980)

composed of two terms: one is light that came from the input and passed through the forward-path filter $\tilde{f}$, and the other is light that transversed the feedback loop and passed both filters. In short, the output is related to the input by

$$A_O = A_I\,\tilde{f} + A_O\,\tilde{f}\,\tilde{g}\,e^{i\beta},$$

where A_I is the Fourier transform of the input

A_O is the Fourier transform of the output

$\tilde{f}$ is the filter in the forward path

$\tilde{g}$ is the filter in the feedback loop

β is a phase factor determined by the spacing between the mirrors,

and we have dropped the transmittance and reflectance coefficients of the mirrors for simplicity.

It is more convenient to describe a system by its transfer function H, which (by definition) directly relates the input to the output: $A_O = H\,A_I$. Simple manipulations show that the transfer function for the above system is

$$H = \frac{\tilde{f}}{1 - \tilde{f}\,\tilde{g}\,e^{i\beta}}.$$

The method of operation is as follows. Given a partial differential equation, we translate it into an expression for a transfer function that relates an input (the boundary conditions) to an output (the solution). We then tailor $\tilde{f}$, $\tilde{g}$, and β so as to realize this transfer function.

4.6.2   Example of the derivation

We now demonstrate the above recipe with a detailed example. The equation that we tackle is

$$\frac{\partial f(x,y)}{\partial x} = b(x,y), \qquad (4.1)$$

with the added conditions

1. $f(x,y) = 0$ for $x < 0$,

2. $f(x,y) \to 0$ for $x \to \infty$,

3. $f(0,y) = d(y)$.

In order to display this as a transfer function, we equate the Fourier transforms of both sides. The right-hand side is simply $B(u,v)$ (we use uppercase symbols for Fourier transforms, and u, v as the coordinates of the frequency domain). The Fourier transform of the left-hand side is

$$\int_{-\infty}^{\infty} \int_{0}^{\infty} \frac{\partial f(x,y)}{\partial x} \, e^{-i(xu+yv)} \, dx \, dy =$$

$$= \int_{-\infty}^{\infty} \left(\left[f(x,y) \, e^{-ixu} \right]_{0}^{\infty} + iu \int_{0}^{\infty} f(x,y) \, e^{-ixu} \, dx \right) e^{-iyv} \, dy$$

$$= \int_{-\infty}^{\infty} f(0,y) \, e^{-iyv} \, dy + iu \int_{-\infty}^{\infty} \int_{0}^{\infty} f(x,y) \, e^{-i(xu+yv)} \, dx \, dy$$

$$= D(v) + iu \, F(u,v)$$

(the definition of the Fourier transform, i.e., eq. C.1, integration by parts, and conditions 1–3 have been used). The solution, $f(x,y)$, may therefore be found if we realize a system whose output is

$$F(u,v) = \frac{B(u,v) - D(v)}{iu}.$$

We will supply $b(x,y) - d(y)$ as an input to the system; hence all that is left is to define $\tilde{f}, \tilde{g}$, and β so that the transfer function will be $\frac{1}{iu}$. It turns out that a possible solution is

$$\begin{cases} \tilde{f} = \frac{1}{u}, \\ \tilde{g} = \sqrt{2} \, u, \\ \beta = \frac{7\pi}{4}. \end{cases} \qquad (4.2)$$

Of course the actual implementation will only approximate this, as $\frac{1}{u}$ tends to infinity at $u = 0$. To summarize, the above mathematical derivation shows that if we create an optical system as depicted in fig. 4.10, with $\tilde{f}, \tilde{g}$, and β as in eq. 4.2, and present it with the input light distribution $b(x,y) - d(y)$, the output light distribution will be $f(x,y)$, i.e., the solution of eq. 4.1.

4.6.3 Evaluation

The advantages of such a feedback system for implementing the required transfer function are twofold:

- The filters $\tilde{f}$ and $\tilde{g}$ can be real-valued, even when the desired transfer function is complex. The imaginary part is supplied by β.

- The dynamic range is increased, compared to systems that do not employ feedback.

The system as described here may be used to solve linear partial differential equations of the second degree, in two variables. Extensions for the solution of equations with three and even four variables, as well as some integral equations, have also been demonstrated [146,146,406].

Other optical systems have also been proposed, notably the use of matrix-vector multipliers to solve a discrete version of the equation [120]. As this involves quite a bit of algebra, and no new optics, it is not treated here.

Possible uses of fast optical analog solutions of partial differential equations are [406]:

- *Parameter determination.* In many cases the general expression of the PDE that models a physical process is known, but the specific parameters are not (e.g., we might know that $\frac{\partial f}{\partial t} = \alpha f$, but not know what is the value of α). With the fast optical system we can create numerous solutions with differing parameters, and then see which best fits the data about the physical process.

- *Design optimization.* In the design of a physical system modeled by a PDE, the choice of parameters might greatly influence the performance. Again, by simulating the behavior of systems with different parameters, we can choose those that give optimal performance according to some predefined measure.

Summary

Light intensities (or amplitudes) may be used to represent numerical values in an analog manner, rather then using a symbolic digital representation such as the binary representation used in conventional electronic computers. With the analog optical representation, the basic arithmetic operations are trivial: addition is done by combining beams of light, and multiplication by the modulation of beams of light. As matrix-vector and matrix-matrix multiplications are based on summing a set of products, these operations are also realizable by optical systems. Completely parallel optical multipliers deserve more attention in this context than systolic architectures, which are also possible with electronic equipment.

Mathematical operations on continuous 2-D data fields that may be considered include differentiation, integration, and the analog solution of partial differential equations. In all cases, the main advantage of the optical systems is their speed.

Upon superficial survey, the potential of these optical systems seems very promising. However, analog optical numerical processors are limited by the low accuracy of the results (errors of less than 1% are considered good), brought about by the low dynamic range. Another limit is on the size of the operands, resulting from the finite space-bandwidth product of the systems.

Bibliographical notes

The ease of performing basic arithmetic operations was noted already by Cutrona et al. [172]; the different methods were tabulated by Häusler [302].

A great deal of research has been directed at matrix operations; a myriad of systolic acoustooptic architectures have emerged. Exhaustive surveys were written by Casasent [114] and Athale [33]. A much more readable review is Caulfield's article in Laser Focus [129].

Specific topics, e.g., parallel matrix multipliers and solution of differential equations, are dealt with only in the few papers cited in the present text.

Chapter 5

Hybrid Optical/Electronic Systems

In chapters 3 and 4 we surveyed the operations that are achievable with analog optical systems. The emphasis was on what happens in the optical domain. The questions of how the input is acquired or what is done with the output were addressed only if these subjects were material for the understanding of the optical system.

In this chapter we examine how analog optical processors fit into the framework of general processing systems, and in particular how they interact with electronic digital computers. We first discuss the characteristics of the optical and electronic systems, and the degree of dependence between them. Then we delve into the details of where and how electronic computers can aid optical processors. Finally a different aspect of hybrid systems is addressed — that of systems incorporating closed circuit television.

5.1 Division of the work

As we saw in the preceding chapters, optical processing systems are inherently different from the more commonplace electronic computers [557]. The main characteristics of optical systems are:

- The input and output are usually 2-D spatial patterns.

- The output is produced by some manipulation of the input — all of it in parallel. Therefore the operation is extremely fast. The manipulation is usually linear. Decision-type operations (branching) are not available.

- The system's operation is embedded in its physical structure. Some component must be physically altered in order to change the operation that is performed on the input.

- The operation is analog in nature, and hence inaccurate.

Electronic computers, on the other hand, are characterized by:

- All data is represented by numbers, at all stages.

- The work is typically done in a sequential manner. Decision operations allow the data to affect the course of the computation.

- The computer is programmable by software.

- The accuracy is practically unbounded.

The above list points out the advantages and disadvantages of hooking optical systems and electronic computers together. We want to marry the speed and parallelism of optical systems with the programmability and accuracy of electronic computers. The price is that the data has to be translated from an analog representation to a digital representation, and vice versa. The hope is that we don't end up with the accuracy of optics and the sequential character of electronics.

5.2 Dependence between optics and electronics

As a rule, analog optical processing systems are not self-supporting. The relations between them and electronic computers may be classified into three levels of dependence:

1. The optical system is a special purpose subunit in an electronic system. It is activated when needed, and serves as an analog special purpose accelerator [354]: the data is fed into it, the optical system operates on the data, and the results are read out (fig. 3.1). The preceding chapters reviewed what optical processors can do. A good example is feature extraction from an image by use of a Fourier transform and a wedge-ring detector (section 3.2.7). The optical system is merely used as a means to compute the Fourier transform and partition the results according to meaningful parameters (spatial frequency and orientation). There is no need to prepare the data or adjust the system.

2. The optical system uses the services of an electronic computer. Note that it may still be part of a larger (electronic) computer system, but part of the activity is directed at operating the optics. This may include (fig. 5.1) [111]:

   (a) Preprocessing of the data.

   (b) Control over optical components.

   (c) Postprocessing of the results.

   These points are the topic of the next section.

3. The optical system is totally independent. The notable (and only) example for such a system is that of processing SAR images (section 3.4). The input is the film exposed in the flight. The output is a film with an image of the terrain. No electronic intervention is needed.

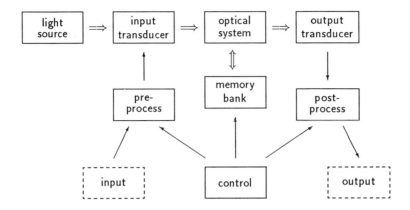

Figure 5.1: *Schematic hybrid optical/electronic system. The optical path is designated by a double arrow; electronic paths are single arrows (figure concept by Gabi Birin).*

5.3   What an electronic computer can do for an optical processor

5.3.1   Preprocessing

The source of the data might be an external sensor, e.g., a video camera, or it may come from the memory of an electronic computer. In any case, it may be necessary to perform some processing on the data before it is fed into the optical system, in order to ensure optimal results. Examples are:

- One of the drawbacks of analog optical systems is that they might be nonuniform. For instance, the intensity of the light falling on the input transducer might not be the same at all points. If the nonuniformities are known, it is possible to compensate for them by modification to the data [95].

- As mentioned in section 3.2.6, correlations with incoherent light are much improved if the model and the input scene are edge-enhanced. As edge enhancement is a *local* operation, it can be done while the video signal is being fed into the input transducer [616]. With proper equipment, any 3×3 convolution of the input image can be achieved at video rate [289].

5.3.2   Control

The ability to control the actions of the optical system might add a measure of flexibility to it. Examples:

- In fig 5.1, the optical system is shown to interact with an optical memory bank. The memory bank signifies the knowledge of the system. For instance, in a pattern recognition system the memory is the set of models the system knows about. The ability to control which filter is placed in the optical path allows us to decide what the system will search for at each moment. More generally, the ability to move optical components furnishes us with a decision-making tool, and we can thus program the system to some degree.

- When the input is a film, a computer may be used to control the switching from one frame to another [288].

- Clock pulsations are required for the correct operation of some optical processors, e.g., the systolic systems that perform matrix operations [95]. This also falls under the heading of control.

5.3.3 Postprocessing

The output from the optical system is usually not fit for direct use by its user. Additional processing steps depend on the specific system being discussed. Some examples are:

- The output from an optical correlator is a point of light. This output can be analyzed and a more convenient display generated [412,479]. For example, the computer may automatically classify the input scene, and print out a diagnosis [288]. It may also make decisions that are based on the optical output.

- The usual correlation process involves a Fourier transform, multiplication by a matched filter, and an inverse Fourier transform. Great flexibility and better signal-to-noise ratio may be achieved, however, if only the first Fourier transform is performed optically, and the rest is done on a digital electronic computer [176,113,644]. This comes, of course, at the expense of speed.

- The chief advantage of optical processors is their speed, while their chief disadvantage is their low accuracy [557]. In some cases we may benefit by using an analog optical processor to get a rough estimate of the result quickly, and then improve the accuracy by digital postprocessing [138,4]. For example, consider the solution of a set of simultaneous linear equations (page 121). While the original problem is defined as $\mathcal{A}\mathbf{x} = \mathbf{b}$, What the analog optical system actually solves is better described as $\tilde{\mathcal{A}}\tilde{\mathbf{x}} = \tilde{\mathbf{b}}$, because even the analog representation of the coefficients is not exact. The result $\tilde{\mathbf{x}}$ is of course also of limited accuracy. A digital electronic computer can, however, use this result to calculate

$$\mathbf{r} = \mathbf{b} - \mathcal{A}\tilde{\mathbf{x}} = \mathcal{A}\mathbf{x} - \mathcal{A}\tilde{\mathbf{x}} = \mathcal{A}\,\Delta\mathbf{x}.$$

The optical processor can now be used again, to solve the new problem $\mathcal{A}\,\Delta\mathbf{x} = \mathbf{r}$. The solution $\Delta\tilde{\mathbf{x}}$ is added to the old result $\tilde{\mathbf{x}}$ to give better accuracy. Additional iterations may further improve the result [138,4].

• Compensations for nonuniformities in the optical system may be done in the output as well as in the input [95].

5.4   Closed circuit television

Television and video equipment have been mentioned a few times already in this book. The use of such equipment in optical computing is not so much a result of its technical merits, as a result of its availability. Closed circuit television is especially well suited to serve as an interface between a parallel optical computer and a sequential electronic one: a TV camera translates a 2-D image into a temporal signal by scanning, while a monitor does the reverse. It is also convenient for use in systems that require some sort of feedback or iteration: the output light distribution is simply detected by a video camera, and displayed again on a monitor that serves as input [445]. The resolution, which is typically about 500×500 points, is usually adequate. Electronic processing of the returning video signal is also possible.

On the other hand, video equipment has two major drawbacks:

• *Low speed.* Television equipment is designed to fool the human eye into seeing a continuous motion. A rate of 25 frames per second[1] is sufficient for that. This relatively low speed, which saves bandwidth in television transmission, is not justified in optical computing applications where bandwidth is not a limiting resource.

• *Noncontinuity.* An additional requirement is to prevent flicker, which makes it necessary to refresh each point on the screen at a rate of 50 Hz. However the low resolving power of the eye allows the following trick: only 25 frames are displayed each second, but each frame is displayed in two parts, during two consecutive scans of the screen. In the first scan, only the odd-numbered lines are displayed, while in the second scan the even-numbered lines are shown. Thus the screen is scanned 50 times a second. This interleaved scanning procedure is unnecessary and annoying from an optical computing point of view.

---

[1]In the United States the rate is 30 frames per second, because the electricity supply has a frequency of 60 Hz.

Summary

The great majority of special purpose optical systems are not self-supporting; they only become useful when combined with an electronic processor. A typical configuration is one in which a host processor preprocesses the input data, controls the operations of the optical system, and then postprocesses the output. Such a scheme allows the optical system to perform its special task efficiently, while leaving all decisions and interfacing to the more flexible electronic components.

A special class of hybrid systems is those that use closed circuit television. Their main advantage is the availability and relatively low price of video equipment.

II

TOWARD A GENERAL PURPOSE DIGITAL OPTICAL COMPUTER

The second part of this book is about recent work towards the realization of a general purpose digital computer based on optical devices. This work is still in its initial stages, and many questions are still open. The survey therefore spreads out and compares different approaches.

Chapter 6 supplies the background in nonlinear optics that is needed for some of these approaches. It can be skipped by readers not interested in the details of optical implementations. Chapter 7 reviews the different ways in which computer components may be realized optically; first internal representations are considered, and then the implementation of logic gates, arithmetic units, memory devices, and interconnections. Finally, possible architectures are considered. Chapter 8 is about integrated optics, which provide a possible fabrication technology following the ideas of integrated circuits. The feasibility and limitations of the projected devices are also discussed in chapter 8.

Chapter 6

Nonlinear Optics

Classical optical systems, such as those described in chapter 2, are typically linear. This means that the light passing through the system is transformed in some way, but the light *does not influence the way the system operates*. As a consequence, these systems cannot perform Boolean logic operations. Consider an AND gate, for example. Its function may be described as

$$a \text{ AND } b = \left\{ \begin{array}{ll} 0 & \text{if } a = 0, \\ b & \text{if } a = 1. \end{array} \right.$$

The first input, a, is seen to dictate how the system operates: if it is 0, the output will be 0 regardless of the second input. If it is 1, on the other hand, the second input b is piped to the output.

Therefore the optical implementation of logic gates, which lies at the heart of an attempt to realize a general-purpose digital optical computer, requires the use of *nonlinear* optics. There are two ways to go about achieving a nonlinearity:

- Use a nonlinear encoding scheme (i.e., encode each input in a different manner), and then use a linear optical system for the processing.

- Use a real optical nonlinearity.

In this chapter we explore optical nonlinearities: first the theory and physical effects, and then bistable devices and phase conjugate mirrors, which are the most important nonlinear devices. The use of nonlinear encoding is discussed in chapter 7.

6.1 Nonlinear effects

When light passes through a crystal, the electric field associated with the light exerts a force on the electrons and ions of the crystal. As a result, the electrons are slightly displaced in one direction, while the nuclei of the atoms are displaced in the opposite direction, thus inducing a *polarization*[1]. The polarization P induced by a field E may be expanded in a power series

$$P = \chi_1 E + \chi_2 E^2 + \chi_3 E^3 + \dots.$$

---

[1]This has nothing to do with the orientation of the electric field in an electro-magnetic wave; the word "polarization" simply has two unrelated meanings.

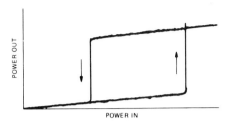

Figure 6.1: *The input-output characteristic of a bistable device, displaying hysteresis.* (Reprinted with permission from the *Bell System Technical Journal* [631], ©1982 AT&T)

Nonlinear optical phenomena arise from large susceptibilities in the nonlinear terms. For example, a large χ_2 causes the crystal to act as a frequency doubler: if an electric field $E = \cos(\omega t)$ impinges on the crystal, the transmitted light will include a component $E' = \cos(2\omega t)$. A large χ_3 causes the index of refraction to change with the intensity of the input light [628].

The nonlinear susceptibilities of most materials are very small, so nonlinear effects are restricted to extremely high light intensities. In the late '70s, however, it was discovered that certain semiconducting crystals (such as $BaTiO_3$, $LiNbO_3$, and $KNbO_3$) display very large nonlinearities. These discoveries spurred the current efforts to realize optical logic gates.

We will not go into the physical details and the material issues of these nonlinearities; they are much beyond the scope of this book (see the bibliographical notes at the end of the chapter for references). We just mention that the most important nonlinear effect is the *photorefractive* effect. This is the change of the refractive index of a crystal when it is illuminated. This effect may be used for both bistable devices and optical phase conjugation. Related effects are listed in appendix G.

6.2   Optical bistability

A bistable device may be regarded as a switch [623]. Think of an ordinary light switch. It has two stable states, in either of which it can remain indefinitely: the "on" state and the "off" state. It can be made to go from one state to the other by an appropriate investment of energy (i.e., by pushing on it). The process of going from one state to the other is nonlinear: when the energy supplied passes a certain threshold, the switch suddenly jumps to the other state where it remains. The threshold for switching up should be higher than the threshold for switching down again. This way the switch will stay in a given state even after the force that brought it there is removed. Such a display of memory is called *hysteresis* (fig 6.1). The region between these thresholds is the bistable region.

What we need for optical logic is an optical switch that is controlled by light. In other words, we need a device that displays *optical bistability*: when illuminated with a given input intensity, there should be two possible output intensities. The output intensity that is observed depends on the history of the input intensity. Such bistability can result from a nonlinear characteristic of the device, along with some sort of feedback mechanism.

A number of optical bistable switches have been proposed recently. The criteria for evaluating their performance are as follows:

- *Switch time.* The amount of time required to switch from one state to the other, to switch back, and the delay before another switching cycle can start.

- *Switching energy.* How much energy is needed in order to switch, and how much of it is dissipated in the device.

- *Stability.* How stable are the two states, and specifically the possibility of spontaneous switching.

The following is a survey of the main methods in which bistable optical devices have been realized [521].

6.2.1 Intrinsic Fabry-Perot resonator bistable device

A Fabry-Perot resonator is a device whose transmittance depends on the wavelength of the incident light. The heart of the resonator is a resonant cavity. This is simply a space bound by two parallel semi-transparent mirrors. Light entering this area through one of the mirrors bounces back and forth in it. At each reflection, some of the light is emitted through the mirrors. We are interested in the light that is transmitted through the device, i.e., light that enters through one mirror and exits through the other (fig. 6.2) [1].

The intensity of the transmitted light depends on the wavelength. The transmitted light is composed of rays that have bounced back and forth a different number of times. If there is constructive interference between all these rays, the transmitted light intensity will be high. Otherwise the rays will cancel each other, and the transmitted intensity will be low. In this case most of the light is reflected backward. The condition for constructive interference, and hence for high transmission, is that the path differences for the various rays will be an integer number of wavelengths. Here the path differences are multiples of twice the resonator length d, so the condition is

$$2\,d \;=\; n\,\lambda \qquad \text{(resonance condition)}.$$

This also gives a condition on the frequency of the light, as the wavelength and frequency are connected by the speed of propagation. Frequencies that fulfill

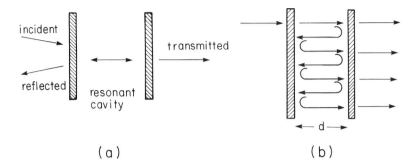

Figure 6.2: *A Fabry-Perot resonator.*
(a) General structure.
(b) The transmitted beam is created by interference between beams that have bounced back and forth a different number of times. The vertical displacement is not real — actually all the beams are collinear. They are drawn this way so that the relations between them are seen.

the condition are called *resonant frequencies*. We can therefore say that high transmission occurs only at the resonant frequencies. Note that high transmitted intensity is coupled with high intensity *inside* the resonator: when constructive interference occurs at the output, it also occurs inside. If the reflectivity of the mirrors is high, the intensity buildup inside the resonator may be rather large.

In order to create a bistable device, a material with an optical nonlinearity is placed in the resonant cavity[2] (fig. 6.3) [632,623,1,720]. A typical nonlinearity is the change of the refractive index with intensity (i.e., the photorefractive effect). When the intensity of light passing through such a material changes, so does its index of refraction. There is consequently a certain degree of tuning of the resonant frequency: when the refractive index becomes larger, the light becomes slower. Therefore the effective path differences between successive beams become longer. The light must now have a longer wavelength (i.e., a lower frequency) in order to fulfill the resonance condition.

Another influence of the nonlinear material in the resonant cavity is that it introduces a feedback effect: when the resonant frequency is present, high intensity results. But the high intensity also determines what the resonant frequency will be. The name "intrinsic bistable device" derives from the fact that the feedback is internal in this way.

The bistable behavior results from the following scenario. In the stable state

---

[2]A simple and much used construction is to use a thin wafer of an optically nonlinear crystal. The sides of the wafer are covered with reflective layers, and so the wafer itself becomes the resonant cavity. This construction is called an *etalon*.

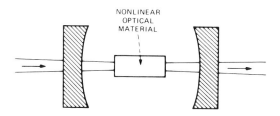

Figure 6.3: *Schematic intrinsic Fabry-Perot bistable device.*
(Reprinted with permission from the *Bell System Technical Journal* [631], ©1982 AT&T)

of low transmission, the illuminating beam of light is somewhat *off* resonance. When its intensity is increased, the characteristic resonant frequency of the cavity changes, and becomes nearer to the frequency of the illumination. At a certain stage it is near enough for the interference between the beams to become constructive, and an intensity buildup occurs inside the resonator. This causes a condition of positive feedback, and very rapidly the intensity increases and the resonance of the cavity comes to fit the input illumination frequency. The positive feedback causes the system to overshoot, and enter a condition with negative feedback, just above resonance: if the intensity rises, the resonance moves away so that the intensity falls again. If it the intensity falls, the device again approaches the resonance condition, so that the intensity goes up. This is therefore a stable state (the high transmission stable state).

When the input intensity is subsequently lowered, it does not immediately affect the intensity buildup in the resonator because of the self maintenance of the buildup. Therefore the input intensity may be lowered to below its initial value while the system stays in the high-transmission state. It should be remembered, however, that the intensity buildup in the resonator depends on the input illumination as a source of energy. When the input intensity is lowered far enough, the intensity in the resonator will not suffice in order to keep the resonator in tune with the input frequency. As soon as the tuning is lost there is no more constructive interference, the intensity in the resonator decreases sharply, and the system switches back to the low-transmission stable state.

A number of bistable devices of this type have been proposed, using various materials [624,152,512, sect. II]. The most promising seem to be semiconducting crystals, especially GaAs and InSb [245,546]. The physics of the nonlinear material, i.e., how and why the index of refraction changes with intensity, is beyond the scope of this book [450,482,483,625].

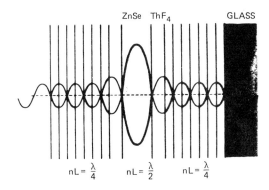

Figure 6.4: *Layered structure of an interference filter.*
(Reprinted with permission from *Optical Engineering* [629], ©1987)

6.2.2   Interference filter bistable device

A similar type of device is based on an interference filter, rather than a Fabry-
Perot resonator [630]. This is a multilayer sandwich of alternate high and low
refractive index material (fig. 6.4). Each layer is one-quarter wavelength thick (or
a multiple of this). The high index material is nonlinear. The required feedback
is obtained from reflections from the interfaces between the layers. This type of
device has been the preferred choice in the first generation of optical gates based
on bistable devices, because it is the most convenient [629].

6.2.3   Hybrid resonator-based bistable device

The basic concept in a hybrid bistable device is identical to that of an intrinsic
one. The difference is in the feedback-nonlinearity mechanism. In an intrinsic
device, the light intensity in the resonator directly causes the nonlinearity. In a
hybrid device, an electronic detector that detects the output intensity causes the
nonlinearity [633] (fig. 6.5).

The nonlinear material in hybrid resonator bistable devices is a material that
changes its refractive index when *a voltage* is applied. The output beam from
the device is split into two: one is used as output, and the other for feedback.
The intensity of the feedback beam is detected, and used to modulate the voltage
that is applied to the nonlinear material. This "artificial nonlinearity" has two
important advantages over intrinsic nonlinearity: the nonlinearity can be much
greater (depending only on the sensitivity of the detector), and it is much more
flexible and controllable (this is especially important for research). On the other
hand it has the disadvantage of being slower: its speed is limited by the response
time of the detector.

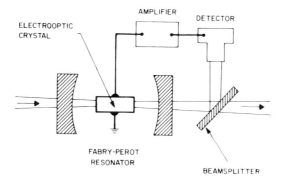

Figure 6.5: *Schematic hybrid bistable device.*
(Reprinted with permission from *Optical Engineering* [633], ©1980)

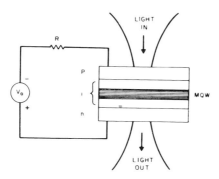

Figure 6.6: *Schematic self-electrooptic effect bistable device.*
(Reprinted with permission from *Applied Physics Letters* [486], ©1984)

6.2.4   Self electrooptic effect device (SEED)

The SEED is based on a multiple quantum well (MQW) structure placed inside a
PIN photodiode detector (fig. 6.6) [735,485,486,487,488,512, sect. III]. The MQW
structure is a stack of a couple of hundred very thin (less than 10 nm) alternating
layers of GaAs and GaAlAs[3]. We shall not go into a detailed discussion of the
properties of this structure. Suffice it to say that when an electric field is applied

---

[3]The GaAs layers have a smaller band gap than the GaAlAs layers (see appendix E), so electrons
in the conduction band of the GaAs are trapped and cannot pass the GaAlAs barriers. These
traps are quantum mechanical energy wells; hence the name "multiple quantum well".

to it, its absorption decreases. Without an electric field it absorbs light readily.

As explained in appendix E, a PIN photodiode detects light by absorbing photons and creating electron-hole pairs. An applied voltage then turns them into a photocurrent. The point is that in the absence of light (and hence the absence of a photocurrent), the applied voltage creates an electric field across the diode. This field affects the MQW structure, and induces low absorption.

As the incident light intensity starts to rise, some of the light is absorbed. As a result, a small photocurrent is generated. This current passes through a resistor (R in the figure), and causes some of the voltage to fall on it. Therefore less voltage is left for the diode, and the electric field on the MQW is weakened. Note, however, that most of the incident light is not absorbed — it is transmitted. Thus when the incident intensity increases, so does the transmitted intensity.

Only when the incident light intensity is high enough to cause an appreciable decrease in the electric field, does the MQW start to absorb strongly; in fact, it absorbs practically all the incident light. At this stage the transmitted light intensity suddenly drops to near zero. This is the switching from the transmitting state to the blocking state. When the input intensity is subsequently lowered, the switch back occurs at a somewhat lower level. Note that in a SEED low inputs are transmitted and high inputs are blocked. In the resonator devices the opposite is true: low intensities are blocked and high ones are transmitted.

SEEDs are favored as candidates for future optical logic gates because of their excellent properties: small size, low power requirements, quick response, and no hard-to-adjust resonators.

6.2.5 Hybrid polarization-based devices

Bistable devices based on polarization changes also do not require resonators. The light just passes through them once, rather than going back and forth many times and building up its intensity. Therefore they are potentially faster than the resonator-based devices. They are also not sensitive to changes in the input wavelength, and may thus utilize a broader band of frequencies.

The nonlinear material in these hybrid bistable devices causes a change of the polarization of the incident light. The amount of change depends on a voltage that is applied to the material. The output light is then passed through an analyzer that only allows light of one polarization to get through. Thus the polarization change is translated into an intensity change. The output intensity is then used to modulate the voltage on the material: this is the feedback.

One implementation uses a liquid crystal light valve (described in section 2.4.6) [632]. Instead of having independent write and read beams, the output beam is split into two, and one part is used as the write beam for feedback (fig. 6.7).

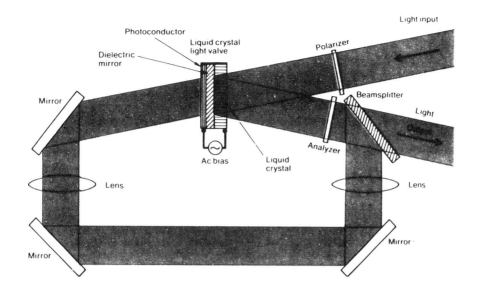

Figure 6.7: *Bistable device based on an LCLV.*
(Reprinted with permission from *IEEE Spectrum* [632], ©1981 IEEE)

6.3 Optical phase conjugation

6.3.1 Definition

An ordinary mirror reflects the light that falls on it. A phase conjugation mirror, on the other hand, *reverses* the propagation of the light. The reversed light exactly retraces the path of the incident light. This difference between the two types of mirrors is depicted in fig. 6.8.

To illustrate the point, think what you would see in a phase conjugation mirror hanging above your bathroom sink: you would see a uniform dark nothing. The reason is that the only light reaching your eyes would be light that *originated in your eyes*, hit the mirror, and was reversed. All the light issuing from your nose, for example, would return to your nose; none will reach your eyes. therefore you will not see your nose or any other part of your face [541].

The term "phase conjugation" derives from the fact that the reversed wave may be described by exactly the same mathematical expression, except for the sign of the phase. As the phase is described by the imaginary part of the complex amplitude, this change of sign is equivalent to conjugation. Specifically, a wave propagating from left to right along the x axis is described by

$$A \cos(\omega t - kx - \varphi) = \text{Re}[\psi e^{i\omega t}],$$

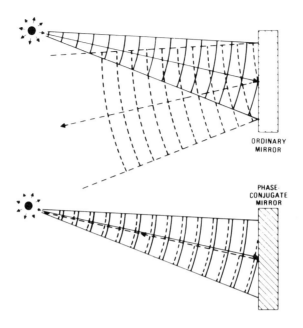

Figure 6.8: *An ordinary mirror redirects the light falling on it (top). A phase conjugation mirror actually reverses the propagation of the light; light issuing from a point source will converge back to it (bottom).*
(Reprinted with permission from *Optical Engineering* [542], ©1982)

where A is the wave's amplitude
        $k = \frac{2\pi}{\lambda}$ is the "wave vector"
        $\omega = 2\pi\nu$ is the "radian frequency".
The equation defines ψ to incorporate all the terms that do not change with time: $\psi = Ae^{-i(kx+\varphi)}$. The reversed wave is then described by

$$A\cos(\omega t + kx + \varphi) = \mathrm{Re}[\psi^* e^{i\omega t}],$$

where ψ^* is the complex conjugate of ψ [542].

6.3.2   Four-wave mixing

When low intensities are involved, phase conjugated waves are created by four-wave mixing (FWM). Three of the four waves are inputs: two *pump* beams, and a *probe* beam. The fourth is the output; it is the conjugate of the probe. Typically all waves have the same frequency. This is called *degenerate* four-wave mixing (D4WM).

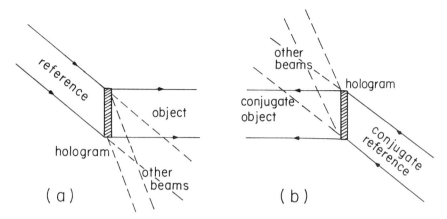

Figure 6.9:
(a) In normal reconstruction from a hologram, a reproduced reference beam is used.
(b) If a conjugate reference beam is used instead, the conjugate of the object beam is created.

Four-wave mixing is analogous in many ways to holography [617,542,273,274, 740,170]. In the normal holographic process, the readout beam used to create a reconstruction of the object beam is a reproduced reference beam (see fig. 6.9 (a). The other two beams that are created do not interest us now[4]). If we use a conjugate reference beam instead, i.e., a reversed version of the original reference, this will create the desired output beam (fig. 6.9 (b)): it is the conjugate of the object beam, and retraces its propagation in the reverse direction.

Four-wave mixing is a real-time version of this holographic process. The creation of the hologram and its use to construct the conjugate object beam occur simultaneously. The configuration is centered around a photorefractive medium [512, sect. IV], in which the three input beams meet. The two pump beams are counterpropagating plane waves; thus each is the conjugate of the other. These beams serve as reference at the hologram creation, and as the conjugate reference readout for the reconstruction. The probe comes in at an angle — this is the object beam in the hologram creation (fig. 6.10 (a)).

What happens may be explained as follows. The probe wave interferes with one of the pump waves. The intensity in the bright fringes of the interference pattern is much higher than in the dark fringes. As the photorefractive material changes its index of refraction with intensity, a phase hologram is created. The second pump wave meanwhile acts as a readout beam for this hologram. As it is

---

[4]The conjugate beam in regular holography is *not* the phase conjugate beam we are seeking now. It has similar characteristics, but it does not retrace the original object beam.

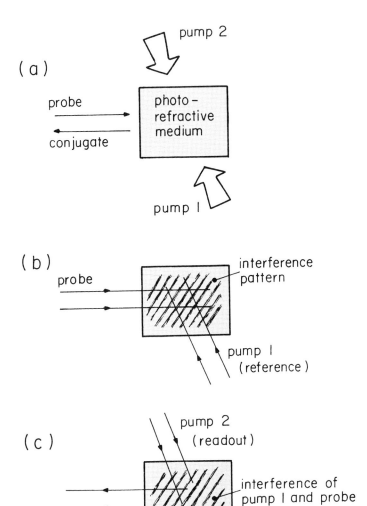

Figure 6.10: *Four-wave mixing is analogous to holography.*
(a) General configuration. The two pumps are conjugate to each other.
(b) While the probe and one pump beam interfere to write a hologram ...
(c) ... the other pump beam serves as readout, and creates the conjugate of the probe.

the conjugate of the first pump, the conjugate of the probe is created. This is the desired output (fig. 6.10 (b,c)).

It should be noted that the two pump waves have equal standing. Therefore the probe wave also interferes with the second pump, creating *another* hologram. The first pump acts as a readout in this case. As the two pumps are conjugates, the conjugate of the probe is generated again.

To summarize, the three input beams interfere in the nonlinear photorefractive medium. The nonlinearity serves to couple the beams to each other, and to generate an output which is the conjugate of the probe beam. An interesting point is that most of the output energy is derived from the pump beams. With proper engineering, a phase conjugator can therefore display gain: The conjugate can be more intense than the original probe.

Mathematical derivation [542]

The creation of the conjugate beam may be derived directly from the nonlinear interaction of the three input beams in the photorefractive medium. The photorefractiver effect is caused by a third order nonlinearity χ_3. The inputs are waves of the form $\cos(\omega t - kx)$. This may be written in complex notation as $E + E^*$, where $E = e^{i(\omega t - kx)}$. The total field from the three inputs is therefore

$$E_{tot} = E_1 + E_1^* + E_2 + E_2^* + E_3 + E_3^*,$$

where E_1 and E_2 are the pumps
E_3 is the probe.
The third order induced polarization is

$$P^{(3)} \propto \chi_3 \, E_{tot}^3.$$

This expression has 216 terms, each incorporating three Es. The interesting ones are those of the form $E_1 E_2 E_3^*$. As the probe beams are conjugate to each other, $E_1 E_2 = E_1 E_1^* = \alpha$, a scalar. Therefore part of the polarization behaves like E_3^*, with gain α. This radiates a wave described by E_3^*, i.e., a conjugate of the probe wave.

6.3.3 Stimulated Brillouin scattering

Brillouin scattering is the scattering of light due to an acoustic wave (see sect. 2.5.1). In *stimulated* Brillouin scattering the acoustic wave does not exist beforehand; it is generated by a positive feedback interaction with the light. This only works for very high light intensities.

The main appeal of stimulated Brillouin scattering is its very simple configuration: the input light beam just shines into a crystal, a glass, or a container holding liquid or compressed gas. No pump beams are needed. If the input intensity is above the system's threshold, a conjugate beam will be reflected. We start by seeing how the light wave is reversed by the acoustic wave. We then investigate how the acoustic wave is generated in the first place [617,542].

The optic and acoustic waves propagate along the same line in this application. As the light is much faster, it passes through the periodic changes from a high to a low refractive index caused by the slower acoustic wave. These changes occur along planes that are perpendicular to the propagation of the light; hence it is not refracted (it does not change its direction). However when light hits an interface between mediums of different refractive indices, part of it is reflected back into the old medium and only part is transmitted into the new medium. When multiple such interfaces exist as in the case of an acoustic wave, the *total* transmission and reflection depend on the spacing between them: if it is such that constructive interference occurs between successive reflections, the total reflection is high. If, on the other hand, reflections cancel out while transmitted rays interfere constructively, the total transmission is high. In the case of stimulated Brillouin scattering, the acoustic wave is such that practically everything is reflected. The condition for this is that the acoustic wavelength be half the optical wavelength.

Having seen how the acoustic wave reverses the propagation of light, we now turn to investigate how the light generates the necessary acoustic wave. Two counter-propagating light waves are needed — the input wave and the reversed output (this is where the positive feedback comes in: the acoustic wave creates the reversed light, which is material in creating the acoustic wave). The sum of two such waves is a so called *standing wave*: at certain points (called "nodes") the two waves always cancel out, while between them large oscillations are observed. Due to the electrostrictive effect, the places where there is a large field are compressed. Thus a pattern of alternating compressed and uncompressed areas is generated.

An acoustic wave is just such a pattern, except for the fact that it moves. This is brought about by a small modification to the above model: there is a minute difference between the frequencies of the two light waves. With this change, the spatial pattern does not stand — it moves with the light waves. The frequency of the generated acoustic wave is exactly the difference between the frequencies of the light waves[5].

So the acoustic wave creates the reversed light, and the reversed light creates the acoustic wave. But how does the whole process start? The initial acoustic wave is supplied by thermal fluctuations in the material, which cause random changes in the refractive index. The instant such changes — in one small area — create a reversed light wave, the positive feedback takes effect: the reversed light interferes with the incident light and strengthens the acoustic wave, which in turn reflects more light, and so on.

---

[5]Another interpretation is that the reflected wave is Doppler shifted; see page 36.

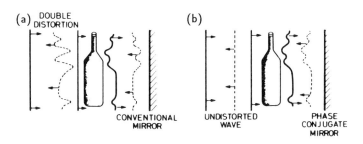

Figure 6.11: *Correction of distortions with optical phase conjugation.*
(a) When a plane wave passes a distorting medium (the bottle), is reflected by a mirror and passes it again, a double distortion results.
(b) If a phase conjugate mirror is used, the distortion is undone.
(Reprinted by permission from *Nature*, Vol. 308, No. 5955, pp. 110–111 [273], copyright ©1984 Macmillan Magazines Limited)

6.3.4   Uses of optical phase conjugation

Optical phase conjugation has some important uses. While they are not directly related to data processing, they accomplish things that would otherwise require intensive computation. The most pronounced examples are the correction of imaging distortions and the self targeting of radiation.

Distortion correction [617,541,516]

Light beams become distorted while traversing certain media. Examples are imaging through inhomogeneous media (e.g., the atmosphere), or the transmission of light pulses through fiberoptics. Such distortions set a limit on the amount of information that can be extracted from the light. The distortions may be undone, however, with a phase conjugate mirror: the distorted light is conjugated, and then passed through the same kind of distorting medium. As the conjugate light retraces its evolution in the medium, it regains its original quality.

Self-targeting [617]

A major problem with space laser weapons is how to aim them at their targets. A possible solution is to illuminate the target with a weak, not very directional laser beam. some of the reflected light is collected into a laser amplifier. The amplified light then hits a phase conjugation mirror; as a result it retraces its propagation through the amplifier, becoming even more amplified, and comes to a focus on the target from which it was originally reflected.

Image processing

Image processing operations are also possible. These include:

- Convolutions and correlations, by imposing a spatial modulation on the beams used in four-wave mixing [731,732].

- Edge enhancement, by having the probe beam much more intense than the pumps [215,732].

- High-resolution imaging: the conjugate beam recreates the object's light distribution [541,732].

Summary

Logic operations are nonlinear; therefore nonlinear optics must be utilized in the realization of a digital optical computer. The chief nonlinear effect that is used is the photorefractive effect. Materials displaying this effect change their index of refraction when the intensity of the light in them changes.

The most important nonlinear devices (with regard to optical computers) are bistable devices; these devices can be switched optically from a transmitting to a reflecting mode and vice versa. Many different implementations have been proposed and demonstrated. The most promising for optical computers are nonlinear etalons and SEEDs.

Optical phase conjugation mirrors are another important nonlinear device. Their principle use is in the compensation for distortions that light suffers when passing through a nonuniform medium. While not performing any computation in the regular sense, such applications may replace intensive computational processes.

Bibliographical notes

Nonlinear optics are *not* treated in most optics textbooks. The original papers or a few lecture notes and collected papers volumes must be consulted. The photorefractive effect is reviewed by Glass [254]; a full mathematical model is given by Moharam and Young [498]. Miller provides derivations of the effect in semiconductors [482,483]. A comprehensive review of nonlinear materials is given in a panel discussion reported in Applied Optics [512]. Nonlinear materials are also addressed in a review by Glass [255].

There are no comprehensive surveys of optical bistability. The papers relating to each device are cited in the text. A collection is the special issue of the IEEE J. Quantum Electronics [521].

A good introduction to optical phase conjugation and its uses is provided by two recent articles in Scientific American [617,541]. More advanced material is gathered in special issues of Optical Engineering [513] and J. Optical Society of America [529].

Chapter 7

Digital Optical Computers

Digital optical computers (DOCs) should appear to their users as general purpose computers, just like the current well-known electronic computers. The only difference will be in the hardware implementation and in their performance. Instead of being based on electrons in silicon integrated circuits, the DOC will be based on photons with some as yet not completely specified technology. As a consequence it is expected to be much faster, perhaps by explicit use of parallel computations. It will also be immune to EMI.

DOCs do not yet exist, and it is debatable whether they ever will. The results to date suggest conflicting predictions. Broadly stated, the claim against DOCs is that it would be impossible to create optical systems that can outperform electronic VLSI circuits in all respects [362,363]. These include not only speed, but also possibility of miniaturization, ease of mass production, reliability, and low power consumption coupled with the ability to dissipate excess heat.

The investment in electronic computers is huge; there must be a very large payoff in order to justify a change of basic technology. DOC researchers claim that their machines will offer the necessary improvements. For example, it is said that the high speed achievable with optics is unrivaled and irreplaceable in some applications [631]. It has also been pointed out that DOCs are better off than electronic computers were in their infancy, because optics is a mature field and much existing knowledge may be used [432]. The growing interest and activity in DOC research in the last years is manifested by the growing number of papers on the subject.

This chapter focuses on the basic issues and components of general purpose computers, and how to address them in DOCs. These issues include internal representations, implementation of logic and arithmetic units, computer memory, interconnections, and architectures. No attempt will be made to assemble the whole thing or to present a proposal for a complete DOC; rather, each issue will be treated individually. The realizability of digital optical computers will be dealt with in chapter 8.

7.1 Internal representations

The strategy for representing information in an electronic computer is well established. The binary system is used [304]. Logical "0" and "1" values are represented

A	B	F		A_3	A_2	A_1	B_3	B_2	B_1	F_3	F_2	F_1
0	0	0		0	0	0	0	0	0	0	0	0
0	1	0		0	0	0	0	0	1	0	0	0
0	2	0		0	0	0	0	1	0	0	0	0
0	3	0		0	0	0	0	1	1	0	0	0
0	4	4		0	0	0	1	0	0	1	0	0
1	0	0		0	0	1	0	0	1	0	0	0
1	1	0		0	0	1	0	0	0	0	0	0
1	2	0		0	0	1	0	1	1	0	0	0
1	3	4		0	0	1	0	1	0	1	0	0
1	4	4		0	0	1	1	0	1	1	0	0
⋮	⋮	⋮		⋮	⋮	⋮	⋮	⋮	⋮	⋮	⋮	⋮

Figure 7.1: *Quinary two-input truth table and equivalent binary six-input table.* (Reprinted with permission from *Optical Engineering* [25], ©1986)

by two distinct voltages (or, in memory systems, by two distinct magnetizations). Numbers are usually represented by the two's complement method.

In optical computers, however, the field of internal representations is still open for debate. The binary system is challenged by multilevel logic. The different logical states may be represented by different intensities, or different polarizations, or different phases, or even by the location of a point of light. Number representation is not limited to two's complement: the residue number system has advantages that become especially important in the context of optical processing. This section surveys the main representation techniques. Subsequent sections will deal with implementation issues, with an emphasis on the simplest and most intuitive representation, i.e., binary logic represented by two intensities.

7.1.1 Multivalued logic

Generally speaking, multivalued logic allows for more information in a basic unit. This may help in increasing effective data rates and storage densities, reducing interconnection requirements, and reducing circuit complexity. As an example, consider the function defined by the truth table in fig 7.1: its implementation in quinary (5 level) logic requires 2 inputs and one output, while an equivalent implementation in binary requires 6 inputs and 3 outputs. The main drawback of multivalued logic is that more elementary values have to be distinguished. Thus it is more sensitive to noise.

The theory of multivalued logic is quite advanced, but it has not gained wide acceptance for use in computers [205,328]. One reason for this might be the staggering amount of choice. With binary logic, a gate with 2 inputs has $2^2 = 4$

possible input combinations, and can perform one of $2^{2^2} = 16$ possible functions. These functions are adequately described by Boolean algebra [457, chap. 2]. If we go to ternary logic, however, a gate with two inputs has $3^2 = 9$ possible input combinations, and performs one of $3^{3^2} = 19,683$ functions. And this is just the smallest possible example. The algebraic formalism that describes these structures exists, and has been applied to various problems (e.g., branching, arithmetic). In specific, well-defined cases, multivalued logic really does contribute to the simplification of problems, or to faster solutions. An example is modular or residue arithmetic (discussed in section 7.4.2). However, a simple and general system that would replace the binary one does not seem imminent.

7.1.2   Representation of basic values

The most common method for representing the different basic values is by distinct intensity levels. In the binary system, for example, logical "1" may be represented by a high light intensity while "0" is represented by low intensity. Such a scheme is called *bright true* logic. If the opposite encoding is used, i.e., "1" is represented by low intensity, it is called *dark true* logic.

Alternatively, the basic values may be encoded into other parameters of the light. For example, orthogonal polarizations may be used for the representation of the binary values [434,446]. This method has the advantage that the light intensity never changes, which means that the energy propagating with the light never changes. In the intensity levels scheme, changing the signal from "1" to "0" requires the absorption and subsequent dissipation of the energy that came with the signal. Changing a signal from "0" to "1", on the other hand, requires an investment of energy. With polarization, these problems do not exist: the polarization is simply changed by a half-wave plate. The energy remains unchanged.

Another advantage for representations by polarization or phase occurs in modular, multilevel systems, where the levels have an intrinsic cyclic relation. For example, counting modulo 3 will be 0, 1, 2, 0, 1, 2, 0, $\cdots$. Representing the levels by distinct polarizations or phases captures this cyclic structure, because polarization and phase are only defined modulo π and 2π, respectively. This can save the need to perform explicit modular arithmetic. Continuing with the above example, let us represent "0" by a complex amplitude of 1, "1" by $\exp\left(\frac{2\pi i}{3}\right)$ and "2" by $\exp\left(\frac{4\pi i}{3}\right)$. Then adding 1 (modulo 3) is equivalent to multiplying by $\exp\left(\frac{2\pi i}{3}\right)$, i.e., to changing the phase by 120°.

A totally different concept is that of representing values by certain *spatial patterns*. This type of representation is especially fitting for optical computers, as it is two-dimensional and thus susceptible to classical optical processing methods. A simple example is the *dual rail* coding scheme, used in conjunction with binary systems. A string of bits is encoded into a double array of cells. Each bit is represented by a pair of adjacent cells, only one of which is bright: in a "1" bit the top cell is bright and the bottom cell dark, while in a "0" bit the order is reversed. Note that in this system the energy content of the different bits is the same, as opposed to simple representation by bright or dark cells. However, the space required to encode each bit is increased.

7.1.3   Number representation

The way numbers are represented has a great impact on the ease and efficiency of calculations [242] (if you are not convinced, try to find the product of CMLIX and CCCXLVIII). In computers, this has three distinct aspects:

- The internal representation should be compatible with the input/output representation. At least translation from one to the other should be easy.

- The internal representation should fit the hardware efficiently.

- There should be simple algorithms to perform the basic required operations (e.g., arithmetic, comparisons) on numbers in the internal representation.

Two types of representations are prominent in the context of optical computing [338]. These are the well known fixed radix system, and the residue system. The residue system has been known for hundreds of years, but has not been popular in computers. The reason it is presently attracting attention in the context of optical computers is that it has some features that are more significant here than in electronic computers. One is that it has a cyclic nature, which is relatively easy to use and which simplifies the computations. Another is that carryless calculations are possible, which prompts increased use of parallelism and hence increased speed. A full description and a discussion of implementation issues is given is section 7.4.

7.2   Implementation of binary logic elements

Combinatorial binary logic elements are the basic building blocks of electronic digital computers. If we know how to build AND gates and inverters, we can build a decoder[1]. This is a major component in any CPU. If we also have XOR and OR gates, we can build a full adder, which is the beginning of an ALU. Pairs of NAND or NOR gates can be wired into flip-flops, the basic one-bit memory element. In short, if we can implement the basic logic gates in optics, we have the components of a complete digital optical computer.

---

[1]A decoder is the circuit that decodes the current instruction and activates the units that will carry it out. CPU is an acronym for "central processing unit". ALU is "arithmetic logic unit", which is part of the CPU.

A large part of the research concerned with the realization of DOCs has concentrated in attempts to make optical binary logic gates. This requires the use of nonlinear optics, because logic operations imply that one beam of light affects another. In linear systems, beams of light do not interact and thus cannot affect each other [628]. The following points may serve as guidelines for evaluation of the different implementations [625,629]:

- What is the switching time? In addition to fast switching, the time to switch up should be equivalent to the time to switch down. This is usually rather hard to assess, because only the feasibility of most of the implementations has been checked and demonstrated, without regard to real-time operation.

- What is the power consumption? Power is usually inversely related to speed — faster gates require more power.

- Are the gates cascadable, i.e., can the output from one gate serve as a direct input to another? This question can be refined thus:

  * Are the logical values represented by different energy levels, or by different parameters but constant energy? A constant energy level makes cascading more natural, as gates along the way do not have to dissipate or invest energy.

  * Are the values restored to their standard values at the output from each gate? If not, signal degradation will occur.

  * Is there any gain? Gain allows for a fan-out of more than one.

  * Is the representation cyclic? In some cases, a cyclic representation coupled with cascadability may save the need for explicit operations.

- Good operating characteristics are needed. This includes stability and high contrast between the different logic states.

- Is it possible to extend the system to accommodate multilevel logic?

- Is it all optical, or does it rely on electronic support, e.g., in the form of detectors or modulators? The response time of electronic components might be a limiting factor.

- Is it possible to create large arrays of logic elements that will operate in parallel?

- Reasonable operating conditions are preferred. This means that the logic devices should not require special low temperatures, unavailable light sources, etc.

A large number of possible implementations have emerged, and the major ones are surveyed in what follows and summarized in table 7.1. In some of these proposals, the logic operation is carried out "directly". Others make use of elementary devices, just as electronic logic gates are based on transistors. The most prominent and promising system, that of threshold logic, is based on bistable optical devices (section 6.2).

7.2.1   Laser logic gates

Probably the oldest idea of how to implement logic gates by optical means is that of using lasers; it was suggested soon after the invention of lasers, in the mid '60s. In order to understand it, the principles of laser action must be known (they are explained in appendix D). A prerequisite for operating a laser is the achievement of a "population inversion" — there should be more electrons in an excited state than in the ground state. A multi-input NOR gate maybe constructed by having one laser provide the output beam, and having a set of other lasers that can turn it off by destroying its population inversion. Each of these lasers represents an input to the gate; it is active if the input is "1". They influence the output laser by illuminating its resonant cavity at an angle. This causes stimulated emission of photons along the illuminating beam. Note that these photons do not contribute to the original output, because they are propagating in a different direction. However their emission *does* deplete the population of the excited state, and hence comes at the expense of the original output. If the illuminating laser beam is strong enough, it can destroy the population inversion altogether, and thus cause the output laser to shut down [399,381].

It soon became evident that the above idea is not practical for the realization of logic gates in a computer. Its chief disadvantages are the size and power requirements of each device. It was therefore dropped, and appears here only for completeness.

7.2.2   Threshold logic

A very simple implementation of binary logic gates uses nonlinear devices, where the nonlinearity consists of a threshold located at some input level. If the input is below the threshold, there is no output. If it is above, there is a constant output level (irrespective of how far the input is above the threshold).

To implement a logic function, the inputs to the gate are summed [596,1]. This sum is fed into the nonlinear device (fig. 7.2 (a)). The exact level of the threshold determines which Boolean function appears at the output. For example, if the threshold is so low that any one input passes it, the output function is OR. If it is so high that only all the inputs together pass it, the output function is AND (fig. 7.2 (b)).

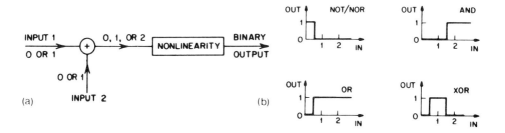

Figure 7.2: *Threshold logic.*
(a) *Schematic representation of a two-input device.*
(b) *Threshold characteristics for some specific functions.*
The extension to n-input logic elements is straightforward.
(Reprinted with permission from the *Proceedings of the IEEE* [596], ©1984 IEEE)

This method works fine for commutative functions, especially if they are mono-tonic and only one threshold is needed (the XOR, for instance, is somewhat more difficult). But it cannot be used to implement all 16 binary logical functions. This is not a grave fault, however, as any complete set[2] will do, and threshold logic is sufficient for that. On the other hand, it is worth mentioning that threshold logic may also be used to implement complex functions directly (e.g., by giving different weights to the inputs) [329,295].

Optical implementation

Optical nonlinear devices with threshold-like characteristics are readily available in the form of optical bistable devices, e.g., those based on a Fabry-Perot resonator (see page 150). If the input frequency is near enough to the resonant frequency, the bistable region becomes very narrow or even disappears. We are then left with a threshold device (fig. 7.3) [716,633,626,627,1,720,344,341]. To use this, the light entering the resonant cavity is the sum of all the inputs to the gate. The transmitted (or reflected) light is the output.

Additional features [624,625,627,629,720]

An important requirement of logic elements is that they be *cascadable*, i.e., that it is possible to use the output from one gate to drive other gates. Another is that the logical values will be *standard* throughout the system at all times: logical "1" must

---

[2]A *complete set* of Boolean functions is one that allows all other functions to be computed by the use of composite circuits. for example, AND and NOT constitute a complete set, as do OR and NOT. NAND and NOR are each a single-element complete set.

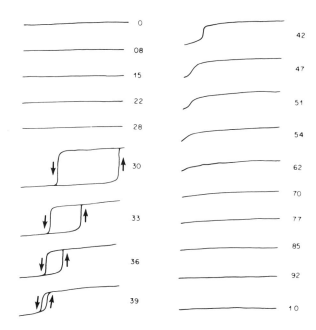

Figure 7.3: *Characteristics of resonator-based nonlinear devices, depending on the initial tuning. Those marked .39 or .42 may be used for threshold logic.*
(Reprinted with permission from *Optical Engineering* [633], ©1980)

always be represented by the same light intensity. Considerations of cascadability and standardization imply that it is undesirable that the whole input intensity for the nonlinear device will come from the outputs of other devices, and also that it is undesirable for the output to depend on the exact values of the input signals. Therefore a gate with N logical inputs will have $N + 1$ incident light beams: N are the signal beams, and the additional one is the *hold* or *bias* beam (fig. 7.4 (a)). The hold beam supplies most of the intensity. It is a very stable beam, and keeps the device just below the threshold. The signal beams only supply the additional intensity needed for switching. The exact relations between the beams and the threshold decide which gate is implemented (fig. 7.4 (b)–(d)). When the gate switches to the "1" state, it is the hold beam that provides the output. This ensures enough intensity to drive a number of secondary gates. It also insures that the output values are standard.

Another problem is that when many gates are interconnected, their response times are longer than the time taken by the signals to get from one to the other. Therefore some sort of *clock* mechanism is needed in order to maintain stability.

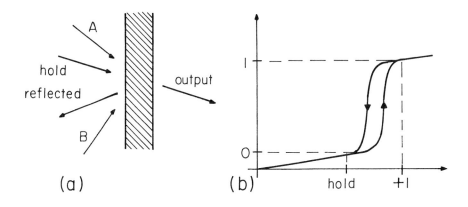

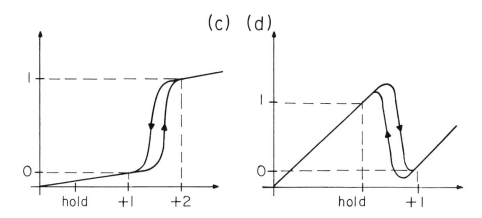

Figure 7.4: *Use of a hold beam in threshold logic.*
(a) The different beams that interact to produce the switching.
(b) input/output characteristic for OR gate.
(c) input/output characteristic for AND gate.
(d) input/output characteristic for NOT gate. Here the reflected beam is used as output.

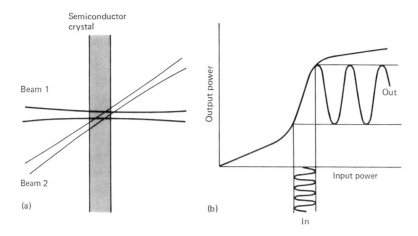

Figure 7.5: *(a) Schematic illustration of an etalon based transphasor.*
(b) Input/output characteristic.
(Reprinted with permission from *New Scientist* [623], ©1980)

This is provided by pulsing the hold beam: instead of being continuous, it switches between its sub-threshold intensity and zero intensity. The hold beams for successive gates are stepped. Each gate is enabled (high hold value) only when its inputs have stabilized. It is disabled again after the gates that use its output have been enabled.

7.2.3 Transphasors

In electronic logic, the different gates are implemented by combinations of transistors etched into the silicon chips. A transistor may be viewed as an amplifier, where a small input may control a much larger output. Therefore another use of transistors is to increase the possible fan-out from a gate.

All this is directly transferable to optics. The optical equivalent of the transistor is the *transphasor*. This device is based on the same threshold-type nonlinear devices already described (page 170), and used to implement the threshold logic components [1,623,484]. The input/output characteristic of light passing through such materials has a region where the slope is very high. A relatively strong main beam (beam 1 in fig. 7.5 (a)) supplies the input intensity needed to reach this region. Small changes in the intensity of a secondary, weak beam then produce large changes in the transmittance of the main beam (fig. 7.5 (b)).

The amount of gain obtained depends on the steepness of the input/output characteristic, and on the modulation parameters of the input [455]. The width of the steep area is also important. If it is very narrow, the main beam must be very stable so as to keep the device near the optimal working point. Gains of about one order of magnitude are easily achievable [633]. Under suitable conditions (e.g., a temperature of $77°K$), gains of more than 4 orders of magnitude have been observed [684]. The switching speed of these devices is expected to be in the picosecond range [1]. These figures can be compared to gains of two orders of magnitude and switching speeds in the nanosecond range, which are standard in silicon electronics.

7.2.4   Logic by four-wave mixing

Logic elements built from a four-wave mixing optical phase conjugator are also possible (see section 6.3.2). The phase conjugation is actually not used; only the dependence of the output on the three input beams is important. An AND gate is created as follows [224]: The two inputs are represented by the pump beams. the probe is a sort of readout beam; its conjugate is the output. Note that the conjugate beam is created as a result of the interaction of all three input beams in the nonlinear medium. If one or both of the pumps is missing, no conjugate will appear. thus is one or both of the inputs is "0", the output will also be "0". This is precisely the definition of an AND gate.

In order to achieve a complete set of logic functions, the NOT gate is also needed. This may be done by a simple interference between the signal beam and a constant reference beam. The reference is adjusted so that when the input signal is present ("1"), destructive interference occurs, so the output is "0". With no input ("0"), the reference gives an output of "1".

Alternatively, all 16 logic functions may be realized in the original four-wave mixing system. To do so the pump beams are modulated by the inputs, while the probe beam is modulated in accordance with the function that is to be realized [199]. The concept is similar to that used in shadow casting logic (described below in section 7.2.7).

Similar logic devices may be made based on the related two-beam coupling phenomenon, in which energy from a pump beam might be transferred to a signal beam [207].

7.2.5   Truth-table look-up

The preceding sections presented optical means to implement active logic gates. By that we mean that the gates really do some computational process and create the output anew each time an input is presented. A totally different strategy is to use a look-up table. With a look-up table all possible input combinations are tabulated in advance, with the corresponding output values. When an input is presented, it is matched with all entries in the table and the corresponding output value is found. This concept is very similar to array logic [223].

The great advantage of look-up tables is that they can implement any function, regardless of complexity or number of inputs. The look-up time is more or less constant and short, even if the time needed to compute the table was very long. The usual problem with look-up tables is their size. The most naive implementation is to store the whole table in memory. With p input bits and a q-bit output, this requires $2^p q$ bits of storage: the input is used as the address to find the output. This requirement may, however, be reduced.

One method is to use efficient representations. For example, the tables needed for residue arithmetic are much smaller than tables for regular fixed-point arithmetic (see page 191). Also, tables for multi-valued logic are smaller than tables for binary logic, because each value conveys more information. Another method is to replace the table by a set of q tables, each containing the set of inputs for which a certain output bit is on (or off). Such tables actually represent formulas in disjunctive normal form. A process of logical minimization [242] is then applied, to find equivalent formulas with a minimal number of terms. Thus the size of the tables is reduced. Using these tables is also potentially simpler: it is not necessary to identify the exact entry that matches the input. Rather, it is sufficient to find out whether the input is present somewhere in the table. The process of table look-up (in reduced tables) can therefore be viewed as an exhaustive search or as a pattern matching process. There are two main ways to do this in digital optics, which we next survey [241].

Exclusive OR method [285]

The table is recorded on a hologram. This means that the reconstructed image will be a 2-D array of small squares. Each line will give the bits of one entry in the table: bright squares represent "1" and dark squares represent "0". To use this table, it is imaged on a detector array: there is one detector for each square. Simultaneously, the input is duplicated and imaged on every line of the detector array. However, the light used to image the input and the light used to reconstruct the table are *out of phase*. As a result, destructive interference will occur in squares where both the table and the input have "1", and they will be *dark*. If only the input *or* the table have a "1", the square will be bright. In other words, the detectors will detect the XOR of the input and the table entries. Therefore, if the input is present in the table, a line of all dark squares will be detected. If it is not, every line of detectors will have at least one bright square.

NAND method

In this method each line in the hologram is one square longer than the entries in the table. This extra square is called the reference bit. At the recording stage, the squares are phase modulated so that the sum of the reference bit and all the "1" bits exactly cancel out, but any other combination will not. A simple way of achieving this is as follows: assume the line has r "1"s. all "0"s will be recorded with phase 0°, and all "1"s with phase 180°. The reference bit will be coded with phase 0°, but with amplitude r times larger than the others (which are all equal).

To use the table, it is illuminated by an *amplitude* modulator, that gives bright light in the "1" bits and in the reference bit. The interaction of this light pattern with the different recordings is imaged on a set of detectors (one detector per line). If the input appears in the table, the corresponding detector will not receive any light, because the reconstructed "1"s will cancel the reconstructed reference bit. If the input does not appear in the table, all detectors will get some light, because the cancellation will not be complete.

7.2.6 Logic by theta modulation and spatial filtering

As mentioned at the beginning of this section, logic operations are nonlinear. This motivates the use of nonlinear filtering techniques for the realization of logic operations. One of these nonlinear techniques is based on theta modulation: the encoding of data values by gratings in different orientations (see page 98). In the case of binary logic, logical "1" may be encoded by a vertical grating while logical "0" is encoded by a horizontal one[3] [46,444].

A logic gate may be realized in a two stage process: first one input is encoded, Fourier-transformed by a lens, and the diffracted light is filtered. An inverse Fourier transform then images what is left on the encoded second input. The result is again Fourier-transformed, and filtered in accordance with the function of the desired gate. A final inverse Fourier transform produces the output, with logical "1" represented by light and "0" by darkness.

An example of an AND gate, operating on a 3 × 3 array of bits in parallel, is given in fig. 7.6. After the first input is Fourier-transformed by a lens, five main light spots may emerge: in the center is the zero-order beam, on the horizontal axis are spots created zones with vertical gratings, and thus representing logical "1", and on the vertical axis are spots representing logical "0" (see fig. 7.7 (a)). Depending on the desired gate, one or the other may be filtered out: for instance, if a NOT gate is being implemented, an input of "1" cannot contribute to the output. In other cases, e.g., OR or XOR, both values must propagate to the second stage. Therefore one of the "1" spots and one of the "0" spots are allowed through[4].

The diffraction pattern after the second input is more complex, as it is formed by two beams. The beam representing "1" in the first stage forms a pattern that is displaced horizontally (around Z_1 in fig. 7.7 (b)). The beam that represents "0" from the first stage forms a pattern that is displaced vertically (around Z_0).

---

[3]Slightly different coding procedures have also been proposed [442,443,444,724].

[4]Using only one of each pair of spots combines the filtering with the decoding: light from both spots in a pair interferes to create a grating pattern. With only one, the output receives uniform illumination.

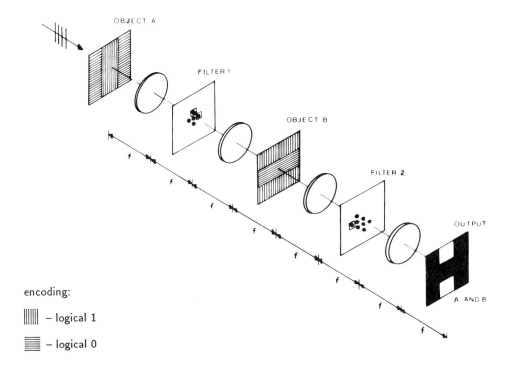

encoding:

|||||| – logical 1

☰ – logical 0

Figure 7.6: *An* AND *gate realized by spatial filtering of theta-modulated data. The squares in the filters indicate holes. All the other spots of light in the diffraction patterns are blocked.*
(Reprinted with permission from *Applied Optics* [444], ©1986)

The figure indicates the different combinations that generate the peripheral light spots.

Logic gates are implemented by filters which are opaque except for holes at the locations of certain light spots. For example, an AND gate is implemented by one hole, that lets the left-most light spot through. This works because this light spot is generated by two consecutive diffractions from a vertical grating. Therefore the presence of light in this location indicates that both inputs were "1". If one of the inputs was not "1", there will be no light at this place.

encoding by polarization

A method for performing logic operations which is very similar to the one described above has also been devised for systems in which the data values are represented by polarizations, rather than by spatial patterns. In this method Wollaston prisms

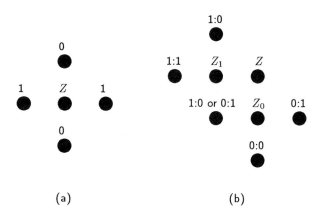

Figure 7.7: *Logic by spatial filtering of theta-modulated data:*
(a) Diffraction pattern of encoded data.
(b) Diffraction pattern at the second filter. Z, Z_1 and Z_0 are zero-order spots. Other spots are labeled by the logical combinations that generate them.

are used. These prisms deflect light in different polarizations by different amounts, and thus allow the logical values to be separated spatially. In this case only four light spots are created, corresponding to the four possible input combinations. To implement logic gates, the polarization of the light is some of these spots is changed by a half-wave plate [446,724]. The advantage of this method is that light is not lost: all the light that enters a gate also exits as useful output.

7.2.7   Shadow casting logic

A totally different way in which to implement binary logic is by means of a shadow casting system [666,332]. This requires special coding of the inputs: one input is coded by horizontal transparent and opaque stripes, and the other by vertical stripes. When the two inputs are superimposed, only one-quarter of the input mask is left transparent. This encodes the input combination (fig. 7.8).

The input mask is illuminated by some combination of 4 LEDs. Each LED casts a shadow in a slightly different direction, but the shadows are interlaced. The geometry of the system is such that the central square of the output pattern may be influenced by all 4 LEDs (depending on the input mask; see fig. 7.9). The following formula gives the exact condition for light in the central square:

$$c = \alpha \wedge (a \wedge b) \vee \beta \wedge (a \wedge \neg b) \vee \gamma \wedge (\neg a \wedge b) \vee \delta \wedge (\neg a \wedge \neg b),$$

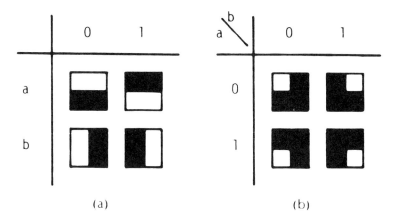

(a)   (b)

Figure 7.8: *Shadow casting logic.*
(a) Coding of the two binary inputs.
(b) Combinations of the two inputs superimposed on each other.
(Reprinted with permission from the *Proceedings of the IEEE* [332], ©1984 IEEE)

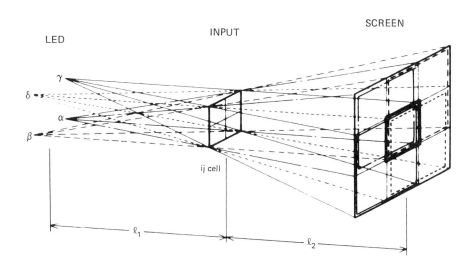

Figure 7.9: *Configuration of a shadow casting system.*
(Reprinted with permission from the *Proceedings of the IEEE* [332], ©1984 IEEE)

LED   INPUT   SCREEN

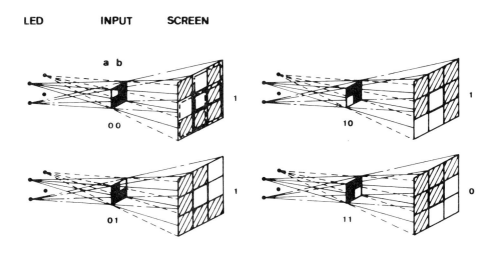

Figure 7.10: *Implementation of a* NAND *gate by shadow casting.*
(Reprinted with permission from the *Proceedings of the IEEE* [332], ©1984 IEEE)

where $\alpha, \beta, \gamma, \delta$ describe which LEDs are lit
        a, b are the two inputs
        $\wedge, \vee, \neg$ denote logical AND, OR, NOT respectively.

Light in the central square is interpreted as an output of a logical "1" value. A dark central square is a logical "0" output. The 16 possible combinations of turning on the 4 LEDs give rise to the 16 possible 2-input binary logic functions.

As an example, we shall see how a NAND is implemented. This function requires three LEDs to be lit: β, γ, and δ in the notation of fig. 7.9. Consequently, an ⌐ shaped light patch is formed on the output screen. When the input mask encodes 00, 01 or 10, the central square is one of the lit squares and we register an output of "1". However when the input encodes 11, the central square turns out to be dark and the output is "0" (fig. 7.10). This exactly matches the definition of a NAND gate.

Shadow casting systems are optically very simple. No lenses or nonlinear devices are needed. In addition they are very flexible: all 16 binary functions may be performed, without making any changes to the system configuration. All that has to be done in order to change the function is to change the lit LEDs. These systems may also be extended to multilevel logic [25], or to image processing systems [667]. However, all is not rosy. Dominant among the drawbacks is the problem of encoding the input, which requires some sort of SLM. The need for encoding also makes direct cascading of gates impossible.

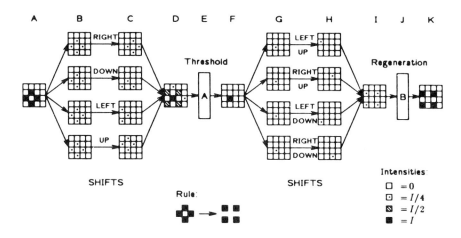

Figure 7.11: *Stages in the optical realization of symbolic substitution.*
(Reprinted with permission from *Applied Optics* [503], ©1987)

7.2.8 Symbolic substitution logic

General purpose digital computers represent all their data in symbolic form. Their logic operations may be viewed as the substitution of the output symbol for the input symbols. An extension of this idea is to use two-dimensional spatial patterns as symbols; The function of a logic gate is then to *recognize* the input pattern, and then to *generate* the corresponding output pattern.

A possible optical implementation is depicted in fig. 7.11 [72,73,503]. The substitution rule turns a pattern of four points arranged as a cross into four points at the corners of a square. This substitution is realized in two steps: first, the input pattern is shifted in accordance with its points, and all these shifted versions are superposed. Only one resulting point has a high intensity — this identifies the center of the input pattern. Then this point is shifted along the diagonals and superposed to generate the output square. Note that if a few instances of the input pattern are present, all of them will be substituted in parallel. An alternative approach is the use of a holographic code translator, as described on page 81 [747].

Symbolic substitution is a very low-level — and hence very general — operation. A machine that performs symbolic substitution is a generalization of a finite automaton. Substitution rules can be designed to implement logic gates, arithmetic operations, interconnections, and even to simulate a Turing machine [72,66]. However the efficiency and practicality of such an approach are not clear; the optical system outlined above suffers from excessive complexity and a requirement for a higher space-bandwidth product than most of the other ideas for optical logic. But additional research that would simplify the optical system [73,747,687] and

represent values by	implementation	all optical	speed	cascadable
intensity	bistable device	yes	μs–ns	yes[d]
	LCLV	yes	ms ?	yes
	four wave mixing	yes	?	yes
phase	none	?	?	?
polarization	spatial filtering	?	?	yes[t]
spatial pattern	shadow casting	no	?	no*
	θ modulation	no	?	no*
	symbolic substitution	yes	?	yes ?
mixed	truth table	no	?	no ?

Table 7.1: *Comparison of the different approaches towards the implementation of optical logic gates.*

find optimal substitution rules might make it worth consideration.

7.2.9   LCLV logic gates

The liquid crystal light valve (LCLV), as previously described in section 2.4.6, acts as a controlled polarization changing mirror: the read beam is reflected with a polarization change that depends on the intensity of the write beam. This happens independently for each point on the LCLV.

In order to implement a logic gate, two areas of the LCLV are used [211,212, 161]. each is controlled by one of the two inputs to the gate. The polarized

constant energy	values restored	gain	possibly multi-level	possibly cyclic	references
no	yes^d	yes^t	yes^t	no	[624,627,629,716]
no	yes ?	no	no	no	[212]
no	yes ?	yes ?	no	no	[224]
yes^t	no ?	?	yes^t	yes^t	
yes^d	yes^d	?	yes ?	yes ?	[446]
(yes)	–	–	yes	(yes)	[666,332]
(yes)	–	–	yes ?	(yes)	[46,444]
yes	yes ?	?	yes	can be	
–	–	–	yes^t	–	[242,496]

* If gates are not cascadable, questions of constant energy, standardization, gain and cyclic nature are irrelevant. The signal has to be encoded anew at each stage.

^{d} This has been demonstrated in laboratory prototypes.

^{t} This derives from the theory, but is undemonstrated yet.

– indicates entries which are not relevant to certain implementations.

? indicates topics which are not discussed in the references.

read beam is reflected from one of these areas, passes through a second polarizer, and is then re-imaged on the other area. The second reflection passes through a third polarizer and the result is the output from the gate (fig. 7.12). Different orientations of the polarizers determine which gate is implemented. Alternatively, only one area of the LCLV may be used, with the second input controlling the readout beam [30].

These LCLV methods have the advantage of using a commercially available device. However they suffer from the slow response time of the LCLV, and are optically more complex. Somewhat simpler systems have also been proposed [369].

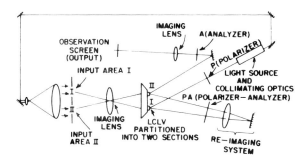

Figure 7.12: *Logic gates by double reflections from an LCLV.*
(Reprinted with permission from *Applied Optics* [212], ©1981)

7.3 Implementation of multilevel logic

Some of the methods for implementation of binary logic elements are extendible
to multilevel logic (see table 7.1). The following is a short list of the important
points relating to each implementation, showing how multilevel logic operations
may be realized directly:

Threshold logic — The bistable devices are replaced by multistable devices that
follow the same principles.

Truth-table look-up — The truth tables themselves present no problem; on the
contrary, using more values reduces the size of the tables. Other reduction
techniques, like logic minimization, may also be applied [495]. In the optical
implementation, the recording of an item with n values is done by assigning
$n - 1$ pixels to it, and using position coding (i.e., at most one pixel will be
transparent) [496].

Spatial filtering — The encoding (either by theta modulation or by polarizations) is enhanced so that more diffracted spots of light are produced. These
spots should represent all the possible input combinations, and their filtering
realizes the desired function.

Shadow casting — A more sophisticated coding of the input is needed, so as to
distinguish the different levels. The number of LEDs is also increased. The
output is again taken from the center of the superimposed shadow pattern
[25].

An alternative to the above ideas is to use binary coding of the multiple levels
[200]. Such a scheme allows the better known and developed methods of binary

logic to be used. This idea is reasonable if the motivation for the use of multilevel logic is its logical structure, e.g., in the case of residue arithmetic. It is unreasonable if the motivation is the desire to encode information by less symbols.

7.4   Implementation of arithmetic units

7.4.1   Fixed radix system

The fixed radix number system is well known [374, sect. 4.1 and 4.2]. A positive integer n is represented in a radix r system by a sequence of digits $x_m x_{m-1} \cdots x_1 x_0$, so that $0 \le x_i < r$ for every i, and

$$n = \sum_{i=0}^{m} x_i \, r^i.$$

Negative numbers are represented in a somewhat roundabout way. The scale is limited to numbers of no more than M digits (i.e., only numbers for which $m < M$ will be represented). The number $-n$ is then represented as $1 \, y_{M-1} \, y_{M-2} \cdots y_1 \, y_0$, and

$$-n = -r^M + \sum_{i=0}^{M-1} y_i \, r^i.$$

It turns out that $y_{M-1} \cdots y_1 \, y_0 = \bar{x}_{M-1} \cdots \bar{x}_1 \, \bar{x}_0 + 1$, where $\bar{x}_i = r - x_i$. Therefore the method is called "r complement". The reason for using this method is arithmetic convenience: it allows positive and negative numbers to be used in the same way. This is well known for the binary (two's complement) case. It is readily extended to any even radix [128,457, sect. 1.5].

Fractions can be accommodated by using negative exponents. The range of exponents used can be constant and embedded into the structure of the computer (fixed point), or else it can be given as part of the representation of each number (floating point). Floating point notation may also be used to represent very large numbers, by specifying large positive exponents.

Arithmetic by logic

The fixed radix method is used in practically all electronic computers (with radix 2, of course). Arithmetic operations are performed by combinatorical logic circuits, that accept the binary representations of the operands as input and produce the binary representation of the result as output [457, chap. 4]. An adder for 5-bit numbers is shown in fig. 7.13 as an example. Equivalent circuits can be made for optical computers, by use of optical logic gates like those described in section 7.2 [30,444].

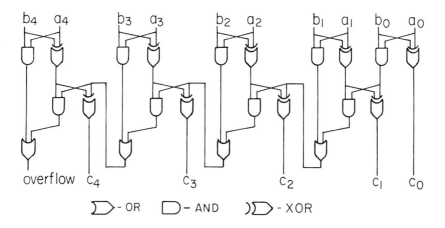

Figure 7.13: *An adder circuit for 5-bit numbers.*

Single-gate adder

The special characteristics of optical logic gates sometimes allow for shortcuts in the implementations of certain circuits. A nice example is given by threshold gates based on Fabry-Perot bistable devices (page 150). As the intensity of the incident light on such a device increases, the transmitted light remains low until a threshold is reached. Then it jumps up, and stays at a high level (fig. 7.14 (a)). The rest of the light is reflected. At low intensities, the reflected intensity increases as the incident intensity increases (fig. 7.14 (b)). When the threshold is reached, the reflected intensity falls because suddenly most of the light is transmitted. Then the reflected intensity increases again.

With careful adjustments, and using *both* the transmitted and reflected beams, a full adder may be implemented [729]. Four beams contribute to the input intensity: the hold beam brings the device to the threshold area, and the two input beams and one carry beam govern the exact state. The output sum is given by the reflected beam: it has a high intensity only if one or three of the signal beams are on. The output carry is given by the transmitted beam: it is high if more than two input signals are on.

Multiplication by convolution

The multiplication of two N-bit numbers is usually done by N additions. An alternative method, which has not gained acceptance in electronic computers but has aroused some interest in the context of optical computers, is that of digital

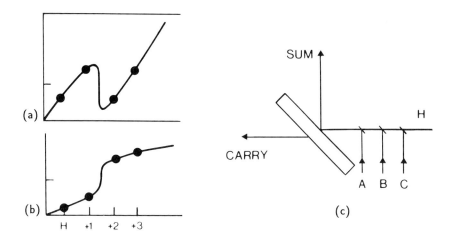

Figure 7.14: *Single-gate full adder based on bistable resonator.*
(a) Reflected characteristic.
(b) Transmitted characteristic.
(c) General configuration.
(Reprinted with permission from *Optics Communications* [729], ©1985)

multiplication by analog convolution[5] [661,568,180,148,335].

The result of multiplying two numbers in binary representation is given by the following equations:

$$c = a\,b$$

$$= \left(\sum_{i=0}^{N-1} a_i\, 2^i \right) \left(\sum_{j=0}^{N-1} b_j\, 2^j \right) \qquad \text{(binary)}$$

$$= \sum_{i=0}^{N-1} \sum_{j=0}^{N-1} a_i\, b_j\, 2^{i+j} \qquad \text{(open brackets)}$$

$$= \sum_{k=0}^{2N-1} 2^k \underbrace{\sum_{\ell=0}^{N} a_\ell\, b_{k-\ell}} \qquad \text{(by setting } k = i + j\text{),}$$

where it is understood that $b_{k-\ell} = 0$ if $k - \ell < 0$ or $k - \ell \geq N$. Note that the

---

[5]The concept of performing multiplication by convolution is well known; in fact, this is the basis of the Schönhage-Strassen integer multiplication algorithm, which is (asymptotically) the fastest one known [8, sect. 7.5]. However, it did not father any practical implementations, as it only becomes advantageous for extremely large numbers.

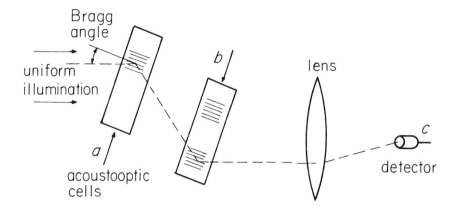

Figure 7.15: *System for binary multiplication by optical convolution.*
(Adapted with permission from *Optical Engineering* [180])

term marked by the underbrace is the kth term of the convolution[6] of the binary representations of a and b. Therefore the whole convolution function gives the set of coefficients for all the exponents of 2.

This is not the final result, as these values are not necessarily binary. Rather, they may assume values in the range 0 to N. Denoting the output by $c_{2N-1} \cdots c_0$, the binary result may be obtained in $\log N$ steps by converting each c_i into a binary representation, and then adding up the $2N$-bit-long bit slices created by the concatenation of all the least-significant bits, those next to them (shifted by one place), and so on, until the most-significant bits are added (shifted by $\log N$) [335]. The need for this additional step of analog-to-digital conversion, and then addition, is the greatest drawback of this method.

This method is attractive for optical computers, because convolution is an atomic operation in optical systems (as shown in section 3.2.2). In this case the data is one-dimensional (an array of bits), so 1-D optical systems suffice. The simplest configuration is as follows (fig. 7.15): Two acoustooptic cells are used. The binary representation of one input is fed into the first, while that of the other input is fed into the other cell, in the opposite direction. Uniform illumination impinges upon the cells at the Bragg angle, so that it is deflected by pulses of the acoustic wave that represent "1" bits. Rays of light that are deflected twice, once from each cell, emerge in their original direction. such rays are focused by a lens onto a detector, to provide the output. Rays that are only deflected once miss the detector, and do not contribute to the output. Rays that are not deflected at all *do* get to the detector, and thus influence the output. This may be avoided by

---

[6]See definition in appendix B or C.

the use of different acoustic frequencies in the two cells, and the appropriate slight change in the geometry of the system [180].

The apparent advantages that this method has in the context of optical computers are:

- It utilizes a well-known analog optical system. Such systems cannot be used in most cases because of dynamic range limitations. For example, an analog multiplication (section 4.1.3) of numbers in the range 0 to 256 requires the distinction between some 65,000 discrete levels in the output. The digital encoding reduces this requirement: when these numbers are coded by 8-bit sequences, only 8 discrete levels appear in the output. Therefore the analog system may be used without loss of accuracy. Note that the accuracy of the result is, nevertheless, 16 bits.

- It is potentially fast, especially if the numbers are not translated back to ordinary binary representation after every operation, but rather when the values attached to each exponent of 2 becomes large [335].

- Only 1-D SLMs are used. Fast and well-developed acoustooptic SLMs are currently available.

However, it is doubtful whether these advantages, coupled with the fact that the basic convolution operation is simple, compensate for the additional work required in order to turn the result back into binary representation. Indeed, given the performance of current devices, this method *does not* provide a viable alternative to the usual multiplication scheme [569].

7.4.2   Residue number system

In the residue number system [672,374, sect. 4.3.2], a set of K moduli $m_1, m_2, \cdots,$ m_K are selected as a base by which numbers are represented. The moduli must have no common factors[7]. A positive integer n that satisfies

$$0 \le n < \prod_{i=1}^{K} m_i$$

is then represented by the K-tuple

$$\left(n_{mod\, m_1}, n_{mod\, m_2}, \cdots, n_{mod\, m_K}\right),$$

where $x_{mod\, y}$ denotes the remainder of the division of x by y. For example[8], 87 will be represented in a residue system with the moduli 5, 7, 9 and 4 as

$$\left(87_{mod\, 5}, 87_{mod\, 7}, 87_{mod\, 9}, 87_{mod\, 4}\right) = (2, 3, 6, 3).$$

---

[7]Such numbers are said to be *relatively prime*.

[8]Examples are adapted from [325].

Negative numbers may be represented by their complements (modulo m_i). Continuing with the above example, -87 will be represented by $(3, 4, 3, 1)$. When this is used, the range of representable numbers changes to

$$-\frac{1}{2} \left(\prod_{i=1}^{K} m_i \right) \leq n < \frac{1}{2} \left(\prod_{i=1}^{K} m_i \right).$$

The advantages of the residue number system over the fixed radix number system is that there is no interaction between the different moduli when arithmetic operations are performed. The calculations for the different moduli can be carried out concurrently and independently, and there is no carry from one digit in the representation to another. The rule for residue arithmetic can therefore be written as

$$(s \Box t)_{mod\ m_i} = ((s_{mod\ m_i}) \Box (t_{mod\ m_i}))_{mod\ m_i}, \qquad i = 1, \cdots, K,$$

where s and t are two numbers in the representable range, and $\Box$ stands for addition, subtraction, or multiplication. This should result in an appreciable speedup when compared to the fixed radix system, where calculation of high order digits must wait for a carry that might be generated in the calculation of lower-order digits. As an example, the addition of 19 to 87 (in the same system as before) proceeds as follows:

$$
\begin{array}{ccccccc}
 & & \mathbf{5} & \mathbf{7} & \mathbf{9} & \mathbf{4} & \\
87 & \mapsto & 2 & 3 & 6 & 3 & \\
19 & \mapsto & 4 & 5 & 1 & 3 & \\
 & & \overline{} & \overline{} & \overline{} & \overline{} & \\
 & & 1 & 1 & 7 & 2 & \mapsto \quad 106
\end{array}
$$

The main disadvantage of the residue number system is the need to translate numbers to and from the residue representation. This is needed both for input/output and for numerical comparisons. These translations are not easy in the general case[9]. Another problem is the detection of overflow conditions. Residue arithmetic does not give any indication of an overflow — it just gives a wrong result. A third drawback is that only integers are accommodated. Scaling does not solve this difficulty, because the range of distinguishable values remains small. Also, division is problematic, as the quotient of two integers may not be an integer. Therefore use of the residue system will only be advantageous if the following conditions are met:

- There is a massive amount of computation involved, so that the time saved by concurrent calculations in the different moduli is significant.

---

[9] One of the methods is the Chinese remainder theorem.

- There is no need for comparisons (or other operations that would necessitate translation) throughout the computation, so that conversion to and from residue would be done only once at the beginning and the end of the computation. For example, many of the iterative matrix-vector multiplication algorithms (section 4.3.2) can be done in residue arithmetic throughout [337].

- It is possible to avoid the need to check for overflow.

- Only integers are needed.

The idea of residue arithmetic has received some notice in the context of optical computing because optical computers are inherently suited for concurrent calculations (this point is elaborated in section 7.7). Residue arithmetic is also appealing because its optical implementations do not entail the realization of Boolean logic functions, and because it retains some of the characteristics of analog optical systems. A number of very different approaches to the optical implementation of residue encoding and arithmetic have been proposed. These include the use of truth tables, permutation mapping devices, and diffraction gratings.

Residue arithmetic by table look-up

Truth-tables are not limited to the tabulation of logical functions — arithmetic functions may be tabulated as well. This means that all the possible calculations are performed in advance, and when the need arises the result is simply looked up. It turns out that if numbers are represented by the residue system, the sizes of the tables that tabulate arithmetic operations are surprisingly small. For example, the residue number system with moduli 5,7,9 and 4 can represent numbers in the range $0 \ldots 1259$. However the computations regarding the first modulus, 5, only deal with the values $0 \ldots 4$. Therefore the truth table for, say, addition modulo 5 requires just 25 entries. A set of four truth tables for addition in all four moduli will total 171 entries. This should be compared with a total of $1259^2 = 1,585,081$ entries that would be required for a direct truth table relating any two numbers to their sum[10]. The combination of residue arithmetic and truth-table look-up has therefore received some attention [284,241,242,495].

---

[10]This is not a strictly valid comparison, because a full truth table will also include information about overflow conditions, while the residue tables do not.

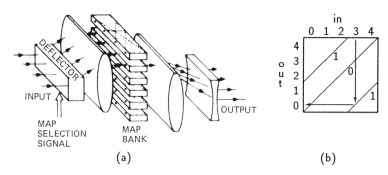

Figure 7.16: *Residue operations by permutation maps:*
(a) Use of a bank of fixed permutation maps.
(b) Optical cyclic permutation by controllable mirrors. If the "0" mirror is activated, no permutation occurs. With the "1" mirrors, the output is permuted as shown.
(Reprinted with permission from *Applied Optics* [325], ©1979)

Residue arithmetic by permutation maps

Many residue operations reduce to permutations of the residues of each modulus; for example, addition of 2 modulo 5 is a cyclic permutation of 2 places:

$$
\begin{aligned}
(\ 0 + 2 \ )_{mod\,5} &= 2 \\
(\ 1 + 2 \ )_{mod\,5} &= 3 \\
(\ 2 + 2 \ )_{mod\,5} &= 4 \quad \text{or symbolically} \\
(\ 3 + 2 \ )_{mod\,5} &= 0 \\
(\ 4 + 2 \ )_{mod\,5} &= 1
\end{aligned}
$$

Such permutations occur all the time in optics. An imaging lens, for instance, casts a *reversed* image of the original object (see fig. 2.5). Hence the points of the image are actually a permutation of the points of the original. A mirror does the same when it reflects a beam of light. These observations motivate the representation of values by the spatial location of a point of light; for example, an array of five points may represent numbers modulo 5 by having light at only one point at a time. Light at the first location signifies a residue of 0, the second point signifies 1, and so on. Arithmetic operations are then performed by moving the input spot of light to another location.

The simplest arithmetic system would have a special optical permutator for each operation. For example, the operation "add 2 modulo 5" would require its own device, which is different from the device for "add 3 modulo 5". These devices may be realized by means of mirrors or prisms that direct the input light to the output. A large bank of permutation-mapping devices is needed in order to implement the whole repertoire of operations. They are activated simply by

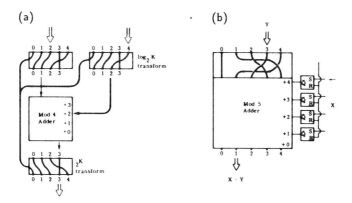

Figure 7.17: *Residue operations may be realized by combinations of adders, which perform cyclic permutations, and additional fixed noncyclic permutations.*
(a) Multiplication, using permutations for logarithms and exponents.
(b) Subtraction, using a permutation of residues to their complements.
(Reprinted with permission from *Applied Optics* [663], ©1979)

having the input directed at them (fig. 7.16 (a)).

A more economic scheme would use controllable permutation mappers, e.g., mirrors that can be switched between a reflecting mode and a transmitting mode (fig. 7.16 (b)). With such a device, one input is represented by the spatial locations, while the binary representation of the other controls the mirrors. Note that mirrors can only provide for *cyclic* permutations. While this is sufficient for addition, it is not good enough for multiplication and subtraction. Multiplication can, however, be decomposed into three stages: take the logarithms of the operands, add, and exponentiate. In residue arithmetic, logarithms and exponents are also just permutations (fig. 7.17 (a)) [663]. Therefore multiplication can be carried out by a controllable cyclic permutation (the addition), sandwiched between two *fixed* noncyclic permutations (the logarithm and the exponentiation). Subtraction may be accommodated in a similar manner, by adding one noncyclic permutation before the addition. This permutation takes residues to their complements (fig. 7.17 (b)).

A modular system based on such combinations has been proposed for the implementation of a residue ALU [663]. The modules used are composed of arrays of elementary switches, that can interchange the light beams propagating in adjacent channels (fig. 7.18. The switches are integrated directional coupler switches, explained on page 237). The input enters through the channels at the top (recall that only one of them will contain light). The top row of switches, controlled

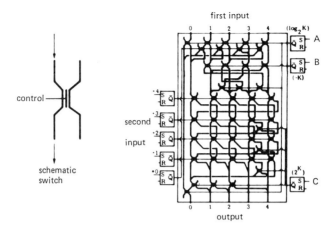

Figure 7.18: *A programmable multipurpose module for residue operations. See explanation in text.*
(Reprinted with permission from *Applied Optics* [663], ©1979)

by A, may perform a logarithmic permutation. The next row, controlled by B, may perform a negation. The main block of switches implements an adder; it is controlled by the inputs from the left (only one of which will be activated — this is also compatible with the representation by spatial location). The bottom row, controlled by C, may perform an exponentiation.

Encoding and decoding

As stated above, one of the main disadvantages of the residue system is the need to encode the data in an unusual way, and to subsequently decode it so that it will be fit for human consumption. The encoding (from binary to residue) is relatively simple, provided that controllable residue adders are available. The residue representation is then generated by adding the values of the bits: if a number is given in binary as $\alpha_n \cdots \alpha_1 \alpha_0$, its residue modulo m is given by

$$\alpha_0 2^0 + (\alpha_1 2^1)_{mod\,m} + \cdots + (\alpha_n 2^n)_{mod\,m}.$$

The decoding is more difficult; one possibility is to use the Chinese remainder theorem. Another is to use a mixed-radix representation as an intermediate step, where the radices are partial products of the set of moduli [325].

A simple optical encoding and decoding scheme uses the multiple diffraction orders produced by a grating (section 2.4.3) [561]. As shown in fig. 7.19, one

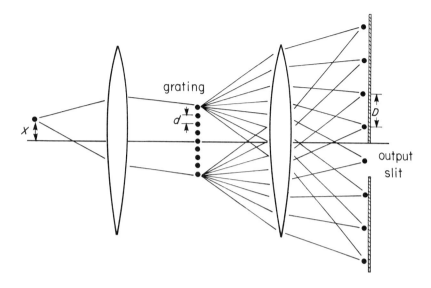

Figure 7.19: *One point of light is transformed into an array of equidistant points through diffraction from a grating.*

point of light is easily transformed into an array of points by this phenomenon. The location of these points depends on the displacement of the original point (x in the figure). The intervals between the produced points (D) are regular, and depend on the grating spacing (d). An output opening of width D blocks all but one point of light. This is used as follows: The number to be converted dictates the displacement x. As x increases, points of light corresponding to different diffraction orders pass across the output opening. The location of the light in the opening represents the residue of x when divided by D[11] (fig. 7.20 (a)). Thus the residue is derived from the number, both being represented by spatial location.

The same system may be used for decoding. if x represents a residue, the locations of the light points represent all the possible numbers that would give this residue when divided by the modulus. By using an array of gratings, each one corresponding to a different modulus, multiple sets of light points are obtained. In general the points of light in distinct sets do not align; the one location where they all do align indicates the number represented by the input residues (fig. 7.20 (b)).

---

[11]This statement is only true in the case of 1:1 magnification. More generally, the location of the light in the opening represents the residue of x divided by a certain modulus. This modulus was used to calculate the grating spacing, and thus also dictates D.

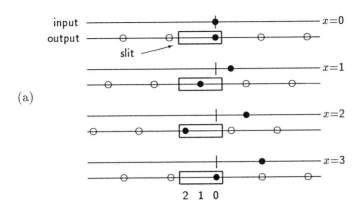

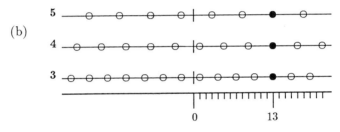

Figure 7.20: *Residue encoding and decoding using diffraction gratings:*
(a) Encoding: only one diffraction order is observed at the output, the others being blocked. Its location indicates the residue of the input displacement x, after division by the modulus used to create the grating, in this case 3.
(b) Decoding: when the residues are used as input, the locations of the diffracted light spots indicate potential encoded numbers. With residues 3,1,1 and moduli 5,4,3, the points of light align in the column that designates 13 as the encoded number.
(Adapted with permission from *Applied Optics* [561])

This system, while being direct and elegant, suffers from one chief drawback: the resolution at the input and output planes must be sufficient to accommodate the whole range of representable numbers. In other words, the range of numbers is limited by the space-bandwidth product of the system. This greatly limits its usefulness.

7.4.3   Modified signed-digit system

The modified signed-digit number representation is an attempt to have the best of both worlds: easy-to-use fixed radix numbers and carry-less concurrent calcu-

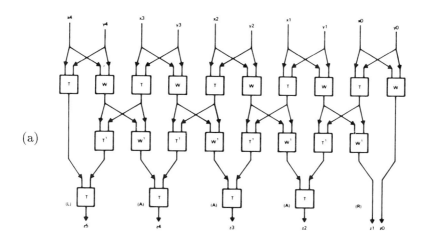

(a)

(b)

T	1	0	-1
1	1	1	0
0	1	0	-1
-1	0	-1	-1

W	1	0	-1
1	0	-1	0
0	-1	0	1
-1	0	1	0

T^1	1	0	-1
1	1	0	0
0	0	0	0
-1	0	0	-1

W^1	1	0	-1
1	0	1	0
0	1	0	-1
-1	0	-1	0

Figure 7.21: *(a) Modified signed digit adder circuit for 5 digits. Note the lack of a carry-chain, in contrast with fig. 7.13.*
(b) Truth tables for gates used in (a).
(Reprinted with permission from *Optical Engineering* [189], ©1986)

lations. The idea behind signed-digit numbers is that the digits are not limited to the range $0 \ldots r - 1$ (where r is the radix). Negative digits may also appear. This causes a redundancy in representation: for example $7 = 0\,1\,1\,1 \equiv 1\,-1\,1\,1$ (in radix 2). This nonuniqueness allows for the design of arithmetic algorithms where each digit depends only on its two neighbors, and no carry chains occur [36].

In the modified signed-digit representation [189], the radix is 2. The possible digits are -1, 0, and 1. To get a negative number, the signs of all digits are simply switched. Addition (or subtraction) is done by a ternary logic circuit of depth 3 (fig. 7.21 (a) is an example for 5-digit numbers). The gates are called T, W, T^1, and W^1, and their truth tables are given in fig. 7.21 (b). It should be noted that the middle three units in fig. 7.21 are identical, and any number of such units may be inserted. Therefore we can make circuits that add numbers of arbitrary length in the same time it takes to add a two-digit number. Multiplication is done by multiplying each digit in the multiplier by each digit of the multiplied, and then summing in pairs.

A possible optical implementation of these gates uses a direct realization of the truth tables [189]. The numbers are coded by position, as they were in the implementations of residue arithmetic devices. An array of nine bistable devices is used to identify the input combination: each bistable device accepts light from one of the positions of each input, and transmits light only if both its inputs are on. A holographic element then directs the output from each bistable device to the appropriate output port, so as to implement the desired gate. Other schemes have also been proposed [573,66].

7.5   Memory

Memory is one of the basic components of any conventional computer. Indeed it is common to view the whole process of computation as a series of transformations on the contents of the memory. Practically speaking, a computer's memory may be divided into three types: primary, secondary and archive[12]. The primary memory is usually a volatile array of elements that are capable of storing one bit or word each. It is directly accessible by the CPU. The secondary memory is a random access magnetic disk or drum. The archive is kept off-line on magnetic tapes and such.

   In optical computing, only two types of memory are discussed. One is more or less equivalent to primary memory, and consists of arrays of one-bit-store elements. The other is mass storage, which is a combination of secondary memory and archive memory. It is implemented by optical disks or by holographic storage systems. This type of memory promises very high capacity and storage density on line, and it has therefore been developed also in the context of electronic computers [153,530]. In reviewing such systems it should be remembered that they interface to electronic devices — converting them for use with optical computers would require some adjustments.

   When designing an optical computer that copies the architecture of existing electronic computers, it is self-evident that appropriate optical memory devices should be included. However, it is not self-evident that optical computers should follow the Von Neumann architecture of conventional electronic computers in the first place. Ideas about a memoryless computer are mentioned in section 7.7, which deals with architectures.

7.5.1   Bit-by-bit storage elements

Flip-flop arrays

The primary memory is actually an array of elements, each of which is able to store one bit. An example of a basic element of this type is the flip-flop, which might

---

[12]We ignore the finer details of cache strategies, etc.

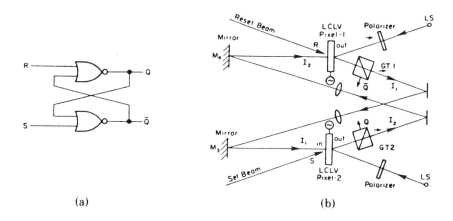

(a)   (b)

Figure 7.22: (a) Electronic flip-flop.
(b) Optical implementation.
(Reprinted with permission from *Applied Optics* [213], ©1984)

be implemented by a pair of NOR gates as depicted in fig. 7.22 (a) [457, sect. 6.2]. As we have seen in the previous section, such gates may be implemented optically, and so it follows that flip-flops may be implemented optically.

fig. 7.22 (b) shows an implementation of a flip-flop based on an LCLV [211, 213,610,341]. Each pixel on the LCLV acts as an OR gate: any one of the beams incident on the write side is sufficient in order to activate it. The inversion needed in order to turn this into a NOR gate is obtained by adjusting the polarizers so that a bright spot on the input side causes a dark output.

Bistable arrays

An electronic flip-flop utilizes two logic gates in order to implement a one-bit storage device. However, this structure is not necessarily needed for this end. For example, The optically bistable devices described in section 6.2 may function as single-element storage devices [633]: they are inherently history-sensitive, and retain their condition until an input change causes them to switch to the other state [243].

This application is not very attractive, however, as the bistable devices require a constant and very stable "hold" beam that will keep them in the bistable region. Switching down necessitates the interruption of this hold beam.

Magnetooptic systems [154,392,391]

The most established technology for bit-by-bit optical storage is that of magnetooptic devices. The underlying idea is the same as in conventional magnetic storage apparatus, such as disks and tapes. There is a thin layer of ferromagnetic material, which may be magnetized in one of two directions. The direction of magnetization corresponds to the stored binary value. The main difference is in the method of writing and reading the stored information.

In conventional systems, the stored information density is no more than 10^6 $bits/_{cm^2}$. This limit is not imposed by the storage medium — it is a result of the reading and writing technology. The read/write heads used must be very near to the storage medium (on a scale of a few microns), because the usable energy is that stored in the bit. This requires operation within very fine mechanical tolerances, and creates the risk of head crashes. Access time is limited by the time needed to mechanically move the heads to the proper position. The data transfer rate depends on the combination of the bit size and the relative speed between the storage medium and the read/write head. The higher the speed, the harder it is to adhere with the required mechanical tolerances. Reasonable data transfer rates are in the range of 10 $^{Mb}/_{sec}$.

Optical systems using magnetooptic effects do not have the above drawbacks. A stored information density of 10^8 $^{bits}/_{cm^2}$ is achievable. There is no risk of head crashes, and the mechanical tolerances are much less restrictive. This is because the distance between the nearest optical element and the storage medium is much larger, approaching a millimeter. The read-out energy comes from the read-out beam. There is no need to mechanically move anything in order to access different bits of information — only an inertialess read-out beam of light is deflected. Data transfer rates surpass 10 $^{Mb}/_{sec}$.

Optical reading of the magnetically stored data is based on the Faraday effect. This is the same as in magnetooptic SLMs (page 31): the polarization of light passing through the magnetized material is rotated, with the direction of rotation depending on the direction of magnetization. The polarization of reflected light is likewise rotated, through the Kerr effect. As a result, when a "0" bit is read, a beam with one polarization emerges. When a "1" bit is read, the read-out beam will emerge with another polarization. These polarization differences are easily changed into intensity differences by an analyzer.

Optical writing of magnetic information involves thermomagnetic effects: the energy in the incident beam is used to heat up the bit area. When the area is heated, an external magnetic field is applied and causes the bit to freeze into the right magnetization. We do not go into the physical details of how exactly this happens. We also ignore the issue of choosing the best materials for these effects [79].

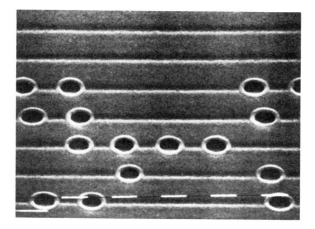

Figure 7.23: *Scanning electron microscope picture of the pits burned on a videodisk. The grooves are formed during the manufacture process; they help align the laser beams. Each white segment in the scale at bottom is 1μm long.*
(Reprinted with permission from *IEEE Spectrum* [88], ©1979 IEEE)

7.5.2 Optical disks

Erasable magnetooptic disks are now at advanced stages of development. Read-only optical disks, however, are already in common use [590]. These devices were developed by the household entertainment industry for the storage and reproduction of video programs and music. Only later were they adapted for computer use. The different types of optical disks will be described here, and will be compared to conventional magnetic disks in table 7.2.

Videodisks

Optical disks were developed primarily for the video industry. These "videodisks" are intended to store half an hour of a video program, in digital format. The information may be embedded in the disk in the manufacturing process, or else it may be written once. The information is then kept indefinitely and may be read as often as desired. Soon after they appeared in the market, it was suggested that these disks may also be used to store general digital data [49,50,361,88,182,710]. The write-once characteristic implies that the most reasonable application is that of archival storage. The capacity is very high: as much as 10^{10} bits on a 30-cm disk. "Jukebox" systems that automatically exchange disks can increase the capacity, at the cost of an access time of a few seconds [12,722].

type	size [cm]	capacity [Mbyte]	transfer rate $\left[\text{Mb}/\text{s}\right]$	access time [ms]	usage	ref
Philips videodisk	30	2500	5–10	100–500	write once	[361]
CD-ROM	12	540	0.15	50–1500	read only	[594]
Toshiba magnetooptic	13.3	268	2.62	100	read write	[502]
IBM 3340	35.6	70	7	35	read write	[361]
floppy	13.3	1.4	0.06	365	read write	[594]

Table 7.2: *Comparison between optical disks and conventional disks.*

The recording medium is a thin, low-reflectance metallic film, deposited on an aluminum reflector. In the writing process, a laser beam burns minute pits (about 1 micron across) in the film, and exposes the reflector. The intensity of the readout beam is much lower, so that it does not affect the film. The reflected readout beam is thus modulated by the pits in the film.

Compact disks (CD)

Another type of disk that utilizes optical readout is the compact disk. This too was developed for the domestic entertainment market, with the intention of replacing LP records in audio recording and reproduction. Therefore the data is usually impressed upon the disk irreversibly by the manufacturer. Again, once these disks and their players were available, it was suggested that they be used to record and distribute digital data [594,155,531].

Optical digital data disks (OD³)

Lately, large efforts have been invested in the standardization of optical disks intended to serve as a secondary computer memory [497,230]. Rather than using the myriad of different commercially available videodisks and compact disks, a totally new standard is being developed. Both write-once disks, following the principles of videodisks, and erasable magnetooptic disks are being investigated

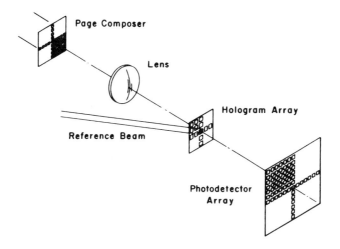

Figure 7.24: *Schematic representation of a holographic memory. The lens is positioned so as to image the page composer on the detector array.*
(Reprinted with permission from *Applied Optics* [697], ©1973)

[502]. The potential advantages of optical disks as secondary storage are [233]:

- High capacity on-line.

- Reasonable access time.

- High data transfer rate.

- No danger of head crashes.

7.5.3   Holographic mass storage

Holographic mass storage systems are intended to store vast amounts of data on-line. The volumes cited are of the order of 10^{12} bits and more. The basic idea behind these systems is simple: the data is arranged in pages, which are rectangular images, and these pages are recorded on holograms. When we wish to retrieve data, the appropriate page is reconstructed from the hologram (fig. 7.24) [572]. The reasons for using holography for this application are the high storage density and the inherent redundancy of holography, which allows tolerance of noise [651].

This type of memory is well suited for archival, read-only applications. In such cases, the hologram is made on film and the film is kept in the system.

However, materials that allow for both writing and erasing of holograms have been developed (e.g., thermoplastics [407,408]). Therefore a holographic storage system based on the appropriate materials and techniques may function as an active memory system.

The capacity limit of one thin hologram is about 10^8 bits [370]. This limit results from diffraction due to the angular size of the hologram and its relations with the other optical components. Higher capacities are achieved through multiple exposures on thick holograms, or the use of sets of distinct holograms.

Page composers

As mentioned above, the first step in the writing process is to arrange the information in pages. These are literally rectangular arrays of bits[13], and not just virtual and shapeless blocks of data, as in conventional computers. The idea is to represent the input by an image, e.g., have a bright pixel for each "1" and a dark one for each "0". The devices used as page composers are simply spatial light modulators, described in section 2.4.6, and everything said there is directly transferable to this application.

In some applications the input data page may not be available at once. Then page synthesis may be used [96]. This means that the hologram of the page is created by superimposing holograms for individual bits. Each input bit is recorded as it comes, and contributes a hologram to the appropriate page. Only at the end of the recording process do the complete holograms emerge.

A consequence of the use of whole pages as the basic element in each memory access is a high equivalent data transfer rate. If the system can access a page every few microseconds, and each page holds a few thousand bits, the resulting data transfer rate may well reach 1 $^{Gb}/_{sec}$. An alternative method of achieving such speeds is by use of multichannel systems, where the input bit stream is demultiplexed and each resulting channel is recorded separately [584].

Volume holography

As mentioned above, the capacity limit of a simple 2-D hologram is about 10^8 bits. However, this limit does not apply to 3-D or *thick* holograms. Technically, thick[14] holograms are the same as thin ones: they just record an interference pattern generated by the combination of an object beam and a reference beam. The difference is that the recorded interference pattern is *three-dimensional* [703]. Instead of the set of parallel lines, we get a set of parallel surfaces. Reconstruction from such a

---

[13]Sometimes line composers are used instead of page composers. Then we have linear arrays of bits.

[14]The required thickness is related to the recording material properties and to the hologram geometry; it should be large enough so that an optical path difference of half a wavelength may be induced. In some materials, "thick" can be as little as 5 μm for visible light.

three-dimensional pattern is reminiscent of diffraction from a crystal lattice: only very specific directions give a strong, constructive interference. Coming back to holography, this means that the reconstruction is very sensitive to the direction of the reconstruction beam. If it is not perfectly identical to the reference beam used in the recording stage, there will be no reconstruction. This points the way to making multiple but distinct holograms on a thick medium: the different holograms are simply made with different reference beams. A single hologram may be individually reconstructed by choosing the direction of its reference beam for the reconstruction beam. Other holograms will not respond to this reconstruction beam, because the direction will not be right for them. If the medium is thick enough, a difference of a few minutes of an arc between the different reference beams is sufficient, and hundreds of distinct holograms may be recorded [232,511].

A possible medium for the recording of thick holograms is simply thick photographic emulsions. Other mediums are various crystals that display some photoelectric or photochromic effect. A prime candidate is lithium niobate ($LiNbO_3$) doped with Fe^{+2} and Fe^{+3}. The illumination of this crystal causes a change in the concentration of the dopants, which causes a change in the space charge and in the refractive index. This change can also be fixed [89].

Proposed systems

A number of holographic optical storage systems have been proposed and even built. This has nothing to do with optical computers; the incentive was the need for mass storage devices for electronic systems. Typically, these systems use photographic film as the storage medium. The needed capacity is obtained by moving the film, both in recording and in retrieval. See the bibliographical notes for references dealing with design concepts and systems.

7.6 Interconnections and communication

The concept of using light to convey information dates back to ancient history; for example, an impressive system of bonfires and torches was used to notify the diaspora of the setting of dates by the elders of Jerusalem, in the Roman era. More recently, the use of a modulated beam of light was used some 100 years ago in Graham Bell's photophone. The technology of creating, modulating, conducting, and detecting beams of light has advanced greatly in the past two decades. In fact, communication systems based on a light carrier are becoming quite commonplace.

This section addresses optical interconnections and communication. Optical interconnection schemes have been developed already in the context of electronic computers; we begin by investigating the reasons that make optical interconnections so appealing. We then deal with the relatively common fiberoptics communication systems, and their possible use in optical computers. Finally, we turn to ideas that were specifically developed for optical interconnections in computers: open-space communication using holograms or lenslet arrays, and optical implementations of a bus, a crossbar switch, and a perfect shuffle network. While most of these ideas were developed with electronic computers in mind, they will only be simplified by a transition to optical computers — the light sources and detectors will become redundant.

7.6.1   Merits of optical interconnections

Large bandwidth

The use of light as a carrier of information is just another step in the continued use of carriers of higher and higher frequencies. The fact that we have special sentiments toward these frequencies because we can see them is irrelevant. The need for carriers with higher frequencies stems from the hunger for larger bandwidth. If the carrier frequency is of the order of 10^{14} cps, a bandwidth near 10^{13} cps should be available. This implies possible data rates in excess of 10^{12} bps. Such rates are 3 orders of magnitude faster than the fastest data rates today.

Communication at a data rate of 10^{12} bits per second means that the modulation of the carrier changes 10^{12} times every second. The simplest modulation is on-off switching: a pulse of light (on) may indicate a "1" bit, while its absence (off) indicates a "0". To utilize the high potential of optical communication, a switch that is capable of turning on and off at a rate of about 10^{12} times a second is therefore required [544]. Electronic switching devices fall at least 2 orders of magnitude short of this objective: the fastest modulation of laser light reported to date is of the order of 10 GHz [401,68]. Therefore optical switches must be used. Good candidates for this job are bistable optical devices, described in section 6.2.

High speed of propagation

Under ideal conditions, electronic signals may propagate as quickly as optical signals. However, the realization of these ideal conditions necessitates coaxial cables and such, which is not practical at the chip level of a computer. When the thin lines of an integrated circuit are considered, it turns out that electronic signals propagate two orders of magnitude slower than light [733]. The reason is that the electronic conductor has a capacitance that has to be charged — it can be described as a pipe that has to be filled before anything arrives at the other end. Therefore the propagation time increases with the length of the connection, and also with the fan-out. With light these problems do not exist — it always propagates at the speed of light (modulo the refractive index of the medium).

No interferences

Electrons interact strongly with each other, through the Coulomb force. This is an asset when designing a logic gate, where one input *should* influence the other. It is a severe limitation in the context of interconnections, where the data should pass unaffected. Electronic interconnections must be laid some distance apart, so as to prevent crosstalk (the undesired leakage of a signal from one channel to another).

Electrons in a metallic conductor also interact with electromagnetic radiation: the conductor simply serves as an antenna. Thus electronic interconnections are susceptible to electromagnetic interference.

Photons, on the other hand, do not interact with each other or with other radiation. This is a drawback in the implementation of optical logic, but a great asset in optical interconnections. Indeed, beams of light carrying information can even cross each other without trouble.

Density and parallelism

Each electronic interconnection path must be wired individually, and these wires must be evenly spaced. The layout of an electronic interconnection system is therefore quite difficult to plan. As light beams do not interact, optical interconnections need not be guided at all — the light can just propagate freely in space, with different communication channels crossing each other. Numerous distinct channels may thus utilize the same space. The possible interconnection density is therefore much larger [301].

Dynamic reconfiguration

As we shall see, optical interconnection patterns are often controlled by holograms and masks. If these elements are implemented by spatial light modulators (SLMs), they can be dynamically reconfigured. Thus the interconnection pattern may be modified in real time [462,262,613]. This is not yet a realistic proposition, as current SLMs are too slow and provide only limited resolution. However, even the possibility of changing the interconnection pattern only once every few milliseconds might be enough in some applications. For example, it would allow for the tailoring of a multiprocessor interconnection network so as to fit the algorithm of the next program to be run on the system [403].

What cannot be done

Two additional properties that are sometimes cited as true of optical interconnection systems are actually not so true:

- Extremely short light pulses, only 8 fs long, have been observed [614]. As data bits are represented by pulses of light, this seems to indicate the possibility of data rates in the 10^{14} bps range. The problem is that with current technology only a few thousand such pulses can be generated each second. If we want a continuous stream of them we must divide each pulse, of duration τ, into $\frac{T}{\tau}$ channels, where T is the cycle time, and then recombine them with delays of $\tau, 2\tau, \cdots, (\frac{T}{\tau} - 1)\tau$ [143]. This is expensive to do.

Another problem with these extremely short pulses is that they are also very short in it length — only about 1μm long. This implies that they cannot be used in free-space interconnection schemes (described in section 7.6.4), as the path differences in such systems are typically at least a 100μm long. The short pulses will be totally smeared and mixed in such systems [611].

- Unlimited fan-in and fan-out are not practical. When N beams are combined with beam splitters or holographic elements, only $\frac{1}{N}$ of the total power finds its way into the combined beam. this is so because the input beams are actually split, and only one part of each one is used. With a fan-out of N the same thing occurs: each channel receives only $\frac{1}{N}$ of the power [266]. However, the possible fan-outs are larger than for comparable electronic interconnection schemes, operating at the same data rate. The limit is set by the sensitivity of the detectors [301].

7.6.2   Interconnection needs

In order to assess the applicability of optical schemes to interconnections inside a computer, let us first look at the requirements and problems of electronic computers. There are three hierarchies of interconnection [262,331,368]:

- *Interconnections on a chip.*
  This is one of the greatest problems in integrated circuits. As the elements on a chip are scaled down, more elements can be packed into a given space. These smaller elements also operate faster. More elements require more connections, and placing all these connections on a 2-D surface (or a number of surfaces) is a difficult optimization problem that makes VLSI layout costly. When this is settled, there are other difficulties: One is that the interconnect delay does *not* scale down. This is because scaling down by a factor of α reduces the capacitance of the lines by a factor of α, but increases the resistance by the same factor. The delay is proportional to their product, and remains constant. Another is that there usually is a large variance in the lengths of different interconnections, and so there is a large variance in delays. This variance might cause synchronization difficulties. As the basic switching times of the elements becomes shorter, these interconnection delay problems become a limiting factor.

- *Interconnections between chips on a board.*
  The number of pins that connect a chip to the outside world is severely limited by size considerations, and the fact that all connections are made along

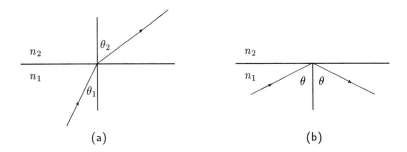

Figure 7.25: (a) A ray is refracted when it passes from a medium of one refractive index to a medium of a different refractive index.
(b) Total internal reflection occurs if the incident angle is above the critical value.

the edges only. The typical solution to this problem is to incorporate multiplexers (i.e., parallel-to-serial converters) in the chip [324], and use the few available connections for a multitude of tasks. This increases the complexity of the system, wastes chip area, and might also degrade performance.

- *Interconnections between boards and modules.*
  At this level a large bandwidth is usually required, coupled with high connectivity. Again compromises are made when the hardware needed in order to meet the requirements is excessive. For example, a bus allows only one interchange of information to take place at a time. A crossbar switch allows multiple interchanges in parallel, but it is more complex and expensive.

7.6.3   Fiberoptics

It is impractical to transmit light through air for long distances as radio waves are transmitted. the reason is the very high frequency of light, which causes it to propagate in a different manner. while radio waves tend to spread out a bit, and thus are able to "get around" obstacles, light beams tend to stay straight. If we do not want to risk a communication failure every time a flock of geese happens to fly through the beam, we must therefore seek a medium that will safely conduct the light to wherever it should go. The chosen medium is one composed of optical fibers.

An optical fiber is a conductor, or *waveguide*, for light. The propagation of light in (bent) optical fibers is explained by the phenomenon of *total internal reflection* (fig. 7.25) [351]. The fiber's cross section has two parts: a core and a cladding. The difference between them is that the core has a higher index of refraction. Denote these indices by n_1 (core) and n_2 (cladding). A beam of light that hits

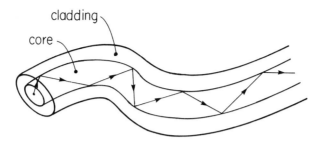

Figure 7.26: *Light advancing in an optical fiber follows a zigzag course.*

the core/cladding interface at an angle θ_1 (from the core side) is refracted, and emerges at an angle θ_2 (on the cladding side). These angles satisfy the relation

$$n_1 \, \sin \theta_1 = n_2 \, \sin \theta_2 \qquad \text{(Snell's law)}.$$

Since $n_1 > n_2$, then $\theta_1 < \theta_2$ (all angles are in the first quadrant).

If θ_1 is larger than the critical value of $\arcsin(n_2/n_1)$, the formula cannot be valid, because it would require that $\sin \theta_2 > 1$. Indeed, for these angles the beam is not refracted. Instead it is reflected back into the core. When a beam of light propagates along an optical fiber, it actually follows the zig-zag path that results from internal reflections each time it hits the core/cladding interface (fig. 7.26). Additional details may be found in appendix H.

The use of fiberoptics has risen steadily in the last few years. Most of the research work in this field, however, relates to problems arising in long-distance communication via fibers, which is largely irrelevant to digital optical computers (see bibliographical notes).

Fiberoptics are already also being used in local area networks, e.g., to connect computers to peripherals (see page 257) It has been suggested that they may be used even at a smaller scale, for connections between boards and chips [262]. Their advantages over electronic interconnections are bandwidth allowing higher data rates), and the possibility of connecting to any point on the chip. If that is the case with electronic computers, then fiberoptics will of course provide good interconnections for optical computers as well. At the chip level it is unreasonable to use independent optical fibers — rather, they too should be integrated into the chip. Such ideas are treated in chapter 8, which deals with integrated optics.

7.6.4   Free-space interconnections

Within the confines of an optical computer, there is actually no reason to conduct the light in optical fibers — the distances are short, and no geese are present. It

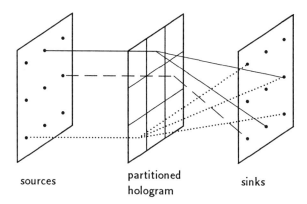

sources   partitioned   sinks
                   hologram

Figure 7.27: *Schematic representation of a holographic interconnection element.*

is perfectly possible for beams of light carrying information to simply crisscross the space between the various elements. As light beams do not interact when one passes through the other, there is no danger of crosstalk. The advantages of the so called *free-space* interconnection scheme stem from the fact that the third dimension of space is utilized, instead of confining the interconnection topology to a 2-D surface. This alleviates many topological difficulties. It also allows for direct communication to the interior of a chip, as opposed to communication only along the edges. As a consequence, it makes many concurrent interconnections possible. These advantages make free-space interconnections seem profitable for inter-chip and even intra-chip communication (see page 260).

The main issue in free-space interconnection is how to direct the many beams of light and focus them on the right ports. Two primary techniques have emerged: one uses holographic optical elements, and the other uses lenslet arrays.

Holographic interconnection

As mentioned in section 2.8.2, holograms (and especially computer generated holograms) may be used to implement optical elements with arbitrary characteristics. Assume a single source of light. A simple hologram, similar to a diffraction grating, can deflect its light in any desired direction (depending on the orientation of the grating), and focus it on a sink[15]. A more complicated hologram can create multiple images of the source, each on a different sink. In the general case we have a set of sources, a set of sinks, and an arbitrary mapping of sources to sinks. In order to implement this mapping, the hologram is divided into subholograms, one

---

[15]Note that we use the term "sink" instead of "detector". This is because in an optical computer we use the light itself — we do not detect it and turn it into an electrical current.

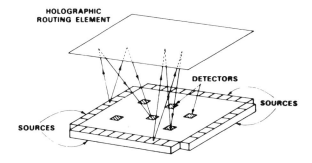

Figure 7.28: *A possible configuration of sources, sinks, and a reflective holographic interconnection element.*
(Reprinted with permission from the *Proceedings of the IEEE* [262], ©1984 IEEE)

for each source [596,340,342,382]. Each subhologram is illuminated by one source only, and it images that source on the appropriate sinks (fig. 7.27).

As each subhologram must have a minimal size, this method limits the number of elements that can be connected. If there is some regularity is the interconnection pattern of different elements, however, the number of subholograms needed may be dramatically reduced. A simple special case is where all sources have the same interconnection pattern (for instance in an implementation of a certain gate array). Then all sources may use the same hologram. Even if the interconnection patterns differ slightly, it might be possible to find a *basis* for the interconnection space. This means that it might be possible to express all the different patterns as combinations of a small number of basic patterns. If this is the case, only the basis interconnections are implemented by the hologram, and each source can implement its specific interconnections by using a linear combination of the basis interconnections. This requires an additional hologram that implements the mapping from sources to linear combinations of basis elements.

Free-space interconnections utilize three-dimensional space. There are various ways in which to set up the sources, sinks, and hologram [262]. The most compact scheme is to have the sources and sinks arranged in a plane, with a reflection hologram suspended above them (fig. 7.28). Other schemes use transmission holograms instead of reflection ones, and then redirect the light with mirrors. If the hologram is implemented by an SLM, rather than being fixed, the interconnection pattern may be changed dynamically [462,262].

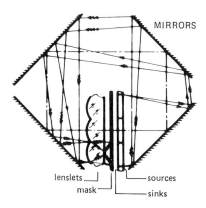

Figure 7.29: *A lenslet array interconnection device.*
(Reprinted with permission from *Optics Letters* [248], ©1986)

Lenslet arrays [248,543]

A lenslet array is just an array of small, simple lenses. These lenses are used to image *all* the sources on each and every one of the sinks. By inserting a mask before the sinks, only light from the desired sources actually reaches the sink. We now describe a possible configuration in more detail (fig. 7.29). Arrange the elements to be interconnected into a square, 2-D planar array. Each element has a source on one side and a sink on the other. A set of mirrors reflects the light distribution of the sources side to the sinks side, where it falls on a lenslet array. There is one lenslet in front of each sink. The lenslet array is placed so that an image of the sources is formed on a mask at the entrance to each sink. Assume we have N^2 elements. Then the mask will be composed of N^2 submasks (one for each element), and each sub-mask will be composed of N^2 small squares (one for each possible connection). If the source at coordinates (i, j) should be connected to the sink at coordinates (k, l), the $(i, j)^{th}$ square in the $(k, l)^{th}$ submask will be transparent. Otherwise it will be opaque (fig. 7.30).

Lenslet arrays have an advantage over holographic interconnections in that they do not require coherent light. They have the disadvantage in that a compact configuration like that of the reflection hologram is not practical — more open space is required to direct the light onto the appropriate sinks. Both methods require careful alignment of the interconnection components: the hologram or the lenslet array and mask [249].

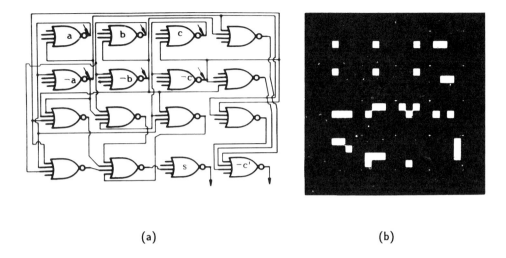

(a)   (b)

Figure 7.30:
(a) One bit full-adder implemented by a NOR *gate array with 16 gates.*
(b) Mask for optical implementation of the interconnections in the gate array, using a lenslet device.
(Reprinted with permission from *Optics Letters* [248], ©1986)

7.6.5   Communication methods from electronic computers

Many different communication schemes have been devised for electronic computers, at the high level of board-to-board communication or communication between modules. Some of these schemes have optical implementations. We shall review three of these: the bus, the crossbar switch, and the perfect shuffle network.

Bus

A bus is a common transmission medium, used by all the communicating entities. At each moment, at most one user is transmitting a message on the bus, while all the others listen. The message begins with an address. A module that finds out that the current message is not addressed to it simply ignores the message. Typical busses in electronic systems are constructed of a number of wires in parallel; each wire serves as a carrier for one bit. Thus a whole word of data may be transmitted in parallel.

The optical implementation of a bus is simply an optical fiber. The different modules access the information flowing in the fiber by means of special couplers. These couplers are curved pieces of fiber that touch the main fiber; their operation is similar to that of directional couplers, explained in section 8.3.2 [491,675]. The bits are transmitted serially, rather than in parallel. In this way, only one fiber is needed, and each port needs only one detector and one laser diode [301].

Crossbar switch

The crossbar is a general switch device that can connect any of N inputs to any of N outputs. The operation of a crossbar can be viewed as a matrix-vector multiplication [596]: the multiplying vector is the vector of inputs. The matrix is a binary one, with the $(i, j)^{th}$ element equal to 1 if input i connects to output j, and 0 otherwise. The product of this multiplication is the vector of outputs.

Matrix-vector multiplications are easily implemented in optics, and crossbar switches have indeed been implemented in this way [469,597,598,159]. The details are given in section 4.3.1. Crossbars are usually not implemented in electronic computers, because they would require N^2 individual switches; they are used in telephone exchanges. However, the optical implementations are also not yet practical, as the time required to set the matrix describing the connections is rather long.

Shuffle-exchange network

One of the alternatives to the costly crossbar switch is the shuffle-exchange network. The "shuffle" operation on a vector means to divide it into two equal parts and then to interleave them (the name derives from the perfect shuffling of a deck of cards). Mathematically this is equivalent to a cyclic permutation (to the left) of the binary addresses of the vector elements (i.e., element 100110 moves to position 001101). When the option to exchange pairs of neighboring elements is added to a perfect shuffle network, any arbitrary permutation of the elements is achievable in a small number of steps. This type of network has received much attention in computer science literature [648,395,736,55].

The perfect shuffle can be realized by using only simple, classical optical components: lenses and prisms (fig. 7.31) [433,432]. A first set of prisms separates the input into two halves. A lens then Fourier-transforms these two halves separately. A second pair of prisms causes a shift in the Fourier plane, and thus stretches each half to the size of the whole input vector. A second lens performs the inverse Fourier transform, and the two interleaved halves emerge. The input elements must not be contiguous, so that they will not overlap after the stretching. Another somewhat different configuration has also been proposed [198].

In order to be useful, the network must also provide for the inverse operation: the "unshuffle". This amounts to separating the even-numbered elements from the odd ones. This operation can be achieved optically by reversing the above system, and adding an array of small prisms that would direct even inputs to one direction and odd inputs to the other direction. Alternatively, a sequence of $\log N - 1$ shuffle operations can be performed; this is equivalent to one unshuffle.

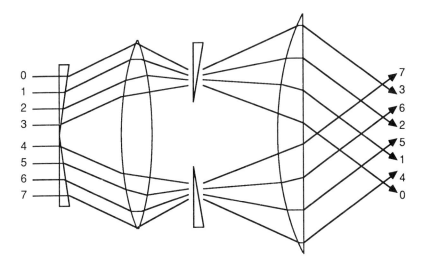

Figure 7.31: *Optical implementation of the perfect shuffle.*
(Adapted with permission from *Applied Optics* [433], ©1986)

This system is easily extended into a 2-D perfect shuffle that performs a perfect shuffle on rows and on columns simultaneously: each prism is just replaced by a pair of orthogonal prisms. The motivation for a 2-D system is that it better utilizes the optical components. It is just as useful, because a 2-D shuffle exchange network of size $N \times N$ can be used to perform the functions of a linear shuffle-exchange network of size N^2 [592].

7.7   Architectures

Broadly speaking, the architecture of electronic computers supports the Von Neumann model: a CPU manipulates the contents of the memory by running through a serial program; for each instruction data is loaded from the memory to the CPU's internal registers, and the result is stored back in the memory. The technology used to implement these computers is based on planar integrated circuits. A possible approach to choosing an architecture for optical computers is to simply copy the very successful electronic precedence, replacing electronic logic elements by optical ones, and interconnection wires by optical waveguides [728]. This results in an "integrated optics" technology, which is surveyed in chapter 8. However, this approach requires each of the optical elements to be highly superior to the functionally equivalent electronic ones in order to justify the transition to optics; specifically, the optical elements should be faster by at least two orders of magnitude [580]. As it is not clear whether such expectations are practical (see the discussion in section 8.6.1), many researchers feel that a radically different architecture should be pursued.

The architecture[16] of a computer should be related to the capabilities of the underlying technology. In the case of optical computers, the possibility of dense interconnections coupled with little interference implies that parallel architectures might be fitting. A beam of light may contain millions of resolvable points, each of which may be used as a distinct data channel. As the beam traverses an optical system, various operations are performed on all the points in parallel. Therefore the parallel architecture that seems most suitable to an optical computer is that of an SIMD (Single Instruction-stream Multiple Data-stream) machine[17] [607,226,227]. It should be noted that this is a low-level SIMD architecture: the parallelism is at the gate level rather than at the processor level. Instead of having multiple processors all running the same program, each *gate* performs its function on all the data in parallel.

The basic data element in this architecture is not a byte or a word but rather a 2-D (binary) image. All the data paths, logic elements, and memory devices should be able to handle a whole image in one step.

7.7.1 Arrays of gates

When we say a gate performs its function on all the distinct data channels concurrently, we are actually speaking of an array of gates, each dealing with one data channel. This is *not* the same as the gate arrays in conventional electronic computers. The conventional gate arrays are arrays of interconnected, identical gates (like the NOR array in fig 7.30 (a)). The data passes from one gate to another in the array. In the optical gate arrays discussed here, there are no interconnections. Each gate operates on a distinct data stream.

All the binary logic implementations described in the preceding sections are easily extended to arrays of logic elements. Indeed, most of them were originally described in the literature as arrays, and not as single elements. For example, in a threshold-logic element based on an etalon, the nonlinearity at each point depends only on the *local* incident light intensity. Therefore spatially distinct areas of the etalon, illuminated by different beams, may implement distinct gates. This conceptual division is enhanced if the etalon is also physically etched into isolated pads, each a few microns across, because then crosstalk is reduced [345]. Arrays of 100×100 devices have already been demonstrated (fig. 7.32) [705]. The

---

[16]Actually the term "structure" might be more appropriate, as we are dealing with how the various components are put together. "Architecture" is also used to define the interface that the computer presents to the operating system software.

[17]This is a parallel architecture in which at any given moment one instruction is being applied to many data elements.

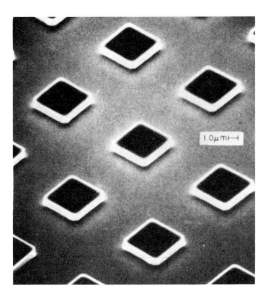

Figure 7.32: *Scanning electron microscope picture of part of a 100 × 100 array of bistable devices, of the Fabry-Perot etalon type. Each device is about 9 μm across.*
(Reprinted with permission from *Applied Physics Letters* [705], ©1986)

same applies to logic gates implemented by reflections from an LCLV. We can conceptually divided the LCLV into numerous elements, each giving an individual reflection. With the shadow casting system, an array of input masks is used instead of one input mask, and an array of detectors instead of one detector (fig. 7.33).

7.7.2   Proposed optical computers

A number of preliminary proposals that attempt to show how a complete processor can be made have been presented over the years. A few are surveyed in the following. These proposals do not enjoy all the possible advantages of optical systems, and do not incorporate all the new ideas. More work is therefore required before an optical computer that satisfies the many expectations will emerge. We start with the proposal that is most similar to conventional electronic computers, and then move on to those that are more and more unique.

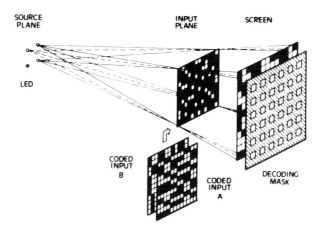

Figure 7.33: *Multiple element shadow casting system.*
(Reprinted with permission from the *Proceedings of the IEEE* [332], ©1984 IEEE)

Hybrid computers

The least ambitious architecture is that of a hybrid electronic/optical computer, in which the processing is done electronically but the interconnections are optical. This idea seeks to combine the mature and proved electronic devices with the improved capabilities of optical communication systems.

A good example is the tse[18] computer, which is actually just a general purpose electronic digital computer, duplicated a large number of times [599]. The optical interconnections are used as a means to achieve a highly parallel architecture.

We consider a 128×128 element tse computer. This means that each and every gate that is used in a conventional computer is duplicated 16,384 ($= 128^2$) times. Each interconnection wire is replaced by a fiberoptic bundle containing 16,384 fibers. The fibers are interfaced with the (electronic) gates by means of detectors and light emitting elements. In places where data links combine or diverge, a special interleaver/duplicator is used. This is a trapezoidal, layered construction of optical fibers, which accepts two input images at the large base and interleaves them to create an output image at the small base. When used in reverse, an input at the small base is duplicated at both outputs at the large base. To do this, even layers contain fibers from one half of the long base to the short base, while odd layers contain fibers from the other half (fig. 7.34).

Thus we have created the equivalent of 16,384 independent computers. The

---

[18]"Tse" is the English transliteration of the Chinese word for "pictograph character". The name derives from the use of images as the basic data element.

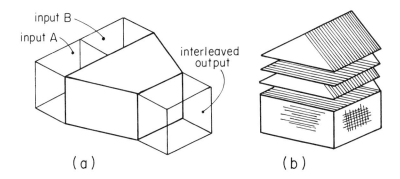

Figure 7.34: *(a) Tse interleaver/duplicator.*
(b) Layered structure used to implement it.

final step in creating a tse computer is to allow all these computers to intercommunicate by the use of "sliders" — optical fiber bundles in which the output is a cyclic shift of the input. Sliders operate in one dimension, and come in various sizes. In order to implement all possible shifts in the vertical direction of a 128×128 image, for example, 7 sliders are required: The first takes the top row and moves it to the bottom, the second takes the top two rows to the bottom, the third four rows etc. The seventh takes 64 rows, i.e., it switches the upper and lower halves of the image. Arbitrary shifts are realized by using a subset of these sliders in sequence.

The structure of a tse ALU is very similar to the ALU of a conventional computer (fig. 7.35): it can perform various arithmetic or logical operations on the data, as dictated by the instructions it receives. One difference is that the option of sliding the input is added. Another is that the instruction lines are also 16,384-fiber bundles, rather than single lines. This allows a tse machine to operate as an MIMD machine, because each of the 16,384 subcomputers may be controlled and programmed independently. Therefore the power of a tse machine is quite formidable: on the one hand it can act as a 16,384-channel SIMD machine, running a conventional program, and on the other it can become a massive MIMD machine, which requires special programming.

A prototype tse had been under development in 1977. The main problem encountered was insufficiently accurate alignment of the short optical fiber bundles that were used to interconnect the various elements of the computer. In 1980 the optical interconnections were dropped in favor of a totally electronic machine. In addition, the concept of sliders was abandoned: the interconnections between processors were limited to the four nearest neighbors. The only mode of operation was SIMD. The final result was the Goodyear MPP (Massively Parallel Processor),

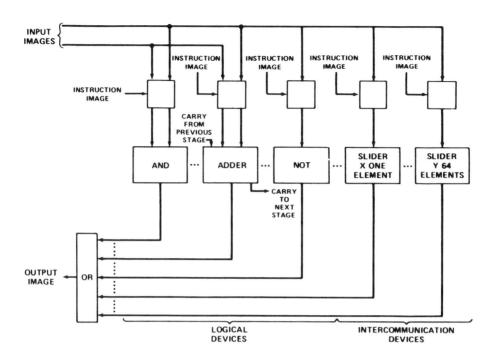

Figure 7.35: *Tse computer ALU.*
(Reprinted with permission from the *Proceedings of the IEEE* [599], ⓒ1977 IEEE)

which was developed for image processing tasks in NASA [600,51,551].

Cellular architectures

The concept of cellular logic is well known and has received much attention, especially in the field of image processing [556,588]. The basic idea is to have a 2-D array of processors, where each is connected to its near neighbors (together they form a "cell"). The primary operations in such a system are those that only require data from near neighbors, e.g., convolutions with a small kernel.

Several ideas concerning optical implementations of cellular logic have been proposed [743]. For example, if the desired operation really is a convolution, analog optical systems can be used to carry it out. Another idea is to use truth-table look-up — this is based on the fact that the cell is small, and therefore the table need not be large (e.g., for a 3×3 cell, there are $2^9 = 512$ possible combinations). Still another idea is to use a lenslet array in order to implement

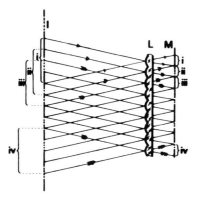

Figure 7.36: *Lenslet array configuration for local interconnections only.*
(Reprinted with permission from *Applied Optics* [249], ©1982)

the local interconnections (fig. 7.36). In this case the lenslets will form an image of a local area only, instead of forming an image of the whole output plane as described on page 214.

The above ideas address the concept of optical cellular operations, but do not go into the details of a whole processor. An attempt to do so is OPALS (Optical Parallel Array Logic System) [668,669,670,671]. OPALS operation is based on shadow casting (section 7.2.7). The input pixels are coded by horizontal and vertical stripes, and superimposed. This gives 4 distinct code patterns, corresponding to the 4 possible input pixel combinations. The resulting image is illuminated by an array of light sources, giving rise to overlapping shadows with various lateral shifts. The LED array is larger than 2×2, so that the shifts allow for interactions between neighboring pixels. The signals sampled at the centers of pixels in the overlapping shadow pattern are the outputs. In OPALS, not all the binary logic functions are used. Rather, the desired functions are viewed in disjunctive normal form and computed in iterations: each time one AND term is computed, and then it is OR'ed with the result of previous iterations. The output is latched for use in the next iteration (fig. 7.37).

Pipelined dataflow machines

In Von Neumann architecture, which is the basis of contemporary electronic computers, the memory is used to store intermediate results for further use. Only a small number of memory elements are accessed in each cycle. This scheme has some disadvantages. One is that the desired memory element must be identified by its address. Indeed, a large portion of the activity of conventional computers

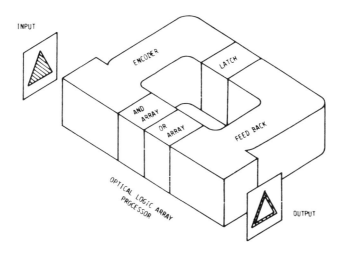

Figure 7.37: *Schematic view of OPALS.*
(Reprinted with permission from *Applied Optics* [669], ©1986)

is devoted to keeping track of where the information is, rather than to performing useful calculations on the information. Another is that most of the hardware is idle most of the time: all the memory cells which do not participate in the current step just sit and wait. A consequence of Von Neumann architecture is the so-called Von Neumann bottleneck [37,38], which refers to the performance limitations imposed by the inherently serial character of the communication between the CPU and the memory.

A possible alternative to Von Neumann architecture is that of a dataflow machine. The idea is that every operation is carried out by its own little module, and these modules send their output directly to the other modules that need to use this data [615]. Thus the data flows through the system in parallel, and it is used as soon as it is produced. The reason that electronic computers follow Von Neumann architecture rather than dataflow architecture is that dataflow is not practical: it requires too many interconnections.

Optical systems are known to be inherently suited to massively parallel communication schemes. This suggests the possibility of creating an optical computer that follows the ideas of dataflow, rather than those of the Von Neumann computer. To simplify matters, some structure ought to be imposed on the interconnection network. For example, the computing modules might be arranged in successive stages, and the data will be pipelined in parallel from one stage to the next [324,326]. A more compact alternative is to create a circular pipeline, in which 2-D arrays of modules alternate with interconnection devices (e.g., holograms) [627,629]. While this undermines the concept of dataflow to some degree, in the sense that local synchronization by the availability of the data is replaced by global synchronization of the whole network, it allows for a feasible architecture that is easier to program.

A few such systems have been proposed[19]. The pipeline scheme has been suggested with logic elements that are either NOR gates with an invariant interconnection pattern, or special function/interconnection modules composed of AND gates. The loop scheme has been used to demonstrate the cascadability of optical logic gates based on bistable devices.

Neural computers [2,565,346,451]

Conventional computers, regardless of their various shortcomings, are very successful in the solution of structured problems. Such problems are characterized by the fact that they are solvable by the repeated application of a sequence of operations, i.e., by an algorithm that may be defined in concise terms. However, not all problems are like that. There are a large number of problems that we do not know how to solve by means of a well-defined proved algorithm. At best we can suggest some sort of heuristic procedure. Examples for such problems are the recognition of a face, or the evaluation of the situation in a chess game.

If we try to analyze how we as humans solve these problems, it seems that we do so by drawing on a large bank of experience, accumulated by trial and error over the years. This suggests that computers with large memories and associative reasoning powers might be needed if we want to solve such problems mechanically. Models with these capabilities have recently been proposed, e.g., the Hopfield model of neural networks (see page 122). As these models lend themselves to optical implementation this is another possible direction for optical computers. It might be misleading to discuss such ideas under the heading of possible architectures for general-purpose digital computers, as they differ radically from conventional electronic architectures. However, optics *is* different from electronics, and maybe this unusual architecture will be the one which allows optical computers to achieve sufficient advantages to make them worthwhile.

The name "neural computer" derives from the fact that a good policy seems to be to mimic the structure of the human brain, or at least a simplified model of it. The architecture is then comprised of multiple simple processing elements that are connected to each other. This is a viable approach for an optical computer, but not for an electronic one, because of the dense interconnection pattern that is necessary. The elements themselves can be electronic to start with, leaving all-optical systems as an ultimate goal. The interconnection scheme dictates the function of the whole, e.g., the extraction of features from a light distribution

---

[19]Usually the somewhat ambiguous term "classical finite state machine" is used to introduce them.

imaged on the top plane of "neural" elements.

Alternative optical realizations of associative memory are reviewed in section 9.3.6.

Summary

Optical computers will use a totally new technology, which is quite different from that of existing electronic machines. Many design decisions have to be made in the process of their development. Even basic issues such as the use of binary or multilevel logic, the representation of the basic values, and the number system, have not yet been resolved.

Numerous techniques for the implementation of optical logic elements have been proposed, and many have also been demonstrated. Some of these techniques follow ideas from electronic computers, e.g., the realization of logic by an optical equivalent of the electronic transistor, or by table look-up. Others resemble classical optical systems, e.g., logic by spatial filtering or shadow casting. The most advanced proposal, that of threshold logic by bistable devices, falls in between. A number of special optical arithmetic units have also been proposed.

Storage schemes for optical computers have not yet been devised; however we can get a good idea of the possibilities from the optical devices created for electronic computers. These include mass storage and archival systems, using holograms or optical disks. If such devices are adopted for optical computers, some changes in the tasks of the operating system are implied.

Optical interconnections have so far been developed more for electronic computers than for optical ones. The guided communication lines known from electronics are augmented by the possibility of free-space interconnections. This is a major advantage, as it alleviates layout problems and allows for much more dense interconnections.

As the development of digital optical computers is still at an early stage, and the it is not yet clear what devices will be used, it is premature to talk about architectures. However, it is already apparent that digital optical computers will be parallel in nature, as their chief advantages stem from their inherent parallelism. More specifically, optical computers are expected to be SIMD machines, i.e., they will perform the same operations on many data streams in parallel.

Bibliographical notes

The best collection of papers about DOCs is probably the July 1984 special issue of the Proceedings of the IEEE [522]. Applied Optics also had a few recent special issues on the subject [523,548]. The January issues of Optical Engineering are also devoted to it [524,185,525]. Individual papers that provide the best introductory surveys are those by Jahns [338] and Sawchuk [596].

The papers relating to each of the optical logic implementations are cited in the text. The threshold method based on optical bistability has been subject to intensive study over the past years, under the European Joint Optical Bistability Project (EJOB). The final report of this project was published by Elsevier Editions, Brussels. It should be noted that only the most prominent proposals for optical logic have been reviewed in the present text; numerous additional proposals have been made lately, based on various phenomena and devices. Most of these ideas have not been followed up even by the people that suggested them; they just show that logic can be done in another way, without showing any distinct advantage over other methods. The most interesting additional methods are those involving optical Fredkin gates [612,174,231], the QWEST effect [728], and the Pockels effect [492,493,494].

In the case of arithmetic devices, the situation is slightly better. Nearly all researchers concentrate on the fixed radix and residue systems. A special issue of Applied Optics is a collection [548]. A few secondary systems and techniques have not been reviewed here [34,142,200,272].

Papers about optical memory devices are collected in a number of special issues [530,710,397]. A table comparing commercial optical disks is given in [182]. Holographic mass storage systems are described in [647,576,697,41,179].

Fiberoptics are reviewed in numerous publications, e.g., [510,163,87,70,358,352, 350,429].

Chapter 8

Feasibility and Technology

In the preceding chapter, the principles underlying possible implementations of digital optical computers were reviewed. We saw that all the basic elements of a digital computer can indeed be implemented by optical devices. However, most of the optical systems involved have only been demonstrated in a laboratory environment. They are usually large and crude, requiring a lot of accurate adjustments in order to function correctly. In addition, they have only been demonstrated on an individual basis — no attempts have been made to actually put them all together, to form one integrated optical computer.

This chapter addresses the feasibility of creating digital optical computers. In doing so, two things have to be taken into account. First come issues related to the individual components: will it be possible to mass produce them at a low price, will they be reliable, will their operating conditions and performance be good? Then issues relating to the computer as a whole need be investigated: these include the interactions among the different components, input and output, and the general performance and capabilities of the machine. These global issues depend to a large degree on the settling of questions regarding the individual components. As this has not yet been done in the case of optical computers, it seems premature to discuss them. We will therefore concentrate once again on the individual devices.

The recent success of electronic computers is largely due to integrated circuit technology. Many people therefore expect that optical computers will also have to rely on similar concepts (e.g., [728]). This assumption rests on the observation that integration will solve a number of general problems that plague bulk optical computing systems [458]:

- The physical space required by bulk systems is usually large. Integrated optical circuits will be much smaller.

- Alignment and adjustment problems are a major factor that contributes to the cost of optical systems. The components of integrated circuits are fabricated in place on a rigid substrate, and therefore do not require individual attention.

- Bulk systems are relatively sensitive to thermal and vibrational influences from the environment — That is why heavy, isolated tables are used in optics laboratories. Integrated circuits will be more robust.

- Bulk systems are hard to reproduce. The possible use of high-precision integrated circuit fabrication techniques for mass production is therefore appealing.

In this chapter we combine a feasibility study of optical computers with the idea of implementing them by using integrated optics technology [334]. Note that this limits the architecture and makes it a copy of conventional electronic machines, with computational elements connected by communication channels. Our discussion begins by considering miniaturization and its applicability to optical circuits. We then look into some details of integrated optics: first the ideas and methods used with thin films, which are the backbone of integrated optics technology, and then the implementation of various devices. Finally the feasibility and limitations of miniaturized optical devices, and integrated optical circuits in particular, are discussed. The last section asks whether the concept of integrated optics is indeed the right thing for digital optical computers, and reviews other possibilities.

8.1   Miniaturization

It is clear that today's electronic computers have greatly benefited from miniaturization[1]. A typical electronic processing element of today may contain thousands of logic gates. These are realized by means of tens or hundreds of thousands of transistors [304]. There are a number of points that motivate attempts to miniaturize these devices [363,475]:

- *Reduced size.* Had components the size of ten years ago been used, the sheer size of a computer with so many of them would have made it unpractical.

- *Speed.* When transistors are reduced in size, their switching time is also reduced. In addition, small devices allow for dense packing and thus shorter communication distances.

- *Low power consumption.* Smaller devices require less power. The excess energy that must be dissipated is also reduced.

- *Economics.* Mass production of miniature components can make the price of each one very low, and also reduce the price of the machine as a whole.

- *High reliability.* The technologies used in the fabrication of miniature devices insure high reliability, meeting the most stringent requirements.

---

[1]There is a problem with terminology here, as "miniaturization" is not an absolute term. What we consider to be miniature today might look like an elephant in a few years. We'll use the word anyway, with the understanding that we refer to the current state of affairs, and that things might change.

It is interesting to note the degree to which these points are also applicable to optical circuits. Reduced size is of course welcome in optical computers too. The obtainable reduction is limited, however. Whereas in VLSI the minimal feature size is determined by the technology and by the microscopic characteristics of the materials, In optics the minimal feature size corresponds to the wavelength of the light [377]. The size of optical elements must be at least a few wavelengths: light simply cannot be confined to a cross section of much less than a wavelength, i.e., approximately 1μm. At the moment it so happens that VLSI technology produces features that are about of this size too. It is already obvious, however, that it will be impossible to miniaturize optical devices to the same degree that is possible in electronics, as it is expected that electronic devices will be reduced by at least another order of magnitude before reaching their limit [608].

Another difficulty with the miniaturization of optical devices is that some devices simply must be large. The reason might be that the device geometry depends on the wavelength in some way; for example, a resonator might be a certain number of wavelengths long. The problem is that when the size of the device is reduced, the wavelength is not: the same light source is used. Therefore the reduced device size will not fit the wavelength, and the device will not function correctly. Another possible reason for not being able to miniaturize a device is that the device might depend on certain interactions between light and matter. If the interactions are weak, a long interaction length must be used to compensate.

Higher speed is an important benefit of miniaturization. The computing time of a logic circuit is the sum of two parts: the switching time of the gates and the interconnection delay. When an electronic circuit is reduced in size[2], it is only the switching time that scales down [595,475]. With current technology, the switching time has been reduced so much that the interconnection delay is becoming the dominant source of timing and synchronization problems. Optical circuits fare better: in optics, the interconnection delay depends only on the interconnection length, so it scales down too. This might prove to be one of the most important advantages of optics over electronics.

When it comes to power consumption, we see that optical circuits relying on optical nonlinearities may require relatively high powers. The reason is that the nonlinear effects only appear at high intensities. When the devices are subject to low power only, their response is linear, and they cannot be used for computation. The reason that power is consumed is that practical computation is irreversible (for instance, you cannot reconstruct the inputs of an AND gate from its output). In theory this need not be so, and a reversible computer can be thought of [231, 57,58,394]. However, such a computer will have to be very slow, so as to always be in thermodynamic equilibrium with its environment.

---

[2]This refers to shrinking in all three dimensions. Specifically, the interconnection line *width* and *height* are diminished in the same manner as the *length*.

The problem is aggravated by the fact that the power consumption increases as the switching time decreases [362]. Let us take a Fabry-Perot bistable device (section 6.2) as an example. If the length of the cavity is reduced, a larger nonlinearity is needed in order to cause switching. This implies higher light intensities. Thus the reduction in size (that reduces the switching time) necessitates an increase in power.

The subjects of cost and reliability strongly depend on the manufacturing technologies. As these technologies are not yet advanced in the case of optical circuits, it is too soon to judge these aspects of miniaturization in regard to optical systems.

8.2 Thin film waveguides

Having outlined the concept of miniaturization and some of its implications in connection with optical devices, we now turn to implementation techniques. Specifically, the next few sections deal with optical integrated circuits [489,680,376,673, 334].

8.2.1 Principles

Up to a certain limit, free-space communication is very attractive for interconnections between devices. On the very small scales typical in integrated circuits, however, diffraction effects become important. Narrow beams of light do not stay narrow and straight — they diverge widely, and even curve around obstacles. As a result, free-space interconnections are usually not appropriate, and the light must be conducted along special waveguides. These waveguides follow the same principles as the optical fibers described in section 7.6.3, but the details are different.

The analog of the fiberoptic core is a thin film of a dielectric material with a high refractive index, that is deposited on (or in) a substrate with a lower refractive index [490,681,162,257]. The difference in refractive indices may be quite small, on the order of 1% [489]. The film may be covered by another layer, also with a lower refractive index, but we consider here the simple case where the cover is air. The film is usually laid down in strips of rectangular cross section, which serve as waveguides that confine the light to a one-dimensional channel. Thus the light is forced to propagate in the desired direction. However not all the energy of the light is confined in the higher-index strip. The light's electromagnetic fields may also be detected a short distance out of the strip[3]. This phenomenon is useful when you want to couple two strips and cause an interaction between them (as we will see in section 8.3.2); it is aggravating when you want to diminish crosstalk.

---

[3]These are called *evanescent* fields.

8.2.2   Materials

The effectiveness of physical processes in integrated circuits depend heavily on the materials employed. Today, electronic integrated circuits utilize silicon as the dominant material, with indications that GaAs may become significant in the future. In integrated optics the quest for materials has not yet ended, with different considerations pointing in different directions [15,255].

Monolithic GaAs

Monolithic gallium arsenide (or rather various alloys of GaAl-As) is probably on its way to becoming the preferred choice. The reason is that this is the only system of materials that enables all the necessary active devices — lasers, modulators, switches, and detectors — to be fabricated together [477]. In particular, the most efficient and useful light source today for fiberoptics and integrated optics is the GaAs double heterostructure injection laser [659,591]. However, differences in the detailed requirements for the laser versus the waveguide applications remain to be resolved before a true monolithic technology emerges.

The GaAs system is the prime representative of a whole new family of semiconductors: the III-V family, so named after the columns of the periodic table from which its elements come. In the case of GaAlAs, Ga and Al come from the third column, and have three valence electrons; As comes from the fifth and has five. On average, the number of valence electrons is four, as in other semiconductors such as silicon. The advantage of this family is that various alloys, with different percentages of Ga and Al, may be fitted together. This is possible because the lattice structures of GaAs and AlAs crystals are nearly identical. Such combinations of different crystals allow for new properties in the materials, e.g., interaction with light of different wavelengths [591,53].

Hybrid LiNbO$_3$

The best active waveguide devices, e.g., modulators and switches, are those fabricated on lithium niobate substrates. However, the sources used are usually based on GaAs, while the detectors employ Si. Hence the hybrid nature of this system. In short, LiNbO$_3$-based integrated optics have the advantage of many superior components, and the disadvantage of the need to couple efficiently with other systems.

Silicon-based [289,69]

Silicon-based integrated optics are nearly monolithic: only the source is in GaAs, and all the rest is in Si. It is also relatively easy to fabricate complete circuits on a single crystal, covered with an insulating layer of SiO$_2$; the mature technology

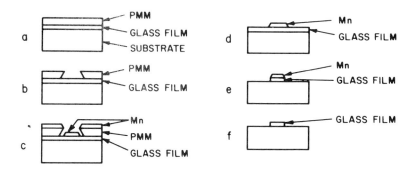

Figure 8.1: *Steps in the fabrication of an integrated optical circuit.*
(Reprinted with permission from *Applied Optics* [258], ©1973)

of electronic integrated circuits may be used. However, the performance of the
devices is inferior to that of devices fabricated on LiNbO$_3$.

8.2.3   Fabrication

Thin films have many applications outside the field of integrated optics, and many
different techniques have been developed for their fabrication and examination
[676]. Basically, the techniques for creating the film and making the required
patterns of strips and optical elements are very similar to those used in electronic
integrated circuits, and therefore we will make do with a short review.

The film is either laid on a substrate, or else it is created by a modification of
the substrate surface. The chief methods are:

- *Diffusion.* The substrate is coated with the film material, or placed in an
  environment rich in the film material, and heated. The film material then
  diffuses into the substrate. This creates a layer which combines the original
  substrate and the added material. It is not a well-defined layer; there is a
  gradual change to pure substrate.

- *Ion implantation.* This is similar to diffusion, except that the added ions
  are driven forcefully into the substrate. Precise control of the energy with
  which they hit the substrate allows for the regulation of the depth they reach
  [550,477].

- *Epitaxy.* Epitaxy is the growth of crystal layers on top of the substrate.
  In molecular-beam epitaxy, a beam of the film molecules is directed at the
  face of the substrate. In vapor-phase epitaxy, a the substrate is exposed to
  a vapor of the film material. As the molecules become attached, the film is

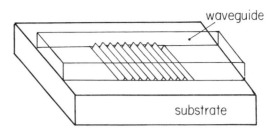

Figure 8.2: *An integrated optics mirror.*

created. This method allows for very accurate structuring of the film, and is used for the creation of heterostructure semiconductors [193].

An example of the creation of an integrated optic circuit is shown in fig. 8.1 [258]. First a planar glass film is made that covers the whole substrate. This is turn is covered by a layer of PMM (Polymethyl-methacrylate) resist (a). The desired pattern of strips is then drawn on the PMM by a deflectable electron beam, and the PMM is developed. This exposes strips of the glass film (b). An electron beam is used instead of a simpler photolithographic technique because it gives better resolution [74], and specifically because it allows for smoother sides. This is important in order to prevent undesired light scattering. After the development, a coat of metal (Mn) is deposited on the whole structure (c). When the remaining PMM and its coating are removed (with acetone), only strips of Mn on the glass film are left (d). These strips protect the glass underneath them, while the rest is etched away (e). The etching can be either wet — using a solvent, or, in the case of glass, dry etching — sputtering by ion bombardment. The dry process is more precise, as the direction of the ions is controlled [514]. Finally the Mn is removed (with hydrochloric acid), and the desired pattern of glass strips is obtained.

8.3   Passive integrated optics devices

The thin strips of high refractive index on a substrate with lower refractive index are the channels that conduct the light from one part of the optical circuit to another. We still have to see how miniature versions of the necessary optical elements are realized. We start with passive elements, i.e., mirrors and couplers.

8.3.1   Mirrors

A thin film mirror is very different from the mirror hanging on your bathroom wall. It consists of a very fine grating [680], etched into the substrate before the film is deposited (fig. 8.2). When light zigzagging along the film hits this grating, most of it is reflected and zigzags back again.

8.3.2 Couplers

A coupler is an interface device that accepts a signal (in our case a beam of light) and enters it into the system (the integrated optics circuit). In the context of thin films, there are two important types of couplers. One type is used to couple an external beam of light to a thin film waveguide. This allows light from an external source to be used. The other type allows waves propagating in distinct waveguides to interact. In particular, light may be switched from one waveguide to another.

End coupling

The most primitive way to get a beam of light into a thin film is to focus it on the film's edge, and hope for the best. A microscope objective is usually used, because the target is very small: a typical film is only about one wavelength wide. However, this method (which is also called "end fire") is not very efficient, and only works if the film is a crystal with cleaved edges.

Prism coupler

As end coupling is inefficient, the light must enter through the surface of the film. A prism coupler [682,683,293] does just that: an incident beam of light with a cross section of hundreds of wavelengths is fed into a thin film waveguide. This is accomplished by use of the phenomenon of tunneling — the passage of energy through a barrier. The configuration is as follows (fig. 8.3 (a)): A prism is placed just above the surface of the thin film. The light enters the prism in perpendicular to one of its faces. It is then reflected internally from the base of the prism. However it is wrong to think that all the light's energy is confined within the prism. The electromagnetic fields that constitute the light exist also outside of the prism, albeit they decay rapidly. But if *another* waveguide passes through these evanescent fields, they may be captured in it. In the case of a prism coupler, the other waveguide is the thin film. Thus it seems as if the light from the prism has passed the narrow gap of air (the barrier), and entered into the thin film. With certain configurations, the coupling efficiency (giving the part of the energy in the incident light beam that is coupled into the thin film waveguide) may approach 100% [294]. The rest is reflected.

Grating coupler

A different method for coupling a light beam to a thin film is to use a grating coupler (fig. 8.3 (b)) [175,739]. This is simply a fine grating that is deposited on

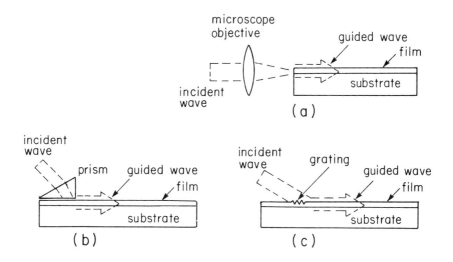

Figure 8.3: *Methods for coupling an external beam to a planar film:*
(a) End coupling. (b) Prism coupler. (c) Grating coupler.
(Adapted with permission from the *IEEE Journal of Quantum Electronics* [490], parts (b,c) ©1972
IEEE)

the film's surface. An incident light beam then suffers a cyclic phase modulation
of its cross section. The resulting field pattern is equivalent to a set of waves
propagating along the film, and indeed such waves are excited. Thus part of the
incident light energy is coupled to guided waves propagating in the film. The
efficiency of a grating coupler is somewhat lower than that of a prism coupler, but
it is much simpler to construct, and its geometry is also compatible with that of
other planar thin film devices.

Directional coupler

The previous couplers all dealt with the coupling of an external beam of light into
an integrated optics waveguide. This coupler is different. If two waveguide strips
laid on the same substrate are close enough to each other, light may pass from
one to the other [638,458]. This is the same tunneling phenomenon that occurs
in the prism coupler, but here it is used to couple two *guided* beams. If the two
guides have identical physical properties, a coupling of 100% may be achieved.
This means that a beam of light can pass completely from one guide to the other.

The degree of coupling strongly depends upon the interaction length; therefore
the guides are usually kept parallel and close for only a limited and controlled

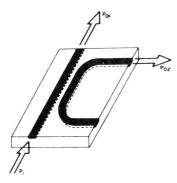

Figure 8.4: *Directional coupler between waveguide strips.*
(Reprinted with permission from the *IEEE Transactions on Microwave Theory and Techniques*
[376], ©1975 IEEE)

length (fig. 8.4). For example, if the interaction length is twice that required for 100% coupling, the net result will be nil: any input beam will be completely coupled from its original waveguide to the other guide, and then it will be completely coupled back again. This is of course not useful; shorter couplers may, however, be used to divide a signal between two guides and for other purposes, e.g., switching (as shown in section 8.4.3). Typical interaction lengths are in the order of 1 mm.

8.4   Active integrated optics devices

Passive devices only route an existing beam of light. Active devices *create* a beam of light or modulate it. Active integrated optics devices are characterized by the use of low power levels. The *power density* in the devices, however, is usually quite high, because the light is confined to an extremely small cross section. This allows for very efficient devices, in comparison with bulk optical systems.

8.4.1   Lasers

Semiconductor light sources, and lasers in particular, may be formed as integrated parts of thin film waveguide structures. The active part of these so called *injection lasers* [609,204,659,537,591] is a thin layer which acts as a junction between two types of crystals (see appendix E). If these crystals are compatible with the materials used in the thin film waveguide, a high coupling efficiency may be achieved.

The needed feedback for laser action may be brought about by the use of integrated optics mirrors, like the ones described in the preceding section [680].

An alternative is to use a periodic structure that causes distributed feedback [376, 378,739]. This means that parts of the wave are reflected throughout the length of the laser, instead of all of it being reflected only at the ends.

8.4.2 Modulators

In the context of integrated digital optical components, the required modulation is a binary change in the intensity of the guided light beam. This allows digital data to be imposed on the light beam. One way to do this is to directly modulate the output of the light source, e.g., a laser, by modulating the power supply to that source. Another is to modulate an existing uniform beam. This may be done with waveguides that display various electrooptic or magnetooptic effects [349,680]. When the appropriate external field is applied to such a waveguide (e.g., by integrated electrodes), the guided wave is phase or amplitude modulated. Phase modulation may be converted into amplitude modulation by use of interference: the waveguide branches into two symmetric paths, which then join again [574]. If the light in only one branch is phase modulated, so that its phase is changed by half a cycle, destructive interference will occur when the branches rejoin. The result is zero amplitude. If, on the other hand, both branches are left untouched, constructive interference will occur, resulting in high amplitude.

Another variant are modulators that cause some of the light to escape from the thin film waveguide into the substrate [505,518]. By regulating the amount of light that escapes, the remaining light is amplitude modulated.

Acoustooptic devices are also used as modulators. Here the idea is to create a surface acoustic wave (SAW) that propagates along the surface of the thin film waveguide. As the propagation speed of the guided light is much higher than that of the SAW, we may say that the light "sees" a standing acoustic wave in the film, in other words, a grating. This grating causes some of the guided wave to be diffracted. Turning the SAW on and off causes the grating to appear and disappear, and so changes the diffraction pattern of the guided light.

8.4.3 Switches and bistable devices

Switches and/or bistable devices are critical for the realization of logic circuits. Therefore we must consider their possible fabrication in the framework of integrated optics. These devices typically rely on interactions between light in neighboring waveguides, or between the light and the waveguide material. As such interactions are usually very weak, the devices must be quite large (a length of 1–2 mm is common). This is a major disadvantage if one is contemplating the use of these devices in optical computers.

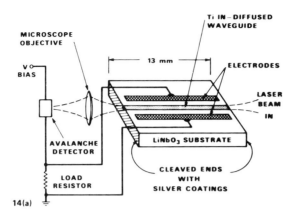

Figure 8.5: *Integrated hybrid bistable device.*
(Reprinted with permission from *Optical Engineering* [633], ©1980)

Hybrid bistable device

Integrated optical hybrid bistable devices that follow the principles outlined in
section 6.2 have been fabricated (fig. 8.5) [633]. The thin film guide is made of
a material that displays an electrooptic nonlinearity. The electrodes needed to
cause the nonlinearity are easy to make with integrated circuits technology. The
resonator, on the other hand, is more difficult. One problem is the long interaction
length required. Another is that the mirrors must reflect the whole wave without
phase distortion, so the regular integrated-grating mirrors cannot be used. Instead,
the crystal with the waveguide is cleaved and the edges are turned into regular
reflective mirrors. The feedback is obtained as in bulk hybrid bistable devices,
by detection of the output beam and application of the resulting voltage to the
electrodes.

Directional coupler switch

The coupling efficiency of a directional coupler, described in the preceding section,
depends on the interaction length and on the physical properties of the waveguides.
It can also be affected by an applied electric field. An especially promising configuration is as follows (fig. 8.6 (a)) [379,645]: The interaction length is divided into
segments. A set of electrodes is made alongside the coupler, so that the electric
field in each segment is reversed from its neighbors. With such a configuration,
the coupling efficiency depends on the voltage applied to the electrodes, and as
the voltage is increased it cyclically changes from very low coupling (nearly all the
light stays in the original waveguide) to very high coupling (nearly all the light

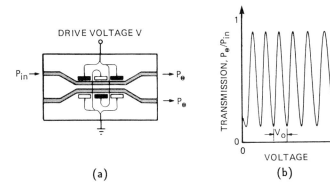

(a)   (b)

Figure 8.6:
(a) Electrically controlled directional coupler switch.
(b) Change of coupling efficiency with applied voltage.
(Adapted with permission from the *IEEE Journal of Quantum Electronics* [171], ©1978 IEEE)

passes to the other waveguide). (See fig. 8.6 (b)).

If one of the outputs of such a switch is fed into a detector, and the resulting voltage is fed back to the switch's electrodes, a bistable device results. Alternatively, such switches can be used to perform logic operations on light beams [674,663]. Their drawback is that the control is electronic, and this severely limits their speed. Still another use is to route optical communication channels [472].

Slightly different configurations (that are also based on a directional coupler) may be used to create extremely short pulses of light (less than 0.1 ps long) [459]. Actually this is a very fast switch that only couples the two waveguides when the voltage applied to it is zero. If one waveguide conducts a constant beam of light, and an alternating voltage is applied, brief couplings will occur whenever the voltage passes the zero point. Thus short pulses will appear in the other waveguide.

Interferometric switch

When a waveguide splits into two, light traveling in it is also divided between the two branches. If the branches subsequently rejoin, the produced light intensity depends on how the light from the two branches interferes[4]. Assuming the branches are symmetrical, the two light beams should interfere constructively. However, if the refractive index of only *one* branch is changed (e.g., by an applied voltage),

---

[4]Indeed, such a structure may be used to measure small differences between the branches by watching how the interference changes; this is the basis of interferometry. Hence the name of this type of switch.

the light in that branch will be delayed relative to the light in the other branch; hence destructive interference will occur. Controlling the voltage thus controls the light intensity in the waveguide after the join.

A slightly more complicated structure allows for optical control. The original waveguide carries a continuous stream of short pulses; these are split into the two branches, and a voltage is applied to one branch so that destructive interference occurs when they rejoin. However, the refractive index is also influenced by the intensity of the light in the waveguide. Therefore optical control pulses, which are selectively fed into one or the other of the branches, may change the relative phase and induce constructive interference. The polarization of the control pulses should be orthogonal to that of the stream that supplies the output, so that the control pulses may be blocked and prevented from reaching the output themselves [400].

8.5   Analog integrated optics devices

Most of this chapter deals with the realization of miniature optical components that may be used in an implementation of a digital optical computer. In this context, the data modulates the light beam by turning it on ("1" bit) or off ("0"). The waveguides considered so far have been narrow strips of thin film, which simply conduct the light from one place to another. This section is a short diversion into the possibility of using integrated optics techniques to implement the analog systems discussed in chapters 3 and 4, or actually 1-D equivalents of those 2-D systems. The systems in those chapters utilized three-dimensional space to operate on light beams with a 2-D cross section; here we talk about systems confined to a two-dimensional film, and light beams with a 1-D cross section. The film will be planar, i.e., it will cover the whole substrate, instead of being deposited in distinct strips.

8.5.1   Lenses

The basic optical elements needed to manipulate beams are lenses (e.g., for 1-D Fourier transforms). It turns out that these are easily implemented in planar thin films [297,16]. Recall that we are talking about thin films with a high refractive index, which we shall denote by n_f, over a substrate with a lower refractive index n_s. Recall also that the light is not completely confined to the film — the electromagnetic fields penetrate the substrate and air to some small degree. Therefore the *effective* refractive index n_{eff} that determines the speed with which the light propagates is not n_f, but some value between n_f and n_s. The important point is that n_{eff} also depends on the *thickness* of the film. An explanation why this is so is given in appendix H.

This dependence of the refractive index on the waveguide thickness may be used to implement lenses. In bulk optics, lenses are specially shaped pieces of

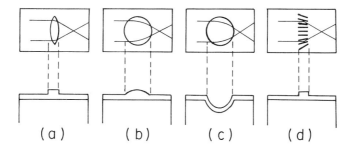

Figure 8.7: *Implementations of integrated optical lenses.*
(a) Flat bump with lens shape.
(b) Luneburg lens (circular bump with varying thickness).
(c) Geodesic lens (circular depression).
(d) Grating lens (Fresnel lens or variable bragg grating).
(Parts (a-c) reprinted with permission from the *IEEE Journal of Quantum Electronics* [696], ©1977 IEEE)

a material with a higher refractive index than the surroundings. In integrated optics, we can simply make specially shaped areas with a uniform, thicker film. The shape will be a two-dimensional cross section of the desired lens (fig. 8.7 (a)) [693,680,618]. Other refractive optical elements may be implemented in a similar fashion. For example, a triangular bump will act as a prism. [680].

Another possibility for integrated lenses is to create a continuous change in the refractive index throughout the lens. Such a lens has less aberrations than a lens whose borders define an abrupt change in the refractive index. This is hard to achieve in bulk optics [460,275], but it is easy in integrated optics: simply create a bump with varying thickness on the thin film. The most common type is a circular bump — called a "Luneburg" lens (fig. 8.7 (b)) [750,640,16]. A rectangular bump is also possible [641].

A third approach is to create depressions in the substrate under the film. The film thickness stays constant. In this case the refractive index does not change, but the path lengths do. The result is called a "geodesic" lens (fig. 8.7 (c)) [355, 639,635,696,582].

Finally, the last technique for integrated lenses is to use a grating structure (fig. 8.7 (d)). The grating may be structured as a 1-D Fresnel zone plate, which acts as a holographic lens (see appendix F) [29,246]. Alternatively, it may be composed of lines in varying orientations. The orientation at each point is set so that the Bragg diffraction condition will be satisfied for rays going through the focus [296].

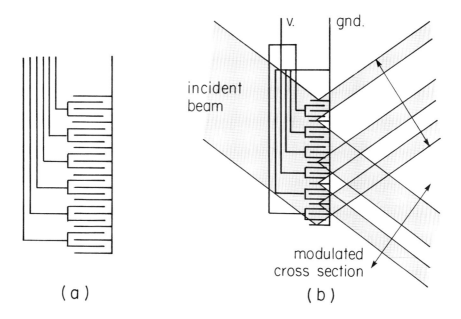

Figure 8.8: *Integrated SLM by interleaved electrodes.*
(a) The electrode structure.
(b) Modulation effect. The light is incident at an angle θ so that $\sin\theta = \frac{\lambda}{2d}$, where d is the grating spacing.

8.5.2   Spatial light modulators

Spatial light modulators are of prime importance in analog optical processing systems, such as those described in chapters 3 and 5: they are the devices that modulate the light beams with the data image, and then operate on these beams. Typical techniques used for the implementation of 2-D SLMs (described in section 2.4.6) require a layered structure which is perpendicular to the direction of propagation of the light. Such a structure is unsuitable for adaptation to 1-D thin film configurations. The one type of SLM that *is* transferable to integrated optics is the acoustooptic SLM (section 2.5.3), which is one-dimensional anyway. Only surface acoustic waves (SAW) are used, generated by interdigital transducers laid on the surface of the film. The theory of the interactions between SAWs and guided optical waves is practically identical to that presented in section 2.5.1 [402,389]. As these SLMs are simple and efficient, very little work has been done in search for alternatives. We describe only one other device.

This integrated SLM [706] is binary, i.e., it does not allow for gray levels. It is based on Bragg's law of diffraction from a grating. Unlike the description in section 2.4.3, here the light comes at an angle of $\arcsin\left(\frac{\lambda}{2d}\right)$. The main beam is then deflected by double this angle, instead of continuing in the same direction. Gratings are created at certain points in the cross section of the beam, and not at others. The incident beam is deflected from the gratings, but passes on undisturbed where gratings do not exist. Thus two complementary beams are generated: a continuation beam with "holes" where gratings caused a deflection, and a deflected beam with "holes" where there were no gratings (fig. 8.8 (b)).

The gratings are created by a system of electrodes with interleaved prongs, that is laid on top of the thin-film waveguide (fig. 8.8 (a))[5]. One common electrode is connected to ground. The other smaller electrodes are either connected to ground or to a certain voltage. If an electrode is connected to ground, there are no electric fields between it and the common electrode. Consequently the part of the beam that passes underneath it goes on in the original direction, undisturbed. If a voltage is applied to an electrode, on the other hand, electric fields in alternating directions appear between its prongs and those of the common electrode. These electric fields modulate the refractive index of the waveguide, and thus create a grating. Light passing under such an electrode will be deflected by this grating.

The use of such SLMs has been demonstrated in integrated optical correlators [706] and matrix multipliers [708,709].

8.5.3   Spectrum analyzers

The integrated optics analog circuits receiving the most attention are radio-frequency (RF) spectrum analyzers, mentioned already in section 3.5.1 [290,14,15,478, 679,28]. The reason is that this technology enables the construction of analyzers that are fast, small, and have a large bandwidth. These properties are difficult to achieve simultaneously by other means.

The principle of operation is straightforward (fig. 8.9). A light beam is spatially modulated by the input RF signal, using acoustooptic or electrooptic techniques. The modulated beam is then Fourier-transformed by an integrated lens, and the result is focused on a detector array (Appendix C deals with Fourier-transforming by a lens). Hence the power spectrum of the signal is obtained in parallel, more or less in real time.

8.6   Properties and limitations

When discussing the feasibility of optical integrated circuits, and their limitations once they are actually realized, one must do so in the context of other, competing

---

[5]Actually there should be a buffer between the waveguide and the electrodes, so that the metallic electrodes do not affect the properties of the waveguide.

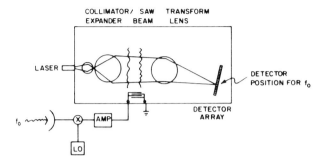

Figure 8.9: *Schematic integrated optical RF spectrum analyzer. The received RF is first converted by an LO and mixer to the frequency range of the analyzer, and then fed to an interdigital transducer. The created SAW modulates a laser beam. Finally, a Luneburg lens focuses the Fourier transform on a detector array.*
(Reprinted with permission from *Optical Engineering* [290], ©1977)

technologies. These include both conventional, silicon-based integrated electronics, and other innovative ideas, like Josephson devices [464,465,396,749,13]. Other optical schemes must also be considered; in fact, most of the following is not limited to integrated optics. We will attempt to introduce the different issues individually, even though they are highly related to each other.

8.6.1   Device speed and power consumption

Speed and power are unseparable when the performance and limitations of minia-turized digital devices are being discussed. The speed at which a device can operate is sometimes limited by its power consumption, rather than by any physical limit on its switching speed [364,366]. The power consumption limit does not arise from an inability to supply the required power — on the contrary, getting rid of the power produced by the device as *heat* is the main problem. If the power consump-tion is greater than the heat removal rate, the device quickly stops computing and starts making tea.

The energy consumption of a device is the product of two parameters: its switching speed and the power needed per switch. Fig. 8.10 compares how various devices fare in regard to different physical limitations [631,632]. The two shaded areas at the bottom left are unaccessible to any switching device. The "kT" region forbids a switching energy of less than the average, randomly fluctuating, thermal energy of a particle at temperature T (The figure uses $T = 300°K$, which is a rather warm room temperature). The "quantum limit" region forbids devices that violate the uncertainity principle, which limits the accuracy with which energy

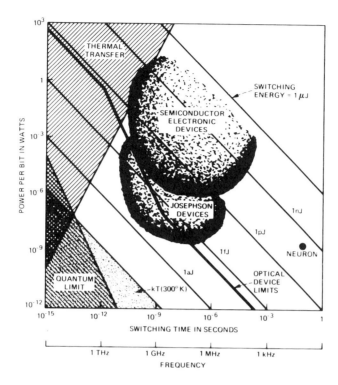

Figure 8.10: *Connection between speed and power consumption for various switches. See text for details.*
(Reprinted with permission from the *Bell System Technical Journal* [631], ©1982 AT&T)

and time may be known simultaneously.

The third shaded area, at top left, is marked "thermal transfer". This is an undesired area, in which a device would create more heat than can be practically carried away [365]. However, a device can operate in this region if its duty cycle is reduced (i.e., it does not work all the time), or if not all the power needed for switching is actually dissipated. Both of these observations are relevant for optical devices [631,632], as we now show.

As an example of a switch that works at a low duty cycle, consider an interface between a limited-speed electronic input and a high-speed optical circuit. This interface will have to multiplex many (slow) electronic data streams into one (fast) optical data stream. Such a multiplexer can be made out of many optical switches, with a high switching speed compatible with the optical system, but a low repetition rate compatible with the electronic input. Each switch will sample its electronic input once in each cycle, which requires the high switching speed, but will wait idle during the rest of the cycle. This time is used to remove more excess heat.

To see how it is possible for power not to be dissipated, we have to distinguish between the power needed to activate the device and the power actually dissipated in it. In optical bistable devices, for instance, they may be quite different. The power that activates the device is the power that causes the nonlinear effect in the material that is placed in the resonant cavity. However, a large portion of this power is eventually carried away in the form of a light beam that is either transmitted through the device of reflected from it. Therefore not all the power need be dissipated in the device.

Fig. 8.10 also displays the operation characteristics of conventional semiconductor electronic devices and proposed Josephson devices. These may be compared with the expected limits on the performance of bistable optical devices (The heavy three-segment diagonal line). We see that at switching speeds of up to about 100 MHz, optical devices require less power than their electronic counterparts. At speeds of up to 100 GHz, the power requirements are very similar. Josephson devices, however, require much less power than either optics or semiconductor microelectronics. The real advantage of optics is in the possibility of subpicosecond switching. No other devices can switch in $10^{-12} - 10^{-14}$ second. Regrettably, this range falls in the area of thermal transfer limitations.

We conclude this discussion with an explanation of how the expected limits on optical bistable devices, depicted in the figure, were derived. The two leftmost segments describe limits in the two main strategies employed in bistable devices. At the far left is the limit on reactive nonlinearity, i.e., bistable behavior that depends on a change of refractive index when the light intensity changes (this is the type that was described in section 6.2). In the middle is the limit on absorptive nonlinearity, where the device operates by absorbing light and saturating some optical transition. The rightmost segment results from a different argument altogether — it represents the minimum number of 1000 photons (at $\lambda = 0.5\mu m$) required for low-noise switching. If too few photons are allowed, statistical fluctuations may cause switching errors.

8.6.2   Interconnection speed

It has been estimated that signals propagate in the conductors of a VLSI circuit at a speed as low as 0.005 of the speed of light [733]. The reason is the low power of the sources used. Changing the voltage of the line from "low" to "high" should be analyzed in terms of a *transient* effect, where a low power source charges a capacitance. Only when the line is charged to a sufficient degree do the components attached to it detect the change of state.

The problem is that the required time does not scale down when the whole circuit is miniaturized. This happens because the time needed to charge the line also depends on the *resistance* of the line[6]. When everything is scaled down, the capacitance scales down too, but the resistance scales up by the same factor [595,475]. Therefore the time needed to charge the line stays the same.

In optical integrated circuits, on the other hand, the signals propagate at about 0.3 of the speed of light in vacuum [377]. With free-space interconnections the speed is of course higher. The interconnection delay also scales down with the interconnection length, regardless of the waveguide width. In addition the bandwidth of each channel is much larger. Thus optical interconnections offer some important advantages over electronic interconnections.

8.6.3   Packaging and size

A chief problem in VLSI design is that of packing the miniaturized components on the chip [64]. The problem stems from communication and interconnection issues. As the components become smaller, their packing density increases and the space between them decreases. As a result the density of communication lines must be greatly increased. This in turn causes problems of layout, signal distortion, and crosstalk.

Another source of packaging difficulties is heat dissipation. As the density of the components increases, more heat is generated in less space; this heat is harder to carry away because of the high density. The chief virtue of Josephson devices is their low power consumption, which is coupled with low heat dissipation. This allows them to be packed at a much higher density than that of conventional semiconductor devices.

In optics, the feature size is limited by the fact that light cannot be confined to a cross section of less than about 1 μm [377]. This is a basic physical limit, and does not depend on the fabrication technology. This limitation is ultimately more restrictive than the technological difficulties encountered in VLSI.

In many optical devices the situation is actually much worse. In these devices at least one dimension must be in the range of hundreds of wavelengths, in order to allow for interactions between beams of light or between light and a material. Examples are lasers, bistable devices, and directional couplers.

The interconnection density of optics, on the other hand, may be much larger than that of electronic devices (see fig. 9.2, p. 260).

8.6.4   Yield and tolerances

The fabrication techniques used for the miniaturized components of integrated circuits create rugged and reliable devices. However, the tolerances in mass-produced

---

[6]Thus the time is the product of the resistance by the capacitance; this is called the *RC time constant* of the line.

miniature components must be high, as it is impossible to fine tune and adjust individual components. Therefore the operation of the components must not be sensitive to variations in their finer details [367]. Unfortunately, most of the optical devices described in chapter 7 do depend on precise fabrication. Therefore it can be expected that the yield in mass production of optical components (i.e., the percentage of fabricated devices that really work) will be lower than the average yield in VLSI. If the yield is too low, production may not be economical.

As an example, consider a three-input AND gate, implemented by way of threshold logic based on a bistable resonator. Minute changes in the length of the resonant cavity will greatly affect its tuning, and thus its threshold value. If the uncertainity about the threshold is big enough, it will become impossible to create a deterministic device that sums the inputs and then compares the sum to the threshold [363]. For instance, if the threshold is $3 \pm 20\%$, each input must be larger than 1.2 so that the sum of all three will pass the highest possible threshold, which is 3.6. On the other hand it must also be less than 1.2, so that only two inputs will not surpass the lowest possible threshold, which is 2.4. Thus it is impossible to create the desired three-input AND gate. Note that it is not practical to change the wavelength in order to compensate for inaccuracies in fabrication. For one thing, the wavelength is determined by the energy levels of the electrons in the source LED or laser; and on top of that, different components might require contradicting adjustments of the wavelength.

8.6.5   Reliability

Integrated circuits tend to be more reliable than larger systems; this is true for electronics, and also for optics. In integrated optics, the improved reliability stems from the fact that the various devices are fabricated together on the same substrate. Hence they cannot move relative to each other. As a result there are no alignment problems, and the system as a whole is not sensitive to vibrations in the environment.

A totally different aspect of reliability is the susceptibility of the computer to soft-fails, i.e., the probability that it momentarily malfunctions as a result of an external influence. The Achilles' heel of electronic computers in this respect is their primary memory, where packets of charge must retain their value for extended periods. The decreased size of these packets has reached a point where spurious charges created by radioactive decay or cosmic rays may change the contents of the memory [473,467,751]. Optical computers, on the other hand, should be free of such problems: They do not utilize electric charges, nor do they interact with electric charges.

8.6.6   Characteristics of the logic devices

The preceding sections highlight the most important properties of miniaturized digital components, and compare microelectronics and proposed optical devices. However, some other less prominent aspects of the operation of computer components also deserve notice. It might happen that these facets will ultimately decide the acceptance or rejection of a new technology. An important feature of silicon microelectronic devices is the way they meet all of these seemingly marginal requirements [363]. A few examples follow.

- *Standardization of values.*
  In electronics, the two basic binary values are represented by two standard voltages (e.g., 0 and 5 volts in TTL). These voltages are distributed throughout the computer by special power supply lines. When the need to set a data line to a certain value arises, a connection to the relevant power line is established. Thus the signal is reconstructed at each step. Optical systems will have to use a light source at each gate to achieve this effect, rather than let the same light beam propagate through a number of gates. Otherwise signal degradation will occur as the computation advances.

- *Switch-up and switch-down symmetry.*
  As a result of the standardization, and a lot of hard work on the part of engineers, it is just as easy to switch up as it is to switch down in electronics. In many optical systems, one direction is much easier and faster than the other.

- *Gain.*
  Microelectronic logic circuits are based upon high-gain transistors. This allows for large noise margins, and also deals with varying fan-outs. Most optical devices do not display any appreciable gain

- *Separation of input from output.*
  In electronic devices, the input and output connect to distinct electrodes. There is no danger of undesired feedback. In optics it often happens that input beams interact with each other to create output beams, and part of the output may go back along the path the input came on.

Among the proposals for optical logic devices, the only one that meets these requirements reasonably well is that of threshold logic by means of a resonator-based bistable device, which uses a pulsed hold beam (a full description is given in section 7.2.2). The standardization is achieved by using the hold beam to generate the output [627,629]. Switch-up is done by the input, while switch-down is done when the hold beam is interrupted; both happen within one cycle. Gain is somewhat problematic, but achievable [685]. Separation of input from output results from having the input and the hold beams propagate along different lines.

8.6.7   Overview

The general trend in the preceding sections was to point out the difficulties and obstacles that optical computing devices will have to overcome. Some of these obstacles are quite formidable, and therefore it seems that optical digital computers will not become a reality in the near future. Many of the problems may be traced to these two sources:

- Electronic devices are based upon interactions between electrically charged particles. This makes the implementation of logic operations easy, because electric charges have an intrinsic tendency to influence each other. It also makes communication difficult because the same influences create crosstalk, and interactions with the conductors limit the bandwidth. Optical devices, on the other hand, are based on light beams. It is difficult to cause an interaction between light beams, and therefore all-optical logic is hard to do. But this lack of interaction is an advantage in the implementation of communication.

  It should be remembered, however, that in Edison's time electronic logic also was impossible. The reason was that devices by which electricity controls electricity did not exist. Electricity could only be controlled by mechanical means. Electronic computers could only be built when the first electronic control was invented — this was a vacuum tube. They only became practical when electronic control became cheap and reliable, with the advent of transistors. Optical computers will need light that controls light. Today we have numerous devices in which electricity controls light, but only a few prototypes of devices by which light controls light. We may hope that continued research will achieve the breakthrough by which light control will become practical [468].

- In electronics, the data is represented by a *potential* (i.e., a voltage), whereas in optics the data is represented by a *packet of energy* (i.e., a light pulse). This causes problems with the cascadability of computing components: dissipation degrades the data, fan-out divides it, etc. The problem of reconstructing the data at each stage in a reasonable manner will also have to be solved in order to create practical optical computers.

8.7   Are integrated optics the right direction?

The concepts of integrated optics were invented in the context of fiberoptics communication systems [489,162]. The object was to make small, durable, and reliable repeaters on long-haul fiberoptics cables. These repeaters would embody a detector, light source and modulator, which would ideally be produced together in a compact package. When the question of planning a digital optical computer came up, it was natural to turn to integrated optics as a potentially promising technology:

- Simple integrated optical circuits were already being discussed and built.

- Integrated optics are reminiscent of integrated electronics, which are the source of the success of electronic computers.

- The mature technology of electronic integrated circuits could be utilized.

- Integrated optical circuits have a few potential advantages over bulk optical systems (see page 227).

It should be remembered, however, that the underlying ideas and concepts of optical computers are very much different from those of electronic computers. Thus it seems unwise just to copy the technology used in electronic computers, with only minor adaptations for optical devices.

Specifically, we showed in section 7.7 that optical computers are inherently suitable for SIMD architectures, with a two-dimensional (binary) image serving as the basic data element. It was concluded that one of the great advantages of optics is the possibility of parallel, free-space communication. All this is lost if we limit our quest to planar, integrated circuits technology. Therefore a totally new, three-dimensional technology might be needed in order to fully realize the potential of digital optical computers. Without such a new technology they might prove to be unattractive; however, developing it is likely to require a massive design and engineering effort.

Ideally, the new technology should incorporate the best of both worlds: it should have the rugged structure and mass production capabilities of integrated circuits, coupled with the use of 3-D space typical in bulk optical systems. Current investigations into multi-layer electronic integrated circuits [9] might provide a starting point, as well as research dealing with large arrays of optical devices (e.g., the array of bistable devices depicted in fig. 7.32). The incorporation of miniature light sources, the manufacture and alignment of routing elements, and input/output interfaces are areas that require much additional research.

Summary

The demonstration that all the devices needed in a computer can be realized by optical means is not enough in order to build one — issues relating to the manufacturing process must also be dealt with. Of primary importance is the choice of technology.

Integrated optics, which follow the principles of the better-known electronic integrated circuits, have been suggested as a viable technology. It is centered around thin films with a high refractive index, deposited on a substrate with a lower refractive index. The film may be etched to form thin strips which confine the light, and thus act as waveguides. This technology was developed in the context of optical communication systems, and is suitable for the mass production of devices.

While many optical devices may indeed be fabricated in integrated optics techniques, the parallel SIMD architecture which is conjectured to be the most fitting for optical computers does not lend itself to a planar integrated implementation. In particular, the free-space interconnections — which are one of the most promising ideas related to optical computers — are not accommodated. Thus a new three-dimensional technology might have to be developed before digital optical computers become a reality.

III

THE IMPACT OF
OPTICAL COMPUTERS

This final part of the book deals with the impact that optical computers may be expected to have. The outlook is from a computer science point of view; therefore the possible influence of optical computers on computer science is the main issue.

Chapter 9 first summarizes the current status of optical data processing systems, and what developments can be reasonably expected in the future. It also includes a short list of new optical devices that might be interesting to design. Chapter 10 deals with the direct influence of optical computers on computer science. This includes both affects on practical aspects of computers, and implications for theoretical computer science.

Chapter 9

Status and Prospects

The first two parts of this book, dealing with special purpose (mostly analog) optical processors and with general purpose digital optical computers, emphasized what theoretically can be done. In this chapter we take a look at what actually *is* being done, and what can be reasonably expected in the future. The first section deals with the status and prospects of special purpose systems, and the second with general purpose digital optical computers. Finally, we review some new optical devices that could be designed to work in conjunction with conventional electronic computers.

9.1 Special purpose (analog) optical processors

Special purpose analog optical processors are the oldest branch of optical computing. A number of such systems are actually in common use, or in advanced stages of development. Others show promise, and are worth further research.

9.1.1 Existing systems

It is difficult to give a precise evaluation of the present status of special purpose optical processors, because most systems that reach advanced stages of design and development do so in a military environment and are therefore classified. The *only* optical processing system that is currently known to be in wide use is that used for synthetic aperture radar imaging; A commercial processor is depicted in fig. 9.1. This was developed under the limitations of military secrecy in the 1950s, but it has since been unveiled.

It seems safe to assume that other systems are now also in use. Coherent, matched-filter pattern recognition systems are known to be in advanced stages of development, if they are not in use already. The probable applications are missile guidance and target registration. RF spectrum analyzers are also good candidates. Here the major application is the real-time identification of hostile transmissions, e.g., a radar whose echos serve as a homing signal for a weapon system.

More peaceful applications are probably also being pursued. The most notable is image processing, or rather image classification. Systems in which thousands of images are acquired daily, e.g., by various satellites, require high processing rates

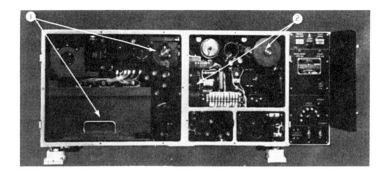

Figure 9.1: *The AN/APQ-102 optical processor for SAR images, manufactured by Goodyear Aerospace Corp.*
(1) Output film and developing tank.   (2) Data film.
(Picture courtesy of Goodyear Aerospace Corp. Previously published in Preston/**Coherent Optical Computers** [555])

that can only be supplied by optics. Simple feature extraction systems, like the wedge-ring detector, are probably sufficient for this application.

9.1.2   Prospects and limitations

Other special purpose processors, while not yet developed, show great promise for the future. The systems that should be considered are those that can be shown to be capable of performance unrivaled by electronic systems. For example, the existing systems cited above fall in this category: SAR processing and pattern recognition both rely on rapid evaluations of the Fourier transform. The optical systems do this instantly; competing serial electronic computers need $O(n \log n)$ steps (for the 1-D transform of n points), and even special purpose parallel networks need at least $O(\log n)$ steps.

Of all the systems described in chapters 3 and 4, matrix multipliers probably have the greatest potential. However, a distinction must be made between systolic multipliers and parallel multipliers. The systolic ones have a number of drawbacks when compared with electronic ones:

- Digital-to-analog and analog-to-digital conversions are necessary. This takes time and reduces accuracy.

- The technology is new, as with all optical systems. Trained technical personnel are not available.

- They offer no drastic improvement over electronic systolic arrays — both require time that is linearly dependent on the input size (i.e., $O(N)$ steps for $N \times N$ matrices).

The first two drawbacks are equally applicable to parallel multipliers. However, the parallel devices *do* offer a great improvement: they turn matrix multiplication into a single-step operation. Because of the importance of matrix multiplication in many algorithms, this property is very attractive.

It should be noted that this potential is yet far from being realized. As noted at the end of section 4.3, both the accuracy of the calculation and the size of the operands are actually limited. These limitations arise form a combination of fundamental reasons (such as those described in section 2.6), and technical limitations of the current state of the art. Parallel matrix multipliers will become attractive only when the state of the art is pushed ahead; if this cannot be done, the promise they hold will not be realized.

9.2 General purpose digital optical computers

9.2.1 Current status

It is much easier to define the current status of general purpose digital optical computers (DOCs). At present they are only at the initial stages of development, and do not yet exist as complete systems. It should be noted, however, that quite a large research effort has been directed towards this goal in recent years. This includes not only sporadic and isolated programs by different teams, but also coordinated efforts such as the European Joint Optical Bistability (EJOB) project.

9.2.2 Existing optical subsystems and their development

Even if a whole all-optical general purpose digital computer is not yet an imminent contraption, optical systems are already being used as subsystems in larger electronic computer systems. This is especially noticeable in the context of interconnections, but also in other areas, e.g., mass storage. All of these systems are undergoing further development that might improve and even revolutionize them.

Local area networks

Perhaps the most common use of optical data manipulation components nowadays is in digital communication networks. This includes both long distance, large capacity telecommunication links, and, more relevant to computers, local area networks (LANs).

A LAN, as its name implies, is designed to supply local interconnections between computers and/or peripherals [664, chap. 7]. Key issues in LAN design
are:

- *Topology* — how the nodes are connected to each other. At one extreme is
  the full mesh, where every node is connected to all the others. This insures
  the ability to fulfill any communication request, at the cost of excessive
  hardware. At the other extreme is the bus, where all the nodes share the
  same communication medium. This saves hardware, but the bus can become
  a bottleneck. In between are various other topologies, e.g., a star or a ring.

- *Protocol* — how communication is established. This is important in every
  network except for a full mesh, where each link is dedicated to a specific pair
  of nodes. Special care must be taken to solve clashes which occur when a
  number of nodes try to use a shared channel simultaneously.

- *Hardware* — how the links are implemented. This dictates the number of
  nodes that may be accommodated, and the data rate.

Optical components are directly related, of course, to the question of the hardware
used. Optical links use fiberoptics technology, and are typified by their large bandwidth [221,218]. This allows for high data rates. The influence of this technology
extends, however, to the other issues as well. For example the high data rate might
make an economical topology practical, whereas with a slower electronic link it
would run into congestion problems.

Contemporary systems operate at data rates of 10–100 ^{Mb}/s [221]. A common
transmission medium is typically used. At low rates (10 ^{Mb}/s) a CSMA/CD protocol is used. This stands for "carrier sense multiple access/collision detection".
It means that each station listens to the medium before starting a transmission
to determine whether another station is already using it, in which case it gives up
and tries again later. If two stations begin transmission simultaneously, both give
up and try again after a random pause. The protocol for higher rates is token
passing or TDMA. Token passing means that only one station is authorized to
transmit at any given time, and the stations pass this authorization among themselves. TDMA stands for "time division multiple access", and means that all the
stations are synchronized and each has a preallocated time slot in which it may
transmit.

The above protocols were developed for electronic LANs, and then adapted for
optical ones. However, the immense bandwidth of optical interconnections allows
for totally new ideas, such as "code division multiple access" (CDMA) [559,560].
A common medium is also used in this method. Each transmitted *bit* is encoded
by a code that specifies its destination. All the nodes of the network continuously
correlate their own codes with the incoming signal. When a bit addressed to
them is received, this is indicated by a high correlation peak; bits addressed to

other nodes give a low correlation value, because the codes are chosen so as to be orthogonal.

The advantages of this scheme are that all stations can transmit asynchronously, without waiting for the medium to be free. In other words, multiple stations may transmit simultaneously, on the same medium. This is so because the correlation operation can extract the right code from a noisy signal created by other bits directed at other nodes (just as it finds a radar echo in a noisy RF signal, section 3.5.2). In addition, adding nodes does not degrade the performance[1]; the new stations just have to be given new codes. Finally, the necessary processing (i.e., the correlation) may be done optically (see section 3.2.2).

Future network nodes with optical processing

Today only the transmission of data in long haul networks is sometimes done by optical fiber. The coding, addressing, routing, parity check, and so on are done electronically. As data rates increase, the delay at the intermediate nodes of the network might become unacceptable. If the node's functions are implemented optically, however, the need for time-consuming optical/electronic conversions is eliminated. It is hoped that the optical processing itself will also be faster than the equivalent electronic processing.

Long-haul networks are often described by the "open systems interconnection" (OSI) model, defined by the International Standards Organization [752,715,664, sect. 1.4]. This model divides a digital interconnection network into seven functional levels. The bottom three levels are called the communication subsystem, and are responsible for all the processing that is done at intermediate nodes in the network. We now survey the functions of these levels, and see how they can be realized by optical systems [330]:

1. *The physical layer.*

   - Switching — Optically controlled light switches are the subject of intensive study, motivated by the needs of optical logic. The same switches can also be used to route information.

2. *The data-link layer.*

   - Synchronization — the recognition of a synchronization signal may be formulated as a pattern recognition problem. It can thus be solved by cross-correlation.

   - Address recognition — same as the above.

   - Parity check — this may be formulated as the multiplication of a matrix by a vector.

---

[1]The quality of the connection depends only on the number of stations that happen to be transmitting simultaneously.

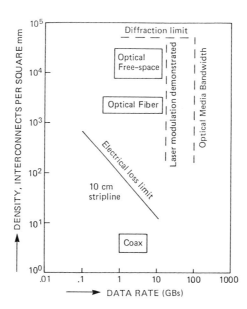

Figure 9.2: *Dependence between interconnection density and data rate for various optical and electronic methods.*
(Reprinted with permission from *Optical Engineering* [301], ©1986)

3. *Network layer.*

- The functions of this level are of the decision-making type: routing, the resolution of collisions, and so on. These functions may be carried out by a finite state machine — the full power of a computer is not necessary. Optical implementations are already beginning to emerge, either by the use of optical logic systems or by simpler formulations.

Future optical interconnections for VLSI

Optical communication started with long haul fiberoptics. today optical local area networks are common, and the ESS-5 (AT&T's digital switching computer, used in the telephone network) even utilizes optical interconnections between boards [54]. As the trend of using optics at lower and lower levels continues, the next step is the interconnection of VLSI components by optical means [262,331,528].

The motivation for this is the high bandwidth available in optical channels. Benefits will include the potential for high interconnection density, negligible crosstalk, and the fact that the interconnection delay scales down as the size

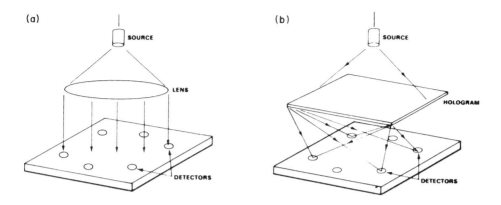

Figure 9.3: *Distribution of a clock signal to a chip.*
(a) Unfocused method — the chip is flooded by the signal.
(b) Focused method — A HOE is used to focus the clock signal onto the detectors, thus reducing the power requirements.
(Reprinted with permission from the *Proceedings of the IEEE* [262], ©1984 IEEE)

is reduced (fig. 9.2). These benefits will hopefully justify the need to translate electronic signals to optical ones and back again.

Each optical link incorporates a driver and laser diode on the transmitting side, and a detector and amplifier on the receiving side. As these devices currently need an area of the order of 100×100 μm, It is not practical to use this technology to replace all the lines on a chip. As a first stage, therefore, it has been suggested that optical interconnections be used for the distribution of clock signals. In this application the source is external to the chip. the chip itself is studded with detectors that receive the clock signal and distribute it to their immediate surroundings. Thus the whole chip receives the same clock signal, and clock-skew problems are diminished (fig. 9.3) [262,159].

The inter-chip situation is different. Only few connections are available in the standard electronic methods. Therefore the high bandwidth of the optical alternative can be enough to justify its implementation, even if only a small number of optical channels are connected to each chip. These channels may be realized by means of optical fibers, or by holographic free-space methods [383]. The design of opto-electronic integrated circuits, which combine light sources and detectors with electronic logic, is now at an advanced stage [528,558].

Optical storage in data bases

Existing optical storage devices, e.g., optical disks or holographic mass memory, are not well suited for primary memory applications. However they *are* useful in the context of archival data bases, which generally have a write-once-read-many-times (WORM) characteristic [61]. Such archives are in wide use, and provide on-line access to data ranging from government publications to the technical specifications of different products (e.g., [540]).

The cumbersome photographic-holographic mass storage systems of the '70s did not gain wide acceptance. Lately, optical disks have been coming into common use, and they are beginning to replace microfilm data bases. The advantages of optical disks over other storage media are:

- They provide high capacity on-line storage.

- Written material is immediately available for reading (i.e., there is no processing step). The material may be written incrementally.

- Data is kept indefinitely. Head crashes do not occur.

- High storage density: more bits in less volume.

- Access time and transfer rate are comparable to those of conventional electronic devices.

- Low cost (and going down).

Even in an archival data base, the need to rewrite some information might arise. For example, some information might need to be updated or corrected. The capability to rewrite (at least to some degree) can be provided in optical disks in one of two ways:

- In the initial writing, some blocks can be left clear. These blocks are later used for newer versions of written blocks [452]. The management of this disk space is similar to the management of conventional magnetic disks by an operating system.

- A set of special codes has been devised, in which each symbol may be represented by several different code words [583]. Initially all the data is written by the version with the least "1"s. The crucial point is that every symbol can then by converted into any other symbol by just adding "1"s to the code-word. Thus a written segment of the disk may be overwritten by new data.

  The simplest encoding system is given in fig. 9.4. It uses three bit positions to write a two-bit word, but allows for one rewrite. The codes for longer words are more efficient.

value	first code	second code
0	0 0 0	1 1 1
1	0 0 1	1 1 0
2	0 1 0	1 0 1
3	1 0 0	0 1 1

Figure 9.4: *To re-write on a write-once memory, the first code is used for the first writing. If the data later needs to be changed, the second code allows each value to be transformed into any other value.*
(Adapted with permission from the Proceedings of the 14th ACM Symposium on Theory of Computing [583], Copyright 1982, Association for Computing Machinery, Inc.)

Optical write-once disks might also be used in data bases where the data is often modified. In such situations they will not be used to store the data; rather the *log* that records the evolution of the data base will be kept on the optical disk. This is convenient because the log need never be rewritten — on the contrary, it should be kept for extended periods [692, page 397].

Possible future trends in storage

The trend in optical digital data disks is towards standard, erasable, high capacity disks. These disks will be able to replace contemporary magnetic disks as a secondary memory for a computer. It is possible, however, that even the existing write-once disks may be found to be useful in this application. This idea is based on the following observations [533]:

- A large cache, with an appropriately large block size, can satisfy up to 90% of all disk accesses. Such a cache can save write-once disk space because, on average, about 50% of all newly written data is deleted or overwritten within 5 minutes. With a large cache, much of it will not reach the disk at all.

- Optical disks are already quite cheap, and their prices are expected to drop further. In addition, their capacity is huge. Therefore the price of the disk space used by a conventional computer user throughout a year will be surprisingly low, even if whatever he writes is written to new disk space. More efficient writing protocols are also possible, e.g., write only a log entry describing the changes made to existing data. This would also allow old versions to be accessed [714].

- There will be no need for backups, because the optical disks themselves act as an archive.

9.2.3   Will DOCs be built?

The success of computers built exclusively from optical components will depend not only on the ability to implement all the functional units optically, but also on how well these units can work together, and on the ensuing performance. These computers will have to outperform todays mature electronic computers in some significant way in order to gain acceptance [580]: maybe they will be much faster, or encourage new parallel architectures, or maybe their immunity to EMI will suffice. But they will also have to be comparable to todays electronic computers in their technical specifications: they should not be excessively large, power consumption should be reasonable, and maintenance must be easy.

To get some insight as to what DOCs are up against, other technologies that were proposed as a replacement for silicon integrated circuits should be reviewed [367]. Semiconductor transistors made of Ge and of GaAs have failed to dislodge the dominant silicon, even though they promise faster switching. So have tunnel diodes. IBM dropped a two-decade project dealing with Josephson devices in 1983, after coming to the conclusion that the potential advantages would not be large enough [585].

The characteristics of the alternative technologies are compared with those of silicon and of optical bistable devices (as the current most likely optical technology) in table 9.1. To summarize, we see that the optical alternative is basically different from the others: it emphasizes parallelism and connectivity rather than raw speed and low power.[2] This is not just an improvement in performance; it is a fundamental change in concepts and architecture. It results from the basic differences between electrons and photons: electrons interact with each other, while photons do not.

The above observations point out the directions in which we might expect optical computers to develop. They will *not* replace PCs used as word processors, nor will they be used as mainframes that supply simple services to a multitude of unsophisticated users. They probably *will* have an impact in the field of supercomputers, Where electronic devices are approaching their limit, and heroic efforts are needed in order to achieve further improvements. Today's supercomputers already employ some degree of parallelism, but except for the Connection Machine [310] the number of processors is small. Interconnections pose a severe problem, and

---

[2]A single proposal that suggests the use of fast optical gates in a conventional architecture and integrated technology has also been made [728]; however, the trend is toward parallelism.

technology	advantages	disadvantages	references
silicon	low price, reliable, not sensitive to variations in manufacture and environment, ease of integration and materials	limited switching speed, packing density, and interconnection speed	
GaAs	very high speed, simple production steps	sensitive to variations in production, VLSI doubtful	[704,195]
tunnel diodes	high speed	unsymmetric switching, sensitive to variations	[367]
Josephson devices	low power consumption, high packing density, high speed	no gain, cryogenic operating conditions	[464,585]
optical bistability	high interconnection density, high speed, inherently suitable for parallelism	sensitive to variations, vibrations, and temperature, fabrication technology uncertain	

Table 9.1: *Comparison between competing technologies for building computers.*

this is where optical systems can come to the rescue. The first foothold of optics in digital computers was the fiberoptic cables used to connect the boards of AT&T's ESS-5 switch. It stands to reason that the next steps will be an extension of this use, in the form of interconnections between chips.

We can only speculate as to further developments. An optimistic scenario leading into the twenty-first century is as follows: with the advance of research, free-space interconnections may will become practical. If so, optical interconnections might penetrate into the intra-chip domain (as described on page 260). At such low levels, the constant need to translate signals from electronic to optic and back again may be expected to be burdensome. This will provide the final push to-

wards the realization of an all-optical general purpose digital computer. Once the
basic development is successfully completed, production experience will contribute
to lowering the costs; thus optical computers will find many computation-intensive
applications, from supercomputers used for weather forecasting and physics simulations to workstations used in logic design.

9.3   New devices for conventional computers

Numerous ideas for new devices present themselves once one starts looking into the
possibilities provided by optics. Here we deal with a few of the more striking ones.
It should be emphasized that these are only preliminary ideas — much research is
still required before operational devices can be realized. Such research might also
reveal problems that will render these ideas unpractical. Special attention should
be given to questions of how these devices interface with their hosts.

9.3.1   One-step generalized matrix-matrix multiplier

A prototype matrix-matrix multiplier is described on page 125. The idea is to
use the capabilities of optical interconnections to duplicate the input data many
times, so that all the N^3 products that are needed will be done simultaneously.
Needless to say, the realization of a practical and commercial device that will
reduce the complexity of matrix multiplication from $O(N^{2.376...})$ to $O(1)$ will be
an unprecedented improvement in the capabilities of computers, especially if large
matrices can also be accommodated.

Many problems in computer science may be solved by a formalism similar to
matrix multiplication, but using different operations. For example, the multiplications might be replaced by boolean AND, while the additions are replaced by
OR (the input in this case is two binary matrices). It seems that such generalized
multipliers are also implementable with optics: Instead of using a transparency
whose transmittance multiplies the amplitude of the incident light, an array of
AND gates may be used. And instead of just summing up the light falling on the
detector, the sum may be fed to a threshold element that operates as an OR gate.
This type of operation is especially suited for the low dynamic range of optics [141].
Thus the flexibility known to us from software, where changing the operations is
trivial, extends (at least to some degree) also to optical computing.

9.3.2   3-D graphic computer output

As we saw in section 2.8, a hologram may be used in order to record the wavefront of the light coming from a 3-D object. That wavefront may subsequently
be reconstructed, and thus a 3-D image of the object is seen. We also saw that

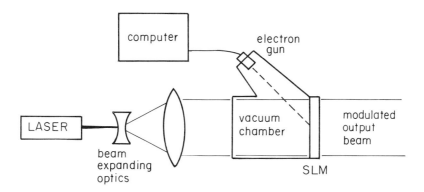

Figure 9.5: *Concept for a 3-D viewing terminal, based on a computer-generated hologram.*

computer-generated holograms (CGHs) may be used to create arbitrary wavefronts. In particular, they can simulate the wavefronts of objects that are not physically available. Computer-generated holograms may therefore be used to create 3-D images as part of a computer's output. The benefits of such an output are obvious for applications such as:

- Medical imaging. Give the doctor a 3-D view of bones or internal organs, constructed from tomographic or other data.

- Computer-aided design (CAD). Give the engineer a 3-D look at the parts he is designing.

- Mathematics. See a 3-D projection of a four-dimensional cube.

- Entertainment. 3-D television, 3-D movies.

We might envision a 3-D viewing terminal as follows (fig. 9.5). The computer calculates the pattern of the CGH, and writes it on an electron-beam-addressed SLM (synthetic interferogram CGHs are especially suited for this). The SLM then acts as a hologram. When it is illuminated by a laser beam, the desired wavefront is constructed.

The idea of 3-D computer output is not new [425,515]; however, such devices do not yet exist. Two basic difficulties dominate:

- The computational complexity of creating the CGH makes the process to slow and expensive. The hard part is the calculation of the wavefront at the hologram, given a mathematical description of the object. Recall that each

and every point in the object influences every point in the wavefront (unless
it is blocked by another part of the object). Tracking all of this is similar to
ideas of ray tracing, used in realistic computer generated pictures.

- The SLM must be large enough so that a reasonably sized image is seen, and
  on the other hand it must have extremely high resolution (a few thousand
  lines per mm). SLMs with both these properties have not yet been devised.

A partial solution, which allows holograms to be created but takes a rather
long time, is to divide the work between the computer and an optical system. The
computer calculates many different projections of the desired object, and displays
them sequentially on a graphic monitor. These images are then combined into a
hologram, by conventional holographic techniques [371].

9.3.3   Atomic set operations

Given a global set of elements, the simplest way to represent various subsets is by
bit vectors. In such a vector there is one bit for every element in the global set. If
the element is a member of the subset, its bit will have a value of "1". If it is not
a member, the bit will be "0". Set operations can then be performed by bitwise
logical operations on these vectors: union is OR, intersection is AND, complement
is NOT, and so on.

In conventional electronic computers, this representation is efficient and easy
to use only for small sets, because the basic data words are small (e.g., 32 bits on
a VAX). If the global set has more elements than a basic word has bits, a number
of words must be used. The set operations are then no longer atomic.

In section 7.7 we mentioned the fact that the natural basic data element in
an optical computer is expected to be 2-D image, with an order of 10^6 resolvable
points. The basic logic gates are expected to deal with such data elements in one
step. Therefore it will be possible to perform atomic set operations on sets of up
to 10^6 elements.

9.3.4   Optical random number generator

Random numbers have become very important in computation in recent years.
They are used where no deterministic algorithm for the solution of a problem is
known. This includes so-called "coin-flipping" algorithms and Monte-Carlo simulations. A computer, however, *is* a deterministic machine (ha ha). Therefore it is
not easy to come by random numbers in a computer — they have to be especially
generated. Two types of random number generators are available: software programs that create pseudo-random sequences of numbers [374, sect. 3.2], or physical
truly random generators [504]. The following points indicate the characteristics of
each type:

- Software generated random numbers are actually periodic (albeit with an extremely large period). Therefore they do not posses all the statistical properties of truly random numbers, and might have some unwanted characteristics.

- The sequence of numbers generated by a software program may be repeated. This is very useful when testing different programs, or when debugging. Physical random number generators cannot repeat their output.

- physical random number generators are much faster.

Physical random number generators are based upon nondeterministic physical phenomena, e.g., radioactive decay or the absorption of cosmic radiation. Optical random number generators are also possible. These devices would exploit the connection between the intensity of a light beam and the probability to detect a photon in it. With low light intensities, the intervals between consecutive photons are large enough for the photons to be counted individually. The arrival times of photons can thus serve as a random variable. Alternatively, A 2-D detector array may be illuminated by a wide beam of light. The location of the detector that detects the next photon is then a random variable. The probability distribution of this random variable is easily determined: it is the intensity distribution in the cross section of the light beam [501,463].

9.3.5 One-step fetch-and-add

One of the proposed architectures for future parallel computers is the so called family of *ultracomputers* [606,268,547]. These machines incorporate a set of N independent processing elements (PEs), N memory modules, and an interconnection network with $\log N$ steps. This network enables each processor to access any memory module in $O(\log N)$ time (one possibility is a set of $\log N$ shuffle-exchange networks, mentioned on page 215).

Ultracomputers are MIMD[3] machines, i.e., each PE runs an independent program. Many synchronization and coordination problems may be solved by introducing a new atomic operation into the underlying hardware. This operation is the "fetch-and-add"[4], denoted by F&A(v,e), where v is a variable in the shared memory and e is an expression [269,387]. This is defined by the *atomic* execution

---

[3]Acronym for "Multiple Instruction-stream Multiple Data-stream".

[4]An earlier version, "replace-add", is similar.

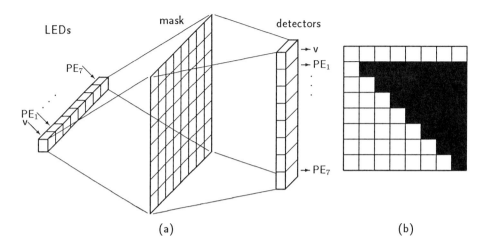

(a)   (b)

Figure 9.6: *Optical interconnection for one-step fetch-and-add.*
(a) Crossbar based on matrix-vector multiplier.
(b) Interconnection mask.

of the following code segment:

```
function F&A( v, e )
var temp;
begin
     temp := v;
     v := v + e;
     return( temp );
end.
```

Thus the value of v is incremented by e, and the *old* value is returned. As an example of the usefulness of this operation, consider a situation where a number of asynchronous processes wish to repeatedly read successive elements of an array. All we need is one shared variable, index, initially 1. Whenever a process wishes to read a new element, it simply executes F&A(index,1). This returns the index of the next unread element, and simultaneously increments index by 1.

The important point in the use of F&A is that distinct F&As aimed at the same variable v are *integrated* by the interconnection network, i.e., they take the same time as only one F&A. This is made possible by the addition of a small amount of hardware at the intermediate nodes of the network. The effect is as if the F&As were executed in an arbitrary serial order. It has been considered impossible to achieve this result in constant time, because of fan-in and fan-out limitations.

With optical interconnection devices, however, these limitations are much less stringent. As a result, A one-step integrating F&A operation is possible. Let us consider a simple case where we have N elements. The first one represents the memory cell $\mathbf{v}$, and the other $N - 1$ are PEs. We connect these elements with a crossbar switch based on a matrix-vector multiplier, like the one depicted in fig. 9.6 (a). Element number i uses LED number i and detector number i. At each cycle, every element transmits a value by lighting its LED, and accepts a return value by means of its detector. Any PE that wishes to perform F&A($\mathbf{v}$,$\mathbf{e}$) emits light proportional to $\mathbf{e}$. PEs that do not wish to perform a F&A do not emit any light and ignore the outputs of their detectors. The memory element emits light that is proportional to the current value of $\mathbf{v}$. The matrix that governs the interconnections is such that every element receives the light from all the preceding elements, except for the memory element that receives the light from all. This mask is shown in fig. 9.6 (b).

The results are as follows: The memory element detects a light intensity proportional to $\mathbf{v} + \sum_{i=1}^{N-1} \mathbf{e}_i$, where $\mathbf{e}_i$ is the value of $\mathbf{e}$ in the F&A coming from PE number i (if PE number i is not performing a F&A, $\mathbf{e}_i = 0$). This is exactly the correct new value for $\mathbf{v}$. PE number j detects a light intensity $\mathbf{v} + \sum_{i=1}^{j-1} \mathbf{e}_i$. Again this is the correct value that would be returned to it, if the F&As were integrated according to the order of the PEs. Thus $N - 1$ F&As aimed at the same memory cell are integrated and executed in a single step.

9.3.6 Associative memory

The memory of everyday computers is location-addressable. This means that the program must specify the location of the data element that it wants to manipulate. The location is typically the serial number of the memory cell holding the data. Keeping track of where the data resides is one of the more time-consuming tasks of a program [37,38].

An attractive alternative is *content-addressable* memory. Here each data element is composed of two fields: a key, and the data itself. When a program wants to manipulate a data element, it only specifies the key. The program[5] does not have to know where in the memory the data is kept. This scheme is also called *associative memory* [292].

In electronic computers, only small associative memories are sometimes provided for the operating system. Large, fast associative memories are not feasible. The difficulty lies in searching for the wanted key among all the memory cells. Two optical schemes have been proposed in order to overcome this problem. One relys on volume holography, while the other uses the Hopfield model of neural networks.

---

[5]Note that the program in question is the machine-language program produced by the compiler, and not the high-level-language program written by the user. Content-addressable memory allows the compiler to enjoy the same freedom from address calculations that users traditionally have.

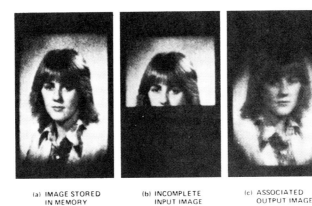

(a) IMAGE STORED   (b) INCOMPLETE   (c) ASSOCIATED
    IN MEMORY   INPUT IMAGE   OUTPUT IMAGE

Figure 9.7: *Example of holographic associative memory capability:*
(a) The image stored in the hologram.
(b) A partial input (the key).
(c) The reconstructed complete output (inversion is due to a mirror).
(Reprinted with permission from *Applied Optics* [535], ©1987)

Holographic associative memory

The roles of the object and reference beams are perfectly symmetric in the holographic process. That means that if we reproduce the object beam, we can reconstruct the reference beam (fig. 3.6). In holographic memory systems, the object is a page composer, i.e., a two-dimensional array of light points that represent bits (one-dimensional line composers may also be used). Therefore it is easy to reproduce, assuming the bit pattern is known.

Holographic associative memory uses volume holography. Volume holography has been mentioned a few times already, as a method by which a large number of images may be recorded on the same medium (see page 204). The different images are distinguished by reference beams that come from different directions. If an image (i.e., a bit pattern) is reproduced, this image's reference beam will be reconstructed. The crucial point in the associative memory application is that even if the image is only *partially* reproduced, the correct reference beam will be reconstructed, albeit with degradation [742].

Readout from a holographic associative memory is a two-step process[6]. In the first step a bit pattern that is a part of one of the stored patterns is produced on the page composer, and used to illuminate the hologram. This is the key (note that *any* part of the pattern can serve as a key). As a result, a reconstruction of one

---

[6]The first step may be skipped, leaving only one step, if the image serves as its own reference [137].

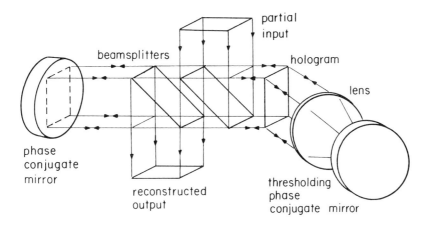

Figure 9.8: *Associative memory system using a phase conjugation resonator for nonlinear feedback. See text for explanation.*
(Adapted with permission from *Scientific American* [541], ©1986)

of the reference beams is created. Thus the correct reference beam is identified. In the second step, this reference beam is reproduced, and the whole data page is reconstructed and read out (fig. 9.7).

The method described above is linear. As a result, the output will contain not only the desired page but also its cross-correlations with the other pages (because the input key also interacts with the other stored pages). The correct page can be enhanced, and the others suppressed, by using some nonlinear feedback. One possibility is to put the system in a resonator created by phase conjugation mirrors[7] (fig. 9.8) [637,535,534,741,742,17,541]. The hologram is situated in the center of the resonator. The input key is injected into the resonator at one side, and impinges upon the hologram. The reference beam is then reconstructed. A phase conjugate mirror reflects this beam onto the hologram, where it reconstructs the object beam. This object beam in turn is reflected back by a second phase conjugate mirror, and so the light goes back and forth through the hologram. These iterations provide the necessary feedback; the nonlinearity is provided by the phase conjugate mirror that reflects the reference beam. This mirror is only active if the light intensity is above some threshold value. The desired reference beam is a plane wave, and is thus focused by a lens to one point. It therefore passes the threshold and is fully reflected. The light corresponding to interactions with other pages is a distorted wave, and therefore the lens does not focus it. As a result it is not reflected. In

---

[7]Phase conjugation mirrors *reverse* the propagation of light, rather than just *reflecting* it as ordinary mirrors do (see section 6.3).

this way each iteration reinforces the desired data page and decreases the noise caused by other data pages[8].

Another possibility is to use a loop that includes a pinhole array and a simple thresholding element, e.g., a liquid crystal light valve (LCLV) [2,536]. The imperfect input image impinges on a hologram, and reconstructs its reference beam. This beam is filtered through a pinhole array, which has holes only in locations that correspond to possible references. Thus light that was diffracted by interaction with the wrong hologram is blocked. The light emerging from the pinhole illuminates a second hologram, identical to the first, and reconstructs the object. This image is cast on the threshold device, and governs its reflectivity: areas corresponding to high light intensities will reflect more. As the original imperfect input is injected into the system by a reflection from this device, this configuration provides the necessary feedback.

The capacity of a holographic associative memory depends on the space-bandwidth product of the hologram, i.e., on the number of resolvable points in it. The number of stored pages can not be more than the space-bandwidth product divided by the number of pixels (i.e., bits) in each page [311].

Neural network associative memory

The Hopfield model of neural networks is described on page 122. There it is noted that the matrix of synapses between the neurons may encode a set of stable states of the system, and that when the system is allowed to evolve from an arbitrary initial state it converges to the nearest stable state. This property may be utilized as follows [209,564]: the initial state is chosen so as to match part of one of the stable states. The matching part is the key (again any part of the whole may serve as key). The system will evolve so as to reach the corresponding stable state. When it does, the values of the other elements may be read. This process is realized by an iterative matrix-vector multiplication, also described on page 122.

A major shortcomng of this method is its low capacity: it turns out that a network with N neurons can only have $0.144N$ stable states [11,169]. Each stable state involves all N neurons, so the information content is actually $0.144N^2$. As the information is kept in the N^2 synapses between the neurons, this means that only about $\frac{1}{7}$ of the information capacity of the system can be utilized.

---

[8]This may also be interpreted as a competition for gain. Any of the stored pages can resonate back and forth between the phase conjugate mirrors. However, if one is stronger than the others, it receives more gain from the mirrors; this gain comes at the expense of the gain that the other pages receive. Thus the strongest page becomes even stronger, and after a few iterations it dominates. Injecting a key that fits one of the pages gives that page an initial advantage in this race [17,741].

Summary

Optical processors for synthetic aperture radar imaging are the only ones currently in wide use. Broadband integrated optics spectrum analyzers, matched filter correlators, and simple image classifiers are probably also being used, or at least in advanced stages of development. The realization of other special purpose (analog) optical processors depends on the resolution of dynamic range and space-bandwidth product problems.

General purpose digital optical computers are still at a very early stage of development, and it is not clear whether they will ever be fully realized. Specific optical devices are, however, already being used (as parts of general purpose electronic computers). These perform the functions of interconnection and mass storage. It might be expected that additional developments, especially in optical interconnections, will pave the road towards an all-optical computer, or at least a hybrid electronic logic/optical interconnection machine.

Along with the quest for a predominantly optical computer, ideas abound for new optical gadgets for conventional electronic computer systems. These are usually special purpose accelerators that can perform some operation accedingly fast. Their implementation and use is, however, limited by interfacing issues.

Bibliographical notes

The optical computing survey by Bell in IEEE Spectrum [54] is the most comprehensive in terms of current status and future prospects. It includes the opinions of many researchers, as well as a listing of major research efforts throughout the world. An interesting collection of perspectives from the forefront of optical computing research is gathered in a special issue of Optics News [526]. The most outspoken critic of optical computing, and indeed of any technology competing with silicon, is Keyes [362,363,367].

Chapter 10

Connections to Computer Science

If we were to summarize the preceding chapters in one sentence, we would say that digital optical computers are still a very long way off. However, some of the optical devices and concepts being developed for optical computers may be used also in conjunction with conventional electronic computers; in fact, some devices are actually designed to interact with electronic computers. They may thus influence various areas of computer science. Such influences are surveyed in the first part of this chapter.

Optical computers (existing and projected) should also be of interest to theoretical computer science, which deals with what can be computed and how. The second part of this chapter is devoted to a study of the impact optical computers might have on conventional models of computation.

A short final section addresses possible influences in the opposite direction, i.e., what computer science can contribute to optical computing.

10.1 Influences on applied computer science

The impact of optical computers on applied computer science ranges from the need to accommodate new optical devices on the one hand, to the replacement of conventional software approaches on the other. We now survey specific possible implications data bases, artificial intelligence, number crunching, operating systems, programming languages, and process control.

10.1.1 Optical storage for data bases

The chief effect on data bases is through the introduction of optical storage devices, specifically optical disks. The characteristics of these devices, and their use in conjunction with data bases, are reviewed on page 262. The challenges that they present to data base researchers are:

- Find the optimal use for this new media. In what cases should it be preferred, and when should it be rejected?

- Develop new protocols for indexing, backup, and recovery that make use of the characteristics of the new medium.

10.1.2   Optical processing for artificial intelligence

The field of artificial intelligence (AI) is ill-defined; we use the term loosely to describe machines that perform actions that we intuitively relate to human intelligence. These include

- Perception and understanding (machine vision, speech comprehension and generation).

- Problem solving (Expert systems, game-playing computers).

- Deduction and inference (in expert systems, mechanical theorem proving, and the use of data bases).

Many of the special purpose optical systems described in chapters 3 and 4 fall into these categories. For instance, pattern recognition is a basic element of machine vision. Optical systems can therefore be used instead of electronic computers that run time-consuming heuristic programs [520]. The following is a short list of other AI tasks and possible optical implementations.

Parsing [201]

Parsing is the analysis of the syntactic structure of expressions. It may be seen as a special case of pattern recognition, where the pattern is in the underlying structure. Two common ways to find the connection between an expression and the grammar that generated it are to start from the grammar and use production rules to create the expression (top-down), or to start from the expression and reduce it to the grammar's start symbol (bottom-up) [7, chap. 4]. In both, pieces of the expression are iteratively exchanged with grammatical symbols. This is actually symbolic substitution, which has received some attention in optics (see section 7.2.8).

Vision and speech data reduction

The human brain deals with visual input by means of a set of receptors and a vast neural system that interconnects them [346]. Various interconnection patterns allow the extraction of different features from the input, and thus a reduction of the data. This can be mimicked in optics by having a large set of matched filters, acting as receptors, and combining their outputs by optical interconnections [307]. The same may also be applied to auditory inputs.

Inference and deduction

One way of approaching inference and deduction is by a matrix-vector formulation [141]. This is easily implemented optically. Another is to use mathematical resolution: if you know that a or b are true, and also a is false or c is true, it means that

b or c are true — which might be easier to check. An optical implementation uses the dual rail encoding scheme for the literals [602]: a would have the top bit lit, while *not a* would have the bottom one lit. To resolve, the representations of two clauses are superposed. A literal that then has both bits lit indicates a possible resolution. Using spreading optics, many resolutions may be done in parallel.

In cases where large data bases are concerned, the crucial step in obtaining an answer is the search of the data base. Large parts of the data base may be searched in parallel using optical pattern matching systems: the key to the desired data (a name, catalog number, etc.) is matched against multiple data entries at once, thus reducing the search time [662]. Optical logic elements may also be used for simple pre-processing, e.g., to check that the data fits a combination of two keys rather than just one [719,61].

Diagnostics [470,471]

Diagnostics may be considered as a special case of inference and deduction: given a set of events (or symptoms), the system is asked to make an educated guess as to what circumstances caused them. The guess is based upon a data base giving the probabilities that certain events will happen, conditioned on the circumstances. This is written $p(e|h)$; it means "the probability that e will happen, when we know that h is true". For example, if $e =$"Joe sneezes", $h_1 =$"Joe has the flu", and $h_2 =$"Joe is fast asleep", we will find a large $p(e|h_1)$ but a small $p(e|h_2)$.

A diagnostic system must use this data to find the opposite probabilities: given that Joe sneezes, is it more probable that he has the flu or that he is asleep? This is done by Bayes' theorem, which states that

$$p(h|e) = \frac{p(e|h)\,p(h)}{p(e|h)\,p(h) + p(e|\bar{h})\,p(\bar{h})},$$

where $\bar{h}$ means that h is *not* true (the theorem is easily extended to multiple events and circumstances). An optical implementation may use a matrix-vector multiplier to pair up all the known events e_i with all the possible circumstances, i.e., to find all the relevant entries $p(e_i|h_j)$ from the data base. The probabilities that the different h_j are the right ones are then calculated in parallel by a set of small electronic processors.

10.1.3   Number crunching

Number crunching is a major application for supercomputers. Its main use is in the simulation of complex physical systems, e.g., the atmosphere, a chemical solution, or the air flow around an airplane.

This application may be a natural one for general purpose digital optical computers, in that they may be able to perform large computations faster through parallelism. On the other hand, it may also be appropriate for special purpose systems. For example, an analog system for the solution of differential equations can do away with the need for quite a lot of numerical calculations.

An important feature of concurrent number crunchers is their programmability. If this is to be extended to optical computers, issues related to parallel programming must be addressed. This is discussed below.

10.1.4   Operating Systems

Electronic special purpose accelerators exist already, and are handled by today's operating systems. There is no reason to believe that optical ones would require any different treatment. They would simply be another resource that the operating system has at its disposal. The operating system would then regulate the use of the optical accelerator, just as it regulates the use of all other devices.

General purpose digital optical computers are another matter. Assuming that these computers will have a parallel architecture, they will need a totally new operating system. As the exact tasks and characteristics of this operating system will be dictated by the details of the architecture, and as these details are not yet known, it is premature to discuss the possible operating system in depth. Suffice it to say that operating systems for parallel computers provide a wide field for research currently being pursued by a number of groups around the world. Key issues in this architecture/operating system interface are:

- Are all the processing elements (PEs) equivalent, or are some distinguishable and capable of controlling others? This architectural decision dictates whether the operating system will be distributed or centralized.

- Will the system be a multi-user one or a single-user one? If it is multi-user, the operating system must deal with the allocation of PEs.

- How are communications between the PEs established? The operating system might have to deal with routing, too.

10.1.5   Programming languages

In this area, too, a distinction must be made between special purpose accelerators and general purpose computers. Special purpose accelerators need not affect programming languages at all; in many cases the operating system governs their use, and allocates them if they are available. If they are not, a conventional software routine is used instead. Alternatively, provisions may be made by which a program can itself activate such a device. This is not possible in the context of a multi-user system, but might be advantageous in a dedicated system, e.g., one used for process control.

As with operating systems, parallel general purpose optical computers will need new programming languages and compilers. Again this is a result of the great difference between any parallel computer and conventional serial computers; a large research effort is now being directed toward new parallel languages. The main approaches to the utilization of parallelism are:

- *Explicit programming.* The programmer is responsible for the individual programming of all the PEs, and has to deal with all the interactions between them.

- *Parallelism by repetition.* Only one process is programmed, but it is duplicated many times in the computer. This is what happens in systolic arrays or SIMD machines, and might therefore be the suitable approach for optical computers.

- *Parallelism by the operating system.* In this method, the burden of taking care of all the interacting PEs is shifted from the programmer to the operating system. The programmer just describes what the program must do, and the operating system activates various parts concurrently whenever possible. An example is the dataflow concept.

- *Parallelism by compilation.* Here the burden is shifted to the compiler. The programmer writes a conventional serial program; the compiler then tries to find parts (especially inner loops) that may be parallelized.

10.1.6   Process control

One of the most common uses of computers is that of controlling various processes, e.g., in an industrial assembly line or a laboratory experiment. This usually involves a combination of sensors that monitor the process, the computer that evaluates the situation and decides how to proceed, and some feedback apparatus by which the computer may influence the process. Optical devices for signal processing and pattern recognition may be helpful in carrying out the processing stage in real time.

10.2   Implications in theoretical computer science

Theoretical computer science is the study of computation. This has two aspects:

- *Algorithms.* The search for recipes that will find solutions to specific instances of various problems. An algorithm provides an upper bound on the amount of work needed to solve a problem, by showing exactly how it can be solved within this bound.

- *Complexity.* What is the minimal amount of work required to solve a given class of problems, irrespective of *how* the solution is obtained; this is the corresponding lower bound. Problems are grouped into complexity classes by the relationship between the size of the input and the amount of work required to deal with it (e.g., logarithmic, polynomial, exponential). Some problems are classified as unsolvable with any amount of work, as no finite recipe can solve them.

Both of these research avenues depend on the underlying *model of computation*, i.e., the capabilities of the machine used to perform the computation. For example, the lower bound on the amount of work[1] required to solve a partial differential equation using a powerful parallel computer will probably be different from the lower bound on the amount of work needed to solve the same problem with a grocery cash register. Algorithms also depend upon the underlying machine, because the sequence of operations used to solve a problem must come from the repertoire of the machine that is being used.

In this section we discuss the question of how optical computers fit into the conventional framework of computational models. We first pose the question of the computational power of special purpose analog systems, and whether or not they are equivalent to Turing machines. We then comment on step-counting when a special purpose accelerator is used. Then we turn to models of parallel computation, and how well they represent the capabilities of projected digital optical computers. Finally we look at how the capabilities of optical systems may prompt changes in specific algorithms.

10.2.1 Computational power of analog systems

The most basic model of sequential computation is the *Turing machine* [312, chap. 7]. This is a finite control with a number of tapes that serve as memory and as input/output devices. The control may be in any one of a finite set of *states*. Two states are distinguished: the *initial* state and the *stopping* state. The tapes are (infinite) linear arrays of cells, each of which may contain one symbol from the machine's *alphabet* (which typically includes the blank and some characters or digits). In its simple version, a Turing machine has three tapes: an *input* tape, an *output* tape, and a *work* tape. Initially the input tape contains some string, while the other two are empty. The reading heads are at the beginnings of their respective tapes, and the control is in the initial state. At each step in the computation, the combination of symbols read from the tapes and the current state of the control dictate what the machine will do: what will be written on the tapes, in which direction the heads will move, and what the new state of the control will be.

---

[1]"Work" should be understood as resources, number of steps, time, etc.

The usefulness of the Turing machine as a model of computation stems from two things. First, it is very simple. Second, it is universal, in the sense that anything that is known to be computable may be computed by a proper Turing machine (this is known as "Church's thesis"). Therefore a Turing machine provides a convenient method for the comparison of various computational processes. Criteria for the comparison are the number of steps until the machine halts, or the number of cells used in the work tape[2].

A good way in which to evaluate the capabilities of optical special purpose (analog) processors is to compare them with Turing machines. This comparison, however, tends to the philosophical, as it involves the notions of what a computer is and how we perceive the physical world. The results are not limited to optics; rather they may be attributed to any physical system.

The simple, classical model of physical (and more specifically, optical) systems regards them as being continuous. for example, the amplitude along the cross section of a light beam is usually described by a continuous function of the spatial coordinates — as we have done throughout this book. This sort of system is inherently stronger than any Turing machine can be, because Turing machines can only compute discrete functions of objects with finite representations. For example, it can be shown that rather simple differential equations with Turing-computable initial conditions can give rise to uncomputable solutions [552,553, 554]. As the equations describe physical phenomena, the correct physical system forced into the initial conditions will evolve naturally so as to "solve" the equation.

While this difference in favor of physical systems is certainly true formally, it is not very convincing practically. For one thing, none of the applications surveyed in this book involves the solution of a problem that is unsolvable on a conventional Turing-like computer. The only difference is that the optical solutions may be faster. Another point is that the continuous, unlimited-accuracy nature of the physical model is actually impossible to realize: the modulation of the input, the operation of the system, and the measurement of the output can only be known to a limited degree of accuracy. A Turing machine with a finite representation can also perform calculations to any desired finite accuracy.

An interesting point is that if the abstract notion of Church's thesis is given a generalized physical interpretation, it turns out to be equivalent to a quantum-physical computer model [184]. Thus it seems that there is an underlying connection between physics and computation, with both disciplines interrelated at the most fundamental level [549].

---

[2]The separation between the input, output, and work tapes is motivated by the desire to be able to note the fact that certain computations need less space than the size of the input or output.

10.2.2   Step-counting with special purpose accelerators

The most basic way in which to compare different algorithms that solve the same problem is by their step counts. For example, the naive algorithm for the Fourier transform requires $O(n^2)$ steps, while the FFT algorithm only requires $O(n \log n)$ steps; thus we conclude that the FFT algorithm is advantageous. In order to get an exact step count (including the constant), the algorithm should be expressed in terms of a simple computer. A Turing machine may be used; however it usually is not because it is unnatural to express algorithms in "Turing language". Instead a random access machine (RAM) is employed as the model of computation.

A RAM is a CPU with a restricted and well-defined instruction set, which operates on data held in a set of registers and in a random access primary memory [8, sect. 1.2]. Hence it is very similar to conventional electronic computers; the difference lies only in the instruction set, which is more limited (on the order of 15 instructions, dealing with register transfers and indexed memory access). Simulation of the execution of an algorithm on this model is straightforward.

Computers with special purpose accelerators, however, cannot be faithfully simulated by a RAM. Some enhancement is needed so as to bring out the advantages gained by using the special purpose device. Without such an enhancement, the special purpose device will not compare favorably with a regular general purpose computer. For example, if we have an optical system that can perform a Fourier transform in one step, we have to build this capability into the RAM. Otherwise the RAM will use $O(n \log n)$ steps to compute the Fourier transform, and will not model our system.

The modification needed in order to allow a RAM to model a special purpose accelerator is simple: a "special purpose co-processor" is added, along with a set of interface registers. When the machine wants to activate the special purpose device, it writes the data for the device in these registers. It is assumed that the special purpose device then performs its task on this data, and writes its output in place of the data. Therefore the regular CPU can start reading the results at the next step. Returning to the Fourier transform example, the RAM will write the data in the special registers. the data is then transformed into its Fourier transform in one step, and the machine then reads the result.

Analogously, a Turing machine may also be augmented with a special purpose tape that interfaces to a *deus ex machina* that performs certain operations instantaneously (fig. 10.1). This is actually equivalent to the use of an *oracle* in the Cook reduction of problems, which is used in order to evaluate the complexity of certain problems relative to subproblems that are computed for free by the oracle [165]. Thus a Turing machine too can easily be adapted for the modeling of computers with special purpose accelerators.

We may therefore conclude that optical special purpose systems do not entail any radical changes in the concepts and techniques of theoretical computer science.

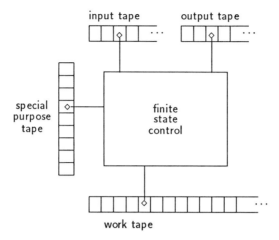

Figure 10.1: *A Turing machine with a special purpose accelerator.*

10.2.3   Optical computers and the PRAM model

The main features distinguishing digital optical computers from conventional computers are parallelism and the use of dense optical interconnections. Parallel computation may be modeled by *nondeterministic* Turing machines — machines that can be regarded as able to fork into a number of submachines that explore different computations in parallel [384,259,192,539]. However, we will concentrate on a more popular model of parallel computation, namely the PRAM, which stands for "parallel random access machine". This is a group of CPUs that can execute a limited and well defined set of instructions. Each CPU has its own bank of registers, and may also have a local memory; the combination of a CPU with its local memory is sometimes called a *processing element* (PE). In addition, all the PEs share the use of a random access primary memory [229].

The rules that govern the outcome when a number of processors access the same memory cell simultaneously dictate a distinction between a number of submodels:

1. EREW — Exclusive Read Exclusive Write.
   In this model, the CPUs may not access the same memory cell simultaneously.

2. CREW — Concurrent Read Exclusive Write.
   In this case, a number of CPUs may read the same memory cell simultaneously, but if a CPU writes something to the memory no other CPU may access that cell at the same time.

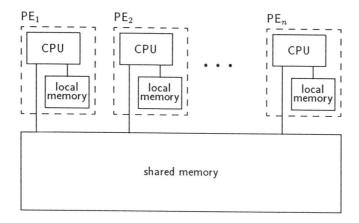

Figure 10.2: *Schematic representation of a PRAM.*

3. CRCW — Concurrent Read Concurrent Write[3].

   Here a few CPUs may also write into the same memory cell simultaneously. The model is further subdivided according to the result:

   (a) Common value only — the software algorithm must ensure that if a number of processors write to the same cell, they all write the same value.

   (b) Garbage — if a number of CPUs write to the same cell, the resulting value will be garbage.

   (c) Arbitrary winner — If a number of CPUs write simultaneously, an arbitrary one will succeed. The data written by the others is lost.

   (d) Priorities — If a number of CPUs write simultaneously, the one with the highest priority succeeds.

Electronic computers, which are modeled by the PRAM, typically have limited fan-in and fan-out. One expression of this fact is that when many CPUs write to the same memory cell, the result relates to at most one of them. Another is that the arithmetic operations performed by the CPUs are binary, i.e., they accept only two arguments. This fundamental limitation directly affects the performance of these machines: whenever data has to be spread out over n CPUs or collected from n locations, this takes at least[4] $\log_k n$ steps, where k is the limit on the fan-in/fan-out.

---

[3]In the original definition of PRAM, this was not allowed [229]. Therefore other names such as WRAM also appear in the literature.

[4]For certain functions of n variables, there exist sophisticated algorithms that may reduce this

Optical interconnections, on the other hand, do not suffer from this limitation. As we saw in section 7.6.4, it is easy to make many *duplicate* copies of the data and to distribute them. Also, a photodetector integrates the light falling on it. Therefore if light from several sources converges onto one detector, the detector's output will be *the sum of the inputs*. These capabilities (which, by the way, are the crucial factor behind the one-step implementations of matrix multiplication and the F&A operation) are unavailable in electronic computers[5]. We must therefore define a new PRAM model, in order to accommodate optical systems.

The new model deviates in two respects from the conventional models. First of all, the notion of "concurrent write" is not powerful enough; we need "duplicate concurrent write". We therefore define[6]:

4. CRDCW — Concurrent Read Duplicate Concurrent Write.
   Each PE may either read from one cell, or write the same value to a set of cells. The set is predefined by the interconnection pattern. In addition, many PEs may access each memory cell, both for reading and for writing. This is conceptually identical to a conventional CRCW model, with each PE that writes to a set of cells replaced by a set of PEs that all write the same value. This similarity is elaborated in appendix I.

The subdivision according to the outcome of concurrent writes, defined above, also holds for this model. However, we again need to add another class in order to accommodate the possibilities of optics:

(e) Sum — a number of simultaneous writes to the same memory cell result in the sum of the individual values being written.

In short, the PRAM model that properly includes the possibilities of optical interconnections is CRDCW-sum. It is interesting to note that this is also the model that is required for the analysis of the computing powers of neural networks:

- Neurons duplicate their action-potential pulses and transmit them to numerous other neurons, via axon branching.

- A neuron sums up the incoming potentials from all its synapses. This sum dictates whether or not it will fire.

---

by a constant factor. For example, the OR of n bits may be computed on a CREW machine in $0.72 \log_2 n$ steps [164].

[5]Analog electronic circuits can also perform these operations: data may be duplicated by amplification and then division among a number of outputs. A number of voltages may be summed by an array of operational amplifiers. However, the fan-ins and fan-outs are still limited by dynamic range, parasitic capacitances, crosstalk, inductance, etc., and the restrictions become more severe as the data rates increase. In addition, the wiring complexity is high. With optics, these restrictions are much less severe.

[6]Equivalently, ERDER and CRDER models may be defined. At present, however, there is no motivation to do so.

In theory, this model is stronger than the conventional CRCW models. This means that anything that could be done on the previous models can also be done on this one, at the same cost. In addition, there are operations that can be done here but cannot be done on the previous models (at least not for the same price). Appendix I proves this claim.

If we turn to practical systems, however, some reservations have to be made. The chief difficulty lies in the analog nature of the representation of values by light intensities. Such a representation is necessarily inaccurate, and therefore both the fan-in and the range of values that may be written are rather limited. This problem may be alleviated if we use a digital binary representation of values, and write each bit separately. This sacrifices the one-step summation and replaces it with a multistep process. However, the number of steps depends on the desired accuracy, and not on the number of inputs that are being summed.

10.2.4 New algorithms

Optical processing systems offer a number of possibilities that are unavailable in conventional computers. It is not that the operations themselves are unavailable, but that they are performed much faster by the optical system. "Fast" is measured here in the number of steps that are required, and the relation between the number of steps and the size of the input. We do *not* take into account the cycle time, i.e., the actual time that each step takes.

The most promising operations are those that can be done optically in constant time, i.e., that are independent of the input size. These operations include:

- *The Fourier transform.*
  An analog 2-D Fourier transform may be done optically in one step. Electronic computers take $O(n \log n)$ steps to calculate a 1-D transform, using the FFT algorithm.

- *Matrix multiplication.*
  Prototype optical one-step matrix multipliers have been demonstrated. Serial algorithms for electronic computers need at least $O(N^{2.376\cdots})$ steps, and the constant hidden in the O notation is large. Systolic architectures require $O(N)$ steps.

- *Multiple products.*
  Multiple point multiplications are performed simultaneously when a light beam passes through a transparency (or an SLM).

- *Large fan-in sum.*
  Optics can sum many analog values in one operation; digital electronics require $O(\log n)$ steps.

Algorithms are stated in terms of the operations that are available. It stands to reason that adding the above operations to the repertoire will enable new algorithms to be developed.

10.3 The contribution of computer science to optical computing

So far the discussion has been rather one-sided: it has only considered how optical computing and optical devices can influence computer science. This section will attempt to balance the picture, by showing how computer science can contribute to optical computing. It should be clear that this is only an attempt to formalize an interaction that has actually been going on all the time, the interaction between the scientist and the engineer. In the case of optical computing the distinction between the two is even harder than usual.

One important contribution that computer science can make is in the area of *directing research efforts*. This has two aspects:

- Point out the most interesting and potentially beneficial research areas.

- Evaluate current results.

These two aspects are strongly interlinked. For example, consider the recent research effort into optical matrix multipliers. The importance of matrix multiplication implies that any breakthroughs in this field will have great impact; the effort is therefore clearly justified. However, it seems that a large part of this effort has been misdirected. While dozens of papers describing optical matrix multipliers have indeed been published, the great majority of these papers delineate systolic architectures which do not have any clear advantage over electronic systolic architectures. Completely parallel multipliers, on the other hand, have been neglected; even the few papers that do deal with them only describe extremely small multipliers, and it is still not clear whether or not efficient parallel multiplies for large matrices can be designed. Thus a reevaluation of results derived from an initially correct approach may help to redirect the effort to a more beneficial direction.

Another example is provided by the analysis in the preceding section. It focuses the attention on a trivial and simple characteristic of optical systems, which is usually taken for granted: the fact that the output from a detector is proportional to the total amount of light that falls on it. If this can be used to create a device that adds a large number of inputs in one step (with digital accuracy), this device may form the basis for a new technology that will surpass the capabilities of electronic machines. In fact, an immediate consequence will be the possibility of designing parallel matrix multipliers. Hence an evaluation in terms of theoretical computer science points out a direction for future research.

Computer science can also contribute to optical computing in terms of *solutions to specific problems*. Good examples for this are provided by coding shemes that solve certain problems that limit the performance of optical devices:

- The code described in figure 9.4 allows a write-once memory to be rewritten. It was developed for optical disks.

- Optical disks also suffer from an unusual type of write errors, namely it might be impossible to write a bit because of a defect in the thin metallic film that serves as a recording medium. Such an error may be called "stuck at 1" or "stuck at 0", as appropriate. A special error correcting code has been developed to deal with this situation; it uses some additional disk space to point back at bits that are wrong [187].

- Error correcting codes may also enhance the performance of optical pattern recognition systems. Instead of using the minimal number of filters, some redundancy is introduced; this allows for the generation of codes by which correct recognition is possible even if one of the filters gives a wrong output [428].

Finally, computer science can make an important contribution in the area of *abstraction and modeling*. It seems that the design procedure is greatly simplified and enhanced by using layers of abstraction. Specifically, the design of a computer system may be viewed as made up of three layers: the top one is the *architecture*; it specifies how the computer behaves from the user's point of view. The second layer is the *implementation*; it details how the architectural concepts are carried out by basic functional elements. The bottom layer is the *realization*; this is where the technical data is given, i.e., which chips are used, how they are connected, etc. It should be noted that numerous implementations of the same architecture may exist; likewise, a given implementation may have a number of distinct realizations.

The would-be designers of optical computers usually just suggest different realizations for some functional unit, without trying to derive a global picture of the machine as a whole. In particular, the low-level abstraction of the implementation layer is missing. Without a clear understanding of what the functionally important characteristics of optical devices are, it is impossible to design a detailed architecture; indeed, the projected architectures are typically cited only in general terms (e.g., "parallel" or "cellular").

A better understanding of the capabilities of optical systems, that would enable the design of viable architectures, may be obtained from new models which describe these systems. Models, by their nature, provide for *simplified* descriptions. A good model is one which expresses the important underlying characteristics, while ignoring the unimportant details. It thus allows a clean analysis of the modeled system. The treatment presented in the previous section is just a preliminary step in the direction of deriving computational models for optics; much research is still needed before a clear and full picture emerges. It may be hoped that collaboration between computer science and optics researchers will someday produce the desired results.

Summary

Optical special purpose processing units, as well as full-scale optical computers, may be expected to have an influence on computer science as their development continues. In practical areas of computer science, the main issue will probably be the question of how to integrate optical devices into existing systems, and how to operate them so as to utilize their full potential. Special purpose optical processors may be treated in the same way as special purpose electronic systems in this respect. Parallel, general purpose digital optical computers (if they become a reality) will share the problems of electronic parallel computers.

In the area of theoretical computer science, the interesting question is how optical computers fit into the existing framework of computational models. This is divided into three subquestions. The first deals with the power of analog systems, and how they relate to Turing machines; while it is true that analog systems are more powerful, it seems that this is more a formal distinction than a practical one. Therefore one should not expect unsolvable or intractable problems to become simple problems on an optical computer. The second question is that of step-counting in the evaluation of algorithms. If special purpose accelerators are used, the count must change accordingly; optical processors are no different from electronic ones in this respect. A possibly real difference does arise in the third field, that of parallelism and interconnections. The possibilities of dense interconnections, duplication, and large fan-in summing greatly exceed those of electronic systems. Therefore a new version of the PRAM model has been proposed in order to allow for the analysis of optical computers.

Computer science may also be expected to influence the future development of optical computers. The techniques and experience gained in connection to electronic computers should be applied to this new field, so as to evaluate current results and point out new directions. New models that would highlight the special capabilities of optics are especially called for.

Appendix A

Taxonomy

The field of optical computing is wide and ill-defined. The following taxonomy is an attempt to classify the many different research efforts in this field. The classification is not hierarchical, like a tree; rather it creates a vector of characteristics for each optical computing project. Nearly all the combinations are possible. The first five points in the classification deal with the nature of the optical system that is addressed:

1. *Analog vs. digital.*
   This is probably the most important distinction. It divides optical computing systems into two groups: those in which data values are represented in an analog fashion (e.g., by different, possibly continuous, light intensities), and those in which the data is encoded in some digital manner. systems which use digital encoding, but represent each digit by an analog quantity, defy this classification.

2. *Special purpose vs. general purpose.*
   This is the second most important distinction, and the major one used in the organization of this book. While general purpose systems are programmable and represent their data in some symbolic form, special purpose systems are further classified according to their use:

   (a) Image processing. This includes pattern recognition, image enhancement, transforms, and filtering.

   (b) Signal analysis. This includes spectrum analysis and the processing of radar signals.

   (c) Numerical processing. Matrix operations are the most prominent example.

   It should be noted that the marriages between "digital" and "general purpose" on the one hand, and "analog" and "special purpose" on the other, do not necessarily apply. The quest for accuracy has sprouted a number of special purpose systems that use analog techniques and digital encoding.

3. *All-optical vs. hybrid.*
   All-optical systems are distinguished from systems that mix electronic devices with optical ones. While "pure" optical systems may be more pleasing

intellectually, hybrid systems are currently more practical. The electronic support can come in one of two forms:

(a) Interleaved individual devices, e.g., electronic logic elements that are interconnected by optical links, using detectors and light sources.

(b) A whole external electronic subsystem, e.g., a microcomputer that controls the operation of the optical devices.

4. *Coherent vs. Incoherent.*
This technical point concerning the light used has far-reaching implications as to the operations that are easy to realize. For example, with coherent light the Fourier transform is a basic operation.

5. *Linear vs. nonlinear.*
Linear systems process all inputs in the same manner. In nonlinear systems, the inputs may interact.

Two additional points classify the type of research that is carried out:

6. *The level being addressed.*
Research related to optical computing may be directed at a number of distinct levels:

(a) Basic optical phenomena and optical materials.

(b) Optical devices.

(c) Complete optical systems that incorporate many devices to achieve a specific goal. This also includes system architecture.

(d) Applications and how they fit into the framework of optical computing.

7. *Practical vs. theoretical.*
While theoretical research deals with explaining why things happen, and with predicting new results, practical research demonstrates new devices.

Appendix B

Linear Algebra

This appendix defines the various algebraic operations and concepts used in the text.

B.1 Matrix operations

A matrix is a rectangular array of numbers. The text uses only square matrices, where the number of rows is the same as the number of columns. Therefore only such matrices are used in the following definitions.

Matrix-vector multiplication

The multiplication of a vector $\mathbf{x}$ by a matrix $\mathcal{A}$ is defined to produce a vector $\mathbf{y}$ whose elements are the inner products[1] of the rows of the matrix with the multiplying vector:

$$\mathcal{A}\,\mathbf{x} = \mathbf{y}$$

is

$$\begin{pmatrix} a_{11} & \cdots & a_{1n} \\ \vdots & & \vdots \\ a_{n1} & \cdots & a_{nn} \end{pmatrix} \begin{pmatrix} x_1 \\ \vdots \\ x_n \end{pmatrix} = \begin{pmatrix} y_1 \\ \vdots \\ y_n \end{pmatrix},$$

where

$$y_i = \sum_{j=1}^{n} a_{ij}\,x_j.$$

Matrix-matrix multiplication

The multiplication of two matrices $\mathcal{A}$, $\mathcal{B}$ is a natural extension of the multiplication of a matrix by a vector. It is defined to produce a third matrix, $\mathcal{C}$, whose elements are the inner products of the rows of $\mathcal{A}$ and the columns of $\mathcal{B}$. Therefore,

---

[1]An inner product of two vectors is the sum of the point multiplications of their respective elements.

$$\mathcal{A}\,\mathcal{B} = \mathcal{C}$$

is

$$\begin{pmatrix} a_{11} & \cdots & a_{1n} \\ \vdots & & \vdots \\ a_{n1} & \cdots & a_{nn} \end{pmatrix} \begin{pmatrix} b_{11} & \cdots & b_{1n} \\ \vdots & & \vdots \\ b_{n1} & \cdots & b_{nn} \end{pmatrix} = \begin{pmatrix} c_{11} & \cdots & c_{1n} \\ \vdots & & \vdots \\ c_{n1} & \cdots & c_{nn} \end{pmatrix},$$

where

$$c_{ij} = \sum_{k=1}^{n} a_{ik}\, b_{kj}.$$

B.2   Linear transforms

An expression $\mathcal{L}$ that depends on a variable x is said to be *linear* if when we replace x by a linear combination of variables, we get a linear combination of expressions:

$$\mathcal{L}(\alpha x + \beta y) = \alpha \mathcal{L}(x) + \beta \mathcal{L}(y).$$

A linear transform is the same thing for functions: if we apply the transformation to a linear combination of functions, we get a linear combination of transformations of the functions (see, e.g., [260, chap. 2]). It turns out that *any* linear transform may be expressed by an integral of the following form (this example is for functions of two variables):

$$g(x', y') = \iint f(x, y)\, h(x, y, x', y')\, dx\, dy, \tag{B.1}$$

where f is the transformed function

g is the result of the transformation

h is the *transformation kernel*. It is sometimes also called the *impulse response* of the system, for it specifies how the system responds at x', y' to an input impulse at x, y.

Shift invariance

A special class of linear transforms is the class in which h does not depend on the absolute values of x, y, x', y'; rather it depends only on the *differences* $x' - x$ and $y' - y$. Therefore h is a function of only *two* variables, and we may write it as

$$h = h(x' - x, y' - y).$$

If the input function f to such a transform is shifted by, say, a in the x direction and b in the y direction, so is the output g. In other words, if we calculate

$$g'(x', y') = \iint f(x - a, y - b)\, h(x - x', y - y')\, dx\, dy$$

we will find that

$$g'(x', y') \equiv g(x' - a, y' - b).$$

These transforms are known as *shift invariant* linear transforms, because the "shape" of g does not change.

The integral that describes shift invariant linear transforms is called a *convolution* integral. The impulse response of such transforms is called their *point spread function* (PSF). The interaction of a shift invariant linear system with its input is often described as a convolution of the input with the point spread function of the system. This is written as

$$g * h \equiv \int\!\!\int\limits_{-\infty}^{+\infty} g(\xi, \eta)\, h(x - \xi, y - \eta)\, d\xi\, d\eta.$$

As we note in appendix C, it is more convenient to handle the convolution operation in the frequency domain, because it is simpler there. Shift invariant linear systems are therefore sometimes defined in terms of their *transfer function*, which is the Fourier transform of their PSF. In the case of optical systems, we talk of the *optical* transfer function (OTF).

Appendix C

The Fourier Transform

C.1 Definition

Given a (complex) function of the spatial coordinates $g(x, y)$, its Fourier transform is defined to be

$$G(\nu_x, \nu_y) = \int\limits_{-\infty}^{+\infty}\!\!\int g(x, y)\, e^{-i2\pi(x\nu_x + y\nu_y)}\, dx\, dy. \tag{C.1}$$

Using the identity $e^{i\theta} \equiv \cos\theta + i\sin\theta$ we see that this is equivalent to the pair of transforms:

$$\int\limits_{-\infty}^{+\infty}\!\!\int g(x, y)\, \cos\left(2\pi(x\nu_x + y\nu_y)\right)\, dx\, dy$$

and

$$-i \int\limits_{-\infty}^{+\infty}\!\!\int g(x, y)\, \sin\left(2\pi(x\nu_x + y\nu_y)\right)\, dx\, dy.$$

Therefore the Fourier transform may be said to give the projection of $g(x, y)$ on the set of all sinusoidal and cosinusoidal spatial patterns that are directed along the axes.

The Fourier transform $G(\nu_x, \nu_y)$ of $g(x, y)$ is also called the *frequency spectrum* of $g(x, y)$. The square of the modulus of the Fourier transform, $|G(\nu_x, \nu_y)|^2$, is called the *power spectrum* or the *Wiener spectrum* of $g(x, y)$.

C.2 Properties

- According to the definition in appendix B, the Fourier transform is a linear transform.

- The inverse Fourier transform is

$$g(x,y) = \int\limits_{-\infty}^{+\infty}\!\!\!\int G(\nu_x, \nu_y)\, e^{i2\pi(x\nu_x + y\nu_y)}\, d\nu_x\, d\nu_y.$$

The only difference is in the sign of the exponent.

- The Fourier transform is not shift invariant: if $g(x,y)$ is shifted by a in the x direction, and by b in the y direction, its transform is multiplied by the phase factor $e^{-i2\pi(a\nu_x + b\nu_y)}$. It should be noted, however, that this does not change the power spectrum of $g(x,y)$, as the modulus of this factor is unity.

- The *convolution* of two functions, $g(x,y)$ and $s(x,y)$, is defined to be

$$g * s \equiv \int\limits_{-\infty}^{+\infty}\!\!\!\int g(\xi,\eta)\, s(x-\xi, y-\eta)\, d\xi\, d\eta.$$

It turns out that the Fourier transform of the convolution is just the point multiplication of the Fourier transforms of g and s. In symbolic notation, if $f = g * s$ and G, S, F are the respective Fourier transforms of g, s, f, then

$$F(\nu_x, \nu_y) = G(\nu_x, \nu_y)S(\nu_x, \nu_y).$$

This points out an algorithm to compute convolutions: first compute the Fourier transforms of the two functions, multiply these transforms, and then take the inverse Fourier transform to obtain the convolution. This procedure is followed both in digital electronic computers (where the Fourier transform is computed using the FFT algorithm), and in optical systems (where the Fourier transform is obtained by means of a lens).

- The *cross-correlation* of two functions is defined as

$$g \star s \equiv \int\limits_{-\infty}^{+\infty}\!\!\!\int g(\xi,\eta)\, s^*(\xi - x, \eta - y)\, d\xi\, d\eta,$$

where s^* is the complex conjugate of s. If we now denote the cross-correlation by f, $f = g \star s$, then

$$F(\nu_x, \nu_y) = G(\nu_x, \nu_y)S^*(\nu_x, \nu_y).$$

In the special case where $g \equiv s$, which is called *autocorrelation*,

$$F(\nu_x, \nu_y) = |G(\nu_x, \nu_y)|^2.$$

Proofs of the above and discussions of further properties of the Fourier transform may be found in many textbooks, e.g., [260, chap. 2] or [587, chap. 2].

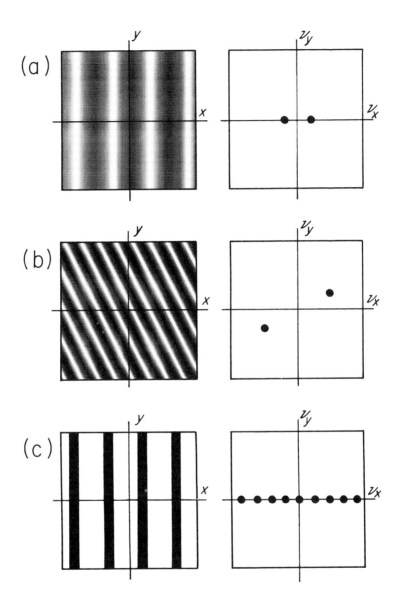

Figure C.1: *Some examples of Fourier transform pairs. At the left is $|g(x,y)|$, and at right $|G(\nu_x, \nu_y)|$. Both the (x, y) and the (ν_x, ν_y) planes should be taken to be infinite. (a,b) The Fourier transform of a bipolar sinusoidal pattern is just two points, whose location depends on the frequency and orientation of the pattern.*
(c) Other periodic patterns generate many harmonic components, displaced by the period frequency.

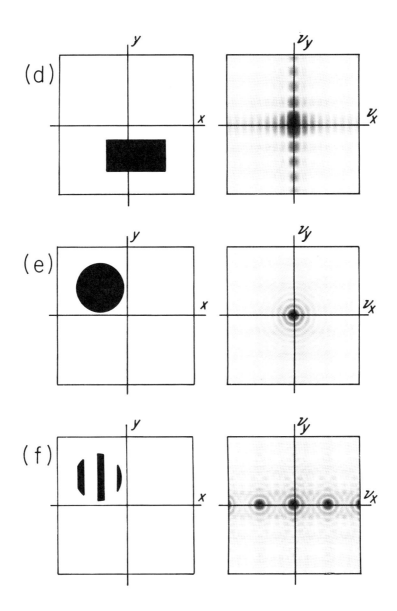

(d,e) A rectangle and a circle have infinite transforms. The smaller the original pattern, the larger the spread of the transform. The transform is always centered around the origin, regardless of the location of the original (only the phase is affected by translation).

(f) When a circle and a periodic pattern are combined, the transform of the circle is repeated on the harmonics of the pattern.

C.3   Meaning

The Fourier transform finds the periodicity in the input function. assume that $g(x, y)$ denotes some image. The claim is that this image may be decomposed into an infinite weighted sum of sinusoidal gratings. These gratings are sets of alternating parallel, equally spaced, straight bright and dark lines[1]. The difference between the gratings is in their periods and orientations. This is analogous to the one-dimensional theorem that any continuous function is decomposable into an infinite weighted sum of harmonic functions.

ν_x and ν_y denote orthogonal spatial frequencies, in the x and y directions. Each pair (ν_x, ν_y) defines a sinusoidal grating. The spatial frequency of the grating is $\sqrt{\nu_x^2 + \nu_y^2}$; this is the number of lines per unit of distance. Its period, i.e., the distance between adjacent lines, is therefore $\frac{1}{\sqrt{\nu_x^2 + \nu_y^2}}$. The orientation of the lines in the grating is $\arctan\left(-\frac{\nu_y}{\nu_x}\right)$.

Given an image $g(x, y)$, its Fourier transform $G(\nu_x, \nu_y)$ says how it is built out of these gratings. If we express the complex G as an amplitude A and a phase ϕ, thus,

$$G(\nu_x, \nu_y) = A(\nu_x, \nu_y)\, e^{i\,\phi(\nu_x, \nu_y)},$$

then $A(\nu_x, \nu_y)$ gives the amplitude of grating (ν_x, ν_y); this is its weight in the sum. $\phi(\nu_x, \nu_y)$ gives its phase at the origin, i.e., at $(x, y) = (0, 0)$. This specifies how it should be placed relative to the other gratings.

In the other direction, if $G(\nu_x, \nu_y)$ is given, the inverse Fourier transform tells us what function $g(x, y)$ will be obtained by summing all the gratings as described by $G(\nu_x, \nu_y)$. Fig. C.1 shows some examples. Other examples that give a good feeling for the connection between an image and its Fourier transform may be found in [420].

C.4   Optical derivation by a lens

In section 2.4.4, a statement was made to the effect that if the light distribution[2] in the front focal plane of a lens has a complex amplitude of $g(x, y)$, the light distribution in the back focal plane will have a complex amplitude $G(\nu_x, \nu_y)$, which is the Fourier transform of $g(x, y)$. The spatial frequencies ν_x, ν_y are connected to the spatial coordinates u, v measured in the back focal plane by the relations:

$$\nu_x = \frac{u}{\lambda f} \qquad \nu_y = \frac{v}{\lambda f},$$

---

[1] Actually there is a gradual change from bright to dark. For simplicity, we will regard this as if we had well-defined lines.

[2] Note that the light must be coherent.

where f is the focal length of the lens
        λ is the wavelength.

There are two ways to go about seeing why this is so. One is by a rigorous mathematical formulation and analysis — this is done in all the optics textbooks, e.g., [260, chap. 5]. The general idea is to divide the space between the front and back focal planes into three, and analyze what happens in each one separately. The analysis of the spaces from the front focal plane to the lens, and from the lens to the back focal plane, is an analysis of *diffraction* phenomena, as described in section 2.4.3. The analysis of what happens when the light passes through the lens simply takes into account the different phase delays suffered at different points, because of the differing thickness of the lens. An elegant alternative to this derivation is presented in [172, app. I]; it uses the fact that a plane wave is focused to a point on the back focal plane.

The other way is to show intuitively how a symmetric pair of light points in one focal plane gives rise to a sinusoidal grating in the other, i.e., to a set of bright and dark lines. It is convenient to regard the first plane as the frequency plane (ν_x, ν_y), and the second as the spatial plane (x, y).

The only prior knowledge we need is that if a plane wave impinges upon a lens, comming along its axis, it converges at the focal point of the lens. The same applies in reverse: light issuing from a point source at the focus of a lens is collimated by the lens, i.e., it turns into a plane wave propagating along the axis. This behavior can be taken as the definition of a lens. Thus a point of light at the center of the ν_x, ν_y plane, which means zero frequency, causes an even illumination of the x, y plane, as we would expect (fig. C.2 (a)).

If the point source is moved, say, a distance u from the focus in the x direction, but stays in the focal plane, the plane wave created by the lens will be tilted with respect to the lens' axis. The tilt angle is $\theta = \arctan\left(\frac{u}{f}\right)$. The intersection of such a wave with the back focal plane will produce a sinusoidal variance of the light's amplitude, i.e., a spatial frequency (fig. C.2 (b)). The spatial frequency is[3] $\frac{1}{\lambda}\tan\theta = \frac{u}{\lambda f}$. It is clear that if the source is moved further away from the focus, a higher spatial frequency is produced (fig. C.2 (c)). Thus we see the connection between distance form the origin on the one hand and spatial frequency on the other [698].

The above discussion shows that at any given moment, a point source, displaced from the focus of a lens, produces a sinusoidal grating at the back focal plane of the lens. But as time advances, the light wave also advances, and the grating moves. In average, therefore, all points will receive an even illumination, instead of maintaining the sinusoidal pattern.

This difficulty is resolved if we notice that

$$|G(\nu_x, \nu_y)| = |G(-\nu_x, -\nu_y)|.$$

---

[3]Actually it is $\frac{1}{\lambda}\sin\theta$, but at small angles $\sin \approx \tan$.

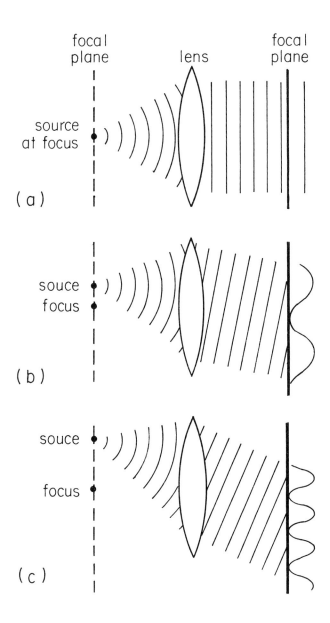

Figure C.2: *Connection between a point source at one focal plane of a lens, and a spatial frequency in the other.*
(a) The focus corresponds to zero frequency.
(b,c) As the transverse distance from the focus increases, so does the frequency.

This means that we must add another point source, displaced from the focus by the same amount but in the opposite direction. The two point sources will then produce two sinusoidal patterns at the back focal plane, and these sinuses will move in opposite directions. The sum of two counter-propagating waves is a standing wave, i.e., a constant pattern of bright and dark stripes, which is what we need.

The relative phases of $G(\nu_x, \nu_y)$ and $G(-\nu_x, -\nu_y)$ determines the phase of the standing grating. If they are in phase, it will have a line of maximum light intensity passing through $(x, y) = (0, 0)$. If they are exactly out of phase, there will be a dark line through $(x, y) = (0, 0)$. Other phase relations will cause intermediate situations.

Appendix D

Lasers

Section 2.3 described the laser as a light source whose output is intense, monochromatic, coherent, and directional. In this appendix, we examine how these properties come about as a result of the laser's principle of operation. An example of an actual laser is given in appendix E.

D.1 Interaction between light and matter

It is well known that the electrons of an atom cannot have arbitrary amounts of energy associated with them; only discrete, *quantized* energy levels are allowed. The energy levels are organized in a system of *shells* and *subshells*, each of which can contain at most a certain number of electrons. Usually the electrons of an atom occupy the positions with the lowest possible energies. For example, given that the capacities of the first three shells are 2, 8, and 8 electrons, and an atom with 14 electrons (Silicon), we will find that two electrons have the lowest energy level (corresponding to the first shell), eight have the next level (second shell), and four have the energy of the third shell. These last four electrons which occupy the outer shell are the most important in the interactions of the atom with its surroundings and with photons of light; they are called the *valence* electrons. The four empty positions are of similar importance. When the electrons are in this configuration, the atom is said to be in the *ground* state. By absorbing an adequate amount of energy, electrons can reach higher energy levels; such configurations are termed *excited* states.

Photons are quanta of energy that may induce transitions of electrons between the different energy levels. There are three basic effects by which photons and electrons interact:

- *Absorption.* If the photon has enough energy, an electron may absorb it and move to a higher energy level (fig. D.1 (a,b)). The photon's energy must be at least as large as the difference between the two levels; any excess energy turns into heat.

- *Spontaneous emission.* An electron in an excited state may move down to a lower energy level. In doing so it releases its excess energy in the form of a photon. The energy of the photon in this case is exactly equal to the difference between the energy levels (fig. D.1 (c)).

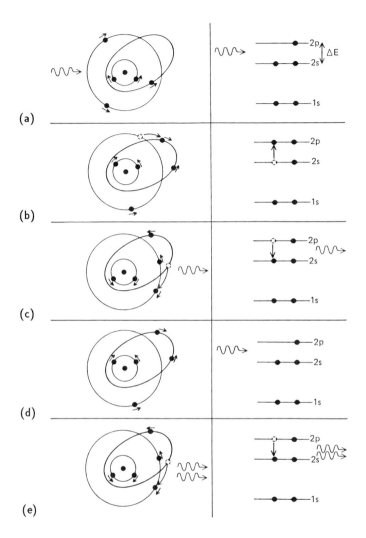

Figure D.1: *Interactions between photons and electrons:*

(a) A photon approaches an atom (with 5 electrons) in its ground state.

(b) The photon is absorbed, and one electron moves from the 2s subshell up to the 2p subshell.

(c) Some time later, the electron moves down again and releases a photon by the process of spontaneous emission.

(d) Alternatively, another photon may arrive...

(e) ... and force a stimulated emission.

(Adapted with permission from *Scientific American* [726], ©1968)

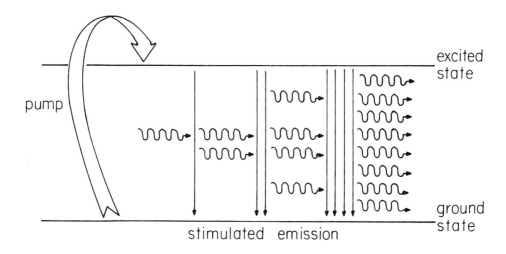

Figure D.2: *Schematic illustration of the principle of laser action.*

- *Stimulated emission.* Given an electron in an excited state, a photon whose energy exactly matches the difference between this excited state and some lower state might come along. Such a photon may cause the electron to go down to the lower state, releasing an additional photon (fig. D.1 (d,e)). The new photon thus created is exactly identical to the photon that induced the transition; they have the same wavelength, phase and direction.

This phenomenon is the basis of the creation of a laser beam. In order to create a monochromatic, coherent and directional laser beam we must guarantee that this process will dominate. Absorption and spontaneous emission should be low.

D.2   Laser action

Consider an ensemble of atoms. In the usual situation, the electrons of the great majority of the atoms will be in the ground state. Only a small number will be excited, because as a rule electrons tend to be in the state of lowest energy[1]. In such a situation, stimulated emission will hardly ever happen: any photon with the right energy has a much higher probability of being absorbed than of inducing the emission of another photon, because there are many more electrons in the ground state.

---

[1] Note, however, that some electrons *will* be excited, because of thermal agitation. The probability of finding an electron with energy E is proportional to the Bolzmann probability function, $e^{-\frac{E}{kT}}$, where k is Boltzmann's constant and T is the absolute temperature (Kelvin's scale).

The solution to the problem is to devise a special *pumping* mechanism, that will pump electrons from the ground state to the excited state, and thus create a *population inversion*. A number of different pumps have indeed been devised; they are somewhat complicated and will not be described here. Once a population inversion has been achieved, however, lasing can begin: one of the electrons eventually goes down to the ground state through the process of spontaneous emission. The generated photon then starts a chain reaction of stimulated emissions, resulting in the creation of a multitude of identical photons, all propagating together (fig. D.2).

However, this is not enough to maintain a continuous coherent laser beam. The lasing material must be placed in a resonator, i.e., between two mirrors. One of the mirrors is a fully reflecting mirror. The other is a partially transparent mirror, through which the laser beam leaks out. Most of the light, however, stays trapped inside the resonant cavity, bouncing back and forth between the mirrors. In the steady state, the pumping mechanism maintains the population inversion, and the intensity of the light in the cavity is such that the stimulated emissions it induces balance the leakage of the output beam through the semitransparent mirror.

Appendix E

Semiconductors and Light

The development of semiconductor devices revolutionized electronic systems, and made them efficient, reliable, and cheap. Semiconductor light sources and detectors will probably play an important part in the realization of optical computers. This appendix reviews the fundamental properties of semiconductor devices, and shows how LEDs, injection lasers, and photodiodes work [186]. It ends with a short section about band-gap engineering. The issue of materials is not discussed [255].

E.1   Semiconductors, impurities, and junctions

Semiconductor crystals are neither conductors nor insulators. Electrons cannot move freely in them, but on the other hand they are also not bound to their places so tightly as to prevent any movement altogether. To understand how this situation comes about, we must acquaint ourselves with the energy structure of these materials.

In appendix D we said that the energies of electrons in an atom are discrete and quantified. In crystals (which are extensive, regular structures of atoms) the interactions between the atoms cause the possible energy levels to change. Instead of discrete energy levels there are allowed energy *bands*. These are separated by *gaps* of prohibited energies. As in individual atoms, the outer energy bands (those occupied by the valence electrons) are the most important for determining the properties of the material. These bands have been named the *valence band* and the *conduction band*; they are separated by the *band gap*. Three classes of materials are identified:

- *Conductors*, in which the band gap is nonexistent, and the conduction band overlaps the valence band. This band is not full, so electrons can move about.

- *insulators*, in which the band gap is extremely large. In all practical situations electrons do not reach the conduction band. The valence band is full, so electrons in it cannot move about.

- *Semiconductors*, which have a small band gap. Normally the valence band is full and the conduction band is empty, so the material acts as an insulator. However, an *electron-hole* pair may be generated: the electron is one that is excited and reaches the conduction band; it is then free to move around. The hole — the empty place it left in the valence band — allows other electrons in the valence band to move about.

A semiconducting crystal also turns into a conductor when it is doped with certain *impurities*. Pure semiconductors are composed of atoms with an average of four valence electrons (either all the atoms are the same and all have four electrons, as in Si or Ge, or else there are equal numbers of atoms with three and five valence electrons, as in GaAs). The impurities can take one of two forms:

- An excess of atoms with five valence electrons. The extra electrons do not fit into the valence band, so they occupy the conduction band. This is called an *n-type* crystal.

- An excess of atoms with only three valence electrons. In this case, the valence band has holes in it, and electrons can move. This is a *p-type* crystal.

All semiconductor devices are based on one simple structure — a *junction* where an n-type crystal and a p-type crystal are brought together. At the junction the extra electrons on the n side combine with the holes on the p side. This leaves a crystal depleted of electrons on the n side; this crystal therefore has a net positive charge. The crystal on the p side, on the other hand, has acquired additional electrons; it therefore has a net negative charge. These net charges prevent more electrons and holes from flowing[1] into the junction, and thus a steady state in which no conduction occurs is reached. This can also be interpreted as a deformation of the energy bands.

E.2   Semiconductor light sources and detectors

LEDs

A simple n-p junction is a diode. When a forward bias is applied, i.e. the n side is connected to the − side of a voltage supply and the p side is connected to the +, this overcomes the electrostatic fields formed at the junction. Electrons and holes start flowing into the junction again, where they combine with each other. In the process, the electrons go down from the conduction band to the valence band, and release a packet of energy equivalent to the band gap. In certain materials (e.g., GaAs), this energy is released in the form of a photon of light. Hence the application of the proper voltage causes this diode to radiate light (fig. E.1).

---

[1] Actually holes aren't physical entities that can move; what realy happens is that an electron in the valence band fills the hole, leaving a new hole in its former location. However, as holes are scarce in the valence band, it is convenient to regard this process as a movement of the hole.

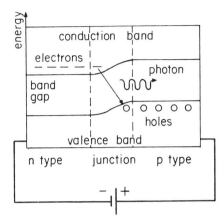

Figure E.1: *Schematic representation of how a LED works: forward bias applied to an n-p junction forces electrons and holes to combine, releasing a photon in the process.*

Lasers [609,659]

As explained in appendix D, the two conditions for the realization of a laser are a population inversion and a resonant cavity. An n-p junction with forward bias already created the population inversion — the power source supplies electrons to the (excited) conduction band on the n side, and removes them from the (ground) valence band on the p side. The resonant cavity is created by cleaving the edges of the crystal so that internal reflection occurs. If the device is part of an integrated circuit, integrated-optics mirrors (section 8.3.1) may be etched on both sides.

This type of laser is called a *laser diode* or an *injection laser*, after the way the electrons are injected into the junction. Greater efficiency is obtained if the electrons, holes, and photons are confined in the junction area. This is achieved by the use of a more complicated structure of n- and p-type crystals of different materials, called a *heterojunction*.

Photodiodes

In the light source applications, the applied voltage injects electrons and holes into the junction. As an electron combines with a hole, a photon is emitted. In a photodiode, the process is reversed. A photon is absorbed in the p-type crystal, and causes an electron to be ejected. Thus a hole is created in the valence band on the p side. The electron receives the energy of the photon, so it is now in the conduction band. A reverse bias applied to the diode pulls the electron and the hole away from the junction, so that they cannot recombine. Hence a photocurrent is generated. The efficiency is increased if an *intrinsic* layer is inserted between the p- and the n-type crystals. Such a structure is appropriately called a PIN photodiode.

E.3 Band-gap engineering

A photon's wavelength λ is linked to its energy E through Planck's equation

$$E = h\nu = \frac{hc}{\lambda},$$

where h is Planck's constant
          c is the speed of light
          ν is the frequency of the light wave.

In semiconductor devices, the energy of the interacting photons must be equal to the band gap. Therefore if we want to be able to create devices that work with light of different frequencies, we must be able to control the band gap.

The band gap is a property of the semiconductor material; different semiconductors have different band gaps. In certain cases, it is possible to tailor the material so that it will have a specific band gap. A well-known example is GaAlAs. In this semiconductor, Ga and Al come from the third column of the periodic table of the elements, and As comes from the fifth column. GaAs and AlAs have widely different band gaps; however, they have a remarkably similar crystal structure. Therefore crystals that incorporate both Ga and Al in any desired ratio can be manufactured. The band gap in the resulting GaAlAs crystals depends on the ratio of Ga atoms to Al atoms, and it can assume any value between the band gap of GaAs and that of AlAs [591,508].

Appendix F

Issues in Holography

Holography is explained in section 2.8. This appendix groups several issues relating to holography which are mentioned in the text, but are not treated in depth.

F.1   Holography and Fresnel zone plates

A three-dimensional object may be regarded as composed of many points. When a hologram of the object is made, it is as if we superpose individual holograms for all these points [586]. In this section we investigate the hologram created by one such point.

Figure F.1: *A hard-clipped Fresnel zone plate.*
(Reprinted with permission from *Optical Engineering* [94], ©1980)

A hologram is actually a recording of the interference pattern of two waves. In the case of a point object, the object beam is a spherical wave diverging from the point. Assuming the point is located at a distance z opposite the origin $(0,0)$ of the hologram, the light distribution it creates on the hologram plane is described by

$$e^{i\frac{2\pi}{\lambda}r} = e^{i\frac{2\pi}{\lambda}\sqrt{x^2+y^2+z^2}}$$

$$\sim e^{i\frac{2\pi}{\lambda}\left(z+\frac{x^2+y^2}{2z}\right)}$$

$$\propto e^{i\frac{2\pi}{\lambda}\frac{x^2+y^2}{2z}},$$

where we assume $z \gg x, y$. If we use a plane wave incident at angle θ as reference, e.g., a wave described by $e^{i2\pi\frac{\sin\theta}{\lambda}x}$, The resulting hologram will record the intensity pattern

$$\left|e^{i\frac{2\pi}{\lambda}\frac{x^2+y^2}{2z}} + e^{i2\pi\frac{\sin\theta}{\lambda}x}\right|^2 = 2 + 2\cos\left[\frac{2\pi}{\lambda}\left(\frac{x^2+y^2}{2z} - x\sin\theta\right)\right]$$

$$\sim 2 + 2\cos\left(\frac{2\pi}{\lambda}\frac{(x-z\theta)^2+y^2}{2z}\right).$$

This is a Fresnel zone plate (see fig. F.1), with its center displaced to $x = z\theta$, assuming that the approximation $\theta \ll \frac{x}{z} \ll 1$ holds. If it does not, the result is a deformed Fresnel zone plate.

It is interesting to note that such a pattern is actually a holographic lens: if it is illuminated by a plane wave, it will focus the light to create a point image.

F.2   Equivalence of holography and spatial carrier modulation

Spatial carrier modulation is a method by which incoherent light may be made to convey complex data values. The idea is to use a high-frequency spatial pattern, and modulate it according to the complex data: the modulus of the data will determine the amplitude of the spatial pattern, while the argument of the data will decide its phase. In section 2.8 it was claimed that holography is equivalent to spatial carrier modulation, or in other words, that holography is a way in which to implement the idea of spatial carrier modulation. We now proceed to show this equivalence ([260, p. 209]).

A hologram is a recording of the interference pattern between the object beam that we wish to record, and a known reference beam. We denote the complex amplitude of the object beam at the plane of the hologram by $\mathbf{O}$, and decompose it thus:

$$\mathbf{O}(x,y) = O(x,y)\,e^{i\varphi(x,y)}.$$

The complex amplitude of the reference beam will be denoted by $\mathbf{R}$. We assume that this is a plane wave, and there is an angle θ between its wavefront and the plane of the hologram. It therefore produces a sinusoidal change of phase along the plane of the hologram, e.g., in the x direction, and may be written thus:

$$\mathbf{R}(x,y) = R\, e^{i\frac{2\pi \sin\theta}{\lambda}x}.$$

At the hologram these two waves interfere, so that the total complex amplitude there is

$$\mathbf{O}(x,y) + \mathbf{R}(x,y).$$

The hologram records the square modulus of this interference pattern, which is

$$|\mathbf{O}(x,y) + \mathbf{R}(x,y)|^2 =$$

$$= |\mathbf{O}(x,y)|^2 + |\mathbf{R}(x,y)|^2 + \mathbf{O}(x,y)\mathbf{R}^*(x,y) + \mathbf{O}^*(x,y)\mathbf{R}(x,y)$$

$$= O(x,y)^2 + R^2 + O(x,y)\, R\, e^{i\left(\varphi(x,y) - \frac{2\pi \sin\theta}{\lambda}x\right)}$$
$$+ O(x,y)\, R\, e^{i\left(-\varphi(x,y) + \frac{2\pi \sin\theta}{\lambda}x\right)}$$

$$= O(x,y)^2 + R^2 + 2\, R\, O(x,y)\, \cos\left(\frac{2\pi \sin\theta}{\lambda}x - \varphi(x,y)\right)$$

$O^2 + R^2$ is just a DC term. The important factor is the spatial pattern described by the third term. Basically this is a cosinusoidal grating with spatial frequency $\frac{\sin\theta}{\lambda}$: this is the spatial carrier. It has, however, been both amplitude and phase modulated. Its amplitude is $2RO(x,y)$, which contains the amplitude of the object beam. Its phase is $-\varphi(x,y)$, which conveys the phase of the object beam. The DC term compensates for any negative values of this modulated carrier. Thus the complex data represented by $\mathbf{O}$ has been incorporated in the real, positive pattern recorded on the hologram, by way of modulating a spatial carrier.

F.3 Holographic spatial filtering

On page 62 we saw how a Fourier hologram may be used as a complex-valued spatial filter. The claim was that when the filter is used, the produced first order beams give the convolution and cross-correlation of the filter's function with the input signal. We now proceed to show why this is so ([260, sect. 7-5]).

The recording stage is the same as for a regular hologram, except that the object light distribution at the hologram is the Fourier transform of the signal $s(x',y')$. We shall denote this by $\mathbf{S}(x,y) = S(x,y)e^{i\varphi(x,y)}$. Using the derivation in the preceding section, the interference pattern recorded on the hologram is described by

$$S(x,y)^2 + R^2 + \mathbf{S}(x,y)\, R\, e^{-i\frac{2\pi \sin\theta}{\lambda}x} + \mathbf{S}^*(x,y)\, R\, e^{i\frac{2\pi \sin\theta}{\lambda}x}.$$

When, after being developed, the hologram is illuminated by the Fourier transform $\mathbf{G}(x, y)$ of the input scene $g(x', y')$, the resulting light distribution is $\mathbf{G}(x, y)$ modulated by the transmittance of the hologram. This transmittance is proportional to the above interference pattern. Denoting the proportionality factor by β, we get

$$\beta \left(S(x, y)^2 + R^2 \right) \mathbf{G}(x, y) + \beta \, \mathbf{S}(x, y) \, \mathbf{G}(x, y) \, R \, e^{-i \frac{2\pi \sin \theta}{\lambda} x}$$
$$+ \beta \, \mathbf{S}^*(x, y) \, \mathbf{G}(x, y) \, R \, e^{i \frac{2\pi \sin \theta}{\lambda} x}.$$

This light distribution is subsequently Fourier transformed by a lens. The first term is the zero-order term, which does not interest us. The second term is a spatial carrier with frequency $-\frac{\sin \theta}{\lambda}$ modulated by $\mathbf{S}(x, y) \, \mathbf{G}(x, y)$. After being Fourier transformed, this gives the convolution $s * g$ (see appendix C), shifted to $x = -f \sin \theta$ (because of the spatial frequency of the carrier). The third term is a spatial carrier with frequency $\frac{\sin \theta}{\lambda}$, modulated by $\mathbf{S}^*(x, y) \, \mathbf{G}(x, y)$. When this is Fourier-transformed, it gives the cross-correlation $s \star g$ shifted to $x = f \sin \theta$. This is exactly the situation described in fig. 3.8.

Appendix G

Physical Effects in Crystals

Quite a few of the devices used in optical computing utilize different physical effects in crystals. The following definitions present these effects in an organized manner.

Background terms

- *Polarization* — The electrons of an atom are normally arranged in a symmetrical distribution around the nucleus. in certain situations, however, the electrons tend to one direction while the nucleus tends to the other. Thus a *dipole* is formed. The vector that describes the shift the center of the positive charge and the center of the negative charge is called the *polarization*. Note that this has nothing to do with the other meaning of "polarization", namely, the orientation of the electric field in an electromagnetic wave.

- *Birefringence* — A property by which the refractive index of a crystal is not a scalar constant; rather, it is different along different axes of the crystal [339, chap. 26]. Thus light beams in different directions or with different polarizations (here it *is* the orientation of the electric field) might "feel" a different refractive index. Typically the electric field component perpendicular to the crystal axis "feels" one index (the *ordinary* one), while an electric field component along the axis "feels" another index (the *extraordinary*).

Effects

Electrooptic effect — A change in the refractive index as a result of an applied electric field. The change depends on the orientation of the field; hence the electrooptic effect often induces birefringence.

Pockels effect — The electrooptic effect in crystals, when the electric field is applied along the crystal axis, and the light propagates along this line.

Electrooptic Kerr effect — The electrooptic effect when the light propagates perpendicularly to the electric field.

Photorefractive effect — A change of the refractive index as a result of the absorption of light. The main mechanism involved is the transportation of electrons that are released by the light and then trapped again in a different location. Thus a space charge is generated in the crystal, which supplies the electric field for the electrooptic effect. The photorefractive effect also causes birefringence.

Bulk photovoltaic effect — The generation of an internal electric field when the crystal is illuminated. This causes the migration of electrons in the photorefractive effect.

Photochromic effect — A change of the absorption coefficient as a result of the absorption of light. This changes the color of the crystal; hence its name.

Magnetooptic effect — A change of the refractive index when a magnetic field is applied to the crystal. This effect too causes birefringence.

Faraday effect — A rotation of the plane of polarization of light passing through certain materials in the presence of a magnetic field. The degree of rotation is linear in the distance and the strength of the magnetic field.

Magnetooptic Kerr effect — A change in the polarization of light reflected from a magnetized material; linearly polarized light becomes elliptically polarized.

Piezoelectric effect — The generation of a polarization as a result of mechanical stress, and vice versa.

Many of these effects are described in [339, chap. 32].

Appendix H

Modes in Waveguides

The explanation of how light propagates in optical fibers (section 7.6.3) used the phenomenon of total internal reflection. It was concluded that the light follows a zig-zag course in the fiber. This appendix elaborates the model and introduces the concept of *modes of propagation*. Modes are then used to explain how changing the thickness of a thin-film waveguide changes the speed of light in it.

H.1 Modes

In microwave radio, specially designed rectangular hollow metal pipes are used as waveguides. The electromagnetic microwaves are reflected from their sides, and thus propagate along them in a zigzag fashion. There is a complication, however: the electric field component of the electromagnetic wave must be zero at each reflection. Otherwise the electric field will induce a current in the side of the metallic pipe, and thus the wave will lose energy and die away. This condition may be fulfilled only if the distance that the wave travels between reflections is $k\frac{\lambda}{2}$, where k is an integer and λ is the wavelength. When this is the case, it is possible that the oscillating electric field will go through the zero value exactly when the reflections occur. In short, we have identified a *constraint* on the way in which the waves propagate in the waveguide. They can only propagate at certain angles, in which the constraint is satisfied (fig. H.1). These are called the *modes* of propagation.

When a light wave propagates in an optical waveguide, a similar constraint

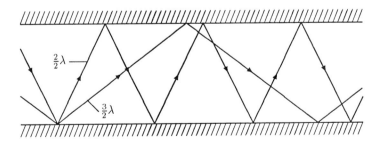

Figure H.1: *Modes for a microwave in a rectangular waveguide.*

holds. Therefore the light too cannot zigzag at any arbitrary angle — it can only propagate in one of a discrete set of modes. Each mode is characterized by the number of wavelengths between reflections. Given that the width of the waveguide is constant, it also dictates the angle at which the light zigzags.

H.2 The speed of light in a thin film

When light propagates along a thin-film waveguide, its *effective speed* depends on the propagation mode. If the mode angle is large, the light zigzags more and thus has to traverse a longer path. It will therefore require more time to get through a unit length of waveguide. If, on the other hand, the angle is shallow, the light propagates more or less in parallel to the surface of the waveguide. In this case the length of its path is minimal, and the light passes through the waveguide quickly[1].

In section 8.5.1 we noted that integrated optics lenses can be made by changing the thickness of the film, because this changes the speed of light in the film. This is so because the propagation modes are *discrete*. Assume a light beam is zigzagging along a thin film; it is of course in some propagation mode, which determines the angle of the zigzags. As the film grows thicker, the angle no longer fits. The light beam must now either switch over to another mode, or else it can stay in the same mode but change the angle slightly, so that it fits the new thickness. As the modes are discrete, it is usually not possible to jump from one to the other. Therefore the angle adjusts. The new angle will be sharper than the previous one, so the effective speed of the light is reduced.

H.3 TE and TM

In a rectangular waveguide, the modes depend on the orientation of the electric field relative to the long side of the waveguide; in other words, the modes depend on the polarization. Two types of mode are distinguished:

TE (Transverse Electric) — The electric field direction is along the width of the waveguide.

TM (Transverse Magnetic) — The magnetic field is along the width. The electric field, which is perpendicular to the magnetic field, is along the shorter height.

This distinction is not important in this book; it is mentioned in case readers see these terms elsewhere.

---

[1] The difference between the propagation speeds of different modes is of great importance in long haul fiberoptics. If a short input pulse excites a number of modes, their different speeds will cause the pulse to be smeared at the output [163]. Thus the possible creation of many modes limits the length or the bandwidth of the link. Single-mode fibers avoid this problem [358,350].

Appendix I

The Strength of the CRDCW Model

I.1 The Hierarchy of PRAM Models

As noted in section 10.2.3, the PRAM model for parallel computation can be partitioned into several submodels. This partition is done according to the rules that determine in what ways the different PEs may access the same memory cell concurrently, and according to the outcome. These submodels form a hierarchal structure, in the sense that some are "stronger" than others. Relative strength is measured by two methods:

- If model A can simulate model B, i.e., the result of each operation available in B can be achieved by a constant number of operations available in A, we say that A is *at least as strong as* B.

  For example, the CRCW model in which a concurrent write results in the highest priority value being written is at least as strong as the model in which an arbitrary value is written. To see this, note that we can arbitrarily choose the highest-priority value to be written each time, so if an algorithm works when an arbitrary writer is chosen it will also work when the highest-priority writer is always chosen. We can thus simulate one model by the other.

- If a problem can be solved in one model within a certain time limit, but *cannot* be solved in second model within the same limit, we say that the first model is *stronger*. Note that this notion depends on the problem in question; a situation might arise in which one problem testifies to the fact that model A is stronger than model B, while another problem shows that B is stronger than A. In such a case we say that the models are *incomparable*. Note that this situation cannot arise if one model can simulate the other, as explained above.

  As an example, consider the calculation of the AND of N bits. This can be done in two steps using a CRCW common-value model in the following fashion: in step 1 the value "1" is written to the result. In step 2, N PEs each examine one input bit, and any PE that finds a logical "0" writes "0" to the result. The value of the result is now the AND of the N input bits.

Using CREW or EREW models, however, calculation of the AND of N bits requires at least $\Omega(\log N)$ steps [164].

I.2   The relative strength of CRDCW-sum

The different models described in section 10.2.3 are listed in order of increasing strength (except for CRCW common-value and CRCW garbage, which are incomparable) [634,219,164]. Therefore if we claim that optical computers modeled by CRDCW-sum are stronger than conventional models, all we have to do is to prove that they are stronger than CRCW with priorities.

Theorem: *The PRAM CRDCW-sum model is stronger than the PRAM CRCW-priorities model.*

Proof: We will show that CRDCW-sum can simulate CRCW-priority, and therefore it is at least as strong as CRCW-priority. Given this result, it is enough to show an example of a problem that is solvable on CRDCW-sum and not on CRCW-priority in order to conclude that CRDCW-sum is indeed stronger. The summing of N inputs furnishes us with the required example: it can be done on CRDCW-sum in one step, by definition. It requires $\log n$ steps on CRCW-priority [480].

Simulation of CRCW-priority by CRDCW-sum

The system is comprised of N PEs, numbered according to the priorities we wish them to assume (no. 1 is the lowest priority; N is the highest). A subset of them wish to write to a shared variable v. We must show that the capabilities of CRDCW-sum are sufficient in order to pick out (in a constant number of steps) the value written by the PE with the highest priority. The following algorithm produces this value in the variable v in 4 steps. The temporary variables `total` and `less-than-me[` N `]` are used (initially set to zero):

1. All PEs that wish to participate (i.e., that want to write concurrently to the variable in question) write 1 to `total`. Using the fact that a concurrent write results in the sum, `total` now holds the number of PEs that participate.

2. For $i = 1 \ldots N - 1$, PE number i writes 1 to `less-than-me[` $i+1$ `]` through `less-than-me[` N `]`. This is just a duplication of data, and therefore possible. As concurrent writes result in the sum, `less-than-me[` i `]` now holds the number of participating PEs with priorities less than that of PE number i.

3. for $i = 1 \ldots N$, PE number i compares `less-than-me[` i `]` with `total`. Only the participating PE with the highest priority will find that `less-than-me[`i`]` = `total-1`. It thus knows that it is the PE with the highest priority.

4. The PE with the highest priority writes its value to **v**. All the others forget about the whole procedure.

Note that this simulation has its **drawback**: the size of the memory must be multiplied by N. In other words, we have reduced the time necessary for certain operations (e.g., summation), at the expense of increasing the *width* of the communication medium (the shared memory). Such tradeoffs are known from other models as well [713].

It is also possible to simulate CRCW-priorities on CRCW-sum, but this requires either an increase in the number of PEs or in the word-size of the computer.

I.3   Is the new model really necessary?

As noted in section 10.2.3, the CRDCW model with n PEs is very similar to a CRCW model with n^2 PEs. It seems that each duplicate write may then be simulated by the CRCW machine in two steps as follows:

1. n intermediate PEs read the value that is to be written. This just uses the concurrent read capability of CRCW. Thus n duplicates have been created.

2. These PEs now write their copies of the data to the appropriate places. If some of them clash with other concurrent writes, this is handled like any other clash.

A somewhat delicate point is that of who takes the initiative. In the CRDCW model, it is clear that the PE that writes decides where he wants to write to. In the CRCW simulation, however, the intermediate PEs have to decide for him, because the writting process proceeds through their activity only. However, this point does not necessarily invalidate the simulation, as it is also not clear how the writing PE (in CRDCW) designates the multiple addresses he is writing to. It is not practical to make a list dynamically for each write, because this would undermine the parallel one-step nature that is the basis of the model. On the other hand, if one of a small set of predefined patterns is used, this can be simulated by the CRCW system. The CRDCW model was introduced in this text because it is more convenient and models the optical systems more directly.

The summing capability is certainly a new one, which changes the properties of existing models. Therefore the "sum" model is interesting and important. However, one can doubt the degree to which it models optical systems, because it mixes characteristics of analog and digital systems. It is not certain yet that optical computers will be able to use this mix, and utilize analog addition. The reason is the limited dynamic range of light detectors.

Glossary

Acoustooptic (AO) — A device that utilizes interactions between acoustic waves and light waves.

Airy pattern — The pattern of concentric rings that is the square modulus of the Fourier transform of a disk.

Avalanche Photodiode (APD) — A semiconductor light detector based on a diode, with internal gain.

Beam splitter — An optical element that splits a light beam that falls on it into two beams: actually a semitransparent mirror. Also used to combine two beams into one.

Bistable Device — An optical device that has two stable states: in one it blocks most of the light falling on it, and only transmits a very small portion of it. In the other it transmits light efficiently.

Bleaching — The removal of the dark grains from a film, thus turning it into a phase filter.

Bragg Angle — The angle between a light beam and a grating, so that light rays interacting with successive lines have path differences of one wavelength.

Bragg Diffraction — The constructive interference (in certain directions) of light coming from a grating.

Bright True Logic (BTL) — An optical logic system in which the logical "TRUE", i.e., the logical value "1", is represented by a bright point of light. Logical "FALSE" ("0") is represented by darkness.

Charge Coupled Device (CCD) — A device that forms and transports small packets of charge. Used in video cameras and other detector arrays.

Coherence — A property of light: when constant phase relationships are maintained between different parts of the light beam.

Coherence Length — The distance that light propagates before coherence is lost. This is a measure of the degree of coherence.

Collimated Beam — A wide, parallel beam of light.

Complex Amplitude — The description of wave amplitude and phase by one complex value. When waves interfere, their complex amplitudes add up.

Computer Generated Hologram (CGH) — A hologram computed and plotted by a (digital) computer, rather than being created photographically.

Dark Current — The current output of a detector even when no light is incident upon it. This is an internal source of noise.

Dark True Logic (DTL) — An optical logic system where "TRUE" is represented by a low intensity and "FALSE" by a high intensity.

Deformable Mirror Device (DMD) — A spatial light modulator consisting of a deformable reflecting membrane suspended above an array of small wells.

Degenerate Four-Wave Mixing (D4WM) — Four-wave mixing where the frequencies of all four waves are the same.

Diffraction — The formation of a light pattern by interference from many sources (or from various parts of an extensive source). Used only in connection with coherent light.

Diffuser — A filter that causes a random loss of phase and direction information of light.

Digital Multiplication by Analog Convolution (DMAC) — An algorithm for binary multiplication that has been popular in digital optical computer research.

Digital Optical Computer (DOC) — A digital computer based on optical hardware. Usually a general purpose computer is meant; this is implemented by mimicking electronic logic devices using optics.

Dispersion — The phenomenon that light waves of different frequencies propagate with different speeds in a medium. This causes problems of pulse deformation in long-distance fiberoptics.

Dynamic Range — The ratio of the highest usable intensity to the lowest usable intensity in an analog optical system. Higher intensities cause nonlinearity problems, while lower ones are indistinguishable from noise.

Electrooptic (EO) — Devices that use physical effects in which electric fields influence the optical properties of certain crystals.

Electrooptic Effect — The change of the refractive index of a crystal as a result of an applied electric field.

Fabry-Perot Resonator — An area bounded by two parallel mirrors; light may bounce back and forth between them. If the distance is an integer multiple of half the wavelength, resonance is achieved.

Fiberoptics — The study of phenomena related to light propagating in optical fibers. Also used to describe the fibers themselves.

F-number — The ratio of the focal length of a lens to its diameter.

Focal Length — The distance from the center of a lens to its focus.

Focal Plane — A plane (perpendicular to the optical axis) passing through the focus of a lens.

Focus — The point to which a lens concentrates the light of an incident collimated beam propagating along the optical axis.

Four-Wave Mixing (FWM) — A method for achieving optical phase conjugation.

Fourier Transform (FT) — The transformation from the spatial (or temporal) domain to the frequency domain.

Fringes — The alternate bright and dark bands that form the interference pattern of two beams. Each fringe represents a relative phase change of 2π radians (one wavelength).

Generalized Matched Filter (GMF) — A matched filter that combines a few versions of the desired object and rejects known noise sources.

Geometrical Optics — The study of optical systems by means of their geometrical properties. The wavelike nature of light does not come into play; rather ray tracing is used.

Grating — A set of parallel lines or surfaces that reflect or transmit light.

Hologram — A recording of the interference pattern between an object beam and a reference beam of light. Such a recording allows for the reconstruction of the wavefront of the object beam.

Holographic Optical Element (HOE) — An optical element that is realized by means of a hologram, rather than by traditional (usually refractive) devices.

Hololens — A holographic lens.

Incoherent Light — Light that displays random phase changes.

Index of Refraction — A characteristic of a medium which dictates the speed of light passing through that medium: it is the speed of light in vacuum divided by the index of refraction.

Injection Laser — A laser implemented by a sandwich of semi-conductor crystals.

Integrated Optics (IO) — The study of optical systems in the form of integrated circuits, on a semiconductor crystal.

Intensity — The energy of a light beam. This is the square of its amplitude.

Interference — The sum of two waves with the same frequency. The result depends on their relative amplitudes and phases; therefore the term is only used in connection with coherent light.

Iterative Optical Processor (IOP) — A special purpose optical processor that works by performing multiple iterations of an operation, e.g., the multiplication of a vector by a matrix.

Kinoform — A phase-only hologram.

LASER — Acronym for Light Amplification by Stimulated Emission of Radiation. This is a light source that produces intense monochromatic, coherent light, in a very directional beam.

Laser Diode (LD) — A miniature semiconductor laser. Also called an "injection laser".

Lens — An optical element that changes the characteristics of a beam of light passing through it from a collimated beam to a converging one, or vice versa. Usually implemented by a specially shaped piece of glass, that exploits the phenomenon of refraction.

Light-Emitting Diode (LED) — A semiconductor diode that emits light when the proper voltage is applied.

Linear System — A system whose response to a linear combination of inputs is the same as the linear combination (with the same coefficients) of its responses to the individual inputs.

Liquid Crystal Light Valve (LCLV) — A spatial light modulator that is based on a liquid crystal.

Magnetooptic — A device or effect in which a magnetic field influences the light.

Matched Spatial Filter (MSF) — A spatial filter (e.g., a transparency) with transmittance proportional to the complex conjugate of the Fourier transform of a given signal (i.e., an image).

Maxwell's equations — A set of four equations that relate the electric and magnetic vector fields of electromagnetic waves.

Monochromatic — Light of only one frequency, and therefore only one color.

Optical Axis — The central axis of an optical system, along which the light propagates. The various optical elements are situated one after the other along the optical axis.

Optical Character Recognition (OCR) — The recognition of printed characters by an optical processor.

Optical Digital Data Disk (OD^3) — An optical disk designed to serve as a secondary memory of a computer.

Optical Path — The distance a ray of light traverses, measured in wavelengths. This takes changes of the refractive index (and hence, changes of the wavelength) into account.

Optical Pattern Recognition (OPR) — The identification of a pattern in a scene by means of optical processing.

Optical Phase Conjugation (OPC) — The generation of a light wave that retraces the propagation of an input wave in reverse.

Optical Transfer Function (OTF) — The effect of an optical (linear, shift invariant) system on a beam of light passing through it, described in the frequency domain. This is the Fourier transform of the system's PSF.

Opto-Electronic Integrated Circuit (OEIC) — An integrated circuit that combines electronic (logic) and optical (interconnection) devices.

OTF Synthesis — The realization of an optical system with a predefined optical transfer function. Usually done by means of a hologram.

Phase — The part of the cycle that a wave is in. With coherent light, the phase relations between different beams decide how they will interfere.

Phase Conjugate Mirror (PCM) — A mirror that reverses a light wave falling on it, rather than reflecting the wave.

Phase Filter — A spatial filter that changes the spatial phase modulation of a beam of light passing through it. It does not change the spatial amplitude modulation.

Photodiode — A light detector based on a diode.

Photochromic Effect — The change of color, and thus also of absorption, as a result of illumination.

Photomultiplier (PMT) — A high-gain light detector, capable of detecting single photons.

Photon — A quanta of light.

Photorefractive Effect — The change of the index of refraction as a result of illumination.

PIN Photodiode — The simplest semiconductor light detector.

Plane Wave — A beam of light whose wavefronts are planar surfaces.

Point Spread Function (PSF) — The response (output) of a linear shift invariant system presented with an impulse input.

Polychromatic — Light composed of waves of many different frequencies, and thus many colors.

Ray Tracing — The tracing of a ray of light as it traverses an optical system, so as to characterize the system.

Refraction — The change of direction that occurs when a light wave passes from one medium to another, e.g., from water to air.

Reflection — The change of the direction of propagation of a light beam at a mirror.

Resonance — The condition in which the frequency of an input wave is the same as an inherent frequency of a physical device, and thus the wave can cause large oscillations.

Ronchi Ruling — A grating where the line width is equal to the spacing between lines.

Self Electrooptic Effect Device (SEED) — A bistable device based on a multiple quantum well structure in a PIN photodiode.

Signal to Noise Ratio (SNR) — The ratio of the power of the desired signal to the background noise power.

Space Bandwidth Product (SBW or SBP) — The product of the aperture of an analog optical system and the highest spatial frequency it can handle. This gives the number of resolvable points, and thus the maximum number of parallel channels that are processed.

Space-Integrating (SI) Element — An optical element that collects light from a large area and focuses it together, e.g., a lens.

Spatial Carrier Modulation — The modulation of a spatial carrier frequency by a complex information signal. The amplitude and phase of the signal govern the amplitude and phase of the carrier.

Spatial Frequency — The number of repetitions in a unit of length that a cyclic pattern goes through.

Spatial Light Modulator (SLM) — An optical device that modulates the cross section of a beam of light passing through it (or reflected from it).

Spatial Modulation — Having some parameter (amplitude, phase) of the light assume different values in different places in the cross section of a light beam.

Spectrum — The frequency content of a signal. In the case of images, this refers to spatial frequencies in two dimensions.

Spherical Wave — A light wave whose wavefronts are spherical, e.g., light diverging from a point source.

Synthetic Aperture Radar (SAR) — A method of radar mapping in which a small antenna carried by a plane or satellite is used to reproduce the effect of a much larger antenna.

Synthetic Discriminant Function (SDF) — A filter that is synthesized out of a training set of objects taken from different classes, so as to discriminate between them.

Thermoplastic (TP) — A material that can be deformed by applying a force when it is heated. Used to record holograms in real time.

Time Integrating (TI) Element — One that adds up its inputs over time, e.g., some detectors.

Transparency — A thin optical element that modulates the light that passes through it, e.g., a slide in a slide projector.

Wavefront — An imaginary surface that connects all points in the cross-section of a light beam that have traveled an equal distance from the source. It fully describes the light beam.

Waveguide — A channel that confines waves and thus guides their propagation, e.g., an optical fiber.

Wavelength — The distance between two consecutive points with the same phase in a wave, e.g., two consecutive crests. Also the distance the wave travels during one period.

White Light — Light composed of all frequencies in a uniform distribution.

Write Once Read Many Times (WORM) — A memory device that can only be written once, and then read many times, e.g., an optical disk. Also called Write-Once Memory or Write-Once Storage (WOM or WOS).

Bibliography

[1] E. Abraham, C.T. Seaton, and S.D. Smith, *"The optical computer"*, Scientific American **248(2)**, Feb 1983, pp. 63–71

[2] Y.S. Abu-Mostafa and D. Psaltis, *"Optical neural computers"*, Scientific American **256(3)**, Mar 1987, pp. 66–73

[3] Y.S. Abu-Mostafa and D. Psaltis, *"Image normalization by complex moments"*, IEEE trans. Pattern Analysis and Machine Intelligence **PAMI-7(1)**, Jan 1985, pp. 46–55

[4] M.A.G. Abushagur and H.J. Caulfield, *"Speed and convergence of bimodal optical computers"*, Optical Engineering **26(1)**, Jan 1987, pp. 22–27

[5] **Acousto-optics**, Proceedings of the IEEE **69(1)**, Jan 1981 (special issue)

[6] R. Adler, *"Interaction between light and sound"*, IEEE Spectrum **4(5)**, May 1967, pp. 42–54

[7] A.V. Aho, R. Sethi, and J.D. Ullman, **Compilers: principles, techniques and tools**, Addison-Wesley, 1986

[8] A.V. Aho, J.E. Hopcroft, and J.D. Ullman, **The design and analysis of computer algorithms**, Addison-Wesley, 1974

[9] Y. Akasaka, *"Three-dimensional IC trends"*, Proceedings of the IEEE **74(12)**, Dec 1986, pp. 1703–1714

[10] G.F. Amelio, *"Charge-coupled devices"*, Scientific American **230(2)**, Feb 1974, pp. 22–31

[11] D.J. Amit, H. Gutfreund, and H. Sompolinsky, *"Storing infinite numbers of patterns in a spin-glass model of neural networks"*, Physical Review Letters **55(14)**, Sep 1985, pp. 1530–1533

[12] G.J. Ammon, *"Archival optical disk data storage"*, Optical Engineering **20(3)**, May/Jun 1981, pp. 394–398

[13] W. Anacker, *"Computing at 4 degrees kelvin"*, IEEE Spectrum **16(5)**, May 1979, pp. 26–37

332

[14] D.B. Anderson, J.T. Boyd, M.C. Hamilton, and R.R. August, "*An integrated-optical approach to the Fourier transform*", IEEE J. Quantum electronics **QE-13(4)**, Apr 1977, pp. 268–275

[15] D.B. Anderson, "*Integrated optical spectrum analyzer: an imminent 'chip'*", IEEE Spectrum **15(12)**, Dec 1978, pp. 22–29

[16] D.B. Anderson, R.L. Davis, J.T. Boyd, and R.R. August, "*Comparison of optical-waveguide lens technologies*", IEEE J. Quantum Electronics **QE-13(4)**, Apr 1977, pp. 275–282

[17] D.Z. Anderson, "*Coherent optical eigenstate memory*", Optics Letters **11(1)**, Jan 1986, pp. 56–58

[18] R.C. Anderson and C.S. Anderson, "*Signal processing using only Fourier phase*", Optical Engineering **25(12)**, Dec 1986, pp. 1316–1319

[19] J.F. Andrus, C.W. Campbell, and R.R. Jayroe, "*Digital image registration method using boundary maps*", IEEE trans. Computers **C-24(9)**, Sep 1975, pp. 935–940

[20] A. Arcese, P.H. Mengert, and E.W. Trombini, "*Image detection through bipolar correlation*", IEEE trans. Information Theory **IT-16(5)**, Sep 1970, pp. 534–541

[21] A. Armand, A.A. Sawchuk, and T.C. Strand, "*Nonlinear optical processing with halftones: accurate predictions for degradation and compensation*", Applied Optics **26(6)**, Mar 1987, pp. 1007–1014

[22] J.D. Armitage and A.W. Lohmann, "*Character recognition by incoherent spatial filtering*", Applied Optics **4(4)**, Apr 1965, pp. 461–467

[23] J.D. Armitage and A.W. Lohmann, "*Theta modulation in optics*", Applied Optics **4(4)**, Apr 1965, pp. 399–403

[24] S.M. Arnold, "*Electron beam fabrication of computer generated holograms*", Optical Engineering **24(5)**, Sep-Oct 1985, pp. 803–807

[25] R. Arrathoon and S. Kozaitis, "*Shadow casting for multiple-valued associative logic*", Optical Enginnering **25(1)**, Jan 1986, pp. 29–37

[26] H.H. Arsenault and Y-N. Hsu, "*Rotation-invariant discrimination between almost similar objects*", Applied Optics **22(1)**, Jan 1983, pp. 130–132

[27] H.H. Arsenault, Y-N. Hsu, and K. Chalasinska-Macukow, "*Rotation-invariant pattern recognition*", Optical Engineering **23(6)**, Nov-Dec 1984, pp. 705–709

[28] G. Arvidsson and L. Thylén, "*Electrooptic integrated optics spectrum analyzer: an experimental investigation*", Applied Optics **21(5)**, Mar 1982, pp. 797–803

[29] P.R. Ashley and W.S.C. Chang, "*fresnel lens in a thin-film waveguide*", Applied Physics Letters **33(6)**, Sep 1978, pp. 490–492

[30] R.A. Athale and S.H. Lee, "*Development of an optical parallel logic device and a half-adder circuit for digital optical processing*", Optical Engineering **18(5)**, Sep-Oct 1979, pp. 513–517

[31] R.A. Athale and W.C. Collins, "*Optical matrix-matrix multiplier based on outer product decomposition*", Applied Optics **21(12)**, Jun 1982, pp. 2089–2090

[32] R.A. Athale, W.C. Collins, and P.D. Stilwell, "*High accuracy matrix multiplication with outer product optical processor*", Applied Optics **22(3)**, Feb 1983, pp. 368–370

[33] R.A. Athale and J.N. Lee, "*Optical processing using outer product concepts*", Proceedings of the IEEE **72(7)**, Jul 1984, pp. 931–941

[34] R.A. Athale, "*Highly redundant number representation for medium accuracy optical computing*", Applied Optics **25(18)**, Sep 1986, pp. 3122–3127

[35] D.A. Ausherman, "*Digital versus optical techniques in synthetic aperture radar (SAR) data processing*", Optical Engineering **19(2)**, Mar-Apr 1980, pp. 157–167

[36] A. Avizienis, "*Signed-digit number representation for fast parallel arithmetic*", IRE trans. Electronic Computers **EC-10(3)**, Sep 1961, pp. 389–400

[37] J. Backus, "*Can programming be liberated from the Von-Neumann style? A functional style and its algebra of programs*", Comm. ACM **21(8)**, Aug 1978, pp. 613–641

[38] J. Backus, "*Function level computing*", IEEE Spectrum **19(8)**, Aug 1982, pp. 22–37

[39] R. Barakat, "*Optical matrix-matrix multiplication based on Kronecker product decomposition*", Applied Optics **26(2)**, Jan 1987, pp. 191–192

[40] R. Barakat and J. Reif, "*Polynomial convolution algorithm for matrix multiplication with application for optical computing*", Applied Optics **26(14)**, Jul 1987, pp. 2707–2711

334

[41] A. Bardos, *"Wideband holographic recorder"*, Applied Optics **13(4)**, Apr 1974, pp. 832–840

[42] E.S. Barrekette, *"Trends in storage of digital data"*, Applied Optics **13(4)**, Apr 1974, pp. 749–754

[43] H.H. Barrett, *"The Radon transform and its applications"*, in **Progress in Optics XXI**, E. Wolf (ed.), North-Holland, 1984, pp. 217– 286

[44] H.H. Barrett, *"Optical processing in Radon space"*, Optics Letters **7(6)**, Jun 1982, pp. 248–250

[45] H.H. Barrett and W. Swindell, *"Analog reconstruction methods for transaxial tomography"*, Proceedings of the IEEE **65(1)**, Jan 1977, pp. 89–107

[46] H. Bartelt, A.W. Lohmann, and E.E. Sicre, *"Optical logical processing in parallel with theta modulation"*, J. Optical Society of America A **1(9)**, Sep 1984, pp. 944-951

[47] H. Bartelt, *"Computer-generated holographic conponents with optimum light efficiency"*, Applied Optics **23(10)**, May 1984, pp. 1499–1502

[48] H. Bartelt and S.K. Case, *"Coordinate transformations via multifacet holographic optical elements"*, Optical Engineering **22(4)**, Jul-Aug 1983, pp. 497–500

[49] R.A. Bartolini, *"Optical recording: high density information storage and retrieval"*, Proceedings of the IEEE **70(6)**, Jun 1982, pp. 589–597

[50] R.A Bartolini, A.E. Bell, R.E. Flory, M. Lurie, and F.W. Spong, *"Optical disk systems emerge"*, IEEE Spectrum **15(8)**, Aug 1978, pp. 20–28

[51] K.E. Batcher, *"Design of a massively parallel processor"*, IEEE trans. Computers **C-29(9)**, Sep 1980, pp. 836–840

[52] P. Baudelaine, *"Linear stretch-invariant systems"*, Proceedings of the IEEE **61(4)**, Apr 1973, pp. 467–468

[53] J.C. Bean, *"The growth of novel silicon materials"*, Physics Today **39(10)**, Oct 1986, pp. 36–42

[54] T.E. Bell, *"Optical computing: a field in flux"*, IEEE Spectrum **23(8)**, Aug 1986, pp. 34–57

[55] V.E. Benes, **Mathematical theory of connecting networks and telephone traffic**, Academic Press, 1965

[56] J. Ben-Haim and J. Shamir, "*Scale- and rotation-invariant pattern recognition*", in **Proc. 1986 Intl. Optical Computing Conf.** Proc. SPIE **700**, July 1986, pp. 25–31

[57] C.H. Bennett, "*Logical reversibility of computation*", IBM J. Research and Development **17(6)**, Nov 1973, pp. 525–532

[58] C.H. Bennett and R. Landauer, "*The fundamental physical limits of computation*", Scientific American **253(1)**, Jul 1985, pp. 38–46

[59] A.A. Bergh and P.J. Dean, "*light emitting diodes*", Proceedings of the IEEE **60(2)**, Feb 1972, pp. 156–223

[60] G.D. Bergland, "*A guided tour of the fast Fourier transform*", IEEE spectrum **6(7)**, Jul 1969, pp. 41–52

[61] P.B. Berra and N.B. Troullinos, "*Optical techniques and data/knowledge base machines*", Computer **20(10)**, Oct 1987, pp. 59–70

[62] L.R. Berriel, J. Bescos, and A. Santisteban, "*Image restoration for a defocused optial system*", Applied Optics **22(8)**, Sep 1983, pp. 2772–2780

[63] W.P. Bleha, L.T. Lipton, E. Wiener-Avnear, J. Grinberg, P.G. Reif, D. Casasent, H.B. Brown, and B.V. Markevitch, "*Application of the liquid crystal light valve to real-time optical data processing*", Optical Engineering **17(4)**, Jul-Aug 1978, pp. 371–384

[64] A.J. Blodgett, Jr., "*Microelectronic packaging*", Scientific American **249(1)**, Jul 1983, pp. 76–86

[65] R.P. Bocker, S.R. Clayton, and K. Bromley, "*Electrooptical matrix multiplication using the twos complement arithmetic for improved accuracy*", Applied Optics **22(13)**, Jul 1983, pp. 2019–2021

[66] R.P. Bocker, B.L. Drake, M.E. Lasher, and T.B. Henderson, "*Modified signed-digit addition and subtraction using optical symbolic substitution*", Applied Optics **25(15)**, Aug 1986, pp. 2456–2457

[67] M. Born and E. Wolf, **Principals of optics**, Pergamon Press, 6th ed., 1980

[68] J.E. Bowers and C.A. Burrus, "*Optoelectronic components and systems with bandwidths in excess of 26 GHz*", RCA Review **46(4)**, Dec 1985, pp. 496–509

[69] J.T. Boyd, R.W. Wu, D.E. Zelmon, A. Naumaan, and H.T. Timlin, "*Guided wave optical structures utilizing silicon*", Optical Engineering **24(2)**, Mar/Apr 1985, pp. 230–234

336

[70] W.S. Boyle, *"Light wave communications"*, Scientific American **237(2)**, Aug 1977, pp. 40–48

[71] B. Braunecker, R. Hauck, and A.W. Lohmann, *"Optical character recognition based on nonredundant correlation measurements"*, Applied Optics **18(16)**, Aug 1979, pp. 2746–2753

[72] K-H. Brenner, A. Huang, and N. Streibl, *"Digital optical coputing with symbolic substitution"*, Applied optics **25(18)**, Sep 1986, pp. 3054–3060

[73] K-H. Brenner, *"New implementation of symbolic substitution logic"*, Applied optics **25(18)**, Sep 1986, pp. 3061–3064

[74] A.N. Broers and M. Hatzakis, *"Microcircuits by electron beam"*, Scientific American **227(5)**, Nov 1972, pp. 34–44

[75] E. Brookner, *"Phased-array radars"*, Scientific American **252(2)**, Feb 1985, pp. 76–84

[76] R.E. Brooks, *"Acoustic wave diffraction for array processing"*, Applied Optics **22(18)**, Sep 1983, pp. 2810–2816

[77] R.E. Brooks, *"Micromechanical light modulators in Silicon"*, Optical engineering **24(1)**, Jan-Feb 1985, pp 101–106

[78] B.R. Brown and A.W. Lohmann, *"Complex spatial filtering with binary mask"*, Applied Optics **5(6)**, Jun 1966, pp. 967–969

[79] B.R. Brown, *"Optical data storage potential of six materials"*, Applied Optics **13(4)**, Apr 1974, pp. 761–766

[80] B.R. Brown and A.W. Lohmann, *"Computer-generated binary holograms"*, IBM J. Research and Development **13(2)**, Mar 1969, pp. 160–168

[81] W.M. Brown, *"Synthetic aperture radar"*, IEEE trans. Aerospace and Electronic Systems **AES-3(2)**, Mar 1967, pp. 217–229

[82] W.M. Brown and J.L. Porcello, *"An introduction to synthetic-aperture radar"*, IEEE Spectrum **6(9)**, Sep 1969, pp. 52–62

[83] O. Bryngdahl, *"Computer-generated holograms as generalized optical components"*, Optical Engineering **14(5)**, Sep-Oct 1975, pp. 426–435

[84] O. Bryngdahl, *"Computer-generated holograms as space-variant optical elements"*, in **Applications of holography and optical data processing**, Proc. Intl. Conf. Jerusalem, Aug 1976, E. Marom, A.A. Friesem, and E. Wiener-Avnear (eds.), Pergamon Press, pp. 507–512

[85] O. Bryngdahl, *"Optical map transforms"*, Optics Communications **10(2)**, Feb 1974, pp. 164–168

[86] O. Bryngdahl, *"Geometrical transformations in optics"*, J. Optical Society of America **64(8)**, Aug 1974, pp. 1092–1099

[87] S.J. Buchsbaum, *"Lightwave communications — an overview"*, Physics Today **29(5)**, May 1976, pp. 23–25

[88] K. Bulthuis, M.G. Carasso, J.P.J. Heemskerk, P.J. Kivits, W.J. Kleuters, and P. Zalm, *"Ten billion bits on a disk"*, IEEE Spectrum **16(8)**, Aug 1979, pp. 26–33

[89] W.J. Burke, D.L. Saebler, W. Phillips, and G.A. Alphonse, *"Volume phase holographic storage in ferroelectric crystals"*, Optical Engineering **17(4)**, Jul-Aug 1978, pp. 308–316

[90] C.B. Burckhardt, *"A simplification of Lee's method of generating holograms by computer"*, Applied Optics **9(8)**, Aug 1970, p. 1949

[91] C.B. Burckhardt, *"Storage capacity of an optically formed spatial filter for character recognition"*, Applied Optics **6(8)**, Aug 1967, pp. 1359–1366

[92] F. Caimi, *"The photodichroic alkali-halides as optical processing elements"*, Optical Engineering **17(4)**, Jul-Aug 1978, pp. 327–333

[93] K. Campbell, G.W. Wecksung, and C.R. Mansfield, *"Spatial filtering by digital holography"*, Optical Engineering **13(3)**, May-Jun 1974, pp. 175–188

[94] T.M. Cannon and E.E. Fenimore, *"Coded aperture imaging: many holes make light work"*, Optical Engineering **19(3)**, May-Jun 1980, pp. 283–289

[95] M. Carlotto and D. Casasent, *"Microprocessor-based fiber-optic iterative optical processor"*, Applied Optics **21(1)**, Jan 1982, pp. 147–152

[96] W.J. Carlsen, *"Holographic page synthesis for sequential input data"*, Applied Optics **13(4)**, Apr 1974, pp. 896–903

[97] D. Casasent, *"Spatial light modulators"*, Proceedings of the IEEE **65(1)**, Jan 1977, pp. 143–157

[98] D. Casasent, *"E-beam DKDP light valves"*, Optical Engineering **17(4)**, Jul-Aug 1978, pp. 344–352

[99] D. Casasent, *"Photo DKDP light valve: a review"*, Optical Engineering **17(4)**, Jul-Aug 1978, pp. 365–370

[100] D. Casasent, *"Acoustooptic transducers in iterative optical vector-matrix processors"*, Applied Optics **21(10)**, May 1982, pp. 1859–1865

[101] D. Casasent, J. Jackson, and C. Neuman, *"Frequency-multiplexed and pipelined iterative optical systolic array processors"*, Applied Optics **22(1)**, Jan 1983, pp. 115–124

[102] D. Casasent, *"Coherent optical pattern recognition"*, Proceedings of the IEEE **67(5)**, May 1979, pp. 813–825

[103] D. Casasent, *"Pattern recognition: a review"*, IEEE Spectrum **18(3)**, Mar 1981, pp. 28–33

[104] D. Casasent and D. Psaltis, *"Deformation invariant, space-variant optical pattern recognition"*, in **Progress in Optics XVI**, E. Wolf (ed.), North-Holland, 1978, pp. 289–356

[105] D. Casasent and D. Psaltis, *"Scale invariant optical correlations using Mellin transforms"*, Optics Communications **17(1)**, Apr 1976, pp. 59–63

[106] D. Casasent and D. Psaltis, *"Scale invariant optical transforms"*, Optical Engineering **15(3)**, May-Jun 1976, pp. 258–261

[107] D. Casasent and D. Psaltis, *"Position, rotation, and scale invariant optical correlation"*, Applied Optics **15(7)**, Jul 1976, pp. 1795–1799

[108] D. Casasent and D. Psaltis, *"New optical transforms for pattern recognition"*, Proceedings of the IEEE **65(1)**, Jan 1977, pp. 77–84

[109] D. Casasent and A. Furman, *"Sources of correlation degradation"*, Applied Optics **16(6)**, Jun 1977, pp. 1652–1661

[110] D. Casasent, F. Caimi, and J.E. Hinds, *"Optical word recognition: case study in coherent optical pattern recognition"*, Optical Engineering **19(5)**, Sep-Oct 1980, pp. 716–721

[111] D.P. Casasent, *"A hybrid digital/optical computer system"*, IEEE trans. Computers **C-22(9)**, Sep 1973, pp. 852–858

[112] D. Casasent, G. Silbershatz, and B.V.K. Vijaya Kumar, *"Acoustooptic matched filter correlator"*, Applied Optics **21(13)**, Jul 1982, pp. 2356–2364

[113] D. Casasent and A. Furman, *"Equalizing and coherence measure correlators"*, Applied Optics **17(21)**, Nov 1978, pp. 3418–3423

[114] D. Casasent, *"Acoustooptic linear algebra processors: architectures, algorithms, and applications"*, Proceedings of the IEEE **72(7)**, Jul 1984, pp. 831–849

[115] D. Casasent and V. Sharma, *"Feature extractors for distortion-invariant robot vision"*, Optical Engineering **23(5)**, Sep-Oct 1984, pp. 492–498

[116] D. Casasent, *"Coherent optical pattern recognition: a review"*, Optical Engineering **24(1)**, Jan-Feb 1985, pp. 26–32

[117] D. Casasent and W-T. Chang, *"Generalized chord transformation for distortion-invariant optical pattern recognition"*, Applied Optics **22(14)**, Jul 1983, pp. 2087–2094

[118] D. Casasent, *"Unified synthetic discriminant function computational formulation"*, Applied Optics **23(10)**, May 1984, pp. 1620–1627

[119] D. Casasent, W. Rozzi, and D. Fetterly, *"Projection synthetic discriminant function performance"*, Optical Engineering **23(6)**, Nov-Dec 1984, pp. 716–720

[120] D. Casasent and A. Ghosh, *"Direct and implicit optical matrix-vector algorithms"*, Applied Optics **22(22)**, Nov 1983, pp. 3572–3578

[121] D. Casasent, S-F. Xia, J-Z. Song, and A.J. Lee, *"Diffraction pattern sampling using a computer-generated hologram"*, Applied Optics **25(6)**, Mar 1986, pp. 983–989

[122] D. Casasent, S-F. Xia, A.J. Lee, and J-Z. Song, *"Real-time deformation invariant optical pattern recognition using coordinate transformations"*, Applied Optics **26(5)**, Mar 1987, pp. 938–942

[123] D. Casasent, L. Cheatham, and D. Fetterly, *"Optical system to compute intensity moments: design"*, Applied Optics **21(18)**, Sep 1982, pp. 3292–3298

[124] D. Casasent and W-T. Chang, *"Correlation synthetic discriminant functions"*, Applied Optics **25(14)**, Jul 1986, pp. 2343–2350

[125] S.K. Case and P.R. Haugen, *"Partitioned holographic optical elements"*, Optical Engineering **21(2)**, Mar-Apr 1982, pp. 352–353

[126] S.K. Case, P.R. Haugen, and O.J. Løkberg, *"Multifacet holographic optical elements for wavefront transformations"*, Applied Optics **20(15)**, Aug 1981, pp. 2670–2675

[127] H.J. Caulfield and S. Lu, **The applications of holography**, John Wiley & sons, 1970

340

[128] H.J. Caulfield, D.S. Dvore, and J.H. Gruninger, "*Efficient real number representation with arbitrary radix*", Applied Optics **23(18)**, Sep 1984, pp. 3149–3151

[129] H.J. Caulfield, J.A. Neff, and W.T. Rhodes, "*Optical computing: the coming revolution in optical signal processing*", Laser Focus **19(11)**, Nov 1983, pp. 100–110

[130] H.J. Caulfield, W.T. Rhodes, M.J. Foster, and S. Horvitz, "*Optical inplementation of systolic array processing*", Optics Communication **40(2)**, Dec 1981, pp. 86–90

[131] H.J. Caulfield, D. Dvore, J.W. Goodman, and W. Rhodes, "*Eigenvector determination by noncoherent optical methods*", Applied Optics **20(13)**, Jul 1981, pp. 2263–2265

[132] H.J. Caulfield and R. Haimes, "*Generalized matched filtering*", Applied Optics **19(2)**, Jan 1980, pp. 181–183

[133] H.J. Caulfield, R. Haimes, and D. Casasent, "*Beyond matched filtering*", Optical Engineering **19(2)**, Mar-Apr 1980, pp. 152–156

[134] H.J. Caulfield, "*Holography: a reassessment*", IEEE Spectrum **19(8)**, Aug 1982, pp. 39–45

[135] H.J. Caulfield, "*Linear combinations of filters for character recognition: a unified treatment*", Applied Optics **19(23)**, Dec 1980, pp. 3877–3878

[136] H.J. Caulfield and M.H. Weinberg, "*Computer recognition of 2-D patterns using generalized matched filters*", Applied Optics **21(9)**, May 1982, pp. 1699–1704

[137] H.J. Caulfield, "*Associative mapping by optical holography*", Optics Communications **55(2)**, Aug 1985, pp. 80–82

[138] H.J. Caulfield, J.H. Gruninger, J.E. Ludman, K. Steiglitz, H. Rabitz, J. Gelfand, and E. Tsoni, "*Bimodal optical computers*", Applied Optics **25(18)**, Sep 1986, pp. 3128–3131

[139] H.J. Caulfield, C.M. Verber, and R.L. Stermer, "*Efficient matrix partitioning for optical computing*", Optics Communications **51(4)**, Sep 1984, pp. 213–216

[140] H.J. Caulfield, "*Role of the Horner efficiency in the optimization of spatial filters for optical pattern recognition*", Applied Optics **21(23)**, Dec 1982, pp. 4391–4392

[141] H.J. Caulfield, *"Optical inference machines"*, Optics Communications **55(4)**, Sep 1985, pp. 259–260

[142] H.J. Caulfield, *"Spatial encoding for optical floating point computation"*, Applied optics **23(2)**, Jan 1985, pp. 239–241

[143] H.J. Caulfield and T. Hirschfeld, *"Optical communication at the source bandwidth limit"*, Applied Optics **16(5)**, May 1977, pp. 1184–1186

[144] J. Cederquist and A.M. Tai, *"Computer-generated holograms for geometric transformations"*, Applied Optics **23(18)**, Sep 1984, pp. 3099–3104

[145] J. Cederquist and S.H. Lee, *"Coherent optical feedback for the analog solution of partial differential equations"*, J. Optical Society of America **70(8)**, Aug 1980, pp. 944–953

[146] J. Cederquist and S.H. Lee, *"Confocal feedback systems with space variance, time sampling, and secondary feedback loops"*, J. Optical Society of America **71(6)**, Jun 1981, pp. 643–650

[147] J. Cederquist, *"Integral-equation solution using coherent optical feedback"*, J. Optical Society of America **71(6)**, Jun 1981, pp. 651–655

[148] V. Chandran, T.F. Krile, and J.F. Walkup, *"Optical techniques for real-time binary multiplication"*, Applied Optics **25(14)**, Jul 1986, pp. 2272–2276

[149] B.J. Chang, *"Dichromated gelatin holograms and their applications"*, Optical Engineering **19(5)**, Sep-Oct 1980, pp. 642–648

[150] I.C. Chang, *"Acoustooptic devices and applications"*, IEEE trans. Sonics and Ultrasonics **SU-23(1)**, Jan 1976, pp. 2–22

[151] I.C. Chang and D.L. Hecht, *"Characteristics of acousto-optic devices for signal processors"*, Optical Engineering **21(1)**, Jan-Feb 1982, pp. 76–81

[152] T.Y. Chang, *"Fast self-induced refractive index changes in optical media: a survey"*, Optical Engineering **20(2)**, Mar-Apr 1981, pp. 220–232

[153] D. Chen and J.D. Zook, *"An overview of optical data storage technology"*, Proceedings of the IEEE **63(8)**, Aug 1975, pp. 1207–1230

[154] D. Chen, *"Magnetic materials for optical recording"*, Applied Optics **13(4)**, Apr 1974, pp. 767–778

[155] P.P-S. Chen, *"The compact disk ROM: how it works"*, IEEE Spectrum **23(4)**, Apr 1986, pp. 44–49

[156] D.C. Chu and J.R. Fienup, "*Recent approaches to computer-generated holograms*", Optical Engineering **13(3)**, May-Jun 1974, pp. 189–195

[157] J.J. Clair and C.I. Abitbol, "*Recent advances in phase profiles generation*", in **Progress in Optics XVI**, E. Wolf (ed.), North-Holland, 1978, pp. 71–117

[158] R. Clark Jones, "*How images are detected*", Scientific American **219(3)**, Sep 1968, pp. 110–117

[159] B. Clymer and S.A. Collins, Jr., "*Optical computer switching network*", Optical Engineering **24(1)**, Jan-Feb 1985, pp. 74–81

[160] W.S. Colburn and B.J. Chang, "*Photoconductor-thermoplastic image transducer*", Optical Engineering **17(4)**, Jul-Aug 1978, pp. 334–343

[161] S.A. Collins, Jr., M.T. Fatehi, and K.C. Wasmundt, "*Optical logic gates using a Hughes liquid crystal light valve*", in **1980 Intl. Optical Computing Conf.**, Proc. SPIE **232**, pp. 168–173

[162] E.M. Conwell, "*Integrated optics*", Physics Today **29(5)**, May 1976, pp. 48–59

[163] J.S. Cook, "*Communication by optical fiber*", Scientific American **229(5)**, Nov 1973, pp. 28–35

[164] S. Cook, C. Dwork, and R. Reischuk, "*Upper and lower time bounds for parallel random access machines without simultaneous writes*", SIAM J. Computing **15(1)**, Feb 1986, pp. 87–97

[165] S.A. Cook, "*The complexity of theorem-proving procedures*", Proc. Ann. ACM Symp. Theory Of Computing, **STOC 3**, May 1971, pp. 151–158

[166] D. Coppersmith and S. Winograd, "*Matrix multiplication via arithmetic progressions*", Proc. Ann. ACM Symp. Theory Of Computing **STOC 19**, May 1987, pp. 1–6

[167] D.M. Cottrell, R.A. Lilly, J.A. Davis, and T. Day, "*Optical correlator performance of binary phase-only filters using Fourier and Hartley transforms*", Applied Optics **26(18)**, Sep 1987, pp. 3755–3761

[168] F.S. Crawford, Jr., **Waves**, Berkeley physics course vol. 3, McGraw-Hill, 1968

[169] A. Crisanti, D.J. Amit, and H. Gutfreund, "*Saturation level of the Hopfield model for neural network*", Europhysics Letters **2(4)**, Aug 1986, pp. 337–341

[170] M. Cronin-Golomb, B. Fischer, J.O. White, and A. Yariv, "*Theory and applications of four wave mixing in photorefractive media*", IEEE J. Quantum Electronics **QE-20(1)**, Jan 1984, pp. 12–30

[171] P.S. Cross, R.V. Schmidt, R.L. Thornton, and P.W. Smith, "*Optically controlled two channel integrated-optical switch*", IEEE J. Quantum Electronics **QE-14(8)**, Aug 1978, pp. 577–580

[172] L.J. Cutrona, E.N. Leith, C.J. Palermo, and L.J. Porcello, "*Optical data processing and filtering systems*", IEEE trans. Information Theory **IT-6(3)**, Jun 1960, pp. 386–400

[173] L.J. Cutrona, E.N. Leith, L.J. Porcello, and W.E. Vivian, "*On the application of coherent optical processing techniques to synthetic-aperture radar*", Proceedings of the IEEE **54(7)**, Jul 1966, pp. 1026–1032

[174] R. Cuykendall and D. McMillin, "*Control-specific optical Fredkin circuits*", Applied Optics **26(10)**, May 1987, pp. 1959–1963

[175] M.L. Dakss, L. Kuhn, P.F. Heidrich, and B.A. Scott, "*Grating coupler for efficient exitation of optical guided waves in thin films*", Applied physics letters **16(12)**, Jun 1970, pp. 523–525

[176] R. Dändliker, K. Hess, and T. Sidler, "*Hybrid coherent optical and electronic object recognition*", Applied Optics **22(14)**, Jul 1983, pp. 2081–2088

[177] S.R. Dashiell and A.A. Sawchuk, "*Optical synthesis of non-linear non-monotonic functions*", Optics Communications **15(1)**, Sep 1975, pp. 66–70

[178] S.R. Dashiell and A.A. Sawchuk, "*Nonlinear optical processing: analysis and synthesis*", Applied Optics **16(4)**, Apr 1977, pp. 1009–1025

[179] L. d'Auria, J.P. Huignard, C. Slezak, and E. Spitz, "*Experimental holographic read-write memory using 3-D storage*", Applied Optics **13(4)**, Apr 1974, pp. 808–818

[180] J.A. Davis, K.D. Jones, and R.A. Lilly, "*Improved system for binary multiplication by optical convolution*", Optical Engineering **25(4)**, Apr 1986, pp. 572–574

[181] L.M. Deen, J.F. Walkup, and M.O. Hagler, "*Representations of space-variant optical systems using volume holograms*", Applied Optics **14(10)**, Oct 1975, pp. 2438–2446

[182] M. de Haan, C. Steenberger, and D. Chen, "*Optical memory research pays off*", Computer Design **23(11)**, Oct 1984, pp. 85–92

[183] N. Demoli, *"Quasiphase-only matched filtering"*, Applied Optics **26(11)**, Jun 1987, pp. 2058–2061

[184] D. Deutsch, *"Quantum theory, the Church-Turing principle and the universal quantum computer"*, Proceedings Royal Society of London A **400(1818)**, Jul 1985, pp. 97–117

[185] **Digital optical computing**, Optical Engineering **25(1)**, Jan 1986 (special issue, mainly about multi-valued logic)

[186] R.W. Dixon and N.K. Dutta, *"Lightwave device technology"*, AT&T Technical J. **66(1)**, Jan/Feb 1987, pp. 73–83

[187] D. Dolev, D. Maier, H. Mairson, and J. Ullman, *"Correcting faults in write-once memory"*, Proc. Ann. ACM Symp. Theory Of Computing, **STOC 16**, May 1984, pp. 225–229

[188] F. Dow Smith, *"How images are formed"*, Scientific American **219(3)**, Sep 1968, pp. 97–108 (reproduced in [398])

[189] B.L. Drake, R.P. Bocker, M.E. Lasher, R.H. Patterson, and W.J. Miceli, *"Photonic computing using the modified signed-digit number representation"*, Optical Engineering **25(1)**, Jan 1986, pp. 38–43

[190] J.G. Duthie and J. Upatnieks, *"Compact real-time coherent optical correlators"*, Optical Engineering **23(1)**, Jan-Feb 1984, pp. 7–11

[191] J. Duvernoy and Y-L. Sheng, *"Effective optical processor for computing image moments at TV rate: use in handwriting recognition"*, Applied Optics **26(12)**, Jun 1978, pp. 2320–2327

[192] P.W. Dymond and S.A. Cook, *"Hardware complexity and parallel computation"*, Ann. Symp. Foundations Of Computer Science, **FOCS 21**, Oct 1980, pp. 360–371

[193] L.F. Eastman, *"Compound-semiconductor transistors"*, Physics Today **39(10)**, Oct 1986, pp. 77–83

[194] J.F. Ebersole, *"Optical image subtraction"*, Optical Engineering **14(5)**, Sep-Oct 1975, pp. 436–447

[195] R.C. Eden, A.R. Livingston, and B.M. Welch, *"Integrated circuits: the case for gallium arsenide"*, IEEE Spectrum **20(12)**, Dec 1983, pp. 30–37

[196] U. Efron, P.O. Braatz, M.J. Little, R.N. Schwartz, and J. Grinberg, *"Silicon liquid crystal light valves: status and issues"*, Optical Engineering **22(6)**, Nov-dec 1983, pp. 682–686

[197] U. Efron, "*Spatial light modulators for optical information processing*", in **Proc. 1986 Intl. Optical Computing Conf.** Proc. SPIE **700**, Jul 1986, pp. 132–145

[198] G. Eichmann and Y. Li, "*Compact optical generalized perfect shuffle*", Applied Optics **26(7)**, Apr 1987, pp. 1167–1169

[199] G. Eichmann, Y. Li, and R.R. Alfano, "*Parallel optical logic using optical phase conjugation*", Applied Optics **26(2)**, Jan 1987, pp. 194–196

[200] G. Eichmann, Y. Li, and R.R. Alfano, "*Optical binary coded ternary arithmetic and logic*", Applied Optics **25(18)**, Sep 1986, pp. 3113–3121

[201] G. Eichmann and S. Basu, "*Parallel optical syntactic pattern recognizers*", Applied Optics **26(10)**, May 1987, pp. 1859–1865

[202] C. Elachi and J. Granger, "*Spaceborne imaging radars probe 'in depth'*", IEEE Spectrum **19(11)**, Nov 1982, pp. 24–29

[203] C. Elachi, "*Radar images of the earth from space*", Scientific American **247(6)**, Dec 1982, pp. 46–53

[204] M. Eleccion, "*The familiy of lasers: a survey*", IEEE Spectrum **9(3)**, Mar 1972, pp. 26–40

[205] G. Epstein, G. Frieden, and D.C. Rine, "*The development of multiple-valued logic as related to computer science*", Computer **7(9)**, Sep 1974, pp. 20–32

[206] S.C. Esener, J.H. Wang, T.J. Drabik, M.A. Title, and S.H. Lee, "*One-dimensional silicon/PLZT spatial light modulators*", Optical Engineering **26(5)**, May 1987, pp. 406–413

[207] Y. Fainman, C.C. Guest, and S.H. Lee, "*Optical digital logic operations by two-beam coupling in photorefractive material*", Applied Optics **25(10)**, May 1986, pp. 1598–1603

[208] R.C. Fairchild and F.J. Fienup, "*Computer-originated aspheric holographic optical elements*", Optical Engineering **21(2)**, Jan-Feb 1982, pp. 133–140

[209] N.H. Farhat, D. Psaltis, A. Prata, and E. Paek, "*Optical inplementation of the Hopfield model*", Applied Optics **24(10)**, May 1985, pp. 1469–1475

[210] N.H. Farhat, "*Nonlinear optical data processor and filtering: a feasibility study*", IEEE trans. Computers **C-24(4)**, Apr 1975, pp. 443–448

[211] M.T. Fatehi, S.A. Collins, Jr., and K.C. Wasmundt, "*The optical computer goes digital*", Optical Spectra **15(1)**, Jan 1981, pp. 39–42

346

[212] M.T. Fatehi, K.C. Wasmundt, and S.A. Collins, Jr., *"Optical logic gates using liquid crystal light valve: implementation and application example"*, Applied Optics **20(13)**, Jul 1981, pp. 2250–2256

[213] M.T. Fatehi, K.C. Wasmundt, and S.A. Collins, Jr., *"Optical flip-flops and sequential logic circuits using a liquid crystal light valve"*, Applied Optics **23(13)**, Jul 1984, pp. 2163–2171

[214] G. Feinberg, *"Light"*, Scientific American **219(3)**, Sep 1968, pp. 50–59 (reproduced in [398])

[215] J. Feinberg, *"Real-time edge enhancement using the photorefractive effect"*, Optics Letters **5(8)**, Aug 1980, pp. 330–332

[216] R.P. Feynman, **QED — the strange theory of light and matter**, Princeton University Press, 1985

[217] R.P. Feynman, R.B. Leighton, and M. Sands, **The Feynman lectures on physics**, vol. I, Addison-Wesley, 1963

[218] **Fiberoptic LANs**, Laser Focus **23(3)**, Mar 1987, pp. 104–120 (special report)

[219] F.E. Fich, P.L. Ragde, and A. Wigderson, *"Relations between concurrent-write models of parallel computation"*, Proc 3rd Ann. ACM Symp. Principles of Distibuted Computing, Aug 1984, pp. 179–189

[220] J.R. Fineup, *"Iterative method applied to image reconstruction and to computer generated holograms"*, Optical Engineering **19(3)**, May-Jun 1980, pp. 297–305

[221] M.R. Finley, Jr., *"Optical fibers in local area networks"*, IEEE Communications mag. **22(8)**, Aug 1984, pp. 22–35

[222] J.B. Flannery, Jr., *"Light-controlled light valves"*, IEEE trans. Electron Devices **ED-20(11)**, Nov 1973, pp. 941–953

[223] H. Fleisher and L.I. Maissel, *"An introduction to array logic"*, IBM J. Research and Development **19(2)**, Mar 1975, pp. 98–109

[224] J. Fleuret, *"Optical comuting units using four-wave mixing and amplitude coding"*, Applied Optics **23(10)**, May 1984, pp. 1609–1612

[225] R.E. Flory, *"Image acquisition thechnology"*, Proceedings of the IEEE **73(4)**, Apr 1985, pp. 613–637

[226] M.J. Flynn, "*Very high-speed computing systems*", Proceedings of the IEEE **54(12)**, Dec 1966, pp. 1901–1909

[227] M.J. Flynn, "*Some computer organizations and their effectiveness*", IEEE trans. Computers **C-21(9)**, Sep 1972, pp. 948–960

[228] S.R. Forrest, "*Optical detectors: three contenders*", IEEE Spectrum **23(5)**, May 1986, pp. 76–84

[229] S. Fortune and J. Wyllie, "*Parallelism in random access machines*", Proc. Ann. ACM Symp. Theory Of Computing, **STOC 10**, May 1978, pp. 114–118

[230] B. Fox, "*Optical storage comes to order*", New Scientist **112(1536)**, 27 Nov 1986, pp. 46–48

[231] E. Fredkin and T. Toffoli, "*Conservative logic*", Intl. J. Theoretical Physics **21(3/4)**, Apr 1982, pp. 219–253

[232] A.A. Friesem and J.L. Walker, "*Thick absorption recording media in holography*", Applied Optics **9(1)**, Jan 1970, pp. 201–214

[233] L. Fujitani, "*Laser optical disk: the coming revolution in on-line storage*", Communications of the ACM **27(6)**, Jun 1984, pp. 546–554

[234] A. Furman and D. Casasent, "*Bipolar incoherent optical pattern recognition by carrier encoding*", Applied Optics **18(5)**, Mar 1979, pp. 660–665

[235] D. Gabor, "*A new microscopic principle*", Nature **161(4098)**, May 1948, pp. 777–778

[236] D. Gabor, "*Microscopy by reconstructed wave-fronts*", Proceedings of the Royal Society of London A **197(1051)**, Jul 1949, pp. 454–487

[237] D. Gabor, "*Microscopy by reconstructed wave-fronts: II*", The Proceedings of the Physical Society B **64;6(378B)**, Jun 1951, pp. 449–469

[238] D. Gabor, "*Character recognition by holography*", Nature **208(5009)**, Oct 1965, pp. 422–423

[239] D. Gabor, W.E. Kock, and G.W. Stroke, "*Holography*", Science **173(3991)**, 2 Jul 1971, pp. 11–23

[240] A.D. Gara, "*Real time tracking of moving objects by optical correlation*", Applied Optics **18(2)**, Jan 1979, pp. 172–174

[241] T.K. Gaylord, M.M. Mirsalehi, and C.C. Guest, "*Optical digital truth-table look-up processing*", Optical Engineering **24(1)**, Jan-Feb 1985, pp. 48–58

[242] T.K. Gaylord and M.M. Mirsalehi, "*Truth-table look-up processing: number representation, multilevel coding and logical minimization*", Optical Engineering **25(1)**, Jan 1986, pp. 22–28

[243] U.H. Gerlach, U.K. Sengupta, and S.A. Collins, Jr., "*Single-spatial light modulator bistable optical matrix device using optical feedback*", Optical Engineering **19(4)**, Jul-Aug 1980, pp. 452–455

[244] P.D. Gianino and J.L. Horner, "*Additional properties of the phase-only correlation filter*", Optical Engineering **23(6)**, Nov-Dec 1984, pp. 695–697

[245] H.M. Gibbs, S.L. McCall, and T.N. Venkatesan, "*Optical bistable devices: the basic components of all-optical systems?*", Optical Engineering **19(4)**, Jul-Aug 1980, pp. 463–468

[246] P. Gidon, S. Valette, and P. Mottier, "*Integrated lenses on silicon nitride waveguides*", Optical Engineering **24(2)**, Mar/Apr 1985, pp. 235–240

[247] I. Glaser, "*Representing bipolar and complex imagery in noncoherent optics image processing systems: comparison of approches*", Optical Engineering **20(4)**, Jul-Aug 1981, pp. 568–573

[248] I. Glaser and L. Perelmutter, "*Optical interconnections for digital processing: a noncoherent method*", Optics Letters **11(1)**, Jan 1986, pp. 53–55

[249] I. Glaser, "*Lenslet array processors*", Applied Optics **21(7)**, Apr 1982, pp. 1271–1280

[250] I. Glaser, "*Information processing with spatially incoherent light*", June 1986, to be published in **Progress in Optics**

[251] I. Glaser, "*Holographic incoherent optical transfer function synthesis: analysis and optimization*", J. Optical Society of America A **3(5)**, May 1986, pp. 681–693

[252] I. Glaser, "*Noncoherent parallel optical processor for discrete two dimensional linear transformations*", Optics Letters **5(10)**, Oct 1980, pp. 449–451

[253] I. Glaser and Y. Katzir, "*Registration fiducials for automated alignment with optical processing*", Applied Optics **21(20)**, Oct 1982, pp. 3695–3698

[254] A.M. Glass, "*The photorefractive effect*", Optical Engineering **17(5)**, Sep-Oct 1978, pp. 470–479

[255] A.M. Glass, "*Optical materials*", Science **235(4792)**, 27 Feb 1987, pp. 1003–1009

[256] A.F. Gmitro, J.E. Greivenkamp, W. Swindell, H.H. Barrett, M.Y. Chiu, and S.K. Gordon, "*Optical computers for reconstructing objects from their x-ray projections*", Optical Engineering **19(3)**, May-Jun 1980, pp. 260–272

[257] J.E. Goell and R.D. Standley, "*Integrated optical circuits*", Proceedings of the IEEE **58(10)**, Oct 1970, pp. 1504–1512

[258] J.E. Goell, "*Electron-resist fabrication of bends and couplers for integrated optical circuits*", Applied Optics **12(4)**, Apr 1973, pp. 729–736

[259] L.M. Goldschlager, "*A universal interconnection pattern for parallel computers*", J. ACM **29(3)**, Jul 1982, pp. 1073–1086

[260] J.W. Goodman, **Introduction to Fourier optics**, McGraw-Hill, 1968

[261] J.W. Goodman and L.M. Woody, "*Method for performing complex-valued linear operations on complex-valued data using incoherent light*", Applied Optics **16(10)**, Oct 1977, pp. 2611–2612

[262] J.W. Goodman, F.J. Leonberger, S-Y. Kung, and R.A. Athale, "*Optical interconnections for VLSI systems*", Proceedings of the IEEE **72(7)**, Jul 1984, pp. 850–865

[263] J.W. Goodman, A.R. Dias, and L.M. Woody, "*Fully parallel, high-speed incoherent optical method for performing discrete Fourier transforms*", Optics Letters **2(1)**, Jan 1978, pp. 1–3

[264] J.W. Goodman and M.S. Song, "*Performance limitations of an analog method for solving simultaneous linear equations*", Applied Optics **21(3)**, Feb 1982, pp. 502–506

[265] J.W. Goodman, "*Operations achievable with coherent optical information processing systems*", Proceedings of the IEEE **65(1)**, Jan 1977, pp. 29–38

[266] J.W. Goodman, "*Fan-in and fan-out with optical interconnections*", Optica Acta **32(12)**, Dec 1985, pp. 1489–1496

[267] E.I. Gordon, "*A review of acoustooptical deflection and modulation devices*", Proceedings of the IEEE **54(10)**, Oct 1966, pp. 1391–1401

[268] A. Gottlieb, R. Grishman, C.P. Kruskal, K.P. McAuliffe, L. Rudolph, and M. Snir, "*The NYU ultracomputer — designing an MIMD shared memory parallel computer*", IEEE trans. Computers **C-32(2)**, Feb 1983, pp. 175–189

[269] A. Gottlieb, B. Lubachevsky, and L. Rudolph, "*Basic techiques for the efficient coordination of very large numbers of cooperating sequential processors*", ACM trans. on Programming Languages and Systems **TOPLAS 5(2)**, Apr 1983, pp. 164–189

[270] J. Götz and J. Jahns, "*An opto-electronic nonlinear component*", Optics Communications **40(5)**, Feb 1982, pp. 325–328

[271] A.P. Goutzoulis, "*Systolic time-integrating acoustooptic binary processor*", Applied Optics **23(22)**, Nov 1984, pp. 4095–4099

[272] A.P. Goutzoulis, "*Systolic time-integrating acoustooptic binary processor*", Applied Optics **23(22)**, Nov 1984, pp. 4095–4099

[273] M. Gower, "*Mirrors that reflect time*", Nature **308(5955)**, 8 Mar 1984, pp. 110–111

[274] M. Gower, "*Dynamic holograms from crystals*", Nature **316(6023)**, 4 Jul 1985, pp. 12–14

[275] **Gradient index lenses**, Applied Optics **25(19)**, Oct 1986, (special issue)

[276] D.A. Gregory and H.K. Liu, "*Large-memory real-time multichannel multiplexed pattern recognition*", Applied Optics **23(24)**, Dec 1984, pp. 4560–4570

[277] J.E. Greivenkamp, W. Swindell, A.F. Gmitro, and H.H. Barrett, "*Incoherent optical processor for x-ray transaxial tomography*", Applied Optics **20(2)**, Jan 1981, pp. 264–273

[278] J. Gruninger and H.J. Caulfield, "*Algorithm improvements for optical eigenfunction computers*", Applied Optics **22(14)**, Jul 1983, pp. 2075–2080

[279] Z-H. Gu, J.R. Leger, and S.H. Lee, "*Optical implementation of the least-squares linear mapping technique for image classification*", J. Optical Society of America **72(6)**, Jun 1982, pp. 787–793

[280] Z-H. Gu and S.H. Lee, "*Recognition of images of Markov-1 model by least-squares linear mapping technique*", Applied Optics **23(6)**, Mar 1984, pp. 822–827

[281] Z-H. Gu and S.H. Lee, "*Classification of multi-classed stochastic images buried in additive noise*", in **Proc. Intl. Optical Computing Conf.**, Proc. SPIE **700**, Jul 1986, pp. 44–54

[282] B. Gu, G. Yang, and B. Dong, "*General theory for performing an optical transform*", Applied Optics **25(18)**, Sep 1986, pp. 3197–3206

[283] B.D. Guenther, C.R. Christensen, and J. Upatnieks, "*Coherent optical processing: another approach*", IEEE J. Quantum Electronics **QE-15(12)**, Dec 1979, pp. 1348–1362

[284] C.C. Guest and T.K. Gaylord, "*Truth-table look-up optical processing utilizing binary and residue arithmetic*", Applied Optics **19(7)**, Apr 1980, pp. 1201–1207

[285] C.C. Guest, M.M. Mirsalehi, and T.K. Gaylord, "*EXCLUSIVE OR processing (binary image subtraction) using thick Fourier holograms*", Applied Optics **23(19)**, Oct 1984, pp. 3444-3454

[286] H. Hacker, Y. Kwon, R. Lontz, and I. Lefkowitz, "*Characteristics of liquid crystal devices with improved response times*", Applied Optics **19(8)**, Apr 1980, pp. 1278–1281

[287] D.G. Hall, "*Survey of silicon-based integrated optics*", Computer **20(12)**, Dec 1987, pp. 25–32

[288] E.L. Hall, R.P. Kruger, and A.F. Turner, "*An optical-digital system for automatic processing of chest X-rays*", Optical Engineering **13(3)**, May-Jun 1974, pp. 250–257

[289] J.E. Hall and J.D. Awtrey, "*Real-time image enhancement using 3 × 3 pixel neighborhood operator functions*", Optical Engineering **19(3)**, May-Jun 1980, pp. 421–424

[290] M.C. Hamilton, D.A. Wille, and W.J. Miceli, "*An integrated optical RF spectrum analyzer*", Optical Engineering **16(5)**, Sep-Oct 1977, pp. 475–478

[291] **Handbook of optical holography**, H.J. Caulfield, (ed.), Academic Press, 1979

[292] A.A. Hanlon, "*Content addressable and associative memory systems: a survey*", IEEE trans. Electronic Computers **EC-15(4)**, Aug 1966, pp. 509–521

[293] J.H. Harris, R. Shubert, and J.N. Polky, "*Beam coupling to films*", J. Optical Society of America **60(8)**, Aug 1970, pp. 1007–1016

[294] J.H. Harris and R. Shubert, "*Variable tunneling excitation of optical surface waves*", IEEE trans. Microwave Theory and Techniques **MTT-19(3)**, Mar 1971, pp. 269–276

[295] M.H. Hassoun and R. Arrathoon, "*Logical signal processing with optically connected threshold gates*", Optical Engineering **25(1)**, Jan 1986, pp. 56–68

[296] G-I. Hatakoshi and S-I. Tanaka, "*Grating lenses for integrated optics*", Optics Letters **2(6)**, Jun 1978, pp. 142–144

[297] G. Hatakoshi, H. Inove, K. Naito, S. Umegaki, and S. Tanaka, "*Optical waveguide lenses*", Optica Acta **26(8)**, Aug 1979, pp. 961–968

[298] R. Hauck and O. Bryngdahl, *"Computer holography: review and digressions"*, in **Intl. Conf. Computer Generated Holography**, Proc. SPIE **437**, Aug 1983, pp. 2–6

[299] R. Hauck, *"Binary coding techniques with emphasis on pulse density modulation"*, in **Proc. 1986 Intl. Optical Computing Conf.**, Proc. SPIE **700**, Jul 1986, pp. 265–269

[300] P.R. Haugen, H. Bartelt, and S.K. Case, *"Image formation by multifacet holograms"*, Applied Optics **22(18)**, Sep 1983, pp. 2822–2829

[301] P.R. Haugen, S. Rychnovsky, A. Husain, and L.D. Hutcheson, *"Optical interconnects for high speed computing"*, Optical Engineering **25(10)**, Oct 1986, pp. 1076–1085

[302] G. Häusler, *"Optical software survey"*, Optica Acta **24(9)**, Sep 1977, pp. 965–977

[303] G. Häusler, *"A method to increase the depth of focus by two step image processing"*, Optics Communications **6(1)**, Sep 1972, pp. 38–42

[304] F.G. Heath, *"Large scale integration in electronics"*, Scientific American **222(2)**, Feb 1970, pp. 22–31

[305] F.G. Heath, *"Origins of the binary code"*, Scientific American **227(2)**, Aug 1972, pp. 76–83

[306] E. Hecht, **Optics**, Addison-Wesley, 2nd ed., 1987

[307] R. Hecht-Nielsen, *"Nearest matched filter classification of spatiotemporal patterns"*, Applied Optics **26(10)**, May 1987, pp. 1892–1899

[308] G.H. Heilmeier, *"Liquid-crystal display devices"*, Scientific American **222(4)**, Apr 1970, pp. 100–106

[309] C.F. Hester and D. Casasent, *"Multivariant technique for multichannel pattern recognition"*, Applied Optics **19(11)**, Jun 1980, pp. 1758–1761

[310] W.D. Hillis, *"The connection machine"*, Scientific American **256(6)**, Jun 1987, pp. 86–93

[311] J. Hong and D. Psaltis, *"Storage capacity of holographic associative memories"*, Optics Letters **11(12)**, Dec 1986, pp. 812–814

[312] J.E. Hopcroft and J.D. Ullman, **Introduction to automata theory, languages, and computation**, Addison-Wesley, 1979

networks and physical systems with emergent col-
ibilities", Proceedings National Academy of Science
). 2554–2558

[314] J.J. _   ons with graded response have collective computational
properties like __ e of two state neurons", Proceedings National Academy
of Science USA **81**, May 1984, pp. 3088–3092

[315] J.L. Horner, "*Light utilization in optical correlators*", Applied Optics
21(24), Dec 1982, pp. 4511–4514

[316] J.L. Horner and P.D. Gianino, "*Phase-only matched filtering*", Applied Optics **23(6)**, Mar 1984, pp. 812–816

[317] J.L. Horner and P.D. Gianino, "*Applying the phase-only filter concept to
the synthetic discriminant function correlation filter*", Applied Optics **24(6)**,
Mar 1984, pp. 851–855

[318] B.A. Horwitz and F.J. Corbett, "*The PROM — Theory and applications
for the Pockels Readout Optical Modulator*", Optical Engineering **17(4)**,
Jul-Aug 1978, pp. 353–364

[319] Y-N. Hsu, H.H. Arsenault, and G. April, "*Rotation-invariant digital pattern
recognition using circular harmonic expansion*", Applied Optics **21(22)**, Nov
1982, pp. 4012–4015

[320] Y-N. Hsu and H.H. Arsenault, "*Optical pattern recognition using circular
harmonic expansion*", Applied Optics **21(22)**, Nov 1982, pp. 4016–4019

[321] Y-N. Hsu and H.H. Arsenault, "*Statistical performance of the circular
harmonic filter for rotation-invariant pattern recognition*", Applied Optics
22(18), Sep 1983, pp. 2804–2809

[322] Y-N. Hsu and H.H. Arsenault, "*Pattern discrimination by multiple circular
harmonic components*", Applied Optics **23(6)**, Mar 1984, pp. 841–844

[323] M-K. Hu, "*Visual pattern recognition by moment invariants*", IRE trans.
Information Theory **IT-8(2)**, Feb 1962, pp. 179–187

[324] A. Huang, "*Architectural considerations involved in the design of an optical
digital computer*", Proceedings of the IEEE **72(7)**, Jul 1984, pp. 780–786

[325] A. Huang, Y. Tsunoda, J.W. Goodman, and S. Ishihara, "*Optical computing
using residue arithmetic*", Applied Optics **18(2)**, Jan 1979, pp. 149–162

[326] A. Huang, "*Design for an optical general purpose digital computer*", in **1980
Intl. Optical Computing Conf.**, Proc. SPIE **232**, pp. 119–127

[327] T.S. Huang, *"Digital holography"*, Proceedings of the IEEE **59(9)**, Sep 1971, pp. 1335–1346

[328] S.L. Hurst, *"Multiple valued logic — its status and its future"*, IEEE trans. Computers **C-33(12)**, Dec 1984, pp. 1160–1179

[329] S.L. Hurst, *"Multiple-valued threshold logic: its status and its realization"*, Optical Engineering **25(1)**, Jan 1986, pp. 44–55

[330] A. Husain, J. Warrior, P.R. Haugen, N. Murray, M. Beatty, and L.D. Hutcheson, *"Optical processing for future computer networks"*, Optical Engineering **25(1)**, Jan 1986, pp. 108–116

[331] L.D. Hutcheson, P. Haugen, and A. Husain, *"Optical interconnects replace hardwire"*, IEEE Spectrum **24(3)**, Mar 1987, pp. 30–35

[332] Y. Ichioka and J. Tanida, *"Optical parallel logic gates using a shadow-casting system for optical digital computing"*, Proceedings of the IEEE **72(7)**, Jul 1984, pp. 787–801

[333] G. Indebetouw, *"Scanning optical correlator"*, Optics Letters **6(1)**, Jan 1981, pp. 10–12

[334] **Integrated optical computing**, Computer **20(12)**, Dec 1987 (special issue)

[335] S. Israel, S.C. Gustafson, and E.S. Cooley, *"Asynchronous integrated optical multiply accumulate with sideways summer"*, Applied Optics **25(14)**, Jul 1986, pp. 2284–2287

[336] S. Iwasa and J. Feinleib, *"The PROM device in optical processing systems"*, Optical Engineering **13(3)**, May-Jun 1974, pp. 235–242

[337] J. Jackson and D. Casasent, *"Optical systolic array processor using residue arithmetic"*, Applied Optics **22(18)**, Sep 1983, pp. 2817–2821

[338] J. Jahns, *"Concepts of optical digital computing — a survey"*, Optik **57(3)**, 1980, pp. 429–449

[339] F.A. Jenkins and H.E. White, **Fundamentals of optics**, McGraw-Hill, 4th ed., 1976

[340] B.K. Jenkins and T.C. Strand, *"Computer generated holograms for space-variant interconnections in optical logic systems"*, in **Intl. Conf. Computer Generated Holography**, Proc. SPIE **437**, Aug 1983, pp. 110–117

[341] B.K. Jenkins, A.A. Sawchuk, T.C. Strand, R.Forchheimer, and B.H. Soffer, "*Sequential optical logic implementation*", Applied Optics **23(19)**, Oct 1984, pp. 3455-3464

[342] B.K. Jenkins, P. Chavel, R. Forchheimer, A.A. Sawchuck, and T.C. Strand, "*Architectural implications of a digital optical computer*", Applied Optics **23(19)**, Oct 1984, pp. 3465–3474

[343] H. Jensen, L.C. Graham, L.J. Porcello, and E.N. Leith, "*Side looking airborne radar*", Scientific American **237(4)**, Oct 1977, pp. 84–95

[344] J.L. Jewell, M.C. Rushford, and H.M. Gibbs, "*Use of a single nonlinear Fabry-Perot etalon as optical logic gates*", Applied Physics letters **44(2)**, Jan 1984, pp. 172–174

[345] J.L. Jewell, Y.H. Lee, J.F. Duffy, A.C. Gossard, and W. Wiegmann, "*Parallel operation and crosstalk measurements in GaAs étalon optical logic devices*", Applied Physics Letters **48(20)**, May 1986, pp. 1342–1344

[346] R.V. Jones, "*Photoneural systems: an introduction*", Applied Optics **26(10)**, May 1987, pp. 1948–1958

[347] R.R. Kallman, "*Construction of low noise optical correlation filters*", Applied Optics **25(7)**, Apr 1986, pp. 1032–1033

[348] R.R. Kallman, "*Optimal low noise phase-only and binary phase-only optical correlation filters for threshold detectors*", Applied Optics **25(23)**, Dec 1986, pp. 4216–4217

[349] I.P. Kaminow, "*Optical waveguide modulators*", IEEE trans. Microwave Theory and Techniques **MTT-23(1)**, Jan 1975, pp. 57–70

[350] C.K. Kao, **Optical fiber systems: technology, design and applications**, McGraw-Hill, 1986

[351] N.S. Kapany, "*Fiber optics*", Scientific American **203(5)**, Nov 1960, pp. 72–81 (reproduced in [398])

[352] F.P. Kapron, "*Fiber optics system tradeoffs*", IEEE Spectrum **22(3)**, Mar 1985, pp. 68–75

[353] M.A. Karim and H-K. Liu, "*All-optical homomorphic image-processing system*", Optics Letters **7(8)**, Aug 1982, pp. 371–373

[354] W.J. Karplus and R.A. Russel, "*Increasing digital computer efficiency with the aid of error-correcting analog subroutines*", IEEE trans. Computers **C-20(8)**, Aug 1971, pp. 831–837

[355] D. Kassai and E. Marom, "*Aberration-corrected rounded-edge geodesic lenses*", J. Optical Society of America **69(9)**, Sep 1979, pp. 1242–1248

[356] H. Kato and J.W. Goodman, "*Nonlinear filtering in coherent optical systems through halftone screen processes*", Applied Optics **14(8)**, Aug 1975, pp. 1813–1824

[357] Y. Katzir, M. Young, and I. Glaser, "*Pattern recognition using incoherent OTF synthesis and edge enhancement*", Applied Optics **24(6)**, Mar 1985, pp. 863–867

[358] D.B. Keck, "*Single-mode fibers outperform multimode cables*", IEEE Spectrum **20(3)**, Mar 1983, pp. 30–37

[359] J. Kedmi and A.A. Friesem, "*Optimal holographic Fourier-transform lens*", Applied Optics **23(22)**, Nov 1984, pp. 4015–4019

[360] P. Kellman, "*Time integrating optical signal processing*", Optical Engineering **19(3)**, May-Jun 1980, pp. 370–375

[361] G.C. Kenney, D.Y.K. Low, R. McFarlane, A.Y. Chen, I.S. Nadan, T.R. Kohler, J.G. Wagner, and F. Zernike, "*An optical disk replaces 25 mag tapes*", IEEE Spectrum **16(2)**, Feb 1979, pp. 33–38

[362] R.W. Keyes, "*Thermal limitations in optical logic*", Applied Optics **8(12)**, Dec 1969, pp. 2549–2552

[363] R.W. Keyes, "*Optical logic — in the light of computer technology*", Optica Acta **32(5)**, 1985, pp. 525–535

[364] R.W. Keyes, "*Fundamental limits in digital information processing*", Proceedings of the IEEE **69(2)**, Feb 1981, pp. 267–278

[365] R.W. Keyes, "*Physical limits in digital electronics*", Proceedings of the IEEE **63(5)**, May 1975, pp. 740–767

[366] R.W. Keyes, "*Power disipation in information processing*", Science **168(3933)**, 15 May 1970, pp. 796–801

[367] R.W. Keyes, "*What makes a good computer device?*", Science **230(4722)**, 11 Oct 1985, pp. 138–144

[368] R.W. Keyes, "*Communication in computation*", Intl. J. Theoretical Physics **21(3/4)**, Apr 1982, pp. 263–273

[369] A.H. Khan and U.R. Nejib, "*Optical logic gates employing liquid crystal optical switches*", Applied Optics **26(2)**, Jan 1987, pp. 270–273

[370] H. Kiemle, "*Considerations on holographic memories in the gigabyte region*", Applied Optics **13(4)**, Apr 1974, pp. 803–807

[371] M.C. King, A.M. Noll, and D.H. Berry, "*A new approach to computer-generated holography*", Applied Optics **9(2)**, Feb 1970, pp. 471–475

[372] G.S. Kino and J. Shaw, "*Acoustic surface waves*", Scientific American **227(4)**, Oct 1972, pp. 50–68

[373] W.R. Klein and B.D. Cook, "*Unified approach to ultrasonic light diffraction*", IEEE trans. Sonics and Ultrasonics **SU-14(3)**, Jul 1967, pp. 123–134

[374] D.E. Knuth, **The Art of Computer Programming**, vol. 2 — **Seminumerical Algorithms**, Addison-Wesley, 2nd ed., 1981

[375] W.E. Kock, "*Side-looking radar, holography, and Doppler-free coherent radar*", Proceedings of the IEEE **56(2)**, Feb 1968, pp. 238–239

[376] H. Kogelnik, "*An introduction to integrated optics*", IEEE trans. Microwave Theory and Techniques **MTT-23(1)**, Jan 1975, pp. 2–16

[377] H. Kogelnik, "*Limits in integrated optics*", Proceedings of the IEEE **69(2)**, Feb 1981, pp. 232–238

[378] H. Kogelnik and C.V. Shank, "*Coupled wave theory of distributed feedback lasers*", J. Applied Physics **43(5)**, May 1972, pp. 2327–2335

[379] H. Kogelnik and R.V. Schmidt, "*Switched directional couplers with alternating $\Delta\beta$*", IEEE J. Quantm Electronics **QE-12(7)**, Jul 1976, pp. 396–401

[380] A. Korpel, "*Acousto-optics — a review of fundamentals*", Proceedings of the IEEE **69(1)**, Jan 1981, pp. 48–53

[381] W.F. Kosonocky, "*Laser digital devices*", IEEE Spectrum **2(3)**, Mar 1965, pp. 183–195

[382] R.K. Kostuk, J.W. Goodman, and L. Hesselink, "*Design considerations for holographic optical interconnects*", Applied Optics **26(18)**, Sep 1987, pp. 3947–3953

[383] R.K. Kostuk, J.W. Goodman, and L. Hesselink, "*Optical imaging applied to microelectronic chip-to-chip interconnections*", Applied Optics **24(17)**, Sep 1985, pp. 2851–2858

[384] D. Kozen, "*On parallelism in Turing machines*", Ann. Symp. Foundations Of Computer Science, **FOCS 17**, Oct 1976, pp. 89–97

[385] A. Kozma and D.L. Kelly, *"Spatial filtering for detection of signals submerged in noise"*, Applied Optics **4(4)**, Apr 1965, pp. 387–392

[386] A. Kozma, E.N. Leith, and N.G. Massey, *"Tilted-plane optical processor"*, Applied Optics **11(8)**, aug 1972, pp. 1766–1777

[387] C.P. Kruskal, *"Algorithms for replace-add based paracomputers"*, Proc. Intl. Conf. on Parallel Processing, Aug 1982, pp. 219–223

[388] G.A. Krusos, *"Restoration of radiologic images by optical spatial filtering"*, Optical Engineering **13(3)**, May-Jun 1974, pp. 208–218

[389] L. Kuhn, M.L. Dakss, P.F. Heidrich, and B.A. Scott, *"Deflection of an optical guided wave by a surface acoustic wave"*, Applied Physics Letters **17(6)**, Sep 1970, pp. 265–267

[390] H.T. Kung, *"Why systolic architectures?"*, Computer **15(1)**, Jan 1982, pp. 37–46

[391] M.H. Kryder, *"Data-storage technologies for advanced computing"*, Scientific American **257(4)**, Oct 1987, pp. 72–81

[392] M.H. Kryder, *"Magneto-optic recording technology"*, J. Applied Physics **57(8);IIB**, Apr 1985, pp. 3913–3918

[393] C.E. Land, *"Optical information storage and spatial light modulation in PLZT ceramics"*, Optical Engineering **17(4)**, Jul-Aug 1978, pp. 317–326

[394] R. Landauer, *"Uncertainty principle and minimal energy dissipation in the computer"*, Intl. J. Theoretical Physics **21(3/4)**, Apr 1982, pp. 283–297

[395] T. Lang and H.S. Stone, *"A shuffle-exchange network with simplified control"*, IEEE trans. Computers **C-25(1)**, Jan 1975, pp. 55–65

[396] D.N. Langenberg, D.J. Scalapino, and B.N. Taylor, *"The Josephson effects"*, Scientific American **214(5)**, May 1966, pp. 30–39

[397] **Laser recording and data handling**, Optical Engineering **20(3)**, May/Jun 1981 (special issue)

[398] **Lasers and light**, Readings from Scientific American, Freeman, 1969 (includes [188,214,351,416,510,601,726])

[399] G.J. Lasher and A.B. Fowler, *"Mutually quenched injection lasers as bistable devices"*, IBM J. Research and Development **8(4)**, Sep 1964, pp. 471–475

[400] A. Lattes, H.A. Haus, F.J. Leonberger, and E.P. Ippen, *"An ultrafast all-optical gate"*, IEEE J. Quantum Electronics **QE-19(11)**, Nov 1983, pp. 1718–1723

[401] K.Y. Lau and A. Yariv, *"Ultra-high speed semiconductor lasers"*, IEEE J. Quantum Electronics **QE-21(2)**, Feb 1985, pp. 121–138

[402] E.G. Lean, *"Interaction of light and acoustic surface waves"*, in **Progress in Optics XI**, E. Wolf (ed.), North-Holland, 1973, pp. 123–166

[403] I. Lee, S. Goldwasser, and D. Smitley, *"Synthesis and mapping algorithms for a reconfigurable optical interconnection network"*, Proc. Intl. Conf. on Parallel Processing, Aug 1986, pp. 394–396

[404] S.H. Lee, S.C. Esener, M.A. Title, and T.J. Drabik, *"Two-dimensional silicon/PLZT spatial light modulators: design considerations and technology"*, Optical Engineering **25(2)**, Feb 1986, pp. 250–260

[405] S.H. Lee, *"Mathematical operations by optical processing"*, Optical Engineering **13(3)**, May-Jun 1974, pp. 196–207

[406] S.H. Lee, *"Optical analog solutions of partial differential and integral equations"*, Optical Engineering **24(1)**, Jan-Feb 1985, pp. 41–47

[407] T.C. Lee, *"Holographic recording on thermoplastic films"*, Applied Optics **13(4)**, Apr 1974, pp. 888–895

[408] T.C. Lee, N.I. Marzwell, F.M. Schmit, and O.N. Tufte, *"Development of thermoplastic-photoconductor tape for optical recording"*, Applied Optics **17(17)**, Sep 1978, pp. 2802–2811

[409] W-H. Lee, *"Computer-generated holograms: techniques and applications"*, in **Progress in Optics XVI**, E. Wolf (ed.), North-Holland, 1978, pp. 119–232

[410] W.H. Lee, *"Sampled Fourier transform hologram generated by computer"*, Applied Optics **9(3)**, Mar 1970, pp. 639–643

[411] W-H. Lee, *"Binary synthetic holograms"*, Applied Optics **13(7)**, Jul 1974, pp. 1677–1682

[412] J.R. Leger and S.H. Lee, *"Hybrid optical processor for pattern recognition and classification using a generalized set of pattern functions"*, Applied Optics **21(2)**, Jan 1982, pp. 274–287

[413] E.N. Leith and J. Upatnieks, *"Reconstructed wavefronts and communication theory"*, J. Optical Society of America **52(10)**, Oct 1962, pp. 1123–1130

[414] E.N. Leith and J. Upatnieks, "*Wavefront reconstruction with continuous-tone objects*", J. Optical Society of America **53(12)**, Dec 1963, pp. 1377–1381

[415] E.N. Leith and J. Upatnieks, "*Wavefront reconstruction with diffused illumination and three dimensional objects*", J. Optical Society of America **54(11)**, Nov 1964, pp. 1295–1301

[416] E.N. Leith and J. Upatnieks, "*Photography by laser*", Scientific American **212(6)**, Jun 1965, pp. 24–35 (reproduced in [398])

[417] E.N. Leith, "*The legacy of Dennis Gabor*", Optical Engineering **19(5)**, Sep-Oct 1980, pp. 633–635

[418] E.N. Leith, "*Complex spatial filters for image deconvolution*", *Proceedings of the IEEE* **65(1)**, *Jan 1977, pp. 18–28*

[419] E.N. Leith and A.L. Ingalls, "*Synthetic antenna data processing by wavefront reconstruction*", Applied Optics **7(3)**, Mar 1968, pp. 539–544

[420] G.G. Lendaris and G.L. Stanley, "*Diffraction-pattern sampling for automatic pattern recognition*", Proceedings of the IEEE **58(2)**, Feb 1970, pp. 198–216

[421] B.A. Lengyel, **Lasers**, 2nd ed., John Wiley & sons, 1971

[422] E.J. Lerner, "*Computers that see*", IEEE Spectrum **17(10)**, Oct 1980, pp. 28–33

[423] L.B. Lesem, P.M. Hirsch, and J.A. Jordan, Jr., "*The kinoform: a new wavefront reconstruction device*", IBM J. Research and Development **13(2)**, Mar 1969, pp. 150–155

[424] L.B. Lesem, P.M. Hirsch, and J.A. Jordan, Jr., "*The promise of the kinoform*", Optical Spectra **4(11)**, Dec 1970, pp. 18–21

[425] L.B. Lesem, P.M. Hirsch, and J.A. Jordan, Jr., "*Computer synthesis of holograms for 3-D display*", Communications of the ACM **11(10)**, Oct 1968, pp. 661–674

[426] Y-Z. Liang and H.K. Liu, "*Optical matrix-matrix multiplication method demonstrated by the use of a multifocus hololens*", Optics Letters **9(8)**, Aug 1984, pp. 322–324

[427] Y-Z. Liang, D. Zhao, and H-K. Liu, "*Multifocus dichromated gelatin hololens*", Applied Optics **22(21)**, Nov 1983, pp. 3451–3456

[428] S. Liebowitz and D. Casasent, "*Error-correction coding in an associative processor*", Applied Optics **26(6)**, Mar 1987, pp. 999–1006

[429] **Lightwave technology**, AT&T Technical J. **66(1)**, Jan/Feb 1987 (special issue, mostly about fiberoptic communication)

[430] R.A. Linke and P.S. Henry, "*Coherent optical detection: a thousand calls on a circuit*", IEEE Spectrum **24(2)**, Feb 1987, pp. 52–57

[431] A.W. Lohmann, "*Incoherent optical processing of complex data*" Applied Optics **16(2)**, Feb 1977, pp. 261–263

[432] A.W. Lohmann, "*What classical optics can do for the digital optical computer*", Applied Optics **25(10)**, May 1986, pp. 1543–1549

[433] A.W. Lohmann, W. Stork, and G. Stucke, "*Optical perfect shuffle*", Applied Optics **25(10)**, May 1986, pp. 1530–1531

[434] A.W. Lohmann, "*Polarization and optical logic*", Applied Optics **25(10)**, May 1986, pp. 1594–1597

[435] A.W. Lohmann, "*Matched filtering with self-luminous objects*", Applied Optics **7(3)**, Mar 1968, pp. 561–563

[436] A.W. Lohmann and H.W. Werlich, "*Incoherent matched filtering with Fourier holograms*", Applied Optics **10(3)**, Mar 1971, pp. 670–672

[437] A.W. Lohmann, D.P. Paris, and H.W. Werlich, "*A computer generated spatial filter, applied to code translation*", Applied Optics **6(6)**, Jun 1967, pp. 1139–1140

[438] A.W. Lohmann and W.T. Rhodes, "*Two-pupil synthesis of optical transfer functions*", Applied Optics **17(7)**, Apr 1978, pp. 1141–1151

[439] A.W. Lohmann and H.W. Werlich, "*Holographic production of spatial filters for code translation and image restoration*", Physics letters **25A(8)**, Oct 1967, pp. 570–571

[440] A.W. Lohmann and D.P. Paris, "*Binary Fraunhofer holograms, generated by computer*", Applied Optics **6(10)**, Oct 1967, pp. 1739–1748

[441] A. Lohmann and B. Morgenstern, "*Azimutalmodulation in der optik*", Optik **20(9/10)**, Sep-Oct 1963, pp. 450–455 (in German)

[442] A.W. Lohmann and J. Weigelt, "*Optical logic processing based on scattering*", Optics Communications **52(4)**, Dec 1984, pp. 255–258

362

[443] A.W. Lohmann and J. Weigelt, "*Optical logic by anisotropic scattering*", Optics Communications **54(2)**, May 1985, pp. 81–86

[444] A.W. Lohmann and J. Weigelt, "*Digital optical adder based on spatial filtering*", Applied Optics **25(18)**, Sep 1986, pp. 3047–3053

[445] A.W. Lohmann, "*Suggestions for hybrid image processing*", Optics Communications **22(2)**, Aug 1977, pp. 165–168

[446] A.W. Lohmann and J. Weigelt, "*Spatial filtering logic based on polarization*", Applied Optics **26(1)**, Jan 1987, pp. 131–135

[447] S.J. Long, D.P. D'amato, and M. Sack, "*OCR in the united states postal service: present status and future needs*", in **Proc. 7ᵗʰ Intl. Conf. on Pattern Recognition**, vol 2, Montreal, Aug 1984, pp. 945–947

[448] J.S. Loomis, "*Computer generated holography and optical testing*", Optical Engineering **19(5)**, Sep-Oct 1980, pp. 679–685

[449] S. Lowenthal and A. Werts, "*Filterage des fréquences spatiales en lumière incohérente à l'aide d'hologrammes*", Comptes Rendus des séances de l'académie des sciences B **266(9)**, Feb 1968, pp. 542–545 (in French)

[450] L.A. Lugiato, "*Theory of optical bistability*", in **Progress in Optics XXI**, E. Wolf (ed.), North-Holland, 1984, pp. 69–216

[451] H. Mada, "*Architecture for optical computing using holographic associative memories*", Applied Optics **24(14)**, Jul 1985, pp. 2063–2066

[452] D. Maier, "*Using write-once memory for database storage*", Proc. ACM Symp. on Principles of Database Systems **PODS**, Los Angeles, Mar 1982, pp. 239–246

[453] W.T. Maloney, "*Lensless holographic recognition of spatially incoherent patterns in real time*", Applied Optics **10(9)**, Sep 1970, pp. 2127–2131

[454] W.T. Maloney, "*Acoustooptical approaches to radar signal processing*", IEEE Spectrum **6(10)**, Oct 1969, pp. 40–48

[455] P. Mandel, "*Dynamic theory of an optical transistor*", Optics Communications **56(1)**, Nov 1985, pp. 53–56

[456] G.R. Mangasaryan, B.E. Khaihin, and V.S. Khitrova, "*Matched filtering on the basis of thick holograms for fingerprint identification*", Optics Communications **22(2)**, Aug 1977, pp. 169–172

[457] M.M. Mano, **Digital design**, Prentice-Hall, 1984

[458] E.A.J. Marcatili, *"Dielectric rectangular waveguide and directional coupler for integrated optics"*, Bell System Technical J. **48(7)**, Sep 1969, pp. 2071–2102

[459] E.A.J. Marcatili, *"Optical subpicosecond gate"*, Applied Optics **19(9)**, May 1980, pp. 1468–1476

[460] E.W. Marchand, *"Gradient index lenses"*, in **Progress in Optics XI**, E. Wolf (ed.), North-Holland, 1973, pp. 305–337

[461] E. Marom, *"Real time image subtraction using a liquid crystal light valve"*, Optical Engineering **25(2)**, Feb 1986, pp. 274–276

[462] E. Marom and N. Konforti, *"Programmable optical interconnects"*, in **Proc. 1986 Intl. Optical Computing Conf.**, Proc. SPIE **700**, Jul 1986, pp. 209–213

[463] J. Marron, A.J. Martino, and G.M. Morris, *"Generation of random arrays using clipped laser speckle"*, Applied Optics **25(1)**, Jan 1986, pp. 26–30

[464] J. Matisoo, *"The superconducting computer"*, Scientific American **242(5)**, May 1980, pp. 38–53

[465] J. Matisoo, *"Overview of Josephson technology logic and memory"*, IBM J. Research and Development **24(2)**, Mar 1980, pp. 113–129

[466] R.L. Mattson, *"Role of optical memories in computer storage"*, Applied Optics **13(4)**, Apr 1974, pp. 755–760

[467] T.C. May and M.H. Woods, *"Alpha-particle-induced soft errors in dynamic memories"*, IEEE trans. Electron Devices **ED-26(1)**, Jan 1979, pp. 2–9

[468] J.S. Mayo, *"Materials for information and communication"*, Scientific American **255(4)**, Oct 1986, pp. 50–57

[469] A.D. McAulay, *"Optical crossbar interconnected digital signal processor with basic algorithms"*, Optical Engineering **25(1)**, Jan 1986, pp. 82–90

[470] A.D. McAulay, *"Real-time optical expert systems"*, Applied Optics **26(10)**, May 1987, pp. 1927–1934

[471] A.D. McAulay, *"Spatial-light-modulator interconnected computers"*, Computer **20(10)**, Oct 1987, pp. 45–57

[472] L. McCaughan, *"Long wavelength titanium-doped lithium niobate directional coupler optical switches and switch arrays"*, Optical Engineering **24(2)**, Mar/Apr 1985, pp. 241–243

[473] R.J. McEliece, "*The reliability of computer memories*", Scientific American **252(1)**, Jan 1985, pp. 68–73

[474] D.H. McMahon, G.J. Johnson, S.L. Teeter, and C.G. Whitney, "*A hybrid optical computer processing technique for fingerprint identification*", IEEE trans. Computers **C-24(4)**, Apr 1975, pp. 358–369

[475] J.D. Meindl, "*Chips for advanced computing*", Scientific American **257(4)**, Oct 1987, pp. 54–62

[476] H. Melchior, "*Detectors for lightwave communication*", Physics Today **30(11)**, Nov 1977, pp. 32–39

[477] M.A. Mentzer, R.G. Hunsperger, S. Sriram, J. Bartko, M.S. Wlodawski, J.M. Zavada, and H.A. Jenkinson, "*Ion implanted optical waveguides in gallium arsenide*", Optical Engineering **24(2)**, Mar/Apr 1985, pp. 225–229

[478] D. Mergerian, E.C. Malarky, R.P. Pautienus, J.C. Bradley, G.E. Mark, L.D. Hutcheson, and A.L. Kellner, "*Operational integrated optical R.F. Spectrum analyzer*", Applied Optics **19(18)**, Sep 1980, pp. 3033–3034

[479] F. Merkle and T. Lörch, "*Hybrid optical-digital pattern recognition*", Applied Optics **23(10)**, May 1984, pp. 1509–1516

[480] E. Meyer auf der Heide and A. Wigderson, "*The complexity of parallel sorting*", Ann. Symp. Foundations Of Computer Science, **FOCS 26**, Oct 1985, pp. 532–540

[481] W. Miceli, "*Optical computing for the strategic defense initiative*", Optics News **12(4)**, Apr 1986, pp. 8–9

[482] D.A.B. Miller, "*Bistable optical devices: physics and operating characteristics*", Laser Focus **18(4)**, Apr 1982, pp. 79–84

[483] D.A.B. Miller, "*Dynamic nonlinear optics in semiconductors: physics and applications*", Laser Focus **19(7)**, Jul 1983, pp. 61–68

[484] D.A.B. Miller, S.D. Smith, and C.T. Seaton, "*Optical bistability in semiconductors*", IEEE J. Quantum Electronics **QE-17(3)**, Mar 1981, pp. 312–317

[485] D.A.B. Miller, A.C. Gossard, and W. Wiegmann, "*Optical bistability due to increasing absorption*", Optics Letters **9(5)**, May 1984, pp. 162–164

[486] D.A.B. Miller, D.S. Chemla, T.C. Damen, A.C. Gossard, W. Wiegmann, T.H. Wood, and C.A. Burrus, "*Novel hybrid optically bistable switch: the quantum well self-electro-optic effect device*", Applied Physics Letters **45(1)**, Jul 1984, pp. 13–15

[487] D.A.B. Miller, D.S. Chemla, T.C. Damen, T.H. Wood, and C.A. Burrus, A.C. Gossard, and W. Wiegmann, "*The quantum well self-electrooptic effect device: optoelectronic bistability and oscilation, and self-linearized modulation*", IEEE J. Quantum Electronics **QE-21(9)**, Sep 1985, pp. 1462–1476

[488] D.A.B. Miller, "*Quantum wells for optical information processing*", Optical Engineering **26(5)**, May 1987, pp. 368–372

[489] S.E. Miller, "*Integrated optics: an introduction*", Bell System Technical J. **48(7)**, Sep 1969, pp. 2059–2069

[490] S.E. Miller, "*A survey of integrated optics*", IEEE J. Quantum Electronics **QE-8(2)**, Feb 1972, pp. 199–205

[491] A.F. Milton and A.B. Lee, "*Optical access couplers and a comparison of multiterminal fiber communication systems*", Applied Optics **15(1)**, Jan 1976, pp. 244–252

[492] T. Minemoto, K. Okamoto, and K. Miyamoto, "*Optical parallel logic gate using spatial light modulators with the Pockels effect*", Applied Optics **24(14)**, Jul 1985, pp. 2055–2062

[493] T. Minemoto, S. Numata, and K. Miyamoto, "*Optical parallel logic gate using spatial light modulators with the Pockels effect: implementation using three PROM devices*", Applied Optics **25(6)**, Mar 1986, pp. 948–955

[494] T. Minemoto, S. Numata, and K. Miyamoto, "*Optical parallel logic gate using light modulators with the Pockels effect: applications to fundamental components for optical digital computing*", Applied Optics **25(22)**, Nov 1986, pp. 4046–4052

[495] M.M. Mirsalehi and T.K. Gaylord, "*Logical minimization of multilevel coded functions*", Applied Optics **25(18)**, Sep 1986, pp. 3079–3088

[496] M.M. Mirsalehi and T.K. Gaylord, "*Truth-table look-up parallel data processing using an optical content-addressable memory*", Applied Optics **25(14)**, Jul 1986, pp. 2277–2283

[497] Y. Mitsuhashi, "*Standardization activities for optical disks in Japan*", Applied Optics **25(22)**, Nov 1986, pp. 4013–4016

[498] M.G. Moharam and L. Young, "*Hologram writing by the photorefractive effect*", J. Applied Physics **48(8)**, Aug 1977, pp. 3230–3236

[499] M.A. Monahan, K. Bromley, and R.P. Bocker, "*Incoherent optical correlators*", Proceedings of the IEEE **65(1)**, Jan 1977, pp. 121–129

[500] F.F. Morehead, *"Light emitting semiconductors"*, Scientific American **216(5)**, May 1967, pp. 108–122

[501] G.M. Morris, *"Optical computing by Monte Carlo methods"*, Optical Engineering **24(1)**, Jan-Feb 1985, pp. 86–90

[502] T. Murakami, K. Taira, and M. Mori, *"Magnetooptic erasable disk memory with two optical heads"*, Applied Optics **25(22)**, Nov 1986, pp. 3986–3989

[503] M.J. Murdocca, *"Digital optical computing with one-rule cellular automata"*, Applied Optics **26(4)**, Feb 1987, pp. 682–688

[504] H.F. Murry, *"A general approach for generating natural random variables"*, IEEE trans. Computers **C-19(12)**, Dec 1970, pp. 1210–1213

[505] M. Nakajima, H. Onodera, I. Awai, and J-I. Ikenoue, *"High efficiency light modulation using guided-to-radiation mode coupling: a proposal"*, Applied Optics **20(14)**, Jul 1981, pp. 2439–2443

[506] M. Nakajima, T. Morikawa, and K. Sakurai, *"Automatic character reading using a holographic data processing technique"*, Applied Optics **11(2)**, Feb 1972, pp. 362–371

[507] H. Nakano and K. Hotate, *"Optical system for real-time multiplication of the multiple matrix with a 2-D light source array"*, Applied Optics **26(5)**, Mar 1987, pp. 917–923

[508] V. Narayanamurti, *"Artificially structured thin-film materials and interfaces"*, Science **235(4792)**, 27 Feb 1987, pp. 1023–1028

[509] J.A. Neff, *"Major initiatives for optical computing"*, Optical Engineering **26(1)**, Jan 1987, pp. 2–9

[510] D.F. Nelson, *"The modulation of laser light"*, Scientific American **218(6)**, Jun 1968, pp. 17–23 (reproduced in [398])

[511] H. Nomura and T. Okoshi, *"Storage density limitations of a volume-type hologram memory: theory"*, Applied Optics **15(2)**, Feb 1976, pp. 550–555

[512] **Nonlinear optical materials**, Applied Optics **26(2)**, Jan 1987, pp. 211–234 (special report)

[513] **Nonlinear optical phase conjugation**, Optical Engineering **21(2)**, Mar-Apr 1982 (special issue)

[514] G.S. Oherlein, *"Reactive-ion etching"*, Physics Today **39(10)**, Oct 1986, pp. 26–33

[515] T. Okoshi, "*Three-dimensional displays*", Proceedings of the IEEE **68(5)**, May 1980, pp. 548–564

[516] T.R. O'Meara, "*Applications of nonlinear phase conjugation in compensated active imaging*", Optical Engineering **21(2)**, Mar-Apr 1982, pp. 231–236

[517] E.L. O'Neill, "*Spatial filtering in optics*", IRE trans. Information Theory **IT-2(2)**, Jun 1956, pp. 56–65

[518] H. Onodera, I. Awai, M. Nakajima, and J-I. Ikenoue, "*Light intensity modulation based on guided-to-radiation mode coupling in heterostrcture waveguides*", Applied Optics **23(1)**, Jan 1984, pp. 118–123

[519] A.V. Oppenheim and J.S. Lim, "*The importance of phase in signals*", Proceedings of the IEEE **69(5)**, May 1981, pp. 529–541

[520] **Optical artificial intelligence**, Applied Optics **26(10)**, May 1987 (special issue)

[521] **Optical bistability**, IEEE J. Quantum Electronics **QE-17(3)**, Mar 1981 (special issue)

[522] **Optical computing**, Proceedings of the IEEE **65(1)**, Jan 1977 (special issue, mainly about analog systems); Proceedings of the IEEE **72(7)**, Jul 1984 (special issue, mainly about digital systems)

[523] **Optical computing, part 1: digital optics**, Applied Optics **25(10)**, May 1986 (special issue)

[524] **Optical computing**, Optical Engineering **23(1)**, Jan-Feb 1984 (special issue); Optical Engineering **24(1)**, Jan-Feb 1985 (special issue)

[525] **Optical computing and nonlinear optical signal processing**, Optical Engineering **26(1)**, Jan 1987 (special issue)

[526] **The coming of age in optical computing**, Optics News **12(4)**, Apr 1986, pp. 5–28 (collection of views)

[527] **Optical information processing**, Optical Engineering **26(5)**, May 1987 (special issue, mostly about SLMs)

[528] **Optical interconnections**, Optical Engineering **25(10)**, Oct 1986 (special issue about optical interconnections for VLSI)

[529] **Optical phase conjugation**, J. Optical Society of America **73(5)**, May 1983 (special issue)

[530] **Optical storage of digital data**, Applied Optics **13(4)**, Apr 1974 (special issue); Applied Optics **25(22)**, Nov 1986 (special issue)

[531] T. Oren and G.A. Kildall, *"The compact disk ROM: applications software"*, IEEE Spectrum **23(4)**, Apr 1986, pp. 49–54

[532] R.K. O'Toole and H. Stark, *"Comparative study of optical-digital vs all-digital techniques in textural pattern recognition"*, Applied Optics **19(15)**, Aug 1980, pp. 2496–2506

[533] J.K. Ousterhout, H. Da Costa, D. Harrison, J.A. Kunze, M. Kupfer, and J.G. Thompson, *"A trace-driven analysis of the UNIX 4.2 BSD file system"*, Proc. 10th ACM Symp. Operating Systems Principles, Washington, Dec 1985, pp. 15–24

[534] Y. Owechko, E. Marom, B.H. Soffer, and G. Dunning, *"Associative memory in a phase conjugate resonator cavity utilizing a hologram"*, in **Proc. 1986 Intl. Optical Computing Conf.**, Proc. SPIE **700**, Jul 1986

[535] Y. Owechko, G.J. Dunning, E. Marom, and B.H. Soffer, *"Holographic associative memory with nonlinearities in the correlation domain"*, Applied Optics **26(10)**, May 1987, pp. 1900–1910

[536] E.G. Paek and D. Psaltis, *"Optical associative memory using Fourier transform holograms"*, Optical Engineering **26(5)**, May 1987, pp. 428–433

[537] M.B. Panish, *"Heterostructure injection lasers"*, IEEE trans. Microwave Theory and Techniques **MTT-23(1)**, Jan 1975, pp. 20–30

[538] D.R. Pape and L.J. Hornbeck, *"Characteristics of the deformable mirror device for optical information processing"*, Optical Engineering **22(6)**, Nov-Dec 1983, pp. 675–681

[539] I. Parberry and G. Schnitger, *"Parallel computation with threshold functions"*, in **Structure in Complexity Theory**, lecture notes in computer science **223**, Springer-Verlag, 1986

[540] P. Penny and M. Picard, *"Application of novel technologies to the management of a very large data base"*, Proc. Intl. Conf. on very large data bases **VLDB 9**, Florence, Nov 1983, pp. 20–29

[541] D.M. Pepper, *"Applications of optical phase conjugation"*, Scientific American **254(1)**, Jan 1986, pp. 56–65

[542] D.M. Pepper, *"Nonlinear optical phase conjugation"*, Optical Engineering **21(2)**, Mar-Apr 1982, pp. 156–183

[543] L. Perelmutter and I. Glaser, *"Digital incoherent optical interconnections"*, in **Proc. 1986 Intl. Optical Computing Conf.**, Proc. SPIE **700**, Jul 1986

[544] S.D. Personick, *"Fundamental limits in optical communication"*, Proceedings of the IEEE **69(2)**, Feb 1981, pp. 262–266

[545] K.E. Peterson, *"Micromechanical light modulator array fabricated on silicon"*, Applied Physics Letters **31(8)**, Oct 1977, pp. 521–523

[546] N. Peyghambarian and H.M. Gibbs, *"Optical bistability for optical signal processing and computing"*, Optical Engineering **24(1)**, Jan-Feb 1985, pp. 68–73

[547] G.F. Pfister, W.C. Brantley, D.A. George, S.L. Harvey, W.J. Kleinfelder, K.P. MaAuliffe, E.A. Melton, V.A. Norton, and J. Weiss, *"The IBM research parallel processor prototype (RP3): introduction and architecture"*, Proc. Intl. Conf. on Parallel Processing, Aug 1985, pp. 764–771

[548] **Photonic logic**, Applied Optics **25(18)**, Sep 1986 (special issue)

[549] **Physics of Computation**, Intl. J. theoretical Physics **21(3/4)**, Apr 1982 (special issue); Intl. J. theoretical Physics **21(6/7)**, Jun 1982 (special issue on computational models of physics); Intl. J. theoretical Physics **21(12)**, Dec 1982 (special issue on physical models of computation)

[550] S.T. Picraux and P.S. Peercy, *"Ion implantation of surfaces"*, Scientific American **252(3)**, Mar 1985, pp. 84–92

[551] J.L. Potter, *"Image processing on the massively parallel processor"*, Computer **16(1)**, Jan 1983, pp. 62–67

[552] M.B. Pour-El and I. Richards, *"The wave equation with computable initial data such that its unique solution is not computable"*, Advances in Mathematics **39(3)**, Mar 1981, pp. 215–239

[553] M.B. Pour-El and I. Richards, *"Computability and noncomutability in classical analysis"*, Trans. American Mathematical Society **275(2)**, Feb 1983, pp. 539–560

[554] M.B. Pour-El and I. Richards, *"Noncomputability in analysis and physics: a complete determination of the class of noncomputable linear operators"*, Advances in Mathematics **48(1)**, Apr 1983 pp. 44–74

[555] K. Preston, Jr., **Coherent optical computers**, McGraw-Hill, 1972

[556] K. Preston, Jr., M.J.B. Duff, S. Levialdi, P.E. Norgrem, and J-I. Toriwaki, *"Basics of cellular logic with some applications in medical image processing"*, Proceeding of the IEEE **67(5)**, May 1979, pp. 826–856

[557] K. Preston, Jr., *"A comparison of analog and digital techniques for pattern recognition"*, Proceedings of the IEEE **60(10)**, Oct 1972, pp. 1216–1231

[558] P.R. Prucnal, E.R. Fossum, and R.M. Osgood, *"Integrated fiber-optic coupler for very large scale integration interconnects"*, Optics Letters **11(2)**, Feb 1986, pp. 109–111

[559] P.R. Prucnal, M.A. Santoro, and T.R. Fan, *"Spread spectrum fiber-optic local area network using optical processing"*, IEEE/OSA J. Lightwave Technology **LT-4(5)**, May 1986, pp. 547–554

[560] P.R. Prucnal, D.J. Blumenthal, and P.A. Perrior, *"Self-routing photonic switching demonstration with optical control"*, Optical Engineering **26(5)**, May 1987, pp. 473–477

[561] D. Psaltis and D. Casasent, *"Optical residue arithmetic: a correlation approach"*, Applied Optics **18(2)**, Jan 1979, pp. 163–171

[562] D. Psaltis and D. Casasent, *"General formulation for optical signal processing architectures"*, Optical Engineering **19(2)**, Mar-Apr 1980, pp. 193–198

[563] D. Psaltis, D. Casasent, and M. Carlotto, *"Iterative color-multiplexed, electro-optical processor"*, Optics Letters **4(11)**, Nov 1979, pp. 348–350

[564] D. Psaltis and N. Farhat, *"Optical information processing based on an associative memory model of neural nets with thresholding and feedback"*, Optics Letters **10(2)**, Feb 1985, pp. 98–100

[565] D. Psaltis, *"Optical realization of neural network models"*, in **Proc. 1986 Intl. Optical Computing Conf.**, Jul 1986, Proc. SPIE **700**, pp. 278–282

[566] D. Psaltis and D. Casasent, *"Deformation invariant optical processors using coordinate transforms"*, Applied Optics **16(8)**, Aug 1977, pp. 2288–2292

[567] D. Psaltis and K. Wagner, *"Real-time optical synthetic aperture radar (SAR) processor"*, Optical Engineering **21(5)**, Sep-Oct 1982, pp. 822–828

[568] D. Psaltis, D. Casasent, D. Neft, and M. Carlotto, *"Accurate numerical computation by optical convolution"*, in **1980 Intl. Optical Computing Conf.**, Proc. SPIE **232**, pp. 151–156

[569] D. Psaltis and R.A. Athale, "*High accuracy computation with linear analog optical systems: a critical study*", Applied Optics **25(18)**, Sep 1986, pp. 3071–3077

[570] D. Psaltis, "*Two-dimensional optical processing using one-dimensional input devices*", Proceedings of the IEEE **72(7)**, Jul 1984, pp. 962–974

[571] C.F. Quate, C.D.W. Wilkinson, and D.K. Winslow, "*Interaction of light and microwave sound*", Proceedings of the IEEE **53(10)**, Oct 1965, pp. 1604–1623

[572] J.A. Rajchman, "*An optical read-write mass memory*", Applied Optics **9(10)**, Oct 1970, pp. 2269–2271

[573] P.A. Ramamoorthy and S. Antony, "*Optical modified signed digit adder using polarization coded symbolic substitution*", Optical Engineering **26(8)**, Aug 1987, pp. 821–825

[574] T.R. Ranganath and S. Wang, "*Ti-diffused LiNbO$_3$ branched waveguide modulators: performance and design*", IEEE J. Quantum Electronics **QE-13(4)**, Apr 1977, pp. 290–295

[575] P.L. Ransom, "*Synthesis of complex optical wavefronts*", Applied Optics **11(11)**, Nov 1972, pp. 2554–2561

[576] B.R. Reddersen and L.M. Ralston, "*Digital optical data storage and retrieval*", Optical Engineering **19(2)**, Mar-Apr 1980, pp. 199–204

[577] W.T. Rhodes, "*Incoherent spatial filtering*", Optical Engineering **19(3)**, May-Jun 1980, pp. 323–330

[578] W.T. Rhodes, "*Acoustooptic algebraic processing architectures*", Proceedings of the IEEE **72(7)**, Jul 1984, pp. 820–829

[579] W.T. Rhodes, "*Acousto-optic signal processing: convolution and correlation*", Proceedings of the IEEE **69(1)**, Jan 1981, pp. 65–79

[580] W.T. Rhodes, "*The optical margin*", Optics News **12(4)**, Apr 1986, pp. 27–28

[581] J. Riggins and S. Butler, "*Simulation of synthetic discriminant function optical implementation*", Optical Engineering **23(6)**, Nov-Dec 1984, pp. 721–726

[582] G.C. Righini, V. Russo, S. Sottini, and G. Toraldo di Francia, "*Geodesic lenses for guided optical waves*", Applied Optics **12(7)**, Jul 1973, pp. 1477–1481

[583] R.L. Rivest and A. Shamir, *"How to reuse a "write-once" memory"*, Proc. ann. ACM Symp. Theory Of Computing, **STOC 14**, May 1982, pp. 105–113

[584] H.N. Roberts, J.W. Watkins, and R.H. Johnson, *"High speed holographic digital recorder"*, Applied Optics **13(4)**, Apr 1974, pp. 841–856

[585] A.L. Robinson, *"IBM drops superconducting computer project"*, Science **222(4623)**, 4 Nov 1983, pp. 492–494

[586] G.L. Rogers, *"Gabor diffraction microscopy: the hologram as a generalized zone-plate"*, Nature **166(4214)**, 5 Aug 1950, p. 237

[587] A. Rosenfeld and A.C. Kak, **Digital Picture Processing** (2 volumes), Academic Press, 2nd ed., 1982

[588] A. Rosenfeld, *"Parallel image processing using cellular arrays"*, Computer **16(1)**, Jan 1983, pp. 14–20

[589] W.E. Ross, D. Psaltis, and R.H. Anderson, *"Two dimensional magneto-optic spatial light modulator for signal processing"*, Optical Engineering **22(4)**, Jul-Aug 1983, pp. 485–490

[590] E.S. Rothchild, *"1985 to be the year of the erasable disk"*, Laser Focus **21(5)**, May 1985, pp. 52–58

[591] J.M. Rowell, *"Photonic materials"*, Scientific American **255(4)**, Oct 1986, pp. 124–134

[592] C. Kruskal and L. Rudolph, *"Observations concerning multidimensional ultracomputers"*, Ultracomputer note #6, Courant Institute, NYU, Jan 1980

[593] Y. Saito, S-I. Komatsu, and H. Ohzu, *"Scale and rotation invariant real time optical correlator using computer generated hologram"*, Optics Communications **47(1)**, Aug 1983, pp. 8–11

[594] Y. Sako and T. Suzuki, *"Data structure of the compact disk — read-only memory system"*, Applied Optics **25(22)**, Nov 1986, pp. 3996–4000

[595] K.C. Saraswat and F. Mohammadi, *"Effect of scaling of interconnections on the time delay of VLSI circuits"*, IEEE trans. Electron Devices **ED-29(4)**, Apr 1982, pp. 645–650

[596] A.A. Sawchuk and T.C. Strand, *"Digital optical computing"*, Proceedings of the IEEE **72(7)**, Jul 1984, pp. 758–779

[597] A.A. Sawchuk, B.J. Jenkins, C.S. Raghavendra, and A. Varma, *"Optical matrix-vector implementation of crossbar interconnection networks"*, Proc. Intl. Conf. on Parallel Processing, Aug 1986, pp. 401–404

[598] A.A. Sawchuk, B.J. Jenkins, C.S. Raghavendra, and A. Varma, "*Optical crossbar networks*", Computer **20(6)**, Jun 1987, pp. 50–60

[599] D.H. Schaefer and J.P. Strong III, "*Tse computers*", Proceedings of the IEEE **65(1)**, Jan 1977, pp. 129–138

[600] D.H. Schaefer and J.R. Fischer, "*Beyond the supercomputer*", IEEE Spectrum **19(3)**, Mar 1982, pp. 32–37

[601] A.L. Schawlow, "*Laser light*", Scientific American **219(3)**, Sep 1968, pp. 120–136 (reproduced in [398])

[602] R.A. Schmidt and W.T. Cathey, "*Optical implementation of mathematical resolution*", Applied Optics **26(10)**, May 1987, pp. 1852–1858

[603] J.L. Schnapf and D.A. Baylor, "*How photoreceptor cells respond to light*", Scientific American **256(4)**, Apr 1987, pp. 32–39

[604] W. Schneider and W. Fink, "*Incoherent optical matrix multiplication*", Optica Acta **22(11)**, Nov 1975, pp. 879–889

[605] A. Schwartz, X-Y. Wang, and C. Warde, "*Electron-beam-addressed microchannel spatial light modulator*", Optical Engineering **24(1)**, Jan-Feb 1985, pp. 119–123

[606] J.T. Schwartz, "*Ultracomputers*", ACM trans. on Programming Languages and Systems **TOPLAS 2(4)**, Oct 1980, pp. 484–521

[607] H.J. Seigel, "*A model of SIMD machines and a comparison of various interconnection networks*", IEEE trans. Computers **C-28(12)**, Dec 1979, pp. 907–917

[608] C.L. Seitz and J. Matisoo, "*Engineering limits on computer performance*", Physics Today **37(5)**, May 1984, pp. 38–45

[609] **Semiconductor lasers**, IEEE J. Quantum Electronics **QE-23(6)**, Jun 1987 (special issue)

[610] V.K. Sengupta, U.H. Gerlach, and S.A. Collins, "*Bistable optical spatial device using direct optical feedback*", Optics letters **3(5)**, Nov 1978, pp. 199–201

[611] J. Shamir, "*Fundamental speed limitations on parallel processing*", Applied Optics **26(9)**, May 1987, p. 1567

[612] J. Shamir, H.J. Caulfield, W. Micelli, and R.J. Seymour, "*Optical computing and the Fredkin gate*", Applied Optics **25(10)**, May 1986, pp. 1604–1607

[613] J. Shamir and H.J. Caulfield, "*High-efficiency rapidly programmable optical interconnections*", Applied Optics **26(6)**, Mar 1987, pp. 1032–1037

[614] C.V. Shank, "*Investigation of ultrafast phenomena in the femtosecond time domain*", Science **233(4770)**, 19 Sep 1986, pp. 1276–1280

[615] J.A. Sharp, **Data flow computing**, Ellis Horwood/Wiley, 1985

[616] R.C. Sherman, D. Grieser, F.T. Gamble, C.M. Verber, and T. Dolash, "*Hybrid incoherent optical pattern recognition system*", Applied Optics **22(22)**, Nov 1983, pp. 3579–3582

[617] V.V. Shkunov and B.Y. Zel'dovich, "*Optical phase conjugation*", Scientific American **256(6)**, Dec 1985, pp. 40–45

[618] R. Shubert and J.H. Harris, "*Optical guided wave focusing and diffraction*", J. Optical Society of America **61(2)**, Feb 1971, pp. 154–161

[619] W.J. Siemens-Wapniarski and M.P. Givens, "*The experimental production of synthetic holograms*", Applied Optics **7(3)**, Mar 1968, pp. 535–538

[620] M.J. Simpson, "*Diffraction pattern sampling using a holographic optical element in an imaging configuration*", Applied Optics **26(9)**, May 1987, pp. 1786–1791

[621] **Spatial light modulators**, Optical Engineering **17(4)**, Jul-Aug 1978 (special issue)

[622] **Spatial light modulators: critical issues**, Optical Engineering **22(6)**, Nov-Dec 1983 (special issue)

[623] D. Smith and D. Miller, "*Computing at the speed of light*", New Scientist **85(1195)**, 21 Feb 1980, pp. 554–556

[624] S.D. Smith, A.C. Walker, B.S. Wherrett, F.A.P. Tooley, J.G.H. Mathew, M.R. Taghizadeh, and I. Janossy, "*Cascadable digital optical logic circuit elements in the visible and infrared: demonstration of some first all-optical circuits*", Applied Optics **25(10)**, May 1986, pp. 1586–1593

[625] S.D. Smith, "*Optical bistability, photonic logic, and optical computation*", Applied Optics **25(10)**, May 1986, pp. 1550–1564

[626] S.D. Smith, I. Janossy, H.A. MacKenzie, J.G.H. Mathew, J.J.E. Reid, M.R. Taghizadeh, F.A.P. Tooley, and A.C. Walker "*Nonlinear optical circuit elements, logic gates for optical computers: the first digital optical circuits*", Optical Engineering **24(4)**, Jul-Aug 1985, pp. 569–574

[627] S.D. Smith, A.C. Walker, F.A.P. Tooley, and B.S. Wherrett, *"The demonstration of restoring digital optical logic"*, Nature **325(6099)**, 1 Jan 1987, pp. 27–31

[628] S.D. Smith, *"Lasers, nonlinear optics and optical computers"*, Nature **316(6026)**, 25 Jul 1985, pp. 319–324

[629] S.D. Smith, A.C. Walker, B.S. Wherrett, F.A.P. Tooley, N. Craft, J.G.H. Mathew, M.R. Taghizadeh, I. Redmond, and R.J. Campbell, *"Restoring optical logic: demonstration of extensible all-optical digital systems"*, Optical Engineering **26(1)**, Jan 1987, pp. 45–52

[630] S.D. Smith, J.G.H. Mathew, M.R. Taghizadeh, A.C. Walker, B.S. Wherrett, and A. Hendry, *"Room temperature, visible wavelength optical bistability in ZnSe interference filters"*, Optics Communications **51(5)**, Oct 1984, pp. 357–362

[631] P.W. Smith, *"On the physical limits of digital optical switching and logic elements"*, Bell System Technical J. **61(8)**, Oct 1982, pp. 1975–1993

[632] P.W. Smith and W.J. Tomlinson, *"Bistable optical devices promise subpicosecond switching"*, IEEE Spectrum **18(6)**, Jun 1981, pp. 26–33

[633] P.W. Smith, *"Hybrid bistable optical devices"*, Optical Engineering **19(4)**, Jul-Aug 1980, pp. 456–462

[634] M. Snir, *"On parallel searching"*, ACM SIGACT-SIGOPS Symp. Principles of Distributed Computing, Aug 1982, pp. 242–253

[635] J. Sochacki, *"Perfect geodesic lens designing"*, Applied Optics **25(2)**, Jan 1986, pp. 235–243

[636] B.H. Soffer, Y. Owechko, E. Marom, and J. Grinberg, *"Programmable real-time incoherent matrix multiplier for optical processing"*, Applied Optics **25(14)**, Jul 1986, pp. 2295–2305

[637] B.H. Soffer, G.J. Dunning, Y. Owechko, and E. Marom, *"Associative holographic memory with feedback using phase conjugate mirrors"*, Optics Letters **11(2)**, Feb 1986, pp. 118–120

[638] S. Somekh, E. Garmire, A. Yariv, H.L. Garvine, and R.G. Hunsperger, *"Channel optical waveguide directional couplers"*, Applied physics letters **22(2)**, Jan 1973, pp. 46–47

[639] S. Sottini, V. Russo, and G.C. Righini, *"General solution of the problem of perfect geodesic lenses for integrated optics"*, J. Optical Society of America **69(9)**, Sep 1979, pp. 1248–1254

[640] W.H. Southwell, *"Index profiles for generalized Luneburg lenses and their use in planar optical waveguides"*, J. Optical Society of America **67(8)**, Aug 1977, pp. 1010–1014

[641] W.H. Southwell, *"Planar optical waveguide lens design"*, Applied Optics **21(11)**, Jun 1982, pp. 1985–1988

[642] R.A. Sprague, *"A review of acousto-optic signal correlators"*, Optical Engineering **16(5)**, Sep-Oct 1977, pp. 467–474

[643] R.A. Sprague and C.L. Koliopoulos, *"Time integrating acoustooptic correlator"*, Applied Optics **15(1)**, Jan 1976, pp. 89–92

[644] H. Stark, *"An optical-digital computer for parallel processing of images"*, IEEE trans. Computers **C-24(4)**, Apr 1975, pp. 340–347

[645] R.A. Steinberg and T.G. Giallorenzi, *"Design of integrated optical switches for use in fiber data transmission systems"*, IEEE J. Quantum Electronics **QE-13(4)**, Apr 1977, pp. 122–128

[646] R.L. Stermer and M. Sokoloski, *"Optical data processing for aerospace applications"*, Optical Engineering **22(5)**, Sep-Oct 1983, pp. SR-146–SR-153

[647] W.C. Stewart, R.S. Mezrich, L.S. Cosentino, E.M. Nagle, F.S. Wendt, and R.D. Lohman, *"An experimental read-write holographic memory"*, RCA Review **34(1)**, Mar 1973, pp. 3–44

[648] H.S. Stone, *"Parallel processing with the perfect shuffle"*, IEEE trans. computers **C-20(2)**, Feb 1971, pp. 153–161

[649] W. Stoner, *"Incoherent optical processing via spatially offset pupil masks"*, Applied Optics **17(15)**, Aug 1978, pp. 2454–2467

[650] T.C. Strand, *"Non-monotonic non-linear image processing using halftone techniques"*, Optics Communications **15(1)**, Sep 1975, pp. 60–65

[651] T.C. Strand, *"Signal/noise in analog and binary holograms"*, Optical Engineering **13(3)**, May-Jun 1974, pp. 219–227

[652] G.W. Stroke and R.G. Zech, *"A posteriory image-correcting "deconvolution" by holographic Fourier-transform division"*, Physics Letters **25A(2)**, Jul 1967, pp. 89–90

[653] G.W. Stroke and M. Halioua, *"A new holographic image deblurring method"*, Physics Letters **33A(1)**, Sep 1970, pp. 3–4

[654] G.W. Stroke and M. Halioua, "*A new method for rapid realization of the high-resolution extended-range holographic image-deblurring filter*", Physics Letters **39A(4)**, May 1972, pp. 269–270

[655] G.W. Stroke, "*Sharpening images by holography*", New Scientist **51(770)**, 23 Sep 1971, pp. 671–674

[656] G.W. Stroke, "*Image deblurring and aperture synthesis using a posteriori processing by Fourier transform holography*", Optica Arca **16(4)**, Jul-Aug 1969, pp. 401–422

[657] G.W. Stroke, M. Halioua, F. Thon, and D. Willasch, "*Image improvement in high-resolution electron microscopy using holographic image deconvolution*", Optik **41(3)**, Nov 1974, pp. 319–343

[658] G.W. Stroke, M. Halioua, F. Thon, and D.H. Willasch, "*Image improvement and three-dimensional recconstruction using holographic image processing*", Proceedings of the IEEE **65(1)**, Jan 1977, pp. 39–62

[659] Y. Suematsu, "*Advances in semiconductor lasers*", Physics Today **38(5)**, May 1985, pp. 32–39

[660] **Surface acoustic waves**, Proceedings of the IEEE **64(5)**, May 1976 (special issue)

[661] E.E. Swartzlander, "*The quasi-serial multiplier*", IEEE trans. Computers **C-22(4)**, Apr 1973, pp. 317–321

[662] H.H. Szu and H.J. Caulfield, "*Optical expert systems*", Applied Optics **26(10)**, May 1987, pp. 1943–1947

[663] A. Tai, I. Cindrich, J.R. Fienup, and C.C. Aleksoff, "*Optical residue arithmetic computer with programmable computation modules*", Applied Optics **18(16)**, Aug 1979, pp. 2812–2823

[664] A.S. Tanenbaum, **Computer networks**, Prentice-Hall, 1981

[665] A.R. Tanguay, Jr., C.S. Wu, P.C. Chavel, T.C. Strand, and A.A. Sawchuk, "*Physical characterization of the variable grating mode liquid crystal device*", Optical Engineering **22(6)**, Nov-Dec 1983, pp. 687–694

[666] J. Tanida and Y. Ichioka, "*Optical logic array processor using shadowgrams*", J. Optical Society of America **73(6)**, Jun 1983, pp. 800–809

[667] J. Tanida and Y. Ichioka, "*Optical-logic-array processor using shadowgrams. II. Optical parallel digital image processing*", J. Optical Society of America A **2(8)**, Aug 1985, pp. 1237–1244

[668] J. Tanida and Y. Ichioka, *"Optical-logic-array processor using shadowgrams. III. Parallel neighborhood operations and an architecture of an optical digital-computing system"*, J. Optical Society of America A **2(8)**, Aug 1985, pp. 1245–1253

[669] J. Tanida and Y. Ichioka, *"OPALS: optical parallel array logic system"*, Applied Optics **25(10)**, May 1986, pp. 1565–1570

[670] J. Tanida and Y. Ichioka, *"Optical parallel array logic system. 2: a new system architecture without memory elements"*, Applied Optics **25(20)**, Oct 1986, pp. 3751–3758

[671] J. Tanida and Y. Ichioka, *"Modular components for an optical array logic system"*, Applied Optics **26(18)**, Sep 1987, pp. 3954–3960

[672] F.J. Taylor, *"Residue arithmetic: a tutorial with examples"*, Computer **17(5)**, May 1984, pp. 50–62

[673] H.F. Taylor and A. Yariv, *"Guided wave optics"*, Proceedings of the IEEE **62(8)**, Aug 1974, pp. 1044–1060

[674] H.F. Taylor, *"Guided wave electrooptic devices for logic and computation"*, Applied Optics **17(10)**, May 1978, pp. 1493–1498

[675] V.J. Tekippe and W.R. Wilson, *"Single-mode directional couplers"*, Laser Focus **21(5)**, May 1985, pp. 132–144

[676] **Thin films**, Physics Today **33(5)**, May 1980 (special issue)

[677] C.E. Thomas, *"Optical spectrum analysis of large space bandwidth signals"*, Applied Optics **5(11)**, Nov 1966, pp. 1782–1790

[678] B.J. Thompson, *"Hybrid processing systems — an assessment"*, Proceedings of the IEEE **65(1)**, Jan 1977, pp. 62–76

[679] L. Thylen and L. Stensland, *"Electrooptic approach to an integrated optics spectrum analyzer"*, Applied Optics **20(10)**, May 1981, pp. 1825–1832

[680] P.K. Tien, *"Integrated optics"*, Scientific American **230(4)**, Apr 1974, pp. 28–35

[681] P.K. Tien, *"Light waves in thin films and integrated optics"*, Applied Optics **10(11)**, Nov 1971, pp. 2395–2413

[682] P.K. Tien, R. Ulrich, and R.J. Martin, *"Modes of propagating light waves in thin deposited semiconductor films"*, Applied Optics **14(9)**, May 1969, pp. 291–294

[683] P.K. Tien and R. Ulrich, "*Theory of prism-film coupler and thin-film light guides*", J. Optical Society of America **60(10)**, Oct 1970, pp. 1325–1337

[684] F.A.P. Tooley, S.D. Smith, and C.T. Seaton, "*High gain signal amplification in an InSb transphasor at 77 K*", Applied Physics Letters **43(9)**, Nov 1983, pp. 807–809

[685] F.A.P. Tooley, "*Fan-out considerations of digital optical circuits*", Applied Optics **26(9)**, May 1987, pp. 1741–1744

[686] E.A. Trabka and P.G. Roetling, "*Image transformations for pattern recognition using incoherent illumination and bipolar aperture masks*", J. Optical Society of America **54(10)**, Oct 1964, pp. 1242–1252

[687] M.T. Tsao, L. Wang, R. Jin, R.W. Sprague, G. Gigioli, H-M. Kulcka, Y.D. Li, H.M. Chow, H.M. Gibbs, and N. Peyghambarian, "*Symbolic substitution using ZnS interference filters*", Optical Engineering **26(1)**, Jan 1987, pp. 41–44

[688] G.L. Turin, "*An introduction to matched filters*", IRE trans. Information Theory **IT-6(3)**, Jun 1960, pp. 311–329

[689] G.L. Turin, "*An introduction to digital matched filters*", Proceedings of the IEEE **64(7)**, Jul 1976, pp. 1093–1112

[690] T.M. Turpin, "*Spectrum analysis using optical processing*", Proceedings of the IEEE **69(1)**, Jan 1981, pp. 79–92

[691] N. Uchida and N. Niizeki, "*Acoustooptical deflection materials and techniques*", Proceedings of the IEEE **61(8)**, Aug 1973, pp. 1073–1092

[692] J.D. Ullman, **Principles of database systems**, Computer science press, 2nd ed., 1982

[693] R. Ulrich and R.J. Martin, "*Geometrical optics in thin film light guides*", Applied optics **10(9)**, Sep 1971, pp. 2077–2085

[694] J. Upatnieks, "*Portable real-time coherent optical correlator*", Applied Optics **22(18)**, Sep 1983, pp. 2798–2803

[695] J.C. Urbach and R.W. Meier, "*Thermoplastic xerographic holography*", Applied Optics **5(4)**, Apr 1966, pp. 666–667

[696] D.W. Vahey and V.G. Wood, "*Focal characteristics of spheroidal geodesic lenses for integrated optical processing*", IEEE J. Quantum Electronics **QE-13(4)**, Apr 1977, pp. 129–134

[697] A. VanderLugt, *"Design relationships for holographic memories"*, Applied Optics **12(7)**, Jul 1973, pp. 1675–1685

[698] A.B. VanderLugt, *"Coherent optical processing"*, Proceedings of the IEEE **62(10)**, Oct 1974, pp. 1300–1319

[699] A. VanderLugt, *"Signal detection by complex spatial filtering"*, IEEE trans. Information Theory **IT-10(2)**, Apr 1964, pp. 139–145

[700] A. VanderLugt, *"Practical considerations for the use of spatial carrier-frequency filters"*, Applied Optics **5(11)**, Nov 1966, pp. 1760–1765

[701] A. VanderLugt, *"The effect of small displacements of spatial filters"*, Applied Optics **6(7)**, Jul 1967, pp. 1221–1225

[702] A. VanderLugt and F.B. Rotz, *"The use of film nonlinearities in optical spatial filtering"*, Applied Optics **9(1)**, Jan 1970, pp. 215–222

[703] P.J. Van Heerden, *"Theory of optical information storage in solids"*, Applied Optics **2(4)**, Apr 1963, pp. 393–400

[704] R. Van Tuyl and C. Liechti, *"Gallium arsenide spawns speed"*, IEEE Spectrum **14(3)**, Mar 1977, pp. 40–47

[705] T. Venkatesan, B. Wilkens, Y.H. Lee, M. Warren, G. Olbright, H.M. Gibbs, N. Peyghambarian, J.S. Smith, and A. Yariv, *"Fabrication of arrays of GaAs optical bistable devices"*, Applied Physics Letters **48(2)**, Jan 1986, pp. 145–147

[706] C.M. Verber, R.P. Kenan, and J.R. Busch, *"Correlator based on an integrated optical spatial light modulator"*, Applied Optics **20(9)**, May 1981, pp. 1626–1629

[707] C.M. Verber, R.P. Kenan, H.J. Caulfield, J.E. Ludman, and P.D. Stilwell, Jr., *"Pipelined polynomial processors implemented with integrated optical components"*, Applied Optics **23(6)**, Mar 1984, pp. 817–821

[708] C.M. Verber, *"Integrated optical architectures for matrix multiplication"*, Optical Engineering **24(1)**, Jan-Feb 1985, pp. 19–25

[709] C.M. Verber, *"Integrated optical approaches to numerical optical processing"*, Proceedings of the IEEE **72(7)**, Jul 1984, pp. 942–953

[710] **Video long play systems**, Applied Optics **17(13)**, Jul 1978 (special issue)

[711] B.V.K. Vijaya Kumar and D. Casasent, *"Eigenvector determination by iterative optical methods"*, Applied Optics **20(1)**, Nov 1981, pp. 3707–3710

[712] B.V.K. Vijaya Kumar and C. Carroll, "*Loss of optimality in cross correlators*", J. Optical Society of America A **1(4)**, Apr 1984, pp. 392–397

[713] U. Vishkin and A. Wigderson, "*Trade-offs between depth and width in parallel computing*", SIAM J. Computing **14(2)**, May 1985, pp. 303–314

[714] J.S. Vitter, "*Computational complexity of an optical disk interface*", in **Automata, Languages and Programming**, Lecture Notes in Computer Science **172**, Springer-Verlag, 1984

[715] J. Voelcker, "*Helping computers communicate*", IEEE Spectrum **23(3)**, Mar 1986, pp. 61–70

[716] A.C. Walker, "*Application of bistable optical logic gate arrays to all-optical digital parallel processing*", Applied Optics **25(10)**, May 1986, pp. 1578–1585

[717] J.F. Walkup, "*Space-variant coherent optical processing*", Optical Engineering **19(3)**, May-Jun 1980, pp. 339–345

[718] C. Warde and J. Thackara, "*Operating modes of the microchannel spatial light modulator*", Optical Engineering **22(6)**, Nov-Dec 1983, pp. 695–703

[719] C. Warde and J. Kottas, "*Hybrid optical inference machines: architectural considerations*", Applied Optics **25(6)**, Mar 1986, pp. 940–947

[720] M.E. Warren, S.W. Koch, and H.M. Gibbs, "*Optical bistability, logic gating, and waveguide operation in semiconductor etalons*", Computer **20(12)**, Dec 1987, pp. 68–81

[721] J.P. Waters, "*Holographic image synthesis utilizing theoretical methods*", Applied Physics Letters **9(11)**, Dec 1966, pp. 405–407

[722] J.W. Watkins, N.A. Boudreaux, and T.H. Otten, "*Large archival mass memory system using optical diskettes*", Optical Engineering **20(3)**, May/Jun 1981, pp. 399–403

[723] C.J. Weaver and J.W. Goodman, "*A technique for optically convolving two functions*", Applied Optics **5(7)**, Jul 1966, pp. 1248–1249

[724] J. Weigelt, "*Binary logic by spatial filtering*", Optical Engineering **26(1)**, Jan 1987, pp. 28–33

[725] C.F. Weiman and G.M. Chaikin, "*Logarithmic spiral grids for image processing*", Proc. IEEE Conf. Pattern Recognition and Image Processing 1979, pp. 25–31

[726] V.F. Weisskopf, *"How light interacts with matter"*, Scientific American **219(3)**, Sep 1968, pp. 60–71 (reproduced in [398])

[727] J.W. Wesner, *"Screen patterns used in reproduction of continuous-tone graphics"*, Applied Optics **13(7)**, Jul 1974, pp. 1703–1710

[728] L.C. West, *"Picosecond integrated optical logic"*, Computer **20(12)**, Dec 1987, pp. 34–46

[729] B.S. Wherrett, *"All-Optical computation — a parallel integrator based upon a single gate full adder"*, Optics Communications **56(2)**, Nov 1985, pp. 87–92

[730] D.R.J. White, K. Atkinson, and J.D.M. Osburn, *"Taming EMI in microprocessor systems"*, IEEE Spectrum **22(12)**, Dec 1985, pp. 30–37

[731] J.O. White and A. Yariv, *"Real-time image processing via four-wave mixing in a photorefractive medium"*, Applied Physics Letters **37(1)**, Jul 1980, pp. 5–7

[732] J.O. White and A. Yariv, *"Spatial information processing and distortion correction via four-wave mixing"*, Optical Engineering **21(2)**, Mar-Apr 1982, pp. 224–230

[733] M.V. Wilkes, *"Size, power, and speed"*, in Conf. Proc. 10th Ann. Intl. Symp. Computer Architecture, **SIGARCH 11(3)**, Jun 1983, pp. 2–4

[734] R.Y. Wong, *"Sequential scene matching using edge features"*, IEEE trans. Aerospace and Electronic Systems **AES-14(1)**, Jan 1978, pp. 128–140

[735] T.H. Wood, C.A. Burrus, D.A.B. Miller, D.S. Chemla, T.C. Damen, A.C. Gossard, and W. Wiegmann, *"High-speed optical modulation with GaAs/GaAlAs quantum wells in a p-i-n diode structure"*, Applied Physics Letters **44(1)**, Jan 1984, pp. 16–18

[736] C. Wu and T. Feng, *"The university of the shuffle/exchange network"*, IEEE trans. computers **C-30(5)**, May 1981, pp. 324–332

[737] R. Wu and H. Stark, *"Rotation invariant pattern recognition using a vector reference"*, Applied Optics **23(6)**, Mar 1983, pp. 838–840

[738] S.K. Yao and S.H. Lee, *"Spatial differentiation and integration by coherent optical correlation method"*, J. Optical Society of America **61**, 1971, pp. 474–477

[739] A. Yariv and M. Nakamura, *"Periodic structures for integrated optics"*, IEEE J. Quantum Electronics **QE-13(4)**, Apr 1977, pp. 233–253

[740] A. Yariv, *"Four wave nonlinear optical mixing as real time holography"*, Optics Communications **25(1)**, Apr 1978, pp. 23–25

[741] A. Yariv and S-K. Kwong, *"Associative memories based on message-bearing optical modes in phase-conjugate resonators"*, Optics Letters **11(3)**, Mar 1986, pp. 186–188

[742] A. Yariv, S-K. Kwong, and K. Kyuma, *"Demonstration of an all-optical associative holographic memory"*, Applied Physics Letters **48(17)**, Apr 1986, pp. 1114–1116

[743] T. Yatagai, *"Cellular logic architectures for optical computers"*, Applied Optics **25(10)**, May 1986, pp. 1571–1577

[744] T. Yatagai, K. Choji, and H. Saito, *"Pattern classification using optical Mellin transform and circular photodiode array"*, Optics Communications **38(3)**, Aug 1981, pp. 162–165

[745] C.Y. Yen and S.A. Collins, Jr., *"Operation of a numerical optical data processor"*, in **1980 Intl. Optical Computing Conf.**, Proc. SPIE **232**, pp. 160–167

[746] F.T.S. Yu, **Optical information processing**, Wiley, 1982

[747] F.T.S. Yu and S. Jutamulia, *"Implementation of symbolic substitution logic using optical associative memories"*, Applied Optics **26(12)**, Jun 1987, pp. 2293–2294

[748] F.T.S. Yu, S. Jutamulia, T.W. Lin, and D.A. Gregory, *"Adaptive real-time pattern recognition using a liquid crystal TV based joint transform correlator"*, Applied Optics **26(8)**, Apr 1987, pp. 1370–1372

[749] H.H. Zappe, *"Josephson quantum interference computer devices"*, IEEE trans. Magnetics **MAG-13(1)**, Jan 1977, pp. 41–47

[750] F. Zernike, *"Luneburg lenses for optical waveguide use"*, Optics Communications **12(4)**, Dec 1974, pp. 379–381

[751] J.F. Ziegler and W.A. Lanford, *"The effect of cosmic rays on computer memories"*, Science **206(4420)**, 16 Nov 1979, pp. 776–788

[752] H. Zimmermann, *"OSI reference model — the ISO model of architecture for open systems interconnection"*, IEEE trans. Communication **COM-28(4)**, Apr 1980, pp. 425–432

Index